Forms of Faith in Sixteenth-Century Italy

Forms of Faith in Sixteenth-Century Italy

Edited by

ABIGAIL BRUNDIN
University of Cambridge, UK

and

MATTHEW TREHERNE
University of Leeds, UK

ASHGATE

Published by
Ashgate Publishing Limited
Gower House
Croft Road
Aldershot
Hampshire GU11 3HR
England

Ashgate Publishing Company
Suite 420
101 Cherry Street
Burlington, VT 05401–4405
USA

www.ashgate.com

British Library Cataloguing in Publication Data
Forms of faith in sixteenth-century Italy. – (Catholic
Christendom, 1300–1700)
    1. Catholic Church – Italy – History – 16th century 2. Religion and sociology
– Italy – History – 16th century 3. Italy – Church history – 16th century
4. Italy – Civilization – 1559–1789 5. Italy – Civilization – 1268–1559
I. Brundin, Abigail II. Treherne, Matthew
306.6'8245'09031

Library of Congress Cataloging-in-Publication Data
Forms of faith in sixteenth-century Italy / [edited by] Abigail Brundin and
    Matthew Treherne.
        p. cm. – (Catholic Christendom, 1300–1700)
    Essays based on a conference held in 2007 at the University of Leeds.
    Includes bibliographical references and index.
    ISBN 978–0–7546–6555–7 (alk. paper)
    1. Christianity and culture – Italy – History – 16th century – Congresses.
    2. Catholic Church – Italy – History – 16th century – Congresses. 3. Italy
    – Church history – 16th century – Congresses.
    I. Brundin, Abigail. II. Treherne, Matthew.

    BX1544.F67 2009
    282'.4509031–dc22
                                          2008050820

ISBN 978–0–7546–6555–7

Printed and bound in Great Britain by
TJ International Ltd, Padstow, Cornwall

Contents

Series Editor's Preface

The still-usual emphasis on medieval (or Catholic) and reformation (or Protestant) religious history has meant neglect of the middle ground, both chronological and ideological. As a result, continuities between the middle ages and early modern Europe have been overlooked in favor of emphasis on radical discontinuities. Further, especially in the later period, the identification of 'reformation' with various kinds of Protestantism means that the vitality and creativity of the established church, whether in its Roman or local manifestations, has been left out of account. In the last few years, an upsurge of interest in the history of traditional (or catholic) religion makes these inadequacies in received scholarship even more glaring and in need of systematic correction. The series will attempt this by covering all varieties of religious behavior, broadly interpreted, not just (or even especially) traditional institutional and doctrinal church history. It will to the maximum degree possible be interdisciplinary, comparative and global, as well as non-confessional. The goal is to understand religion, primarily of the 'Catholic' variety, as a broadly human phenomenon, rather than as a privileged mode of access to superhuman realms, even implicitly.

The period covered, 1300–1700, embraces the moment which saw an almost complete transformation of the place of religion in the life of Europeans, whether considered as a system of beliefs, as an institution, or as a set of social and cultural practices. In 1300, vast numbers of Europeans, from the pope down, fully expected Jesus's return and the beginning of His reign on earth. By 1700, very few Europeans, of whatever level of education, would have subscribed to such chiliastic beliefs. Pierre Bayle's notorious sarcasms about signs and portents are not idiosyncratic. Likewise, in 1300 the vast majority of Europeans probably regarded the pope as their spiritual head; the institution he headed was probably the most tightly integrated and effective bureaucracy in Europe. Most Europeans were at least nominally Christian, and the pope had at least nominal knowledge of that fact. The papacy, as an institution, played a central role in high politics, and the clergy in general formed an integral part of most governments, whether central or local. By 1700, Europe was divided into a myriad of different religious allegiances, and even those areas officially subordinate to the pope were both more nominally Catholic in belief (despite colossal efforts at imposing uniformity) and also in allegiance than they had been four hundred years earlier. The pope had become only one political factor, and not one of the first rank. The clergy, for its part, had virtually disappeared from secular governments as well as losing much of its local authority. The stage was set for the Enlightenment.

Thomas F. Mayer,
Augustana College

Acknowledgements

We are grateful to the following funding bodies, who provided financial support for the conference on *Forms of Faith: The Influence of Religious Change on Artistic, Musical and Literary Culture in Sixteenth-Century Italy* (Leeds, 30–31 March 2007): the Leeds Humanities Research Institute, the Modern Humanities Research Association, the British Academy, the Society for Italian Studies and the Society for Renaissance Studies. Our thanks are due to the Departments of Italian at the Universities of Leeds and Cambridge for their general support, and to the Department of Italian at the University of Cambridge for funding to cover the cost of illustrations, as well as to Ruth Chester for her work on the index. Thanks, too, to Tom Gray of Ashgate, for his patience and help; and to Tom Mayer, editor of the *Catholic Christendom, 1300–1700* series. We would also like to record our thanks to the delegates who took part in the conference in March 2007, especially to Brian Richardson for acting as a respondent at the end of the conference, and to Letizia Panizza, who helped with numerous funding applications and was sadly prevented from contributing to the current volume by other circumstances.

Editions and Translations

Quotations from prose works in languages other than English that appear in the main body of the essays have been translated, and originals provided in the footnotes. Unless otherwise indicated, the translations are the editors'. Poetry in Italian has been left in the original. Biblical quotations are taken from the Douay-Rheims Bible, based on the Latin Vulgate.

Notes on Contributors

Stephen Bowd is Senior Lecturer in European History at the University of Edinburgh. He published *Reform before the Reformation: Vincenzo Querini and the Religious Renaissance in Italy* (Brill, 2002), and is currently working on a study of Gian Pietro Carafa.

Abigail Brundin is Lecturer in Italian at the University of Cambridge, and a fellow of St Catharine's College. Her recent books are *Vittoria Colonna: Sonnets for Michelangelo* (Chicago University Press, 2005), and *Vittoria Colonna and the Spiritual Poetics of the Italian Reformation* (Ashgate, 2008).

Antonio Corsaro is Associate Professor in the Faculty of Literature and Philosophy at the University of Urbino. His recent books are *La regola e la licenza. Studi sulla poesia satirica e burlesca fra Cinque e Seicento* (Manziana (Rome), 1999), a critical edition of the *Paradossi* of Ortensio Lando (Rome, 2000), and *Percorsi dell'incredulità. Religione, amore e natura nel primo Tasso* (Rome, 2003).

Chrysa Damianaki is Associate Professor of Art History at the Università del Salento (Italy). Her recent publications on the Reformation include: 'La porta della Sagrestia di San Marco di Jacopo Sansovino: implicazioni ideologiche e culturali', in *Il Rinascimento italiano di fronte alla Riforma: Letteratura e Arte* (Vecchiarelli, 2005), of which she was co-editor, together with P. Procaccioli and A. Romano; and 'La capella Capponi di Jacopo Pontormo in Santa Felicita a Firenze: per un riesame dei contenuti iconografici e religiosi', in *Officine del nuovo. Sodalizi fra letterati, artisti ed editori nella cultura italiana fra Riforma e Controriforma*, ed. H. Hendrix and P. Procaccioli (Vecchiarelli, 2008).

Iain Fenlon is Professor of Historical Musicology, University of Cambridge, and a Fellow of King's College. His most recent book is *The Ceremonial City: History, Memory and Myth in Renaissance Venice* (Yale University Press, 2008).

Harald Hendrix is Chair of Italian Studies and head of the Department of Modern Languages at the University of Utrecht. He is the editor of *Writers' Houses and the Making of Memory* (Routledge, 2008) and co-editor of *Autorità, modelli e antimodelli nella cultura artistica e letteraria* *tra Riforma e Controriforma* (Vecchiarelli, 2007; with Antonio Corsaro and Paolo Procaccioli), and *Officine del nuovo. Sodalizi fra letterati, artisti ed editori nella cultura italiana fra Riforma e Controriforma* (Vecchiarelli, 2008; with Paolo Procaccioli).

Tom Nichols is Senior Lecturer in the History of Art at the University of Aberdeen. His recent publications include *The Art of Poverty: Irony and Ideal in Sixteenth Century Beggar Imagery* (Manchester, 2007) and *Others and Outcasts in Early Modern Europe: Picturing the Social Margins* (Ashgate, 2007).

Noel O'Regan is Senior Lecturer in Music at the University of Edinburgh. He has published a Royal Musical Association monograph entitled *Institutional Patronage in Post-Tridentine Rome: Music at Santissima Trinita, 1550–1650*, and is completing a study of music at Roman confraternities.

Matthew Treherne is Lecturer in Italian in the University of Leeds, and co-director of the Leeds Centre for Dante Studies. Forthcoming publications include *Dante's* Commedia: *Theology as Poetry*, co-edited with Vittorio Montemaggi (University of Notre Dame Press, 2009), and *'Se mai continga che il poema sacro …': Exile, Politics and Theology in Dante*, co-edited with Claire Honess (Longo, 2009).

Raymond B. Waddington is Professor Emeritus at the University of California, Davis, and senior editor of *The Sixteenth Century Journal*. His book *Aretino's Satyr* (University of Toronto Press, 2004) received the 2005 Scaglione Prize for Italian studies from the Modern Language Association of America.

List of Figures

Introduction

Abigail Brundin and Matthew Treherne

The field of Reformation studies has long been established as an important area of academic endeavour, with an impeccable pedigree of seminal and path-breaking texts and analyses beginning in the nineteenth century.[1] Attention to the period of the European Reformation underpins our understanding of much of our own religious and political climate, equally riven by religious dissent and doctrinal disagreement, by casting light on the pivotal period of religious unrest, suppression and violence in the sixteenth century that still helps shape societies and cultures to this day. In this context, however, Italy's own experience of reform and Reformation has remained relatively unexplored, generally because it is deemed in traditional historiographies to have lasted only for a brief moment in the 1530s and early 1540s, with any religious renewal effectively stamped out after the re-establishment of the Roman Inquisition in 1542, and the subsequent zeal in prosecuting heresy on the peninsula.[2]

This volume, which brings together essays building on papers delivered and discussed at a conference organized at the University of Leeds in 2007,[3] aims to be part of the current and ongoing process of rethinking the experience of an 'Italian Reformation', in all its many forms and manifestations throughout the sixteenth century.[4] The essays consider religious reform through the lens of cultural production, via an examination of what was written, painted, sung, or performed in the period, and the manner in which religious belief is woven through these modes of cultural and personal expression. Crucially, such an approach permits contributors

---

[1] A useful summary of works in the field of Reformation Studies beginning in the nineteenth century is provided in John W. O'Malley, *Trent and All That: Renaming Catholicism in the Early Modern Era* (Cambridge, MA and London: Harvard University Press, 2000).

[2] See, for an example of this traditional view of Italy's experience of Reformation, G.R. Elton, *Reformation Europe, 1517–1559*, 2nd edn (Oxford: Blackwell, 1999), pp. 122–46.

[3] *Forms of Faith: The influence of religious change on artistic, musical and literary culture in sixteenth-century Italy*, Bodington Hall, University of Leeds, 30–31 March 2007.

[4] For a useful bibliography of other recent works that begin this process, see *The Italian Reformation of the Sixteenth Century and the Diffusion of Renaissance Culture: A Bibliography of the Secondary Literature (Ca. 1750–1997)*, ed. by John Tedeschi in association with James M. Lattis, with an Historiographical Introduction by Massimo Firpo (Modena: F.C. Panini, 2000).

to pay attention to the full richness of that expression, showing how the details of music, art and literature present patterns of belief that often tell a different story from that of official doctrine and decrees, over the course of a century of profound transition and upheaval.

A focus on cultural production, and more specifically on cultural *forms* and the manner in which they respond to religious change, is foregrounded in this volume in a variety of different ways. Essays examine changing techniques and approaches in the visual arts, in literary expression, and in musical composition, and consider how these relate to changing modes of religious worship and to variances in the interpretation of doctrine and theology. Equally, such a focus on form enables essays to emphasize the ways in which music, art and literature not only reflect developments in doctrine and religious practice, but also helped shape sixteenth-century religious sensibilities in new and often unexpected ways.

Precisely in light of the results that this mode of cultural analysis throws up, the definition of Italian reform and Reformation suggested by the scope of the essays contained here is deliberately broad and all encompassing. It ranges from early manifestations of reformed sentiment at the turn of the sixteenth century (in the case of conceptions of 'religious friendship' in the circle of Pietro Bembo, Tommaso Giustiniani, Vincenzo Querini and Gasparo Contarini, for example), to the end of the century and the period of the so-called Counter-Reformation (to include, for example, the development of mythological painting in late-century Venice, or reformed musical practice inspired by Florentine models in the Congregation of the Oratory in Rome). Traditional dividing lines between a pre- and post-Tridentine Italian experience are questioned, in recognition of the lines of continuity that span the century, the slow evolution and renegotiations of cultural and religious practices rather than their overnight transformation. Equally, the immediate impact of Tridentine decrees and of the Italian indexes is called into question, in recognition of a reality that was altogether more complex.

As well as complicating any straightforward notions of periodization, the essays in this volume present Italian reform as being more indigenous than is often assumed: while an interest in, and reaction against, Lutheran and other transalpine currents of spirituality played an important role in influencing Italian thinking and theology, currents of reformed thought on the peninsula also had their own particular forms and internal influences. Thus, for example, it was possible to arrive at an interest in *sola fide* – justification by faith alone – via the influence of a certain kind of distinctively Italian Christian humanism, and to hold such a belief in the context of an ardent Catholic faith, as the example of the poet and reformer Vittoria Colonna makes clear.[5] Equally, cultural and religious tendencies in the later century were not solely reactionary, the result of the changed environment in the wake of the Council of Trent, but rather, as a number of the essays seek to stress, continuities with earlier reformed currents persisted and developed in new directions, allowing for a period of cultural growth and renewal in the late century that has often been overlooked.

One of the thorniest problems faced by any scholarly approach to religious culture in the sixteenth century is that of terminology. Many of the terms available for use for this period of religious history – Italian Reformation, Catholic Reformation, Counter-Reformation, evangelism and so forth – provoke negative reactions from scholars on a variety of grounds.[6] It seems a pressing task in a field that is changing shape before our eyes to find a term that does not hint at failure by nominating a Reformation of the established Church that never came to pass. In addition, it is important to avoid terminology that was too closely tied to the transalpine reform movement, carrying overtones of Lutheran and Calvinist doctrine and thus perhaps suggesting that the discussion here would be limited to Italian heretics who held on to certain beliefs in defiance of Church decree and censorship. This is not to argue that the study of Italian heretics is unimportant, nor to deny that they were often harshly punished for their beliefs, but only to maintain that the experience of reform in Italy encompassed this experience alongside numerous others that had less to do with Protestant beliefs. The term that is so much desired, yet still frustratingly elusive, is one that suggests a distinct, Italian experience of reform, taking place both within and outside the Catholic establishment, both before and after agreement with the Protestant reformers was still held to be a possibility, at the level of official doctrine and also, crucially, at the level of popular piety and vernacular cultural practice.

In the continuing absence of any such resonant and useful term, we have been unwilling, as editors, to impose a uniformity of approach on contributors who necessarily and fruitfully approach the question of Italian reform from many different angles, in different historical periods and cultural and political contexts. This book in a sense sidesteps such dangerous terminological terrain altogether by focusing on the arena of cultural production, deliberately seeking out a plurality of viewpoints

---

5   See on this topic, Concetta Ranieri, 'Premesse umanistiche alla religiosità di Vittoria Colonna', *Rivista di Storia e Letteratura Religiosa*, 32 (1996), 531–48; as well as Ranieri, 'Imprestiti platonici nella formazione religiosa di Vittoria Colonna', in *Presenze eterodosse nel Viterbese tra Quattro e Cinquecento*, ed. by Vincenzo De Caprio and Concetta Ranieri (Rome: Archivio Guido Izzi, 2000), pp. 193–212.

6   A summary of the ongoing debates is given in O'Malley, *Trent and All That*.

and trying to understand the myriad ways in which religious change was negotiated by different communities of artists, writers, musicians and believers. A focus on the formal properties of cultural production in particular, that is to say, on innovative formal responses to religious change, allows contributors to explore the manner in which culture responded to and spoke the language of religious belief at the most intimate, and often at the most popular, level.

The volume aims to offer a wide range of approaches, cutting across disciplines, rather than a single programmatic account. Such interdisciplinarity of course reflects the fundamental interdisciplinarity of Renaissance cultural life, which eschewed the concern with boundaries and disciplinary divisions that exists in academia today. One can argue that the subject matter itself demands to be studied in ways that traverse disciplinary divides. Three examples of literary figures who are central to this volume make the point well. The author Pietro Aretino was known for his engagement with the work of Renaissance artists, in particular Titian, and his achievement as a writer on art is beginning to be widely acknowledged in scholarship. The poet Vittoria Colonna corresponded on the subjects of art and religion with Michelangelo (who himself wrote an important corpus of poetry, frequently concerned with religious themes).[7] Torquato Tasso was closely involved with debates on the proper nature of music.[8] More broadly, the close interrelation of cultural and religious life saw the promotion to cardinal of a figure such as Pietro Bembo, key sponsor and practitioner of the new vernacular literary culture of the period. Later in the century, Counter-Reformation theologians played an active role in attempting to redefine musical, literary and artistic culture.[9] Such fundamental interdisciplinarity is exemplified in a work such as Gregorio Comanini's *Il figino* (1591), a dialogue that attempts to define

---

[7]   See, in addition to work in this volume, the recent book by Abigail Brundin, *Vittoria Colonna and the Spiritual Poetics of the Italian Reformation* (Aldershot: Ashgate, 2008), pp. 67–100.

[8]   See Tasso's 1584 dialogue *La Cavaletta, overo della poesia Toscana*. For a discussion of Tasso's engagement with music theory, and of composers' responses to his poetry, see the essays in *Tasso, la musica, i musicisti*, ed. by Maria Antonella Balsano and Thomas Walker (Florence: Olschki, 1988).

[9]   On endeavours by Counter-Reformation theologians to define cultural production, see the following useful studies: Franco Buzzi and Danilo Zardin (eds), *Carlo Borromeo e l'opera della 'grande riforma': Cultura, religione e arte del governo nella Milano del pieno Cinquecento* (Milan: Silvana, 1997); John M. Headley and John B. Tomaro (eds), *San Carlo Borromeo: Catholic Reform and Ecclesiastical Politics in the Second Half of the Sixteenth Century* (Washington, DC: The Folger Shakespeare Library; London and Toronto: Associated University Presses, 1988); Gabriele Paleotti, *Discorso intorno alle immagini sacre e profane (1582)*, ed. by Stefano Della Torre, trans. by Gian Franco Freguglia (Citta del Vaticano: Libreria editrice vaticana, 2002).

the role of art in the light of the Council of Trent by bringing together the voices of a prelate, a painter and a poet.[10] Like Comanini, we too have aimed to unite disparate voices in a search, if not for definitions or consensus, then for the same kind of useful marriage of viewpoints and areas of expertise.

The contributors to this volume are throughout concerned to demonstrate how a full understanding of Cinquecento religious culture might be found as much in the details of the give and take between cultural and religious developments, as in any grand narrative of the period. Indeed, whether examining the vibrant musical culture of confraternities in the Tridentine period, or the reformed ideas encoded in Pontormo's (now destroyed) frescoes for San Lorenzo, clear-cut distinctions between periods are complicated. And, as several of these essays argue, such complication is as evident in the formal aspects of art, music and writing – in the relationship between techniques of different modes of painting in Venice, for instance; or in the interpenetration of styles of popular and art music in Tuscany throughout the century – as it is in explicit statements or representations of doctrinal propositions. As well as challenging strict periodization, the essays also frequently demonstrate the close interaction of religious and humanist culture – an alliance which was repeatedly renegotiated in the period, but which needs to be seen as a dynamic part of the relationship between culture and religion.

The shifting relationship between humanist and religious concerns in the sixteenth century is central to Stephen Bowd's examination of the practice and ideal of friendship in the Cinquecento. Through his close readings of the rhetoric of friendship in the private and public writings of key intellectual figures, Bowd offers a fresh reappraisal of Burckhardtian notions of the Renaissance individual. In developing a language which presented Christological and sacramental dimensions to friendship, at the same time as drawing on classical notions of friendship, Venetian intellectuals tied friendship to *caritas* and, at least implicitly, were able, through friendship, to undercut the authority of the Church. In Bowd's account, this notion of friendship came to be institutionalized and ultimately restricted in the later years of the century.

Antonio Corsaro's essay also discusses the development of religious culture through private relationships, in analysing the restricted circulation of spiritual poetry in manuscript form. The selectivity this circulation permitted enabled the development of devotional books, especially for a sophisticated audience, which often showed strong affinities with reform

---

[10]   Gregorio Comanini, *Il Figino overo del fine della Pittura* (1591), in Paola Barocchi (ed.), *Trattati d'arte del Cinquecento fra Manierismo e Controriforma*, 3 vols (Bari: Laterza, 1960–62), III, pp. 237–379.

movements. Vittoria Colonna's work was a key model for these texts, although Corsaro focuses largely on less well-known authors to demonstrate the range of poetic output produced in non-printed form. Colonna was a key figure, too, for the Academicians of the Florence of Cosimo I; as Abigail Brundin shows in her essay, private and public discussions of her poetry link together literary, religious and linguistic debates. In this particular context, poetry was considered a vehicle for religious truths. The analysis of Colonna's sonnets in the Florentine Academy, as well as that of the works of Dante and Petrarch, therefore permitted vibrant discussion, creating an energetic intellectual environment, which stands at odds with what is often presented as a general move, across the middle decades of the century, towards a 'stagnant' culture, in conformity with the demands of the Counter-Reformation.

The character of Cosimo's Florence as a centre for Reformist culture is further elucidated by Chrysa Damianaki's essay, which examines one of its major works of visual art: Pontormo's frescoes for San Lorenzo. Through a painstaking discussion of the complex process of determining the intended arrangement of the frescoes, and presenting new insights into the ways the frescoes would have been read, Damianaki's chapter enables the frescoes to emerge in their full richness, as a key work of the Reform movement in Florence. An interesting part of her argument is that Giorgio Vasari, one of the most prominent sources for our knowledge of the frescoes, perhaps deliberately protected both Pontormo and Cosimo from later accusations of Protestant sympathies, by being dismissive of the artist's abilities at this point in his career.

Of course, in the later part of the century such protection was often required. In his essay, Tom Nichols offers an account of how a secular genre of paintings adapted to the new religious climate, discussing how Venetian mythological paintings came to be affected by religious models. Where mythological paintings of the first part of the sixteenth century clearly signalled – through a range of aspects of form – their separation from religious art, close examination of Titian's classical paintings, especially the *poesie* of 1550–62, demonstrates a new proximity between secular and Christian painting, which complicates the meanings of both. Titian's *poesie* engage visual traditions that are clearly linked with Christian art. Such an engagement with sacred traditions is also found in Tintoretto's depictions of the nude form, which visually encode a hybridity of the religious and the secular, adding layers of religious and moral meaning.

Harald Hendrix also focuses in his essay on the meeting of classical and Christian models in Venice, discussing the ways in which the notion of 'delightful horror' brought newly discovered elements of classical culture together with Protestant currents, using 'horror' as a means of communicating the Gospels to a wider audience; Hendrix then examines the ways in which that notion of horror gave way, in the Counter-Reformation, to a new concern with instilling piety and devotion. Paying particular attention to the works of Titian and Aretino, Hendrix suggests that whilst Aretino's *Poetics* was to provide a central touchstone for later theoretical debates on the moral value of 'horror', it was in the artistic and literary work of these two figures that the debate on horror was first fully worked out, with distinctly Reformist emphases. Also examining Aretino and Titian, Raymond Waddington discusses in his essay the ways in which reformed ideas recur in the two figures' work: in the case of Aretino, through personal associations outlined in his letters; in the case of Titian, through a close reading of paintings such as the *Ecce Homo* (1543). The emphasis on the humanity of Christ evident in such works, within the relatively heterodox context of Venice in the 1540s, suggests Titian's Reformist sympathies. Still more significantly, the famous depiction of Aretino as Pilate in this portrait, in Waddington's reading, illustrates a principle deeply held by Titian: a commitment, like that of Pilate himself, at least in the account of the Gospel of John, to bear witness to revealed truth itself.

The last three essays examine the relationship between ritual performance and cultural production in Tridentine Italy. As Iain Fenlon points out in his essay, the traditional starting-point for scholars – the Council of Trent's own *Canon* on music for the Mass – is in fact not particularly instructive, and has tended to lead scholars to pay too much attention to settings for the Mass, and in particular to overstate the influence of Palestrina's *Missa Papae Marcelli*. Against that tendency, Fenlon examines the *lauda* tradition in Florence and Tuscany, a musical tradition associated with a Savonarolan brand of piety, showing how this tradition in many ways escaped the dictates of the Tridentine reformers. Indeed, in many ways, that tradition challenges accepted distinctions between secular and sacred music, popular and art music, liturgical and non-liturgical settings; it offers a far richer picture of musical development than that which is obtained through the established emphases on Mass settings. Focusing on the confraternities of sixteenth-century Rome, Noel O'Regan's chapter shows how their use of music demonstrates the persistence of pre-Tridentine models after the 1560s. The devotional music they used was much broader than the Mass, including *sacre rappresentationi* and processions. Although the surviving documentation on that music is relatively sparse, O'Regan shows that these performances were an important part of the city's musical and devotional life. Not only were they, in many ways, impervious to the changes in Church music brought about in the wake of Trent, but they also came eventually to influence 'art' music.

The potential importance of ritual in literary production is also examined in Matthew Treherne's essay, which considers how Torquato Tasso's work in the last decade of the sixteenth century made use of liturgical reference, not simply as a means of signalling the poet's orthodoxy in a superficial way, but as a way of enriching the theological dimensions of his work. In this way, Treherne argues, it is possible to see in Tasso's work a response to the religious climate of Tridentine Italy in which the poet's self-conscious conformity to the Church forms part of a deeper reflection both on theological questions and on the discourse within which those questions can articulate themselves.

Taken as a whole, these essays make a case for a reading of religious culture in the sixteenth century that remains alert to the formal texture of the changes that take place. By placing this attention to texture and detail ahead of any desire definitively to categorize periods, movements, or figures, this volume adds to the growing body of scholarship that challenges the view that the Cinquecento in Italy was a time in which Reform in any real sense was absent, and Counter-Reform a universally deadening force. The volume speaks of a very different Cinquecento: one in which religious culture was not always at ease with itself and the changing world around it, but was none the less vibrant and plural.

CHAPTER 1

Swarming with Hermits: Religious Friendship in Renaissance Italy, 1490–1540[1]

Stephen Bowd

'When friendship ends as an ideal there is nothing left but authoritarianism.'[2]

The 'development of the individual' – of men and women highly conscious of their personal abilities and supremely assured of their place in the secular world – was regarded by the nineteenth-century historian Jacob Burckhardt as one of the defining moments of the Renaissance in Italy and one of the period's most distinctive contributions to the modern age.[3] After 1300, Burckhardt suggested, men and women increasingly substituted corporate loyalties with the pursuit of personal advancement, fame, or individual artistic expression in the growing cities and courts of the Italian peninsula. Burckhardt described an Italy 'swarming with individuals' after 1300, as the 'ban laid upon human personality was dissolved'. This dynamic but paradoxical image suggests that the emergence of individuals and of secular individualism could undermine traditional corporate structures like the monastery and the church and Burckhardt viewed this process

[1] I would like to record my gratitude to the late D. Francesco Andreu for providing me with access to the Theatine archive at Sant'Andrea della Valle in Rome, and to Dr David Rundle for guiding me through the Vatican Library. For their comments on earlier versions of parts of this essay, I am grateful to Professors Elisabeth Gleason, John Martin and Tom Mayer. I am also grateful to audiences in Edinburgh, San Francisco and Leeds for criticism and encouragement. Finally, I would like to thank Dr Abi Brundin and Dr Matthew Treherne for inviting me to present this paper at the 'Forms of Faith' conference.

[2] Brian Patrick McGuire, 'Jean Gerson and the End of Spiritual Friendship: Dilemmas of Conscience', in *Friendship in Medieval Europe*, ed. by Julian Haseldine (Phoenix Mill: Sutton, 1999), pp. 229–50 (p. 243). See also *idem, Friendship and Community: The Monastic Experience, 350–1250* (Kalamazoo, MI: Cistercian Publications, 1988).

[3] Jacob Burckhardt, *The Civilization of the Renaissance in Italy: An Essay*, trans. by S.G.C. Middlemore, 4th edn (London: Phaidon Press, 1951), pt. II.

with decidedly mixed feelings.[4] The restless individual might be inspired by new philosophies exalting human creativity, but equally could be driven by selfish desires into credulity, superstition, irreligion and immorality. For every Leonardo da Vinci whose discovery of the self was the source of abundant creativity, Burckhardt therefore identified a despot like Pandolfo Petrucci of Siena whose rampant egotism was the spur to psychopathic action:

> Insignificant and malicious, he governed with the help of a professor of jurisprudence and of an astrologer, and frightened his people by an occasional murder. His pastime in the summer months was to roll blocks of stone from the top of Monte Amiata, without caring what or whom they hit.[5]

The human energy released in Italy after 1300 contained the seeds of its own destruction and it seems as if Burckhardt was appalled by the spiritual debasement which accompanied the rise of the modern individual and left each man or woman isolated from each other and from God.

Although many of Burckhardt's conclusions have been challenged, his fundamental assumptions about the emergence of Renaissance individualism and its relationship to society and religion continue to inspire debate. John Martin has recently explored the variety of ways in which Renaissance men and women struggled to resolve the problem of the relation of their 'inner experience' to their 'experience in the world'.[6] Martin argues that this resolution took place in the production of what he labels 'social', 'prudential', 'performative', 'porous', or 'sincere' selves, and was complicated by growing religious doubt and the pressing need to act prudently or to find a social role which offered some resolution of inner doubts. In place of man's confidence in his divine similitude there arose 'an increasingly complex dilemma of not knowing if those whom one addressed would ever understand one's deepest feelings, concerns, or hopes'.[7] In other words, where once the boundaries between men and women had been 'porous', by the end of the sixteenth century, men and women stood increasingly alone and forced to rely on 'sincerity' of feeling and emotion to gain trust and to create close bonds.

---

[4]   Ibid., p. 81. Lionel Gossman, *Basel in the Age of Burckhardt: a study in unseasonable ideas* (Chicago, IL: University of Chicago Press, 2000); John R. Hinde, *Jacob Burckhardt and the Crisis of Modernity* (Montreal and Kingston: McGill-Queen's University Press, 2000).

[5]   Burckhardt, *Civilization*, p. 22.

[6]   John Martin, *Myths of Renaissance Individualism* (Basingstoke: Palgrave Macmillan, 2004).

[7]   Ibid., p. 117.

Renaissance friendship, in theory and practice, involved the production of self in all of the ways described by Martin and it can provide a fresh perspective on Burckhardt's Renaissance individualism.[8] Renaissance Italians inherited a rich legacy of discussions of ideal or perfect friendship from classical and post-classical sources.[9] The classical ideal reflected an appreciation of man's inherently sociable nature but equally was shaped by the ancient Greek preoccupation with the perfection of wisdom. As far as it concerned friends, this process of perfection was based on their mutual love for the virtue which they found in each other and was marked at its most metaphysical level by the holding of all things in common and the mingling or merging of souls.[10] In this Platonic sense, the perfection of friendship was a means to a wise end and it reflected the older master-younger pupil relationship illustrated by the Socratic dialogues, notably the discussion of love in the *Symposium*.

Plato's own pupil Aristotle in his *Nicomachean Ethics*, and the Roman lawyer Cicero in his *Laelius* or dialogue on friendship, placed a somewhat greater emphasis on ideal friendship as a practical end in itself. Both men noted that virtuous friends were necessary for the enjoyment of a fully virtuous and civil life and as Cicero remarked:

> For what person is there … who would wish to be surrounded by unlimited wealth and to abound in every material blessing, on condition that he love no one and that no one loves him? Such indeed is the life of tyrants – a life, I mean, in which there can be no faith, no affection, no trust in the continuance of goodwill; where every act arouses suspicion and anxiety and where friendship has no place.[11]

---

[8]   Martin does not discuss friendship although he mentions the 'inwardness' of St Aelred of Rievaulx's work on spiritual friendship and Montaigne's friendship with Etienne de La Boëtie: ibid., pp. 48, 117.

[9]   Much of the discussion in this paragraph is based on the essays in Haseldine, *Friendship* and Reginald Hyatte, *The Arts of Friendship: The Idealization of Friendship in Medieval and Early Renaissance Literature*, Studies in Intellectual History, 50 (Leiden: Brill, 1994).

[10]   Erasmus traced the origins of the adage 'Between friends is all common' to Pythagoras. However, he notes fourteen other classical instances of its use. See David Wootton, 'Friendship Portrayed: A New Account of *Utopia*', *History Workshop Journal*, 45 (1998), 29–48 (pp. 31–2).

[11]   'Nam quis est, pro deorum fidem atque hominum, qui velit, ut neque diligat quemquam nec ipse ab ullo diligatur, circumfluere omnibus copiis atque in omnium rerum abundantia vivere? Haec enim est tyrannorum vita nimirum, in qua nulla fides, nulla caritas, nulla stabilis benevolentiae potest esse fiducia: omnia semper suspecta atque sollicita, nullus locus amicitiae': *De amicitia*, xv. 52–3; Cicero, *De re publica, De legibus, Cato Maior de senectute, Laelius de amicitia*, ed. by J.G.F. Powell (New York: Oxford University Press,

Christians from St Augustine of Hippo and St John Cassian to St Bede and St Aelred of Rievaulx adapted both metaphysical and practical views of the ideal of friendship to discussions of divine love and the Christian duty of charity. For these writers, *amicitia* (or *philia*) between men was a function of *caritas* (or *agape*) in the person of Christ.[12] In this way, all friendships between men of virtue operated as a communion in Christ who had laid down his life for his friends.[13] During the Middle Ages, this type of friendship-love relationship in Christ was institutionalized in the communal setting of the monastery, and subsequently found a place in the world among the men and women who were drawn to each other as confessor and mystic. As Alan Bray has argued, the 'wedded brothers' of the medieval and early-modern periods were also engaged in a communal participation in the love of God outside the monastery by jointly partaking in the body of Christ through friendship ceremonies attached to eucharistic devotion.[14]

The 'monastic' and 'religious' ages of medieval friendship were followed by a humanist cult of friendship during the Renaissance, which may be symptomatic of a 'crisis' in the history of friendship. Peter Burke has treated this 'turning-point in the history of friendship' as essentially a 'secularization of the spiritual and especially the monastic friendships of the Middle Ages', and like Burckhardt he has suggested that there may be a connection between the intensification in the 'emotional and religious rhetoric of friendship' among humanists, notably Erasmus, and the more widespread decline of the social role of religious confraternities, trade guilds, brothers-in-arms, and youth groups.[15] Alan Bray observed that, although the ceremony of wedded brothers was intensely spiritual, it went into decline in the sixteenth century when the privatization and secularization of friendship were accompanied by a growing fear of carnality in homosocial bonds, the stigmatization of the 'sodomite', and

2006), trans. by William Armistead Falconer, *De senectute, de amicitia, de divinatione* (London: William Heinemann, 1923). Cf. ibid., vi. 22.

[12]   The Christian reception and adaptation of classical ideals is succinctly explored by Julian P. Haseldine, 'Love, Separation and Male Friendship: Words and Actions in St Anselm's Letters to His Friends', in *Masculinity in Medieval Europe*, ed. by D M. Hadley (London: Longman, 1999), pp. 238–55.

[13]   Common fellowship is expressed in Acts 2:42, 44, 4:32–5, 5:12–16. See also Psalms 133:1. On the sacrifice which is to be made for friends, see John 15:12–15, 17.

[14]   Alan Bray, *The Friend* (Chicago, IL: University of Chicago Press, 2003).

[15]   Peter Burke, 'Humanism and Friendship in Sixteenth-Century Europe', in *Friendship in Medieval Europe*, pp. 265, 270.

the conquest of the kinship network by the institution of publicly avowed marriage.[16]

In order to test these hypotheses about a crisis in friendship and its relationship with broader social or religious change, the nature of the humanist cult of friendship in Renaissance Italy will be outlined in the first part of this chapter. The spiritual and religious aspects of this cult will be addressed and particular attention will be paid to a group of friends for whom friendship, in its monastic, religious *and* humanist senses, was important. Pietro Bembo, Gasparo Contarini, Tommaso Giustiniani and Vincenzo Querini lived during the thirty years either side of 1500 and have received a great deal of scholarly attention both as individuals and as a group of friends.[17] Their letters and writings give an extraordinary insight into the struggle to resolve the tension between the individual and the universal, or indeed the 'external' and 'internal' selves.[18] This struggle was initially couched in the language of ideal friendship and drew heavily on neo-Platonic and Petrarchan ideas or literary forms. However, like earlier Christians, the Venetian friends were equally concerned with forms of faith, and especially with the means of securing assurance of divine grace.

The reordering of man's understanding of God has, until recently, been cast in terms of a private and individual 'crisis' over the question of the reciprocal nature of the Christian sinner's relationship with a forgiving God. Yet such dramas of individual isolation can obscure the fact that the production of the self can be an act of affirmation of communal solidarity and of engagement with the world even when, in the case of Querini and Giustiniani, it results in the adoption of an eremitic life. The exchange of letters that bound the group of friends together was instrumental in these religious choices, and alongside an Italy 'swarming with individuals', it is instructive to examine a landscape swarming with hermits for whom religious friendship was an effective means of the production of the self.

---

[16]   Bray, *The Friend*, p. 293. Bray's conclusions here should be read in conjunction with his *Homosexuality in Renaissance England* (London: Gay Men's Press, 1982), where he outlines early modern understanding of the sodomite, and the relationship between fear of sodomy and friendship between men. On the relationship between ideals of male-male friendship and ideals of marriage, see Reginald Hyatte, 'Complementary Humanistic Models of Marriage and Male *Amicitia* in Fifteenth-Century Literature', in *Friendship in Medieval Europe*, ch. 14. On carnality and the decline of religious friendships, see Johan Huizinga, *The Autumn of the Middle Ages*, trans. by Rodney J. Payton and Ulrich Mammitzsch (Chicago, IL: University of Chicago Press, 1996), ch. 8.

[17]   Notable in this latter respect is James Bruce Ross, 'Gasparo Contarini and His Friends', *Studies in the Renaissance*, 17 (1970), 192–232, and Constance M. Furey, *Erasmus, Contarini, and the Religious Republic of Letters* (Cambridge: Cambridge University Press, 2006), pp. 86–98.

[18]   Martin, *Myths*, p. 7.

In tracing the fortunes of one group of friends it is possible to discern the basis for the cult of Renaissance friendship but also the outlines of new religious priorities, which increasingly circumscribed that cult. The resolution of inner and outer selves was achieved by emphasizing inwardness but also the porousness of soul and spirit 'in an act of ... divine love' centred on friendship.[19] However, as Martin has argued, this porousness, or potential for the merging of souls, gave way under the pressure of religious change in the course of the sixteenth century to a stronger sense of the individual's isolation before God, and the need for closer supervision of individual feeling and action by means of new institutions which are examined in the final part of this chapter. It seems as if the nature of friendship was transformed in public discourse, as corporate structures placed it in the service of charitable action.

A key phase in the history of friendship began in Florence in the fifteenth century with the work of Marsilio Ficino on Plato and the neo-Platonic corpus of writers. Ficino, the head of a 'Platonic academy' in Florence,[20] outlined a view of Platonic love in which the lovers' souls, recognizing the divine in each other, would direct them towards the divine by means of the will and intellect. Their ultimate goal was wisdom since it was 'one of the most beautiful things', as Diotima says in the *Symposium* where Socrates and Alcibiades provided the model of chaste love for Ficino.[21] The Platonic ideal seems to have animated Ficino's personal relationship with Giovanni Cavalcanti, as demonstrated in the loving letters he addressed to the younger man, exalting true friendship as a permanent union, and placing it on a philosophical and sacred plane like that of Orpheus and Museus, or even Hermes Trismegistus and Aesculapius.[22]

Ideal friendship and love between men was also used as a yardstick for vulgar heterosexual love and marriage by Ficino and other Italian humanists, and in this way the ideal undermined or complicated social

---

[19]   Ibid., p. 18.

[20]   David S. Chambers has reviewed the cases for and against the existence of the Florentine academy and he has commented on the flexibility with which the term 'academy' was used in fifteenth- and sixteenth-century Italy in 'The Earlier "Academies" in Italy', in *Italian Academies of the Sixteenth Century*, ed. by D.S. Chambers and F. Quiviger (London: The Warburg Institute University of London, 1995), pp. 1–14.

[21]   Plato, *Symposium*, ed. and trans. by C.J. Rowe (Warminster: Aris and Phillips, 1998), p. 83.

[22]   Marsilio Ficino, *The Letters of Marsilio Ficino*, trans. by Members of the Language Department of the School of Economic Science, London, 6 vols (London: Sepheard-Walwyn, 1975–99), I (1975), pp. 96–7.

hierarchies.[23] For example, Lorenzo de' Medici 'il Magnifico' addressed a letter to Ficino in which he declared:

> You therefore belong not to Marsilio but to your Lorenzo, who is no less yours than you are your own. In which case, if you wish to be restored to yourself know that it will be on the condition that whenever you take account of yourself you must equally take account of me at the same time. For those whom immortal God has joined together let no man put asunder.[24]

This passage could be analysed at length in terms of the playfulness with which Lorenzo uses notions of equality and exclusivity in perfect friendship and the mingling of souls to highlight the social inequality existing between the two men. The most important point to be made here is that the letter reflects an ideal of friendship that elevates virtue attained by study above the social inequality that might otherwise have divided the two men. A similar rhetorical conceit was expressed in visual terms in the near-contemporary double portrait of two Florentines of unequal social status by Filippino Lippi.[25] In general, this idealization may have mitigated some of the worst excesses of Florentine social relations that have been regarded as especially antagonistic.[26]

Lorenzo de' Medici employed the language of the marriage ceremony in his letter to Ficino, and such 'sacramental male bonding' stands in close proximity to the world of Alan Bray's 'wedded brothers'. The 'wedded brothers' discovered by Bray surprisingly do not include any Italians. However, two men in Ficino's circle who absorbed neo-Platonic ideas of love and friendship were Giovanni Pico della Mirandola and Girolamo Benivieni, and like other 'wedded brothers', the two men are buried together, in this case in a tomb in the left side of the nave in the Dominican church of San Marco, under a tombstone set up some time after the death of Benivieni in 1542. Below an inscription recording the death of Pico are the following words: 'Girolamo Benivieni provided for his burial in this soil so that after death location would not separate the bones of those

---

[23]   On the relationship between exemplary friendship between men and the ideal of marriage, see Hyatte, 'Complementary Humanistic Models'.

[24]   'Iam igitur non Marsilii es, sed Laurentii tui, non minus tui quam tu ipsius. Qua in re, si teipsum tibi reddi vis, scito id ea conditione futurum, ut nullam de te habere possis rationem, quin aeque de me ipso eodem tempore habiturus sis. Quos enim immortalis Deus coniunxit, homo non separet' (Ficino, *Lettere I: 1460–1474*, ed. by Riccardo Fubini (Florence: Giunti Barbera, 1977), pp. 155–56; translation in Ficino, *Letters*, I (1975), p. 64.

[25]   Jill Burke, *Changing Patrons: Social Identity and the Visual Arts in Renaissance Florence* (University Park: Pennsylvania State University Press, 2004), p. 86.

[26]   See Ronald F.E. Weissman, *Ritual Brotherhood in Renaissance Florence* (New York and London: Academic Press, 1982), ch. 1 'Judas the Florentine'.

whose souls had been joined in life by Love.'[27] Such an inscription in so prominent a position has no other Italian parallels, as far as I have been able to discover, but can clearly be associated with Ficinian discussions of love and perfect friendship in the pursuit of wisdom. In this respect it is worth noting that Benivieni wrote a poetic exposition of Ficino's commentary on the *Symposium*, and Pico added his own commentary on it in 1486.[28]

The Pico-Benivieni tomb can also be read in a distinctively religious light, as the rather brooding figure of Fra Girolamo Savonarola placed in front of it at a later date should remind the viewer. Pico and Benivieni have been closely associated with the Dominican friar: Pico's work against astrology was the basis for an Italian epitome by Savonarola, the *Trattato contra li astrologi* (1497), while Benivieni in his turn acted as a translator of Savonarola's works and was the composer of *canzone* for Savonarolan festivals.[29] The 'tension between the Neoplatonic ideals which had influenced him during his association with the Ficinian circle and the more sober vision of Christianity which Savonarola had imparted to him' are apparent in Benivieni's commentary on his *canzone*, written in 1500 while he was in disgrace after Savonarola's fall from power.[30] Here, according to Lorenzo Polizzotto, Benivieni Christianized his earlier amorous *canzone* and rejected a purely contemplative and philosophical approach to the soul's union with God in favour of a more Savonarolan style of reform, which buttressed the contemplative ascent with faith, humility, meekness, living well and conformity to the will of God.

Similar tensions between neo-Platonism, literature, theology and active reform of Church, state and individual can be found in the lives of Pietro Bembo, Gasparo Contarini, Tommaso Giustiniani and Vincenzo Querini, who were friends of Benivieni and of other Florentine

---

[27]   'Hieronymus Beniveni ne disiunctus post / mortem locus ossa separet quos animos / in vita coniunxit amor: hac humo / svpposita poni curavit'. A poem on the reverse of the tomb runs: 'Io priego Dio Girolamo che 'n pace / così in ciel sia il tuo Pico congiunto / come 'n terra eri, et come 'l tuo defunto / corpo hor con le sacr'ossa sue qui iace'. Isidoro del Lungo, *Florentia* (Florence: Barbera, 1897), p. 278.

[28]   Lorenzo Polizzotto, *The Elect Nation: The Savonarolan Movement in Florence, 1494–1545* (Oxford: Clarendon Press, 1994), pp. 141–7.

[29]   Patrick Macey, *Bonfire Songs: Savanarola's Musical Legacy* (Oxford: Clarendon Press, 1998). I am grateful to Dr Noel O'Regan for this reference. In the context of my argument here it is worth pointing out that Psalm 133 'Ecce quam bonus' ('Behold how good and how pleasant it is for brethren to dwell together in unity!') had particular significance to Savonarola and his followers: ibid., pp. 23–7.

[30]   Polizzotto, *Elect Nation*, p. 149.

piagnone.[31] The Venetian patricians forged their friendships during the 1490s at the University of Padua: a masculine environment which might be characterized as a Socratic-Platonic academy where communal life was marked by the signs of social status such as clothing and banquets.[32] Drawn together by their literary and philosophical interests, these friends formed a 'Compagnia degli amici' for which Bembo provided the rules in *c*.1500.[33] The *compagnia*, with its medals inscribed 'Sodality of Friends' ('amicorum sodalitati'), provisions for a portrait of each friend who joined and for a mourning period after the death of each member, is as redolent of the rambunctious patrician companies of hose in Venice and Padua as the Platonic academy.[34] The laws of the company acknowledged that friendship ('amistà') was the sweetest and most joyful thing in human life. As a token of the classical root of this notion, Bembo quoted the Greek proverb usually attributed to Pythagoras that 'Friends hold all things in common' ('Sieno tra essi tutti le cose communi'). For the members of the 'compagnia', these 'cose communi' included both spiritual and earthly goods. The rules stated that all good and bad fortune would be shared and no literary enterprise could be undertaken without the consent of the others. Significantly, the rules admitted no rupture in the company except in the case of war when the demands of the members' 'patrie' might supersede those of loving friends.

Alessandro Ballarin has emphasized the neo-Platonic background to this group and has highlighted the important role of Petrarchism, especially as expressed in Bembo's *Gli Asolani* (1505), in providing a sort of poetic theology.[35] As Constance Furey has recently argued in relation to Erasmus and his 'religious republic of letters', and also in respect of the Venetian friends with whom he had some contact when he stayed in the city, the private communal world of poetry and scholarship could offer an alternative to the institutional public realm in which many humanists were more or less unhappily involved. Such withdrawal into letters did

---

[31]   Stephen D. Bowd, *Reform Before the Reformation: Vincenzo Querini and the Religious Renaissance in Italy*, Studies in Medieval and Reformation Thought, 87 (Leiden: Brill, 2002), pp. 180–87.

[32]   On expressions of masculinity at university, see Ruth Mazo Karras, *From Boys to Men: Formations of Masculinity in Late Medieval Europe* (Philadelphia: University of Pennsylvania Press, 2003), ch. 3. I am grateful to Dr Jonathan Davies for this reference.

[33]   Pietro Bembo, *Prose e rime*, ed. by Carlo Dionisotti (Turin: Einaudi, 1960), pp. 699–703.

[34]   L. Venturi, 'Le Compagnie della Calza: sec. XV–XVI' (part 2), *Nuovo archivio veneto*, n.s. 17 (1909), 140–233. Matteo Casini is writing a study of these companies.

[35]   Alessandro Ballarin, 'Giorgione e la Compagnia degli Amici: Il "Doppio ritratto" Ludovisi', *Storia dell'arte italiana. Parte seconda: Dal Medioevo al Novecento. Volume primo: Dal Medioevo al Quattrocento* (Turin: Einaudi, 1983), pp. 479–541.

not necessarily constitute 'resistance' or 'desertion', but could be a means towards engagement and constructive action, or reform through discussion and meditation with others on sacred and profane letters. Nevertheless, such action eschewed worldly priorities and formal hierarchies and therefore encouraged a form of friendship that respected rank but permitted men *and* women to transcend it with literary skill, notably in poetry as a form of theology.[36]

Informal and semi-formal literary associations or friendships such as the *compagnia degli amici* dedicated to Latin and neo-Petrarchan verse seem to confirm Furey's thesis about the primacy given to poetry in the republic of letters, as a form of theology and an expression of ambivalence towards formal political networks.[37] The potential for the admission of women to the *compagnia*, stated in one of its rules, reflects Bembo's own rejection in his *Gli Asolani* of the conventional hierarchies that displayed some hostility towards feminine involvement in literary matters.[38] Bembo's position may owe something to his contact with the Duchess of Urbino, who was in exile in Venice in 1501–02, and was based on his own practice as his correspondence with his lover Maria Savorgnan and his admirer Lucrezia Borgia reveals.[39] Bembo's resistance to, or ambivalence about, the requirements of service in the Venetian state are quite well known and he spent the first decade of the sixteenth century pursuing religious withdrawal, courtly isolation and literary *otium*. As Bembo wrote to his brother Carlo around 1500: 'Siano pur degli altri le mitre e le corone, *Rura*

---

[36]   Furey, *Erasmus, Contarini*. On 'poetry as true theology' expressing 'transcendent truth' for Petrarch and others see ibid., pp. 67–8. See also Ronald G. Witt, 'Coluccio Salutati and the Conception of the *Poeta Theologus* in the Fourteenth Century', *Renaissance Quarterly*, 30 (1977), 538–63.

[37]   On the shared Platonic and Christian ideal of friendship as common ownership of all goods, and its political implications, see Wootton, 'Friendship Portrayed'. On the reception of Platonic political ideals, including the emphasis on wisdom acquired and exercised by the philosopher-prince, see Alison Brown, 'Platonism in Fifteenth-century Florence and its Contribution to Early Modern Political Thought', *The Journal of Modern History*, 58 (1986), 383–413.

[38]   Bembo, *Prose e rime*, 701; *idem, Gli Asolani*, ed. by Giorgio Dilemmi (Florence: Accademia della Crusca, 1991), p. 182.

[39]   Maria Savorgnan and Pietro Bembo, *Carteggio d'amore (1500–1501)*, ed. by Carlo Dionisotti (Florence: Felice Le Monnier, 1950). The Petrarchan playfulness of Savorgnan and Bembo is analysed by Gordon Braden, *Petrarchan Love and the Continental Renaissance* (New Haven, CT: Yale University Press, 1999), pp. 92–6. The theme of love surpassing earthly considerations, ambitions and riches is addressed in a letter from Bembo to Savorgnan: *Lettere*, I (1987), pp. 77–8. Bembo also declares to Savorgnan that '*di pari* Amore tutto può', ibid., p. 46 (this is an adapted reading of the text following Gordon Braden, 'Applied Petrarchism: The Loves of Pietro Bembo', *Modern Language Quarterly*, 57 (1996), 397–423 (p. 422)). On the notion of the lover living only in the beloved, see Bembo, *Lettere*, I (1987), pp. 106–7.

mihi, et rigui placeant in vallibus amnes.[40] Bembo's retreat involved a return
to source in order to produce philologically correct or improved editions
of Dante and Petrarch in 1501 and 1502: quite a distance from Girolamo
Benivieni's highly 'political' Dante dressed as a *piagnone* prophet.[41]

A similar case of resistance and ambivalence through Petrarchism can
also be made for Querini. Although he served as an ambassador for Venice
on several occasions, in letters to his friends, Querini frequently makes
plain his disgust with earthly ambition and political demands. Querini's
verse may also be interpreted as a retreat from formal political engagement
and as an adumbration of his eremitical withdrawal in 1512. In one of the
posthumously published sonnet sequences, Querini traces the arc of his
tormented state. He has been impelled to experience 'fosco piacer …colmo
d'inganni …vera noia …falso diletto …speranza dubbiosa, e 'l dolor
certo',[42] on account of the passion which the holy appearance of his divine
beloved has aroused. His intellect turns to this object but the flight of his
soul towards his beloved can only be achieved when it is inflamed by her
glances. However, just as Querini dwells on her beauty, her 'angelica fronte'
and the 'chiaro, e vivo raggio' which shines from her eyes, he falters, his
hopes are dashed and he returns to his state of 'dolce pena, /
Temperando
quell'ardor, che sì l'offende.' Querini the hopeless lover therefore hopes
to be revived by the sweet sight, sound and smell associated with 'il ben
Pianeta' and nature itself is renewed by her light. After reaffirming the
single focus of his love and pleading for her pity, the concluding sonnets
return to the theme of the words and beauty of his beloved that inflame
his heart and which, Querini concludes, are immortal.[43] In another lyrical
and plaintive sequence of mock-heroic *ottava rima*, Querini evokes a
Giorgionesque nocturnal scene: the anguished lover pours out his swan-
song to the countryside, lamenting his many 'martiri', the war he has lost
and the prison in which he finds himself chained. Finally, the nightingale
joins in his lament, signalling the approach not of love but of death (or, in
Christian terms, the arrival of Christ, the light of the world) that comes

---

[40]   Ibid., p. 121.

[41]   Sherry Roush, 'Dante as Piagnone Prophet: Girolamo Benivieni's "Cantico in laude
di Dante" (1506)', *Renaissance Quarterly*, 55 (2002), 49–80. See *idem, Hermes' Lyre:
Italian Poetic Self-Commentary from Dante to Tommaso Campanella* (Toronto: University
of Toronto Press, 2002).

[42]   'Sombre pleasure … heights of deception … true boredom … false delight …
doubtful hope and certain suffering'.

[43]   Lodovico Dolce (ed.), *Il primo volume delle rime scelte da diversi autori, di nuovo
corrette, et ristampate* (Venice: Gabriel Giolito de' Ferrari, 1565), pp. 410–15.

with the sunrise, and is welcomed by the lover with joyful feelings of serenity.[44]

In signalling his debt to Petrarch in a multitude of stylistic and linguistic ways, Querini's imitation attempted to universalize Petrarchan form and to diminish the historical distance between his own time and that of Petrarch. This denial of rupture and emphasis on continuity marks for some literary critics the 'humanist crisis of receptivity' and the beginning of a descent into stale academic repetition, but it may also be read as a flight from the distractions of earthly business and ambition towards universal and constant truths embodied in a love of Christ.[45] Giustiniani and Querini, like their friend the poet Girolamo Benivieni, rejected the classical notion of love and friendship that found its highest expression in human virtue, and moved closer to the ideal beloved of Christ, and especially Christian 'caritas', through vows of chastity, solitude and ultimately withdrawal to the hermitage of the Camaldolese order at Camaldoli in the Tuscan Appenines during 1511–12.

The break-up of the *compagnia degli amici* and of the wider circle of friends signals the Venetians' decisive movement from the philosophical or poetic basis of friendship to an eremitic or religious friendship. The seeds of this process lay in the neo-Platonic mysticism or theology of Ficino and it grew by way of the Petrarchan verse already briefly addressed. The way in which the latter could provide a bridge between both worlds is suggested by the bishop of Padua, Pietro Barozzi – much admired by Querini, Giustiniani, and Contarini – for he included a Latin translation of Petrarch's *canzona* ccclxvi ('Vergine bella che di sol vestita') among his prayers for personal use.[46] More directly, a document recently discovered by Alessandro Gnocchi shows how Giustiniani sought to give a more pronounced spiritual spin to the literary laws of the *compagnia*, when he added to the requirements for mutual aid the desideratum that members also hold 'i beni del animo' in common. These spiritual goods could include skills or knowledge acquired by study but also by daily reflection before sleep. '[L]e amice exortationi et le amorevole reprensioni' would drive the

44   *Rime diverse di molti eccellentiss[imi] auttori nuovamente raccolte. Libro primo con nuova additione ristampato* (Venice: Gabriel Giolito di Ferrarii, 1549), pp. 195–203.

45   Thomas M. Greene, *The Light in Troy: Imitation and Discovery in Renaissance Poetry* (New Haven, CT: Yale University Press, 1982), p. 151. See also Roland Greene, *Post-Petrarchism: Origins and Innovations of the Western Lyric Sequence* (Princeton, NJ: Princeton University Press, 1991). I am grateful to Dr Abigail Brundin for these references.

46   Pierantonio Gios, *L'attività pastorale del vescovo Pietro Barozzi a Padova (1487–1507)*, Fonti e ricerche di storia ecclesiastica padovano, 8 (Padua: Istituto per la storia ecclesiastica padovano, 1977), p. 76 n. 61.

soul along the path of virtue, while friendly advice would be given to any member undertaking religious vows, new studies, or love affairs.[47]

However, physical separation put the ideal of friendship under pressure. Aristotle stated that not only must a friend be good, he must be good for the loving friend as an individual, and he should normally be present in order to maintain the friendship. Plato presented a more open and universal form of friendship.[48] In its Christian adaptation by St Gregory of Nazianus, this was a friendship that could overcome distance and console in absence by uniting friends in the spiritual body of Christ through letters.[49] Petrarch's letters provided a powerful and influential Italian example of the way in which absence might not lead to a breach in friendship for, as Petrarch remarked, the ideal friends are as one soul and in each other's prayers.[50]

The problem of separation was felt especially strongly by Gasparo Contarini, whose letters show that he struggled to overcome the absence of his friends. Contarini's epistolary friendship with the new hermits Fra Paolo (Giustiniani) and Fra Pietro (Querini) echoes the medieval genre of friendship letters of conversion in which a monk addresses a friend in the world, describes the advantages of monastic life, and invites him in. The correspondence may also be compared with that of Petrarch where the pleasure of friendship is praised as an honourable thing and strong feelings of inadequacy before God are moderated. Contarini remained in Venice and read Plato, Aristotle and Augustine as he underwent a spiritual crisis which was deepened by the physical distance of his friends: he tried to accept that his justification was inherent but could also be imputed through the actions of will and intellect.

Contarini dwelled on the 'caritas' he received from his friends, even at a distance, and he recognized that 'caritas' could work in this way since it was founded in the love of Christ rather than in earthly or material considerations. Contarini therefore suggested that Giustiniani's absence, which conventionally philosophers said should moderate the warmth of friendship, had in fact led Giustiniani to love Contarini more tenderly.

---

[47]   Alessandro Gnocchi, 'Tommaso Giustiniani, Ludovico Ariosto e la compagnia degli amici', *Studi di filologia italiana. Bollettino annuale dell'accademia della crusca*, 57 (1999), 277–93.

[48]   Eoin G. Cassidy, '"He who has friends can have no friend": Classical and Christian Perspectives on the Limits to Friendship', in *Friendship in Medieval Europe*, ch. 2.

[49]   Caroline White, 'Friendship in Absence – Some Patristic Views', in ibid., ch. 3.

[50]   Francesco Petrarca, *Letters on Familiar Matters. Rerum familiarum libri IX–XVI*, trans. Aldo S. Bernardo (Baltimore, MD and London: Johns Hopkins University Press, 1982), IX, 9; X, 4; XII, 16; XIII, 10; XVIII, 8; *idem, Letters of Old Age. Rerum senilium libri I–XVIII*. Vol. 2, Books X–XVIII, trans. Aldo S. Bernardo, Saúl Levin and Reta A. Bernardo (Baltimore, MD and London: Johns Hopkins University Press, 1992), XIV, 1, 9; XVI, 4. I am grateful to Dr Alexander Lee for his advice on Petrarch.

Contarini ascribed this to the fact that Giustiniani's love 'is not a love or earthly friendship founded in the enjoyment of conversing and living with friends, which philosophers have known, but is founded in Christian charity', which caused one to love God before rational creatures, and which related an increase of love towards him with a corresponding increase in love for those who are near or far from oneself.[51] By means of those who are a 'sweet focus of divine love' such as Giustiniani, Contarini hoped 'occasionally at least to break the ice of my adamantine heart'.[52] As he wrote to Querini:

> I am sure that the good will which you bear towards me, and your increased charity towards God – which means that your charity towards your neighbour has increased also, for in him you love God – will not allow you to omit that action of piety and mercy towards us.[53]

As Contarini noted here, the Aristotelian ideal of friendship as material aid was necessarily transformed into spiritual aid. Such friendship imitated that of Christ for his disciples when he commanded: 'That ye love one another as I have loved you'.[54]

---

[51]   'Dil che altro causa non puol esser, se non che l'amor vostro non è amor nè amicitia mondana fondata ne la delectatione di conversar et viver con li amici, la qual i philosophi hanno cognosciuta, ma è fondata ne la charità christiana la qual prima è verso Dio et dapoi verso le creature rationale, come quelle che la divina bontà ha voluto far partecipe et communicar con loro quella felicità la qual lei sola per natura possiede': Contarini to Giustiniani, Venice, 10 August 1511, in Hubert Jedin, 'Contarini und Camaldoli', *Archivio Italiano per la Storia della Pietà*, 2 (1959), 53–118 (pp. 65–6). For Giustiniani's 'tenerezza di charità verso la persona mia', see Contarini to Giustiniani, Venice, 24 April 1511, in ibid., p. 62.

[52]   'Non me meraveglio adonque se, con più fervente amor, essendo ne l'Heremo lontano, amate più li amici vostri, che non facevi essendoli presente, dil che io, per mia parte, ne resto tanto contento, quanto forse de ogni altra cosa, perchè pur spero, se per me son luntano da quel dolce foccho de l'amor divino, per mezo di tal persone, qual seti vui, qualche volta saltem romper questo giazo del mio adamantino core': ibid., p. 66.

[53]   'Son certo che la benivolentia me portate et la charitate vostra cresciuta verso Dio et, per consequente, cresciuta etiam verso el proximo vostro, in el quale amate Dio, non vi lassarà pretermeter questo offitio di pietade et misericordia verso de nui': Contarini to Querini, Venice, 10 March 1512, in ibid., p. 85.

[54]   'Se Aristotele, privo del lume vero et di quella charitate, la qual sola Iesu Christo ha lassato per precepto a tuti nui, dice nel nono Libro de la Hetica sua che, essendo officio de ogni amico subvegnir a l'amico suo ne li besogni sui circa le cose pertinente al corpo et a la fortuna, molto più debbe esser officio de l'amico subvegnire l'altro amico ne li deffecti sui circa li beni de l'animo, li quali veramente son beni et veramente sonno nostri: Che adonque dirà uno christiano, el qual ha udito nel sacro Evangelio da la boccha de Iesu Christo [John 15:12]: Questo è il precepto mio: che ve amate insieme come io ve ho amato vui, zoè praecipue ne li beni di l'animo, ne li quali Christo ne ama et amò li discipuli sui? Perché ne

Contarini's understanding that practical and moral virtues are inferior to intellectual or contemplative virtues echoes the *Nicomachean Ethics*, but also follows Cicero in his *Laelius* where the true friend subordinates the individual's will and the friends' common will to the higher interests of the state, especially concord within the republic. Contarini's position also reflects Augustine's emphasis on the power of Christ's 'caritas' and the possibility of redemption that Christ's sacrifice for humans had admitted. Contarini's letters are studded with comments on his own 'basezza' but equally they dwell on the figure of the crucified and redemptive Christ.[55] Contarini declared that he did not merit the 'benivolentia' of Giustiniani, which increased in absence rather than diminished. He was aware of his past sins and felt that, despite all the penitence he showed, he would never be able to merit that happiness. However, the passion of Christ might be sufficient to make an accounting for the world's sins. He paraphrased Paul (Rom. 12:3–6):

> And although everyone cannot have the grace of being members close to the head [that is, Christ], yet everyone who is connected to that body by the influence of the virtue of the satisfaction that our head carried out, can hope to make more satisfaction for his own sins with a little effort.[56]

Such a union had to be made with faith, hope and love. Contarini therefore allowed his spirit to soar to that highest happiness ('summa bontà'), and he saw Christ 'on the cross with his arms open and breast opened to the heart' ready to accept him.[57] Contarini declared:

> Therefore will I not sleep securely, although in the midst of the city and without having satisfied the debt that I have contracted, having such a one to pay for my debt? Truly I sleep and I live thus securely as if I stayed all my life in

---

li altri beni ben sappeti che li electi de Dio in questa peregrination spessissime volte sonno molto percossi': Contarini to Querini, Venice, 10 March 1512, in ibid., p. 85. Contarini's idea of material friendship is here drawn from Aristotle, *Nicomachean Ethics* (Cambridge, MA: Loeb Classical Library, 1968), IX, 8, 11.

[55]   Bowd, *Reform*, pp. 88–101.

[56]   'Et benchè tutti non possi haver tanta gratia di esser membri propinqui al capo, pur tuti coloro che saranno connexi a questo corpo per influxo di la virtù de la satisfaction che ha fato el capo nostro, potrà con poccha fatiga sperar di satisfar i suo' peccati': Contarini to Giustiniani, Venice, 24 April 1511, in Jedin, 'Contarini und Camaldoli', p. 64.

[57]   'Per il qual pensiero io di gran timor et assai tristizia converso in alegreza, commenciai con tuto el spirito voltarmi a quella summa bontà, la qual vedeva per amor mio esser in croce con le bracie aperte et con el pecto aperto in fin al core ... ': ibid.

the hermitage, with the intention of never becoming dissatisfied with such a support.[58]

He reiterated that he would live secure and without fear of his own wickedness because of Christ's mercy ('misericordia'). This thought constantly nourished him, despite the fact that Contarini lived among the multitude of the city.

Contarini's use of the imagery of Christ's wounds in this letter is striking, and echoes the letters of Querini where he wrote that he could achieve salvation by turning from Aristotle and looking into his own soul, abandoning his worldly thoughts, and turning them towards

> ... your Saviour, to your Redeemer, to the Creator of all things visible and invisible; and you will see him upon the hard wood of the cross, all bloodied and with his open and cruelly nailed arms, calling to you: Come, my son, come, and do not be afraid; for if I wash your wounds with my own blood you will be most speedily restored to health.[59]

Giustiniani's choice of the eremitic life had also been closely connected with his experience of the redemptive powers of Christ who he describes, in an echo of Petrarch's *canzona* cclxiv ('Quelle pietose braccia / in ch' io mi fido veggio aperte ancora'), as having

> ... opened his Holy arms on the wooden cross in order to embrace, and not only his arms, but his flank to his heart opened to accept me to his heart, if I would wish to love him more than human things.[60]

---

[58] 'Non dormirò adonque io securo, benchè sia in mezo la città, benchè non satisfaci al debito che ho contracto, havendo io tal pagatore del mio debito? Veramente dormirò et vegierò cusì securo come se tuto el tempo di la vita mia fosse stado ne l'Heremo, con proposito di non mi lassar mai da tal apozo': ibid.

[59] 'Drizza l'occhio della mente tua nella più intime parti dell'animo tuo, e chiaramente vedrai esser egli per le molte ed assai recenti piaghe più di quello, che talora pensi indebolito: e se vuoi giovevole medicina ad esse ritrovare, lasciando oggimai da canto li tanti e sì diversi pensieri del mondo, inalza la mente tua al Salvator tuo, al Redentor tuo, al Creatore di tutte le visibili ed invisibili cose, e lo vedrai sopra il duro legno della Croce tutto insanguinato con le aperte e crudelmente confitte braccia richiamarti: Vieni, figliuolo, vieni, e non temere, che con il proprio sangue mio lavando le tue ferite sarai presto presto risanato ...': Lycenope [pseud. Querini] to Giustiniani, n.p., n.d. [c.1511], *Annales Camaldulenses ordinis Sancti Benedicti*, ed. by J.B. Mittarelli and A. Costadoni, 9 vols (Venice, 1755–73. Facsimile reprint, Farnborough: Gregg, 1970), IX, cols 507–8.

[60] '[C]he apriva sul legno della Croce le sue sante braccia per abbracciarmi, e non pur le braccia, ma il fianco fino al cuore avea aperto per accettarmi nel petto suo, se io vorrò amare più lui, che le cose umane': Giustiniani to all of his friends, December 1510, in ibid., col. 475.

Giustiniani was convinced that he could reach their 'eternal blessed homeland' by means of the 'merits of Jesus Christ, and not by my works'.[61]

It is clear then that, although a physical distance opened up between them, the friends worked towards a religious friendship which contained echoes of Petrarchan torments of love and, like the relationship between the 'wedded brothers', was based on a eucharistic devotion and communion in Christ. However, Giustiniani's emphasis on justification by faith over works would have appeared heretical in the decades which followed Martin Luther's attack on the Roman Church and his promotion of the 'priesthood of all believers'. The intense inner spiritual experience of individuals and groups of friends became associated with mystic women, Erasmians and Valdesian sects, and was suspected or suppressed by the Roman authorities after 1540 in favour of a religious life channelled through corporate structures supported by Church and state.

The suppression of Erasmianism and heresy, and the promotion of institutional means of charity and communal religious experience, are closely linked to the name of Gian Pietro Carafa who was elected Pope Paul IV in 1555, and it is useful to close by comparing the Venetians with Carafa, who set a new and more authoritarian tone. Carafa's friendly relations with Tommaso Giustiniani and Gasparo Contarini began around 1522 when he was active in Rome as a member of the Company of Divine Love, which cared for men and women afflicted by syphilis and some other incurable diseases at the hospital of San Giacomo.[62] Giustiniani and Carafa met in Rome in 1523 and they may have been drawn to each other by their shared personal asceticism and by a mutual appreciation of the rewards of contemplation and eremitic withdrawal.[63] Carafa may have

---

[61] '[E]terna beata patria'; 'meriti della passione di Gesucristo, e non per le opere mie': ibid., col. 476.

[62] Jon Arrizabalaga, John Henderson and Roger French, *The Great Pox: The French Disease in Renaissance Europe* (New Haven, CT and London: Yale University Press, 1997), pp. 153–8.

[63] Giustiniani to Carafa, Hermitage of San Girolamo di Pascelupo, 4 August 1523: Frascati, Sacro Eremo Tuscolano (hereafter Tusc.), cod. Q III, fols 101r–2r. Note also Giustiniani to Cardinal Lorenzo Pucci, *c.*1524: Tusc., cod. F VIII, fol. 16v, cited in Eugenio Massa, *I manoscritti originali del b. Paolo Giustiniani custoditi nell'eremo di Frascati. Descrizione analitica e indici con ricerche sui codici avellanesi di san Pier Damiani*, 2 vols (Rome: Edizioni di storia e letteratura, 1967–74), I, 200. Following his visit to Rome during the summer of 1523, Giustiniani praised Carafa for his holiness (Giustiniani to Thiene, Grotte del Massaccio [Cupramontana], 1 December 1523: Marino Sanudo, *I Diarii*, ed. Rinaldo Fulin et al., 58 vols (Venice: F. Visentini, 1879–1903), XXXV, col. 252). He also wrote later that Carafa (and another bishop) 'in quelli cose [that is, programmes of reform] per diversi rispetti existimo li piu sani et piu oculari iuditij de Italia et non dico per adulatione ma perche cosi sento in verita' [in those matters they are in many ways the soundest and most

considered joining the Camaldolese order and it was reported in Venice that Carafa 'si fe' remito.'[64] Giustiniani was informed by one of his monks that Carafa needed greater solitude in order to achieve that tranquility of the soul, which led to religious perfection and a 'total spirituality of life'. Carafa, he added, had taken vows and his 'fratelli' were interested in achieving separation and distance from the world and retiring to cells in some place of solitude. Giustiniani was full of praise for this scheme and recommended several cells and oratories held by the Camaldolese in the Marche, near Ancona.[65] He also recommended another place deserted by a group of hermits who, he said, lived without any rule.[66]

Carafa did not pursue this scheme and the report that Carafa 'si fe' remito' was a reference to the new order of regular clerics called Theatines that was founded by Carafa and his friend Gaetano Thiene and recognized in a papal bull of June 1524.[67] Members of this order were to take vows of poverty, chastity and obedience, and to live communally in a religious or secular location. The order did administer the sacraments, but they did not

---

clear-sighted judges in Italy; and I do not say this in adulation, but because I feel it to be true]: Giustiniani to Galeazzo Gabrielli, n.p. , n.d., (c.1524): Tusc., cod. Q V, fol. 27v. Giustiniani's 'Meditation on the Resurrection' is dated, in a later note, 'in domo D.ni ep(iscop)i theatini', 27 March 1524, in Tusc., cod. Q III, fols 150bis r–53v: cited by Massa, *Manoscritti originali*, I (1967), pp. 271–2.

[64]   Sanudo, *Diarii*, XXXVI, col. 527 (summary of letters on 15 August 1524). See also Luca Eremita Hispano, *Romualdina, seu eremitica Montis Coronae Camaldulensis ordinis historia* (Padua: Hermitage of Rua, 1587), fol. 135v; Giuseppe Silos, *Historiarum clericorum regularium a congregatione condita* ... 3 vols (Rome-Palermo, 1650–66), I, part 3, book 1, fol. 25; and Agostino Romano Fiori, *Vita del B. Michele eremita Camaldolese* (Rome: Antonio de' Rossi, 1720), p. 260.

[65]   Giustiniani to Carafa, n.p. (Grotte del Massaccio [Cupramontana]?), n.d.: Carlo Bromato [pseud. Bartolomeo Carrara], *Storia di Paolo IV, pontefice massimo*, 2 vols in 1 (Ravenna: Antonmaria Landi, 1748–53), pp. 136–7.

[66]   The hermit Niccolò Morosini's departure from Venice is noted in Sanudo, *Diarii*, XXVI, col. 29 (under the date 11 September 1518). Note also the work of Paduan patrician Marco Mantova Benavides, *L'heremita* (Venice: Zorzi Ruscone, 1521) discussed by Thomas F. Mayer, 'Marco Mantova and the Paduan Religious Crisis of the Early Sixteenth Century', in *Cardinal Pole in European Context: A via media in the Reformation* (Aldershot: Ashgate Variorum, 2000), ch. 9.

[67]   *Bullarum diplomatum et privilegiorum sanctorum Romanorum pontificium* ... , ed. by Sebastiano Franco and Enrico Dalmazzo (Turin: A. Vecco, 1860), VI, 73–4. On the Theatines, see Ludwig von Pastor, *The History of the Popes, from the Close of the Middle Ages*, ed. by Ralph Francis Kerr, 40 vols (London, 1891–1953), X, 407–19; Pio Paschini, *S. Gaetano Thiene, Gian Pietro Carafa e le origini dei chierici regolari Teatini* (Rome: Scuola tipografica Pio X, 1926). I have gleaned some information on the Theatines in Venice from a late seventeenth-century manuscript history in Rome, Archivio Generale Teatino, Casettino 14, no. 3, 'Annali dei Padri Teatini della Casa di Venezia sul principio dell'anno 1524. 24. di giugno'; and *Theatine Spirituality: Selected Writings*, ed. and trans. by William V. Hudon (Mahwah, NJ: Paulist Press, 1996).

normally undertake works of charity and did not act as a lay confraternity, although it would be fair to say that the emphasis on friendship in Christ through charity found in the Company of Divine Love was conspicuous in the Theatine rules drafted by Carafa.[68] In these rules, Carafa invited the potential novice to come and observe the order's practices, including 'what care must be taken with respect to literary studies', and enjoined him to follow Christ through the 'narrow gate', to walk 'amidst the sorrow of repentance' and come finally to 'the haven of the fullest charity'. The initiate 'will judge all to be vanity, even among those who have renounced the world' unless he 'makes every effort to conquer concupiscence and attain the charity of the Fathers'.[69] This 'blessed' charity is preserved, as St Augustine says, by a 'manner of life', language, and general appearance which 'are all appropriate to charity … and, if the vow, the profession, the entire religious life all zealously serve charity'. It is wrong, Carafa states, to dishonour charity as it is wrong to dishonour God, for it is recommended by Christ and the apostles and 'if it is absent … everything is empty, but if it is present, all things are full.'[70]

Carafa, like Giustiniani, fled Rome in 1527 to escape the devastating sack of the city, and it was to Venice that he brought the Theatines and established links with Gasparo Contarini and other prominent patricians who admired him. Contarini and Carafa shared an interest in promoting charitable fraternities and institutions that might aid lay religiosity. For example, both men visited the hospital of the *incurabili* in the city 'molte volte'.[71] The Theatines and the *incurabili* were closely related in terms of aims and personnel from their inception, and Gaetano Thiene played a key role in the establishment of the Venetian *incurabili* in 1522. The Theatine

[68]   Gian Pietro Carafa, 'The Theatine Rule of 1526', in John C. Olin (ed.), *The Catholic Reformation: Savonarola to Ignatius Loyola* (New York: Fordham University Press, 1992), pp. 128–32 (pp. 129, 131). A habit for the new company is described in a letter from Unknown (Valerio Lugio?) to Pietro Contarini q. Zaccaria, Rome, 21 October 1524: Sanudo, *Diarii*, XXXVII, col. 90. However, the rule of 1526 states: 'No colour of dress or specific habit is prescribed among us, nor is any prohibited' (Carafa, 'Theatine Rule', p. 131).

[69]   Concupiscence is the 'inordinate desire for temporal ends which has its seat in the senses' and was, according to Augustine, transferred to man with the Fall of Adam when the desires of the flesh were no longer subject to reason. Aquinas regarded it as the material (passive) element of original sin, while the formal (active) element was the loss of original righteousness. It is also a desire that prompts hope (while benevolence, a good worthy in itself, animates the justifying power of charity) and therefore 'provides reason and will with opportunities for resisting the disordered movements of the senses'. Protestants regarded it as a sin in itself and an offence against God. See *The Oxford Dictionary of the Christian Church*, ed. by F.L. Cross (London: Oxford University Press, 1957), s.v. 'concupiscence'.

[70]   Olin, *Catholic Reformation*, p. 132.

[71]   Piero Contarini to Paul III, Venice, 4 March 1540: Pietro Tacchi Venturi, *Storia della Compagnia di Gesù in Italia, narrata col sussidio di fonti inedite* (Rome, 1910), 1, p. 445.

bull of 1533 explicitly mentioned ministering to the ill as an activity of
the brotherhood and one example of service in a hospital as part of the
novitiate is recorded the following year.[72] Contarini's consistent support
for the new order of Jesuits may have been prompted by reports of their
work in the Venetian *incurabili*, as well as by the pronounced scholastic
and Augustinian elements of the *Spiritual Exercises* that he possibly
undertook with Loyola in Rome before Easter 1538. Contarini presented
the constitution of what he called 'li preti riformati del Iesu' to Pope Paul
III in person, and he added his own annotations to it.[73] Loyola wrote that
Contarini was 'factor' in all their matters, and the 'instrument' of their
affairs with the pope.[74]

`   However, there were also marked differences in the attitudes of Contarini
and Carafa towards lay religiosity and the authority of the church, which
stem from their different backgrounds and diverse experiences. Contarini's
realization that he could find salvation in the midst of the city did not
preclude his friendship with Giustiniani and Querini and was made possible
by a strong sense of the 'caritas' borne towards him by them. Contarini's
decision was also marked by an acute awareness of the limits of religious
friendship, for he sensed that his friends' love would not be enough to

[72]   The 1533 bull mentions pious activities in general, and caring for the sick in
particular: *Bullarum diplomatum*, VI, 161. The example of 1534 is recorded in a letter from
Carafa to Thiene, Venice, 18 January 1534: Paschini, *San Gaetano Thiene*, p. 72. But note
Ignatius of Loyola's comment that the Theatines 'do not preach or engage in any of the
corporal works of mercy': Loyola to Carafa, n.p. , n.d., [1536?], *Letters of St. Ignatius
of Loyola*, selected and trans. by William J. Young, S.J. (Chicago, IL: Loyola University
Press, 1959), p. 30. There is a facsimile and transcription of this letter – a partially and
carefully corrected draft and one of the earliest in Loyola's hand – in Georges Bottereau,
S.I., 'La "Lettre" d'Ignace de Loyola à Gian Pietro Carafa', *Archivum Historicum Societatis
Jesu*, 44 (1975), 139–51 (plate, pp. 149–51) ('avnque no prediquen, nj enlas otras obras de
mjsericordia corporals tanto no se exerçiten al parescer externo', ibid., p. 150). Was there
a change in the rule between 1533 and 1536? Was Loyola simply misinformed? Or, is he
referring to a different order? It has also been argued that Loyola never sent this letter:
ibid., pp. 142, 146–7, or that it was intended for someone else: Paschini, *S. Gaetano Thiene*,
p. 138 n. 1.
[73]   Vatican City, Biblioteca Apostolica Vaticana (hereafter BAV), Arch. Arcis S. Angeli,
Arm. XVII, Ord. 2. C., fols 145r–8r, printed in Tacchi Venturi, *Storia*, I (1910), pp. 554–
67. Another autograph annotation to the document by Contarini is at ibid., p. 566. The
document has been translated and published as 'The First Sketch of the Society of Jesus
1539', in *Catholic Reform From Cardinal Ximenes to the Council of Trent, 1495–1563:
An Essay with Illustrative Documents and a Brief Study of St. Ignatius Loyola*, ed. by John
C. Olin (New York: Fordham University Press, 1990). Contarini's meeting with the pope at
Tivoli and presentation of the 'cinque capitoli' is described in a brief letter from Contarini to
Loyola, Tivoli, 3 September 1539: *Cartas de San Ignacio de Loyola*, I, 433–4.
[74]   '[I]nstrumento y medio cerca de Su Santidad': Loyola to Piero Contarini, Rome, 18
December 1540, in ibid., pp. 98–9. See also John W. O'Malley, *The First Jesuits* (Cambridge,
MA: Harvard University Press, 1993), p. 315.

sustain a perfect religious friendship in which he achieved mystical or neo-Platonic union with the divine. However, Contarini accepted that this love would help him in the inferior exercise of moral virtues in the world. Accordingly, Contarini's model bishop of 1517 is full of practical virtues that elevate him *above* the monk and he dispenses charity from the comfort of his study with an urbane simplicity and sincerity.[75] Similarly, Contarini's *c*.1523 model of the machinery of Venetian government is predicated on the same Aristotelian and Thomist ideals of the public utility of association and friendship that emerge in his agonized letters to his friends.[76]

Contarini's attitude was certainly shaped by his Venetian values, for there was a 'secular bias' in Venetian government noted by William J. Bouwsma, and an 'obligation of the laity to supervise the church' embedded in Venetian tradition.[77] For example, as Brian Pullan has pointed out, in 1539 the *incurabili* hospital was given protection against being treated as an ecclesiastical benefice, while lay governors took control of Venetian hospitals more generally.[78] Contarini defended local ecclesiastical liberties and tolerated heretical books, much to the alarm of the papal legate in Venice and Spanish Inquisition respectively.[79] He deprecated the forced religious unity of the Inquisition and any arbitrary exercise of papal power that conflicted with human free will.[80] He disliked the Spanish Inquisition and its power to inspire fear in Catholics, and he also disapproved of

---

[75]   Gasparo Contarini, 'De officio episcopi' in *Gasparis Contareni Cardinalis Opera* (Paris: Sebastianus Nivellius, 1571), pp. 401–31. See *idem, The Office of a Bishop* (De Officio viri boni et probi episcopi), ed. and trans. by John Patrick Donnelly, S.J. (Milwaukee, WI: Marquette University Press, 2002). An English translation of about a half of the treatise is also in Olin, *Catholic Reformation*, ch. 7. The treatise is discussed by Gigliola Fragnito, *Gasparo Contarini, un magistrato veneziano al servizio della cristianità* (Florence: Leo S. Olschki, 1988); and Elisabeth G. Gleason, *Gasparo Contarini: Venice, Rome, and Reform* (Berkeley and Los Angeles: University of California Press, 1994), pp. 93–8.

[76]   Gasparo Contarini, *De Magistratibus et republica Venetorum* (Paris: M. Vascosan, 1543). See also *The Commonwealth and Government of Venice. Written by the Cardinall Gasper Contareno, and translated out of Italian into English, by Lewes Lewkenor Esquire …* (London: John Windet for Edmund Mattes, 1599), pp. 8–9, 13–14.

[77]   William J. Bouwsma, *Venice and the Defense of Republican Liberty: Renaissance Values in the Age of the Counter Reformation* (Berkeley and Los Angeles: University of California Press, 1968), pp. 64, 83.

[78]   Brian Pullan, *Rich and Poor in Renaissance Venice: The Social Institutions of a Catholic State, to 1620* (Oxford: Basil Blackwell, 1971), p. 333.

[79]   Girolamo Aleander to Pietro Carnesecchi, Venice, 14 March 1534: *Nunziature di Venezia*, vol. I: *(12 marzo 1533 – 14 agosto 1535)*, ed. by Franco Gaeta, Fonti per la storia d'Italia, 32 (Rome: Istituto storico italiano per l'età moderna e contemporanea, 1958), p. 191; *idem* to *idem*, Venice, 21 April 1534, in ibid., pp. 206–207; *idem* to *idem*, Venice, 23 April 1534, in ibid., pp. 210–11.

[80]   'Gasparis Contareni cardinalis, ad Paulum III. pont. max. de potestate pontificis in compositionibus epistola', in Josse Le Plat, *Monumentorum ad historiam Concilii Tridentini*

the way in which the administration of justice in Spain, although 'great' (*grande*), nevertheless 'soon declines more quickly to cruelty, than to any clemency'.[81] It is perhaps no surprise then that Contarini worked so hard in the years before his death to extend concordance to the Lutherans in Modena and at the Colloquy of Regensburg.[82]

By contrast, Carafa was disgusted with the involvement of lay people in administering the sacrament to the residents of the *convertite* (the home for reformed prostitutes) – which was uncanonical, and which he may also have felt smacked a little too much of Lutheranism and its 'priesthood of all believers'.[83] Carafa's solutions to heresy and corrupt clergy in Venice were outlined in his famous memorial of 1532, where he eschewed the strong Venetian tradition of independence from Rome and reliance on reforming and beneficent episcopal control in favour of new military orders and papal fiat.[84] Carafa supported – and headed – a reinvigorated Holy Office

---

potissimum illustrandum spectantium amplissima collectio, 7 vols (Louvain: Ex typographia academica, 1781–87), II, 608–15, esp. p. 614.

[81]   'In Ispagna si fa grande giustizia, la quale però declina più tosto a crudeltà, che ad alcuna clemenza', Contarini's 1525 *relazione* of his mission to Emperor Charles V: *Relazioni degli ambasciatori veneti al Senato*, ed. by Eugenio Albèri, 15 vols (Florence: Società editrice fiorentina, 1839–63), ser. 1, II, 44. In 1525, Contarini (as Venetian ambassador to the Emperor) came before the inquisition in Madrid seeking the release of three Venetian captains (including his brother) who had been seized on suspicion of selling a Bible printed in Hebrew, Latin and Chaldaic, with rabbinical annotations. Contarini reported to Venice, 'I spoke for a long time, explaining to them that the practice in Italy as well as in the whole Catholic church was to tolerate any infidel author, such as Averroës and many others, although, as it seemed to them, he contradicted the faith. I adduced many reasons why it would be wrong not to permit our adversaries to be heard and read': Contarini to Federico Contarini and his other brothers, Madrid, 7 February 1525: Sanudo, *Diarii*, XXXVIII, cols 202–3. I quote from the translation (slightly adapted) in Gleason, *Gasparo Contarini*, pp. 35–6. Contarini reported to the Venetian government that 'the inquisition in this kingdom is a most terrible thing, and not even the king has power over it. As far as the New Christians [*conversos*] are concerned, what appears to us insignificant seems serious to the inquisition': diplomatic dispatch, Madrid, 7 February 1525: National Archives: Public Record Office, MS 31/14/71, fols 184r–5r [stamped foliation].

[82]   Peter Matheson, *Cardinal Contarini at Regensburg* (Oxford: Clarendon Press, 1972); Gleason, *Gasparo Contarini*, ch. 4.

[83]   Carafa to Giberti, Venice, 31 March 1533: BAV, cod. Barberini Lat. 5697, fol. 62r–v. Note also his later critical remarks – in a 1539 appeal to Paul III – about rectors of the Church and presbyters not in sacred orders who take the sacrament to the sick: ibid., fol. 130v. The Fourth Lateran Council prohibited laypeople from interfering with Church property or any 'adjuncts of spiritual authority': X 3. 13. 12; *Corpus iuris canonici*, ed. by E.L. Richter and E. Friedberg, 2 vols (Leipzig: Tauchnitz, 1879–81), II, 516; *Decrees of the Ecumenical Councils*, ed. by N.P. Tanner, S.J., 2 vols (London: Sheed & Ward, 1990), I, 254.

[84]   BAV, cod. Barberini Lat. 5697, fols. 2r–11r; Gian Pietro Carafa, 'Memorial to Pope Clement VII (1532)', ch. 5 in Elisabeth G. Gleason, ed. and trans., *Reform Thought in Sixteenth-Century Italy* (Chico, CA: Scholars Press, 1981).

of the Inquisition in Rome, and his support for individual inquisitors was a matter addressed in letters written during his Venetian sojourn.[85]

These examples suggest how the institutions that evolved to dispense charity under the supervision of parish, confraternity, local government, or papacy left much less room for religious friendship. The necessity of control was made more urgent, of course, by the fear of heresy, and this accounts for the change in the texture of religious and cultural life in Italy after *c*.1500. As Brian McGuire has bluntly put it: 'When friendship ends as an ideal there is nothing left but authoritarianism.' However, in painful recollection of his own spiritual struggles, Contarini was concerned that the less adept among the faithful would find this solitude and authoritarianism too much. In an unstable and declining world, divine truth achieved through neo-Platonic contemplation or the assertion of theological clarity was the only constant. Contarini's work on political and ecclesiological structures is informed by this realization and he strove to clarify this framework and make it more flexible.

As Elisabeth Gleason has suggested, Contarini was also troubled by a fear that his solutions were more congenial to the literate or social elite of his friends than to the population as a whole. His pronounced support for the Jesuits may have arisen from an appreciation of their role in bridging the social gap and offering a religion accessible to as many as possible.[86] However, the growls of Carafa about Contarini's 'softly softly' approach to heresy and other matters in the 1530s, as well as his suspicious comments about the Venetian cardinal's friends (he is supposed to have commented of Pietro Bembo's election as cardinal in 1539: 'We don't need any more poets for cardinals')[87] suggest the limits of the republic of letters, religious friendships and the Renaissance, and in this way mark one point where the Counter-Reformation began.

---

[85]   Carafa to unknown, Venice, 3 July 1536: BAV, Cod. Barb. Lat 5697, fols 116r–v, 118r–v; Carafa, 'Memorial', p. 60. In 1552, Pole, who had resigned from the commission of the Inquisition, told Carafa that he objected to its harsh procedures: see Thomas F. Mayer, *Reginald Pole: Prince and Prophet* (Cambridge: Cambridge University Press, 2000), pp. 192, 197.

[86]   On this theme in Venetian religion and culture, see Harald Hendrix, 'Pietro Aretino's Humanità di Christo and the Rhetoric of Horror', in *Il rinascimento Italiano di fronte alla riforma: letteratura e arte. Sixteenth-century Italian art and literature and the Reformation, Atti del colloquio internazionale, London, The Warburg Institute, 30–31 gennaio 2004*, ed. by Chrysa Damianaki, Paolo Procaccioli and Angelo Romano (Rome: Vecchiarelli Editore, 2005), pp. 89–114.

[87]   In 1539, Bembo sent a *canzona* to Lisabetta Querini with the proviso that she tell no one about it nor show it to any 'persona del mondo': Bembo, *Lettere*, IV (1993), p. 245. Gordon Braden cites a manuscript (BAV, Vat. Lat. 6207, fol. 59r) attacking Bembo's lyrics for 'peccati mortali gravissimi' and speculates that this may have been 'part of a move against Bembo by the Inquisition': Braden, *Petrarchan Love*, pp. 101, 182 n. 57.

CHAPTER 2

Manuscript Collections of Spiritual Poetry in Sixteenth-Century Italy

Antonio Corsaro

It is not my intention in this chapter to explore systematically the entire corpus of Italian vernacular spiritual poetry of the sixteenth century, its general features and its most notable authors. Rather, my aim is to consider in detail a limited number of collections of varying renown, all notable because they circulated principally in manuscript form. A preliminary remark seems necessary in this regard: namely, that any discussion of the scribal circulation of poetry in the mid-sixteenth century necessarily restricts itself to a small number of examples, compared to the more mainstream production of printed books of verse that was fed by ongoing and fruitful communication between poets, printers and readers. A further preliminary remark concerns the choice of the term *spiritual* poetry. It is legitimate to call spiritual that particular kind of lyric poetry that originated from Petrarch's *Rerum vulgarium fragmenta*, frequently found within many works of the sixteenth century, usually occupying the final section of a profane collection of love lyrics and concentrating on matters of repentance and prayer. On the other hand, it is also evident that, especially during the watershed years between the Reformation and the Counter-Reformation, this way of conceiving of spiritual poetry is superseded by an alternative model, the production of collections of spiritual poems as intentionally separate and distinguished from collections of profane verse.

As far as chronology is concerned, the beginning of this new trend for discrete collections of spiritual verses is traditionally associated with the first appearance of the *Petrarca spirituale* by Girolamo Malipiero (1536), as well as the religious poetry of Vittoria Colonna. Malipiero's *Petrarca spirituale* is a book in which Petrarch has undergone a thorough rewriting, transforming his profane *Canzoniere* into a grotesque sequence of religious poems, and taking possession of the main linguistic, stylistic and metrical characteristics of Petrarchan poetry while simultaneously negating its essential contents.[1] This was a book that was reprinted several times after

---

[1]   See Amedeo Quondam, 'Riscrittura, citazione e parodia. Il "Petrarca spirituale" di Girolamo Malipiero', in Amedeo Quondam, *Il naso di Laura. Lingua e poesia lirica nella tradizione del classicismo* (Ferrara-Modena: Panini, 1991), pp. 203–62.

its first edition and highly rated by its early readers, but was incapable, none the less, of changing the fortunes of the Italian lyric tradition, essentially because it consisted of a sort of parody, or paradox. Vittoria Colonna's lyric production, on the other hand, represents a different and much more important case, which truly served to modify the practice of religious reading and meditation thanks to a self-conscious and deliberately innovative formal approach based on open competition with the profane lyric code. Of Colonna's poetic production I intend to consider the early dissemination, which seems to have taken place by means of selective and semi-private circulation.

A well-known letter, dated 12 June 1536 and addressed by Carlo Gualteruzzi to Cosimo Gheri, explains the definitive inclination of Vittoria Colonna towards spiritual production:

> Madam the Marchesa of Pescara has turned her attention wholly to God, and writes of nothing else, as you will see from the enclosed sonnet, which I am sending you as evidence of her changed style; I would appreciate it if you would show it to Monsignor Bembo and let me know his opinion, as well as the opinion of Mr Priuli, if he also retains some memory of Rome and of the many souls here who wish him well.[2]

As far as the dissemination of this spiritual production is concerned, the manuscript tradition of Colonna's sonnets allows us to circumscribe quite precisely a period between the end of the 1530s and the beginning of the 1540s, when a selection of manuscripts of Colonna's spiritual verse, intentionally kept separate from her amorous lyric production, were circulated independently from the printed editions, that is to say, not destined for the great mass of readers but jealously safeguarded, and addressed (through carefully selected channels) to exceptional readers, that is, those best able to share the doctrinal and intellectual interests of the poet.

The names of the recipients are among the most illustrious men of letters of that age, and several studies have succeeded in verifying the relationship between them and the surviving manuscripts. In 1900, Domenico Tordi identified the famous ms. Ashburnham 1153 of the Laurentian Library in Florence with the manuscript sent to Marguerite Queen of Navarre. The

---

2 'La signora marchesa di Pescara ha rivolto il suo stato a Dio, et non scrive d'altra materia, sì come per l'inchiuso sonetto potrà vedere, il quale le mando per mostra di questo suo cangiato stile; havrò caro che 'l facciate legger a Monsignor Bembo et me ne scriviate il giudicio di Sua Signoria et anchora al Signor Prioli, s'egli pure serba alcuna memoria di Roma et di tante anime care et amorevoli sue': Ornella Moroni, *Carlo Gualteruzzi (1500–1577) e i corrispondenti* (Città del Vaticano: Biblioteca Apostolica Vaticana, 1984), p. 65.

manuscript dates to 1540 and is entitled *Sonetti de più et diverse materie della divina signora Vittoria Colonna Marchesa di Pescara*. Its content is only partially religious, since the spiritual poems appear disguised within a more conventional literary gift.[3] Carlo Dionisotti has demonstrated elsewhere that the manuscript contains many erroneous readings and attributions; in addition to this (as noted by Tobia Toscano), the collation of Alan Bullock's 1982 critical edition of Colonna's *Rime* has shown that many of those erroneous readings coincide with those of the first edition of the *Rime* (Pirogallo, 1538), famously derived from uncertain and unidentified sources.[4] In conclusion, the Laurentian manuscript should be considered a collection that was not directly controlled by the poet, but was probably put together in Ferrara and sent from there to Marguerite via the orator to the Este Dukes, Alberto Sacrati.

The same Florentine manuscript had been associated by Tordi with an unsigned letter, kept in two copies (Archivio Segreto Vaticano and Fondo Serassi in the Biblioteca Civica of Bergamo), where one can read the following address to the Queen of France:

---

[3]   Domenico Tordi, *Il codice delle rime di Vittoria Colonna marchesa di Pescara appartenuto a Margherita d'Angoulême regina di Navarra* (Pistoia: Flori, 1900). A recent description by Antonio Corsaro (with bibliography) is in Pina Ragionieri (ed.), *Vittoria Colonna e Michelangelo, Firenze, Casa Buonarroti 24 maggio – 12 settembre 2005* (Florence: Mandragora, 2005), pp. 129–30: 'Codice pergamenaceo, sec. XVI, mm 210x150x16 … La parte originale consta di cc. 57, cui fui apposta una numerazione moderna a matita sul recto … A c. 3r l'intitolazione: Sonetti de piv et di/verse materie della / divina signora vittoria / colonna marchesa di / pescara con somma dili/genza revisti et / corretti nel / anno .M. / .D. / .XL. / . / giglio. A c. 3v, centro pagina: La / divina / vitto/ri/a … Le poesie terminano a c. G3v, ove segue la sigla: P.P.C.R. / .S., che Tordi congetturò come Petrus Paulus (de Sanctinis) Civis Romanus, allora agente di Ascanio Colonna fratello di Vittoria. La c. G4r è occupata da un sonetto in francese di altra mano, che sempre secondo Tordi andrebbe attribuito alla destinataria Margherita di Navarra, oppure a sua figlia Giovanna. Il codice contiene 102 sonetti, di cui tre ripetuti con varianti (cc. 4 e 23, 10 e 11, 16 e 18). Di essi 49 risultano editi all'altezza del 1539, ai quali sono da aggiungere 7 nuovamente apparsi nell'ed. 1540 (Comin da Trino) e possibilmente noti all'estensore del codice; mentre altri 22 apparvero nell'ed. 1546 delle Rime, e i restanti solo nell'Ottocento e poi pubblicati dal medesimo Tordi … Vi figurano anche quattro sonetti di Molza, uno di Ippolito de' Medici (o Claudio Tolomei?), uno scambio fra Bembo e Veronica Gambara, un ulteriore sonetto di Bembo in scambio con Vittoria: rime di corrispondenza cioè, che lo scriba assimilò al corpus senza specificarne la diversa paternità, e che sovente hanno portato a attribuzioni erronee o discutibili.' The ms. has now been studied by Abigail Brundin, 'Vittoria Colonna and the Virgin Mary', *Modern Language Review*, 96 (2001), 61–81.

[4]   See Vittoria Colonna, *Rime*, ed. Alan Bullock (Roma-Bari: Laterza, 1982), pp. 360 ff. and tables 16–20. This evidence has been ignored by Bullock himself, who consented passively to Tordi's conclusions (including the hypothesis that Gualteruzzi was secretary to Vittoria). On this matter, see also Vittoria Colonna, *Sonetti in morte di Francesco Ferrante d'Avalos Marchese di Pescara*, ed. Tobia R. Toscano (Milan: Mondadori, 1998), pp. 24–5.

To the Queen of France,
Since we have recently learned that Your Highness wished to have a copy of the *Rime spirituali* by the most illustrious Marchesa of Pescara, and had thus given orders that they be sought out and sent to you with certain haste, and since when she gave them to me I made copies of them one by one and kept them all (which was easy enough for me to do given my longstanding service to Her Excellency), I have decided that it would be a Christian impiety to refrain from sending them to you. So I have had them transcribed and made up into a little volume, free from any exterior decoration, as is fitting to the state and profession of the aforementioned lady, who is turned towards the ornaments of the soul and rejects those of the body as vile and unworthy. This volume is presented by me to Your Highness, and I trust will be received by you, and I appeal to the regal nobility of your great and kind soul that you will not consider it too bold or presumptuous of me to have undertaken a task that was not given to me nor asked of me.[5]

Tordi believed the author of the letter to be Carlo Gualteruzzi, whom he believed to have been the secretary of Vittoria Colonna. This identification, however, has been refuted by Carlo Dionisotti, who clarified that Gualteruzzi never acted as Colonna's secretary, that the letter comes instead from Pietro Bembo, and that it refers to the sending of a different manuscript which has not survived.[6] On this point, evidence is also provided by a further letter written by Bembo in the name of Gualteruzzi:

---

[5]   'Alla Regina di Francia, Essendosi nuovamente inteso V. M.tà desiderar di aver copia delle *Rime spirituali* della Ill.ma Sig.ra Marchesana di Pescara, e sopra ciò aver dato ordine che elle siano cercate e mandatele con buona diligenza, io, il quale mi trovo averle di mano in mano mentre ella donate le ha, copiate e conservate tutte, la qual cosa a me è stata assai agevole per l'antica servitù che io con Sua Exc.za tengo, ho giudicato di non poter senza nota di Cristiana impietà restare di mandargliele. Laonde mi sono messo a farle trascrivere e ridurre in picciolo volumetto, nudo d'ogni esteriore ornamento, siccome appunto conviene allo stato e professione della prefata Sig.ra, la quale volta agli ornamenti dell'anima, quelli del corpo sprezza come cose vili e caduche. Il qual volumetto se fie per parte mia presentato a V. M.tà, siccome spero che al ricevere della presente sarà, prego l'altezza e nobiltà del suo gentile e grande animo a non volermi per ciò riputar troppo ardito e prosuntuoso trapponendomi in cosa a me non imposta né da me richiesta': Pietro Bembo, *Lettere*, ed. Ernesto Travi (Bologna: Commissione per i Testi di Lingua, 1993), vol. IV, p. 606.

[6]   Carlo Dionisotti, 'Appunti sul Bembo e su Vittoria Colonna' [1981], in Carlo Dionisotti, *Scritti sul Bembo*, ed. Claudio Vela (Turin: Einaudi, 2002), pp. 115–40. Ibid., p. 135: 'è affatto improbabile che a [Gualteruzzi] solo faccia capo una tradizione manoscritta delle rime stesse, che non è uniforme e che a volte si presenta con tratti esclusivi di una corresponsabilità del Gualteruzzi. Che è per l'appunto il caso del ms. Laur. Ashb. 1153 illustrato dal Tordi, nel quale figurano mescolate indistintamente alle rime di Vittoria Colonna rime d'altri poeti contemporanei, persino un sonetto di Veronica Gambara dedicato al Bembo e la risposta di lui.' See also Colonna, *Sonetti in morte di Francesco Ferrante d'Avalos*, p. 25: 'Se invio di rime alla regina Margherita da parte del Bembo (per interposto Gualteruzzi) vi sia stato non bisogna certo pensare al ms. L, ma sempre a rime esclusivamente spirituali.'

Most Serene Highness. Cardinal Bembo has received one hundred most beautiful sonnets by the illustrious Marchesa of Pescara, all religious and holy, dictated by her excellent intellect in such a short time that one would not believe it, if one did not really know it to be true, as he does; this lady was begged and prayed by him to consent to send the poems out into the public realm, still more urgently at this time which is, as we know, so contrary and dangerous for our true religion. But he could not persuade her, for she is wholly turned to contemplation of divine things and cares nothing for the matters of this world, so instead he asked her to have the poems back so that he could better review them, and once he had them he immediately made a copy and sent it to me, so that I could send it on to Your Highness … [Bembo] does this to please you for the Marchesa complains to him for having acted thus, when in fact she should be glad that the fruits of her soul, which is totally dedicated to the service of God, should reach Your Highness, who are yourself so dear to God.[7]

As to the identity of the recipient, Dionisotti thought tentatively of Eleonore Queen of France.[8] However, a passage from a letter sent by Pierpaolo Vergerio to Bembo (Summer 1540?) complicates this hypothesis: 'Your own Mr Carlo da Fano went to the effort of collecting the Marchesa's poems. I have seen the Queen in possession of those that he sent here, and will get hold of what I can myself.'[9] In this case, 'the Queen' is certainly Marguerite of Navarre, so that we must conclude that, at the same time that the Ashburnham manuscript was being compiled, Bembo and

---

[7]   'Serenissima Reina. Essendo a mano venuti del Cardinal Bembo cento molto belli sonetti della Ill.ma Sig.ra Marchesana di Pescara, tutti religiosi e santi, dettati dal suo leggiadrissimo ingegno in così breve spazio che non si crederebbe di leggieri da chi veramente nol sapesse, come sa egli; fu dallui confortata e pregata la detta Madonna a dovergli fuori mandare in mano degli uomini, massimamente a questi tempi alla vera nostra religione così contrari e disagiosi, come si vede che sono. La qual cosa non avendo S. Sig.ria ottener dallei potuto, ché alle divine cose e alla contemplazion di loro in tutto volta niente si cura delle mondane, raddomandatole i detti scritti per meglio rivedergli, ed avutigli, se ne fece subitamente scrivere uno essempio per darlo a me, affine che io il mandassi a V. M.tà. … Né cura [Bembo] per piacerle che la S.ra Marchesa di Lui si dolga che così adoprato abbia, quando tuttavia dee allei esser in grado che i frutti della sua al servitio di Dio volta e dedicata anima a V. M.tà, che a Dio tanto grata è, pervengano': Bembo, *Lettere*, vol. IV, pp. 606–7. Partially edited in Dionisotti, 'Appunti', p. 139. See Colonna, *Sonetti*, ed. Toscano, p. 25: 'ancora una volta sullo sfondo [fa] apparizione una Vittoria Colonna del tutto aliena da cure dirette per la sua produzione poetica.'

[8]   Dionisotti, 'Appunti', p. 139: 'Viene fatto di pensare una volta ancora a Margherita di Navarra, ma i riferimenti della lettera sono generici, applicabili anche alla cognata di lei Eleonora, regina di Francia, più cara a Dio che al marito.'

[9]   'M. Carlo vostro da Fano fece la fatica di raccoglier le rime della Marchesa. Ho veduto in mano della Regina ciò che egli scrive in qua, et haverà anchor me, tale quale io sia procuratore': *Lettere volgari di diversi nobilissimi huomini et eccellentissimi ingegni scritte in diverse materie, Libro primo* (Venice: In Casa de' Figliuoli di Aldo, 1542), p. 129.

Gualteruzzi (on behalf of Vittoria) produced another collection of poems, which reached Marguerite's hands and is now lost.

Carlo Gualteruzzi's contribution to the earliest manuscript circulation of Colonna's poems can be discerned from a letter sent to him on 30 January 1540 by Francesco Della Torre, who was close to the bishop of Verona, Cardinal Giberti:

> I have learned from a letter from Mr Lattantio [Tolomei] of a manuscript of many beautiful sonnets: I have a great desire to have these, if I can without causing inconvenience. I wished you to know of my desire: the rest is up to you: but I well know how much I can trust in the generosity of that Lady and your own friendly interventions … From Verona, 30 January 1540.[10]

We know that Della Torre actually received the poems mentioned in the letter, as he himself confirms in a further letter, dated February 1541, to the same Gualteruzzi:

> I must beg your pardon if I do not send them this time: I will send them soon but first must make a copy, with the promise not to let them out of my sight: and I make this promise solemnly … since I would not wish such rare compositions to get into other hands than mine in these lands.[11]

Della Torre's manuscript was identified by Bullock as one containing love poems now in the Biblioteca Nazionale in Florence, II.IX.30. The identification has however been rejected by Dionisotti, and more recently by Toscano, who challenged what appeared to be an unpersuasive chronology of events, as the manuscript refers to a period in which Vittoria had definitively abandoned love poetry. The recipient (Della Torre) was also notoriously involved in religious matters.[12]

---

[10]   'Ho inteso per lettere di M. Lattantio [Tolomei] d'un parto di molti bellissimi sonetti: ho gran desiderio d'haverli: se si può senza importunità. Ho voluto, che sappiate il mio desiderio: il resto sarà ad arbitrio vostro: ma so ben, quanto debbo confidare nella benignità di quella Signora, & nell'officio vostro amorevole … Di Verona. Alli XXX di Gennaro. MDXL': *De le lettere di tredici huomini illustri libri tredici* (Rome: Dorico, 1554), pp. 211–12.

[11]   'Vi piacerà impetrarmi perdono se non li mando questa volta: che li manderò col primo, ma toltone prima copia, con promessa di non lasciarmeli uscir di mano: la qual promessa fate per me sicuramente … sì che non vorrei che sì rare compositioni fosser in altre mani, che nelle mie in questi paesi': *Lettere di XIII huomini illustri, alle quali oltra tutte l'altre fin qui stampate, di nuouo ne sono state aggiunte molte da Thomaso Porcacchi* (Venice: Giorgio de' Caualli, 1565), pp. 156–7.

[12]   Alan Bullock, 'A Hitherto Unexplored Manuscript of 100 Poems by Vittoria Colonna in the Biblioteca Nazionale Centrale, Florence', *Italian Studies*, 21 (1966), 42–56; Colonna, *Rime*, ed. Bullock, pp. 325 sgg.; Colonna, *Sonetti*, ed. Toscano, pp. 22 ff.

Another well-known manuscript is Vatican Library, Vat. Lat. 11539, which was first identified by Enrico Carusi as the one given by Vittoria to Michelangelo around 1540. This manuscript was kept with great care by the artist, who mentioned it in a famous letter of 1551. Following Carusi's contribution, further studies by Bullock, Dionisotti and Toscano appeared on the same topic, and we are now able to read a transcription (with accompanying English translation) of the texts in Abigail Brundin's recent publication, so that I can omit a detailed description of this work.[13] For the purposes of the current argument, if the dating and intended recipient of the Vatican manuscript are indeed genuine (as they seem to be), this would seem to be further evidence of a period of production in which scribal circulation was chosen and promoted by the poet. On this point I should recall a few significant details. The Vatican manuscript, unlike the Ashburnham manuscript, shows features typical of a product that has been directly supervised by the poet. It consists of 103 sonnets entirely dedicated to spiritual subject matter, of which only twenty-six are reproduced in the Ashburnham manuscript. Ten of these sonnets failed to make their way into subsequent editions of the *Rime*, thus remaining unknown until their modern publication. (Tordi published eight of them in 1900, but from another source; one had been published in the 1840 Visconti edition of Colonna's *Rime*. The only sonnet that remained unpublished, 'Suol nascer dubbio se di più legarsi', was edited by Carusi, n. XXXIX, p. 241 of his essay). In other words, as Carusi puts it, 'even after 1551 the manuscript remained unavailable.'[14]

In conclusion, we have information about at least four manuscripts containing collections of spiritual poetry by Vittoria Colonna (of these four manuscripts we can only examine the two that have survived). All four of them belong to the same span of years; they are collated according to an overall coherent design; they are supervised, with varying degrees of attention, by the poet herself; and in each case they are intended for a select public if not for individual recipients. On this final aspect, a more general consideration is provided in a recent article by Brian Richardson on

---

[13]   See in order: Enrico Carusi, 'Un codice sconosciuto delle "Rime spirituali" di Vittoria Colonna, appartenuto forse a Michelangelo Buonarroti', in *Atti del IV Congresso Nazionale di Studi Romani*, ed. Carlo Galassi Paluzzi (Rome: Istituto di Studi Romani, 1938), vol. IV, pp. 231–41; Bullock, 'A Hitherto Unexplored Manuscript'; Dionisotti, 'Appunti', p. 138; Vittoria Colonna, *Sonnets for Michelangelo. A Bilingual Edition*, ed. and trans. by Abigail Brundin (Chicago, IL and London: University of Chicago Press, 2005). A description is also in Codices Vaticani Latini (codd. 11414–709), *Schedis Henrici Carusi adhibitis recensuit José Ruysschaert, Bibliothecae Vaticanae scriptor* (In Bibliotheca Vaticana, MCMLIX), pp. 272–6.

[14]   '[A]nche dopo il 1551 il codice restò inaccessibile': Carusi, 'Un codice sconosciuto delle "Rime spirituali" di Vittoria Colonna', p. 233.

scribal culture in the sixteenth century, where the phenomenon is studied as one that 'fostered, and was fostered by, a sense of close communication between the like-minded', leading to forms of 'scribal publication [which] could make donors and recipients believe, rightly or wrongly, that they were sharing exclusive, select access to texts that were not available on the open market'.[15]

On the other hand, it is evident that the first group of printed editions of the *Rime* offered, in the same span of years, a quite different impression of Colonna's poetry. What is revealed, ultimately, is

> ... the ambuigity of Vittoria Colonna's attitude towards her own poetic oeuvre, which she considered to be important for herself and for others, such that it should be made available to people in its entirety, not just bit by bit, and yet up until the end she continued to refuse and deplore any form of print circulation.[16]

Printers and publishers made the greatest effort to overcome her reluctance to print, but succeeded in publishing only a few spiritual poems together with the love poems. An eloquent example is that of the *Dichiaratione fatta sopra la seconda parte delle Rime della divina Vittoria Colonna*, printed in 1543 by the Bolognese publisher Faelli. The volume, which includes thirty-eight spiritual poems together with an extensive commentary by the young student Rinaldo Corso, as an annotated edition of the work of a living poet represented a great novelty, even if the poems had already been printed in previous years.[17] Although published separately with perfect

---

[15]   Brian Richardson, 'Print or pen? Modes of Written Publication in Sixteenth-Century Italy', *Italian Studies*, 59 (2004), 39–64 (p. 43). Concerning the participation of Vittoria in the construction of the ms. Vat. Lat. 11539, see also the hypothesis of a 'documentabile ... presenza-assenso' made by Toscano (in Colonna, *Sonetti*, ed. Toscano, p. 24).

[16]   '[L]'ambiguità dell'atteggiamento di Vittoria Colonna nei confronti dell'opera sua poetica, che essa sentiva importante per sé e per altri, tale da potere e dover essere comunicata ad altri nel suo insieme, non soltanto a spizzico, e di cui essa però fino all'ultimo rifiutò e deplorò la pubblicazione a stampa': Dionisotti, 'Appunti', pp. 131–2.

[17]   A description of the edition by Antonio Corsaro is now in Ragionieri (ed.), *Vittoria Colonna e Michelangelo*, p. 136. See also Colonna, *Rime*, ed. Bullock, pp. 262–3: '[Faelli edition] contiene 38 poesie di VC comprendenti le dodici composizioni inedite in Rime 1540 & Rime-I 1540, le dieci poesie inedite in Rime-3 1539 e sedici sonetti stampati per la prima volta in Rime 1538. L'ordine è diverso dalle stampe precedenti.' The printed text appears as quite a poor edition, lacking in iconographic ornament, particularly in the context of the high cost and often monumental production of Faelli. It appeared, in addition, as a sort of gift on the occasion of a Lenten sermon, as we can see in the dedicatory letter to Veronica Gambara ('Di Bologna il XV di Febbraio. M.D.XLII'): 'Gli sacri tempi, che hoggimai poco appresso di Quaresima sono, Illust. Madonna m'invitano a mandar senza la sorella in luce questa seconda parte delle Rime della divina VITTORIA da me le state passata isposte, & a voi dedicate ... ritenendo appresso

timing and good commercial intuition, the commentary – as has now been demonstrated – was only the second section of a *corpus* of notes that also included Colonna's love poems, which Corso had conceived according to the traditional passage from human to divine love.[18] After that episode, it was not until 1546 that common readers could read Colonna's spiritual *corpus*, when the famous Valgrisi edition was published in Venice as a wide-ranging and coherent collection, probably approved by the poet herself as a form of poetic testimony.[19]

After the appearance of the 1546 Valgrisi edition of Colonna's poetry, the 'rivoluzione strutturale' of spiritual poetry became increasingly radical. When they appeared on the literary scene, Colonna's poems

> ... did not claim to be the final expiation of a canzoniere, and did not narrate an affair of love and death, senescence and conversion, nor the strictly chronological examination of a soul. Rather this garland of sonnets offers a meditation on the mysteries of faith.[20]

---

di me la prima parte di gran lunga più, che questa, difficile, & oscura, farò con questa saggio, se delle mie fatiche potrò giamai frutto veruno aspettare, & più secura aprirò la strada a far, che la pria si veggia: osservando in ciò l'ordine delle Philosophiche scuole, dove quelli, che le frequentano, sogliono gli Argomenti più debili proporre nel principio, gli più forti riserbando al fine.' Two recent studies are now available: Monica Bianco, 'Le due redazioni del commento di Rinaldo Corso alle Rime di Vittoria Colonna', *Studi di Filologia Italiana*, 56 (1998), 271–95, and Monica Bianco, 'Rinaldo Corso e il "Canzoniere" di Vittoria Colonna', *Italique*, 1 (1998), 35–45. On the author of the commentary, see the article by Giovanna Romei, 'Rinaldo Corso', in *Dizionario Biografico degli Italiani*, 29 (1983), pp. 687–90.

18   The book containing the two sections together was published in 1558 by Girolamo Ruscelli: Tutte le rime della Illustriss. et Eccellentiss. Signora Vittoria Colonna, Marchesana di Pescara, con l'espositione del Signor Rinaldo Corso ... , (In Venetia, per Giovan Battista et Melchior Sessa fratelli). A bibliographical description by Antonio Corsaro is in Ragionieri (ed.), *Vittoria Colonna e Michelangelo*, p. 190. According to a recent study, in 1543 the Prima parte 'doveva essere già almeno sbozzata, ma certo non ancora pronta ad un'uscita in pubblico', whereas 'la revisione del primo abbozzo e la stesura definitiva del commento alla 'Prima parte' avvennero presumibilmente tra il 1543 e il 1550': C. Cinquini, 'Rinaldo Corso editore e commentatore delle "Rime" di Vittoria Colonna', *Aevum*, 73 (1999), 669–96 (p. 675). In the Ruscelli edition, the second section differs in many ways from the text published in 1543. According to Bianco, 'Le due redazioni del commento di Rinaldo Corso alle Rime di Vittoria Colonna', p. 283, the collation 'permette di rilevare tali e tante varianti da imporre l'evidenza che i due testi afferiscano a due redazioni distinte ...È difficile dire con esattezza quando il Corso abbia rimaneggiato l'opera.'

19   Dionisotti, 'Appunti', p. 132: '[edizione] allestita da uomini vicinissimi e devoti a lei, stampa che certo non sarebbe apparsa se il rifiuto di lei fosse stato perentorio.' See also Simone Albonico, 'La poesia del Cinquecento', in *Storia della letteratura italiana, X. La tradizione dei testi*, ed. Claudio Ciociola (Rome: Salerno, 2001), pp. 725–8. A description of the edition is in Colonna, *Rime*, ed. Bullock, pp. 263–4.

20   '[N]on si proponevano come lo scontato finale d'un canzoniere, non raccontavano una vicenda d'amore e morte e senescenza e conversione, né in termini strettamente

The most recent bibliographical surveys allow us to ascertain how popular spiritual poetry became in the aftermath of the Valgrisi edition of Colonna's work, and how it came to nourish a good part of the book trade. As already mentioned, the change concerned the elimination of the traditional ambiguity between spiritual and profane inspiration through the simple, radical abandonment of the latter. On this point, Gabriel Fiamma was explicit in the introductory letter to readers of his book of *Rime* of 1570:

> [Petrarch] has illustrated, enriched, and raised to glory our language, and Poetry, and the art of writing well and wisely. None the less one cannot deny that he who is able to teach about Platonic and philosophical love to those who are mature, more often than not teaches about lascivious love to the young … I have tried, therefore, to offer to our Christian youth a Poetry in which one can learn both the good and correct way to use the Tuscan language … and also one in which they can find that pleasure, which Poetry by its very nature brings … and finally, learn to place all their love in God.[21]

In addition, Fiamma was equally explicit in praising highly the pivotal role played by Vittoria Colonna's example in this process:

> Vittoria Colonna … was the first to write with dignity in verse of spiritual matters, and she forged the way and opened up the route to follow, in order to reach the place where God has chosen to lead me.[22]

As Clara Leri puts it:

> Despite … the penitential sonnets and the canzone to the Virgin, it is not legitimate to claim that the archetypal canzoniere necessarily reserved some

---

cronologici la storia di un'anima. Sono piuttosto, in corona di sonetti, la meditazione sui misteri della fede': Carlo Vecce, 'Petrarca, Vittoria e Michelangelo. Note di commento a testi e varianti di Vittoria Colonna e di Michelangelo', *Studi e Problemi di Critica Testuale*, 44 (1992), 102–25 (pp. 104–5).

21   '[Petrarch] ha illustrata, accresciuta, e posta in dignità la lingua nostra, e la Poesia, e l'arte dello scriver bene, e giudiciosamente, nondimeno non si può anco negare, ch'egli, che a persone mature può insegnar l'amor Platonico, e filosofico; a' giovanetti molte fiate insegna l'amor lascivo … ho pensato di poter dare alla gioventù Christiana una Poesia, nella qual si potesse imparare e la buona, e regolata maniera del parlar Toscano … e appresso trovarvi quel piacer, che per natura sua apporta la Poesia … ; e finalmente imparare a mettere il suo amor in Dio:' *Rime spirituali del R. D. Gabriel Fiamma, Canonico Regolare Lateranense; esposte da lui medesimo* (Venice: Francesco de' Franceschi Senese, 1570), 'Lettera A' lettori', p. a5v.

22   'Vittoria Colonna … è stata la prima, c'ha cominciato a scrivere con dignità in Rime le cose spirituali, e m'ha fatta la strada, & aperto il camino di penetrare, e giungere ove è piacciuto a Dio di condurmi': *Rime spirituali del R. D. Gabriel Fiamma*, 'Lettera dedicatoria a M. Antonio Colonna', p. a4r.

kind of rhetorical autonomy for the spiritual experience; this did appear to be the case, however, in the sixteenth-century laceration of the Catholic spirit, permeated by mediating glimpses of evangelism, in tune with the transalpine cultures of the Reformation. On the other hand, Vittoria Colonna ... represented the unique founding moment of modern Christian poetry, drawn into the broad arena of devotional literature from the courtly and aristocratic environs of her circle.[23]

In other words, Colonna's poetry became a model, provoking some important changes in the use and development of devotional books. These became an increasingly sophisticated product, up-to-date in their language and metrical features and appealing to educated ears for the purposes of private reading. Furthermore, Colonna's doctrinal grammar, although it was clearly based on a reformed religious faith, was accepted by the culture of the Counter-Reformation, its original aristocratic, selective and Nicodemian attitude being ignored in favour of its adoption as a formal model.[24]

Not all subsequent production of spiritual poetry followed Vittoria Colonna's model, however. I now intend to focus my attention on some exceptions, or rather, on some marginal cases that were limited to manuscript production and enjoyed only moderate success. Of particular interest is the case of Antonio Brucioli's collection entitled *Dello amore divino cristiano*, extant in two manuscript copies and known indirectly from a lost third manuscript. The two surviving manuscripts are Paris, Bibliothèque de l'Arsenal, n. 8554, and Florence, Biblioteca Nazionale Centrale, Magl. VII.116.[25] The former consists of three books: *Hymni,*

[23]   [M]algrado ... i sonetti penitenziali e la canzone alla Vergine, non è legittimo sostenere che l'archetipo di ogni canzoniere avesse riservato all'esperienza spirituale uno statuto di autonomia retorica, quale sembrava essere necessaria, invece, nella lacerazione cinquecentesca dell'anima cattolica, penetrata dalle istanze mediatrici dell'evangelismo, in sintonia con le culture oltremontane della Riforma. D'altra parte, Vittoria Colonna ... rappresentò l'irripetibile occasione fondativa della moderna poesia cristiana sottratta alla vasta area della letteratura devozionale dall'orizzonte colto e aristocratico dei medesimi destinatari': Clara Leri, 'Esercizi metrici sui "Salmi": la poesia di Gabriele Fiamma', in Maria Luisa Doglio and Carlo Delcorno (eds), *Scrittura religiosa. Forme letterarie dal Trecento al Cinquecento* (Bologna: Il Mulino, 2003), pp. 127–59 (p. 132).

[24]   For a recent analysis of Colonna's poetry, concerning both doctrinal and stylistic implications, see Giorgio Forni, 'Vittoria Colonna, la "Canzone alla vergine" e la poesia spirituale', in Maria Luisa Doglio and Carlo Delcorno (eds), *Rime sacre dal Petrarca al Tasso* (Bologna: Il Mulino, 2005), pp. 63–94. On the subsequent vicissitudes of Colonna's poetry, and its eventual suppression during the final years of the century, see Gigliola Fragnito, *Proibito capire. La Chiesa e il volgare nella prima età moderna* (Bologna: Il Mulino, 2005), pp. 133 ff., 202, 284–5.

[25]   See in order: Giuseppe Mazzatinti, *Inventario dei manoscritti italiani delle Biblioteche di Francia*, III (Rome: presso i Principali Librai, 1888), p. 129; Henry Martin, *Catalogue des*

cantici et psalmi dello amore divino christiano di Antonio Brucioli libri tre (323 pp.), including 208 hymns, 104 *cantici* and twenty-one psalms, as well as a dedicatory letter to Caterina de' Medici. The latter (440 pp.) illustrates further evolution in the architecture of the book, which has been highlighted by Karl Benrath and more recently by Giorgio Spini and Edoardo Barbieri. Brucioli wrote of his intention to dedicate the poems to Duke Cosimo I de' Medici in a letter of 1549, in the introduction to his work *Del governo dello ottimo Principe et Capitano dello esercito* (Florence, Biblioteca Nazionale Centrale, Magl. XXX. 11,19). There the author spoke of 'tre libri di Hymni, Cantici et Psalmi dello Amor di Dio christiano, che sono 200 Hymni (madrigali) et 100 Cantici (canzoni) et 20 Psalmi (capitoli)'; he added: 'la quarta parte serbo per buon rispetto in altro loco.' In fact, the project changed and evolved over time, since the Florentine manuscript is a fair copy in five books, including exactly four hundred poems (two hundred hymns in the first book (pp. 5–92), and fifty *cantici* in each of the following four (pp. 94–182, 183–256, 257–348, 350–438), but lacks the *Psalms*, which Brucioli described as *capitoli*). It is notable that the author has limited himself to only two metrical forms (short ones, that is, madrigals, and long ones, that is, *canzoni*), and excluded *capitolo in terza rima*. In the same period, Brucioli wrote to Aretino about his collection:

[20 January 1551] I enclose a book of mine, which I composed with much effort, and beg, good sir, that you will be so kind as to read it, and review it a little for love of me; on the first day of Lent I mean to leave the house and come to visit you, to ask for help and advice concerning a drawing. So, dear friend, do not fail to have a little browse before I come and see you, and above all please do not let anyone else see it.

[28 January 1551] In truth my spirits are somewhat low, and I wish to know as soon as possible what might be done with my book; so I beg you dear sir with all my heart to go to the most honourable Legate [Beccadelli], making the necessary overtures that I know you are capable of, and ask him if he might see his way, as quickly as possible, to presenting my book to the Pope with a letter of recommendation to His Holiness, and another either from you or him to his Excellency Cardinal di Monte.[26]

manuscrits de la Bibliothèque de l'Arsenal, VI (Paris: Plon, 1892), p. 489; Antonio Marsand, *I manoscritti italiani della Regia Biblioteca Parigina*, II (Paris: Dalla Stamperia Reale, 1838), pp. 237–39; Giovanni Maria Mazzuchelli, *Gli scrittori d'Italia* (Brescia: Bossini, 1763), vol. II. IV, p. 2144; Karl Benrath, 'Poesie religiose di Antonio Brucioli', *Rivista Cristiana*, 7 (1879), 3–10; Giorgio Spini, *Tra Rinascimento e riforma. Antonio Brucioli* (Florence: La Nuova Italia, 1940), pp. 194 ff., 243–8; Edoardo Barbieri, 'Tre schede per Antonio Brucioli e alcuni suoi libri', *Aevum*, 74 (2000), 3, 709–19 (pp. 717–19).
26   '[M]ando al presente un mio libro, che in questi miei travagli ho composto, prego vostra Signoria che sia contenta di leggerlo, e scorrerlo un poco per mio amore; perché il

In other words, Brucioli was asking both for a poetic judgement and for a recommendation to the *nuncio* Beccadelli in order to obtain an official introduction to the Pope. It seems a typical case of the type that Armando Petrucci has described as *libro manoscritto di lusso*, a product prepared in one or more copies and offered to some illustrious recipient not as an alternative, but rather in anticipation of the impending print run.

In any case, and in spite of a certain fame (as demonstrated by Doni's citation of 'ANTON BRUCIOLI. *Rime spirituali*', in the second treatise of the *Libraria*[27]), the poems were never published. To explain this, it is useful to examine the information we have concerning a third manuscript, sent to the Duchess of Urbino Vittoria Farnese. This is mentioned in a letter from Girolamo Muzio to the *nuncio* Lodovico Beccadelli, dated 8 February 1554:

> A few days ago Brucioli sent a large volume of verse dedicated to our most noble Duchess. But once it was examined here neither the letter nor the spirit met with our approval, and since the words hardly matter if their meaning is suspect, I will speak only of the latter and not the former.
>
> His manner of proceeding is not obviously blameworthy, yet it arouses suspicion, firstly because all his prayers are in some way directed at Christ, implying that the intercession of the saints is unnecessary, and then he has composed a canzone modelled on *Vergine bella che di sol vestita* in which all the things he says of Our Lady in fact concern Christ. I am not saying this is bad, yet it implies that these virtues are not her own and that we should turn to Christ and there is no other form of intercession. In many places he speaks of the persecution of the Church in such a way as to show that he means the inquisitions that the Catholic Church launches against heretics, and he complains greatly about this.
>
> Having seen that the book is of this nature, it seemed wise to pass over it without further comment. Yet, while trying to make it seem the last thing in the

---

primo dì di quaresima spero d'uscire di casa, e verrò a trovare vostra Signoria, per chiedergli aiuto e consiglio sopra un mio disegno. Siché, caro Signor Compare, non lasciate di leggerlo un poco infino a che io possa venir da voi, e sopra tutto vi priego che non lo lasciate vedere a altri ... [P]erché in verità le acque mie sono un poco basse, io desidero il più presto che sia possibile vedere quel che abbia a essere del mio libro; e però prego V. S. con tutto il cuore che vadia, come disse al Reverendissimo Legato [Beccadelli], facendo que' buoni uffizii che sa fare la bontà vostra, e in somma pregarlo che sia contento per qualche modo, il più destro che può fare, che detto libro sia presentato ai piedi del Papa con una lettera di raccomandazione a sua Santità, e con una o vostra, o sua, al Reverendissimo Cardinal di Monte': *Lettere scritte a Pietro Aretino*, ed. Paolo Procaccioli, vol. II. 2 (Rome: Salerno, 2004), 369 and 370, pp. 347–8. See also Spini, *Tra Rinascimento e Riforma*, p. 114.

27   Anton Francesco Doni, *La libraria*, ed. Vanni Bramanti (Milan: Longanesi, 1972), p. 268.

world that he expected, he kept on writing in such a way that, if the Duchess were as proud as she is modest, she would probably have admonished him for modesty. The result was that he sent the book intending to offer it to her, and he spent money on having it copied and bound. The Duchess reponded most kindly to him, saying that the book was not for her and she would send it back, and so she did, and also sent him a donation of ten scudi.

I wanted to alert your Holiness to this because it seems that he plans to print the verses in Venice. He appears to have enough of them for two volumes, the fourth and fifth, as large as all Petrarch's collected sonnets and canzoni put together. Good trees produce sound fruit, and bad ones, rotten fruit.[28]

As one can see, the core of Muzio's argument against the text concerns the emphasis given by Brucioli to prayers offered to Christ, which he perceives as suspect since they bring his argument close to reformed doctrines. On this point Muzio, who was certainly well informed about Brucioli's religious career, demonstrates his skill in turning a literary judgement into a doctrinal trial, as well as his anxiety about an eventual printing of the book. Brucioli had attempted in previous decades to establish a relationship with the dukes of Urbino, as we learn from the dedicatory letters of four of his five books of *Dialogi*, published in 1537–38 (addressed to Francesco Maria,

---

[28] 'Già più giorni il Brucioli mandò un suo gran volume di rime intitolato a questa Signora nostra illustrissima duchessa. Il quale veduto qui non è stato approvato né in parole né in sentenze et, percioché le parole poco sarebbono importate quando le sentenze fossero state approbabili, quelle lasciando, dirò di queste. Il suo procedere non è già in maniera che si possa manifestamente riprendere, ma è tale che dà molta suspitione, ché prima tiene tutte le sue preghiere dirizzate in un certo modo a Christo, che si vede che vuol dire che il ricorrere alla intercessione de' santi sia di soverchio, poi fa una canzone ad imitazione di *Vergine bella che di sol vestita* et le cose che in quella si dicono di nostra Donna le rivolge a Cristo. Il che non dico che sia male, ma che vuole inferire che quelle cose a lei non si convengono et che a Cristo si debbia ricorrere et che altra intercessione non ci sia. Poi in molti luoghi parla delle persecutioni della Chiesa in modo che si comprende che parla delle inquisitioni che fa la Chiesa catholica contra gli eretici et di quella ne fa i rammarichi et le querele. Vedutosi questo libro tale, parve bene passarlo senza altra risposta. Ma esso, non volendo apparir cosa che gli aspettasse, tornò a scrivere in modo che quando che questa Signora fosse così altera come ella è modestissima, ella haverebbe forse fatto ammonir lui di modestia. La somma fu che haveva mandato quel libro con intentione che gli fosse donato et che haveva speso in farlo legare et iscrivere. La Signora humanissimamente gli rispose che quel libro non faceva per lei et che gliele haverebbe rimandato et così gliele rimandò et con esso gli mandò anche a donar dieci scudi. Io ho voluto dare questa notitia alla Signoria Vostra Reverendissima percioché io penso che colui peravventura penserà di fare stampare quelle sue rime in Vinegia. Mostra di haverne assai che questi erano due libri, il quarto et il quinto et non era minor volume di tutti i sonetti et canzoni del Petrarca. I buoni arbori partoriscono i buoni frutti et i cattivi i cattivi': Parma, Biblioteca Palatina, ms. Pal. 1033/31. I quote from the article by Valentina Grohovaz, 'Girolamo Muzio e la sua "battaglia" contro Pier Paolo Vergerio', in Ugo Rozzo (ed.), *Pier Paolo Vergerio il Giovane, un polemista attraverso l'Europa del Cinquecento* (Udine: Forum, 2000), pp. 179–206 (pp. 204–6).

Guidubaldo, Giulio Della Rovere, and eventually to Eleonora Gonzaga, who was bound by a close friendship to Federico Fregoso and inclined to share his ideas on the subject of religion).[29] According to Dionisotti, Brucioli's efforts found the support of Giovan Iacopo Leonardi, an agent of the dukes in Venice; it is likely, however, that the connection went through Pietro Panfilo, a courtier suspected of heresy, and a character in the second and third books of the *Dialogi*.[30] In any case, either due to the disinclination of the Urbino dukes to spend money on literary patronage, or to the duke's death in 1538, Brucioli's dedications failed to achieve their end. Fifteen years later, Brucioli made a further attempt at achieving patronage from Urbino through the dedication to Vittoria Farnese, the second wife of Duke Guidubaldo II (married in 1547 after Giulia Varano's death). In 1550, Vittoria had been the dedicatee of the Italian translation of Erasmus' *Institutio cristiani matrimonii* (Venice: Francesco Rocca e fratelli, 1550). But the religious environment of Urbino had changed by 1554, and the new duchess, although a woman 'of culture and sincere faith who demonstrated her Catholic beliefs, in no way a fanatic, who intervened on behalf of those condemned by the Inquisition for heresy and suspect priests', was not inclined to be involved with the promotion of a doctrinally suspect work.[31]

To return to Brucioli's poetic manuscripts, their fate seems to have been the opposite of Colonna's: where she was reluctant to see the publication of her verse in print, Brucioli desired it but could not obtain it, despite the high demand for the genre. Clearly, doctrinal censorship has a role to play in this; however, other reasons must also be brought into play. The initial statement in Muzio's letter, in which he claims that the book 'non è stato approvato *né in parole* né in sentenze', suggests doubts raised by formal issues and uncertainty about the quality of Brucioli's poetry. On this point,

---

[29]   To Eleonora Brucioli dedicated the *Dialogi della metafisical filosofia* (Venice: Zanetti, 1538). See Giorgio Spini, 'Bibliografia delle opere di Antonio Brucioli', *La Bibliofilia*, 42 (1940), 5–7, 129–80 (pp. 135–6).

[30]   See Carlo Dionisotti, 'La testimonianza del Brucioli', in Carlo Dionisotti, *Machiavellerie* (Turin: Einaudi, 1980), pp. 193–226 (p. 198). On Panfilo and the dissemination of reformed ideas in Urbino, see Alessandro Pastore, 'Pietro Panfilo cortegiano ed eresiarca (1505 c.a.–1574?)', *Rivista Storica Italiana*, 94 (1982), 635–63.

[31]   '[D]i cultura e di sincera pietà [che] manifestò una religiosità cattolica, immune da fanatismi [e] intervenne a favore di eretici condannati dall'Inquisizione e di predicatori sospetti': Salvatore Caponetto, 'Motivi di riforma religiosa e inquisizione nel ducato di Urbino nella prima metà del Cinquecento', in Salvatore Caponetto, *Studi sulla Riforma in Italia* (Florence: Università degli Studi – Dipartimento di Storia, 1987), pp. 259–74 (p. 273). On the religious books dedicated to Vittoria Farnese, see also Silvana Seidel Menchi, *Erasmo in Italia 1520–1580* (Turin: Bollati Borighieri, 1987), pp. 166, 229, 427, 429.

there is no reason to suppose that Muzio was not sincere. Giorgio Spini's recent judgement of Brucioli's collection is useful here:

> His poetry is neither *lied* not *lauda*, but rather it is the expression of the religious sentiment of one man, rather than of a group ... At his shoulders stands Petrarch, with his soul pulled between earth and heaven ... And when it is not Petrarch it is the Psalms ... or other prophetic and poetic books of the Old Testament, which he often translates into verse without even paraphrasing the biblical passages.[32]

If we compare Brucioli's collection with others issued in the same period, we are immediately made aware of some unusual metrical choices, such as the insertion of madrigals and *canzoni* into the collection and the exclusion of the sonnet (which was the staple metre of spiritual as well as amorous poetry). In addition, the stylistic tribute to the Petrarchan model, although evident, is servile and unoriginal, and Brucioli seems to be incapable of adapting a form of collective prayer (psalms, hymns, and so on) to the individual intonation of the Petrarchan lyric. The modest poetic results, in conclusion, help explain the reasons for the poet's failure. Antonio Brucioli, a Florentine educated in a humanistic environment that resembles that of Machiavelli, and subsequently devoted to the study of the Holy Scriptures, was not able to fall in line with the demands of the new kind of spiritual poetry, which in the meantime had attained a highly sophisticated level. In other words, his readers, whilst not approving of the religious content, did not much like the poetry either.

As scholars have ascertained, the general development of the practice of spiritual verse-writing during the sixteenth century reflects a profound change in the activities of the publishing trade. As Edoardo Barbieri has pointed out in relation to the publisher Giolito, it is possible to single out

> ... in the years around 1560 a profound editorial change of direction, the abandonment (or reduction) of the production of books aimed at the 'courtier' in favour of those aimed at the 'believer', through devotional and religious works. Giolito does not seem to have been put under any pressure in this regard – not least because of the status of his press: instead, he seems to have moved with the times, and applied himself to increasing the market for such works, beyond responding to direct requests. From the editorial point of view one can

---

[32] 'La sua poesia non è né *lied* né lauda, è espressione del sentimento religioso di un uomo, più che di una collettività ... Alle sue spalle sta il Petrarca, col motivo ... dell'anima contrastata tra il mondo e il cielo ... E quando non è il Petrarca sono i *Salmi* ... oppure altri dei libri profetici e poetici del Vecchio Testamento, che il nostro non di rado traduce senz'altro in versi, quasi senza neppure parafrasare il testo biblico': Spini, *Tra Rinascimento e Riforma*, p. 196.

thus confirm that, albeit indirectly, the post-Tridentine epoch did 'create' what can best be defined as the 'spiritual' book.[33]

This assertion can certainly be applied to books of spiritual poetry, as is demonstrated by the contents of one of the most recent bibliographical repertories provided by Amedeo Quondam.[34] Nevertheless, a few important collections of poetry must be located outside this general phenomenon.

An interesting case is provided by Luca Contile's *Rime cristiane*, an autograph manuscript rediscovered in the last century and now kept in the Angelica Library in Rome (ms. 2407), whose contents have been published by Amedeo Quondam together with a critical study.[35] The unusual features of this codex allow us to distinguish two separate stages in the ordering of

---

[33] '[N]egli anni intorno al 1560 il momento di una profonda svolta editoriale, per la quale viene abbandonata (o ridotta) la produzione di libri per il 'cortigiano' a favore di quelli per il 'fedele', cimentandosi in testi devoti o religiosi. Non sembra che il Giolito – anche per l'importanza della sua azienda – abbia subito pressioni in tal senso: piuttosto ha colto una certa svolta epocale e si è dedicato egli stesso ad alimentare la domanda di tali libri, oltre a rispondere a sollecitazioni esterne. Dal punto di vista editoriale si può quindi affermare che, sia pur indirettamente, l'epoca post-tridentina 'crea' quello che deve essere più propriamente definito come il libro spirituale': Edoardo Barbieri, 'Fra tradizione e cambiamento: note sul libro spirituale del XVI secolo', in Edoardo Barbieri and Danilo Zardin (eds), *Libri, biblioteche e cultura nell'Italia del Cinque e Seicento* (Milan: Vita e Pensiero, 2002), pp. 3–61 (p. 22).

[34] Amedeo Quondam, 'Note sulla tradizione della poesia spirituale e religiosa (parte prima)', *Paradigmi e tradizioni. Studi (e testi) italiani*, 16 (2005), 213–82. For general bibliographical information, see also Italo Pantani, *La biblioteca volgare. I. I libri di poesia* (Milan: Editrice Bibliografica, 1996). Traditionally, the new vogue for printed spiritual collections is dated from the *Libro primo delle rime spirituali* (Venice: al segno della Speranza, 1550), a general collection where one finds better-known and more minor authors, including Malipiero and Colonna according to the Valgrisi edition of 1548. On this work, see Ginetta Auzzas, 'Notizie su una miscellanea veneta di rime spirituali', in Doglio and Delcorno (eds), *Rime sacre dal Petrarca al Tasso*, pp. 205–20 (pp. 219–20): '[the book represents] un'impresa conforme a esigenze ormai diventate prioritarie. In quella che come sappiamo era una fase di crescita e di cambiamento della letteratura religiosa, i Libri delle Rime spirituali, nella loro idea di partenza se non nella perfetta attuazione, realizzano l'intento di rinnovare un patrimonio illustre ma ormai anacronistico, in linea con le esigenze di un pubblico che, nella mutata sensibilità e nella aumentata alfabetizzazione, cercava prodotti nuovi. Emblematica è in tal senso … l'assunzione delle rime del Malipiero e di Vittoria Colonna … Se questa impresa fu possibile fu grazie all'esistenza del retroterra, un retroterra squisitamente veneto, delle miscellanee di rime allora in auge, che, al di là di un'abbondante messe di testi, in misura più sostanziale offrivano lo schema organizzativo, essendo apportatrici, insieme, di un ordine e di un decoro linguistici nuovi, essi pure negli auspici degli utenti.'

[35] Amedeo Quondam, 'Le "Rime cristiane" di Luca Contile', *Atti e Memorie dell'Arcadia* (1974), pp. 171–316. The same critical analysis is now also published as 'Le rime cristiane di Luca Contile', in Quondam, *Il naso di Laura*, pp. 203–62. A description of the ms. is also provided, pp. 185 ff. On the fate of the manuscript, from its original ownership by Contile's nephew Bernardino after the author's death, see Piero Misciattelli,

the collection, both due to distinct initiatives on the part of the author. The first project, datable after 1546, was structured around a spiritual core but included profane verse. The collection was sent in this form to Pietro Aretino, who wrote to Contile in January 1546:

> ... if it is still the case that you plan to let me read your most Christian verses, before anyone else sees them. I thank you for this, and await the poems; yet I do not wish our different characters to lead to different intentions.[36]

The book was not published, however, probably due to the death of the Marchese del Vasto, Contile's patron.[37] Many years later, in 1560, the author decided to prepare a traditional profane collection, and on that occasion he used a small group of poems extracted from the manuscript, added a number of others, and eventually published his famous book of *Rime* with a commentary by Francesco Patrizi.[38] Nevertheless, the project of the *Rime cristiane* was not abandoned. Contile went back to the original manuscript, eliminating the twenty-eight published profane poems, and adding 140 spiritual verses, as well as a self-commentary. For the dating of this second stage, Quondam has proposed the years 1561–62, when Contile was in Pavia in the circle of the Accademia degli Affidati, relying on the letter sent by him to Isabella Gonzaga, marchioness of Pescara, on 19 August 1561:

> I would often visit Your Excellency with some worthy or engaging entertainment, yet with due respect I fear (for I feel my own compositions to be lowly and probably ugly) causing offence to the heroic harmonies of your great mind,

---

'Luca Contile e il ritrovamento delle "Rime cristiane"', in Piero Misciattelli, *Studi senesi* (Siena: La Diana, 1931), pp. 89–124.

[36] '[S]e ben son per sempre essere servo de la opinione che mostrate circa il consentire ch'io vegga le cristianissime rime vostre, prima che vengano in luce d'ogniuno. Ma in mentre di ciò vi ringrazio, cotal versi aspetto; imperocché non voglio ne la diversità che aviamo circa l'essere, che la volontà sia più d'una': Pietro Aretino, *Lettere*, ed. Paolo Procaccioli, vol. III (Rome: Salerno Editrice, 1999), 664, p. 495.

[37] According to Quondam, 'Le rime cristiane di Luca Contile', pp. 264 and 266: 'le Rime cristiane risultano pronte per la stampa già nel 1546: e forse il ms. 2407 dell'Angelica offre, almeno nella zona dei testi poetici, proprio la copia allestita a quella data per il tipografo'; but Contile's plan 'fu annullato dalla morte ... di Alfonso d'Avalos, Marchese del Vasto, che era stato il gran committente degli scritti religiosi di Aretino, e che in ogni caso doveva esserlo anche di queste rime.' With Contile's help, Aretino was trying, in those years, to find favour with the Marquis del Vasto (see the letter from Aretino of October 1545, in Aretino, *Lettere*, vol. III, 327, pp. 287–8).

[38] *Le rime di messer Luca Contile divise in tre parti, con discorsi ed argomenti di messer Francesco Patrizio e messer Antonio Borghesi, con le sei canzoni dette le Sei sorelle di Marte* (Venice: Sansovino, 1560).

and although I spoke just now of worthy or engaging entertainments, I did not name them as such due to my own liking for them, but because other people have so described them, above all in speaking of my book of Christian poems. Yet since I have other compositions to hand, on the topic of worldly matters, I will leave those to one side, yet if your Excellency has any desire to see some example of the poems, I can produce them forthwith.[39]

A more recent hypothesis concerning the period of the revision of the *Rime cristiane* has been made by Daniele Ghirlanda, according to whom a more probable dating falls in the period before the publication of Contile's *Rime* in 1560.[40] In any case, and despite its very advanced state of preparation, the revision did not lead to a printed edition, and this fact (excluding the obvious possibility of some unexpected impediment) tempts us to seek for an explanation. If we look at the external features of the manuscript, they prove that Contile, who was at the time a well-known writer, worked at it on two separate occasions with a clear intention to publish it.[41] If, on the other hand, we consider the contents, it is apparent, following Quondam's analysis, that the *Rime cristiane* do not illustrate any 'private religious practice', but rather 'a public treatment of religious and spiritual issues, a worldly practice'.[42] Contile, who was first of all a man of letters, had been in touch with Vittoria Colonna and in some way involved in the religious debate of the 1540s, especially at the time when he was engaged in the writing of his *Dialoghi spirituali* (1543). When he celebrated Vittoria in a sonnet, he did not fail to pay the traditional tribute to her spiritual poetry:

---

[39] 'Io spesso visitarei V. Eccell. con qualche vertuoso, et ingegnoso trattenimento, tuttavia rispettosamente temo (perché tengo le cose mie per basse, et forse dissonanti) di non offendere la heroica armonia del suo alto intelletto, & benché io habbia detto vertuoso, et ingegnoso trattenimento, non ho così detto perché paia a me, ma perché così mi dicono molti, massimamente sopra il mio libro delle rime Cristiane, imperò havendo alcune altre cose, che hanno suggetto di scienze mondane, parmi di lasciarle per hora addietro, pure volendo V. Eccell. qualche saggio di esse, non mancarò': *Delle lettere di Luca Contile secondo volume, diviso in due libri* (Pavia: Girolamo Bartoli, 1564), III, pp. 312v–13r.

[40] Daniele Ghirlanda, 'L'idea di un canzoniere: le "Rime cristiane" di Luca Contile', in *Luca Contile da Cetona all'Europa. Atti del seminario di studi Cetona 20–21 ottobre 2007*, ed. by Roberto Gigliucci (Manziana: Vecchiarelli, forthcoming).

[41] The external vicissitudes of the manuscript, as narrated by Misciattelli, 'Luca Contile e il ritrovamento delle "Rime cristiane"', pp. 116 and ff., indicate a product which always remained essentially private, and only later was passed on to Contile's nephew Bernardino. On the other hand, Quondam is certain that 'a Pavia … nell'ambiente dell'Accademia degli Affidati (ricostituita nel 1562), di cui Contile fu celebrato membro, le sue Rime cristiane erano note e circolavano': Quondam, 'Le "Rime cristiane" di Luca Contile', p. 270.

[42] '[P]ratica religiosa privata'; 'un consumo pubblico della problematica religiosa e spirituale, una pratica mondana': Quondam, ibid., p. 273.

> Donna, ch'avete aperto a' vani ingegni
> la tenebrosa vista e sparso il suono
> che 'l tristo placa e stabilisce il buono,
> deh, soccorrete agli alti miei disegni.[43]

On the other hand, whilst some Valdesian elements are evident in his poetry, Contile was not a 'heretic' as Vittoria was, and we find nothing that might cause suspicions of unorthodox religious content (as in the case of Brucioli). If we look at the first draft of the collection as it can be reconstructed from the manuscript, we find instead a personalized *canzoniere*, where spiritual verse is mingled with other kinds of profane and occasional poetry in line with the traditional standard. In other words, this is a collection that is varied and innocuous, where devotional but also occasional and philosophical verses mingle with poems of exchange, poems on the death of illustrious persons, and even a few translations.[44] From another perspective, the *Rime cristiane* seem to be characterized by the strong persistence of Platonic elements, clearly detectable in the stylistic treatment of religious themes.[45]

To summarize, a first approach to Contile's collection reflects the idea of a *cortigiano* poet, a man of letters who, in the particularly propitious circumstances of the 1540s, *also* felt authorized to write religious verse (exactly what Aretino was also doing in the same period). From the point of view of language and style, Contile was well aware of the fundamental relationship between Petrarchan models and the new vogue for spiritual poetry, and on such matters he tried to state his relative autonomy:

---

[43]   I quote from ibid., p. 205.

[44]   On the *Dialoghi spirituali* (Rome, 1543) and in general on Contile's cultural attitudes to religion, see Abdelkader Salza, *Luca Contile uomo di lettere e di negozi del secolo XVI* (Florence: Carnesecchi, 1903), pp. 111–12; and see also the information (perhaps overly rigid) in the article on Contile by Claudio Mutini, *Dizionario Biografico degli Italiani*, 28 (Rome, 1983), pp. 495–502 (p. 497): 'Nel complesso l'opera, priva di ogni interesse speculativo, può considerarsi una rigida chiusura verso ogni istanza di ordine riformistico in base al concetto di un'ortodossia che deve salvaguardarsi, manu armata, da qualsiasi forma di tralignamento all'interno o di un attacco dall'esterno della Cristianità. All'implacabile odio contro Lutero si unisce nel C. il risentimento contro l'alleanza franco-turca … non è da sottovalutare la perentorietà con cui il letterato senese si libera dai residui di una tradizione riformistica (accreditata, se non altro, dai rapporti con la Colonna) per imboccare la strada maestra dell'autoritarismo tridentino.'

[45]   This aspect has been treated in particular in the contribution by Daniele Ghirlanda, cit. n. 40.

Non vorrei che 'l mio verso fosse scabro
ne gli eterni concetti, anzi alto e grave,
non duro sì che gl'intelletti aggrave,
anzi grato qual croco e qual cinabro.
Ma 'n qual ruscello l'uno e l'altro labro
bagnar poss'io, onde chiara e soave
cavarò l'acqua che la voce lave?
O qual fia, che la limi, il dotto fabro?
O voi che l'universo rivolgete
e con le quattro e con le diece corde
di misura ogni cosa fate opima,
piacciavi col pensier che 'l dir s'accorde,
gli acuti e gravi accenti miei reggete,
essendo voi la mia fonte e la mia lima.[46]

An engaged and sequential reading of his texts encourages us to reach the conclusion that Contile's aspirations to a style that was *alto e grave* does not rest upon any deliberate distancing of himself from the *vario stile*, that is, the sweet, moderate style of the lyric code. His aim was rather to impose a religious and devotional mood onto a style of poetry that was the direct descendent of the profane canon. (The title of the work itself, *Rime cristiane*, deliberately selected by the author in place of *Rime spirituali*, was no casual choice.) This is even more evident when we look at the second stage of Contile's revisions. In this second stage, the author decided to turn his original collection into a purely spiritual one, thus following a tendency observable in many other contemporary poets. The age did indeed seem to favour such a change, in the 1560s and the new climate of the Counter-Reformation. But Contile only partially succeeded in making this transformation. He was, in the end, a typical Renaissance man of letters, representative of a lay and courtly culture, and his approach to the religious lyric could only produce a mechanical substitution for his original polyvocal inspiration. The most reasonable explanation for Contile's failure appears to reside in his inability to expunge the original hybrid nature of his book. The final result failed to impress the author himself, and was abandoned.

Conclusion

As we have seen, the separation of profane from religious verse was the dominating feature of production in the second half of the sixteenth century.

---

[46]   I quote from Quondam, 'Le "Rime cristiane" di Luca Contile', p. 204.

This model looks back to Colonna's collections, and was progressively confirmed by the lyrical poetry of authors such as Benedetto Varchi and Antonio Minturno, and later by Tasso and Marino.[47] A meaningful example is that of the poet Laura Battiferri from Urbino, who married the Florentine architect Bartolomeo Ammannati and moved to Florence in 1555, where she became famous thanks to two books: *Il primo libro dell'opere toscane* (Florence: Giunti, 1560), and *I sette salmi pentitentiali del Santissimo profeta Dauit, tradotti in lingua Toscana da Madonna Laura Battiferra degli Ammannati ... insieme con alcuni suoi sonetti spirituali* (Florence: Giunti, 1564). The first collection is essentially a profane one, with the occasional inclusion of religious verse, whereas the latter is a short and coherent selection of translations from the Psalms together with a small group of sonnets of prayer. In later years, Battiferra's spiritual production increased, as is made clear by the final significant sample of her poetry, the ms. 3229 of the Biblioteca Casanatense in Rome, entitled *Rime di M. LAURA Battiferra degli Ammannati*, which should be considered the definitive collection of her *oeuvre*, organized by her husband after the poet's death according to her will.[48] Without dwelling upon the details of its structure, it is notable that this collection, planned as Battiferri's poetic will, presents a clear division between profane and religious verse, the latter being situated in the second section and including all the religious works that she composed after the publication of the two books.

It is quite rare to find evidence of the inclusion of religious poems in strictly 'Petrarchan' profane collections, with a few illustrious exceptions (from Della Casa to Celio Magno[49]) some of which never led to a printed

---

[47]   See Stefano Carrai, 'La lirica spirituale del Cinquecento', in Stefano Carrai, *L'usignolo di Bembo. Un'idea della lirica italiana del Rinascimento* (Rome: Carocci, 2006), pp. 123–35.

[48]   Information about Ammannati's intention to collect his wife's poems can be found in Pietro Pirri, 'L'architetto Bartolomeo Ammannati e i Gesuiti', *Archivum Historicum Societatis Iesu*, 12 (1943), 1–2: 5–57. Ibid., p. 40: 'Egli pensava di raccogliere in volume gli scritti inediti di Madonna Laura, e a tal fine pregò il P. Generale di volergli accordare il padre Giulio Mazzarino ... L'Acquaviva ... promise nondimeno all'Ammannati che, o da lui o da altri, sarebbe stato soddisfatto ... A Firenze infatti mandò per rettore il letteratissimo Orazio Torsellino; ma forse la morte troncò a mezzo questi disegni, giacché una edizione postuma di scritti della Battiferri è affatto sconosciuta.' The discovery of the manuscript was made by Victoria Kirkham: see 'Laura Battiferra degli Ammannati benefattrice dei Gesuiti fiorentini', *Quaderni Storici*, 104 (2000), 2, 331–54 (pp. 341 ff.), and Kirkham, *Laura Battiferra and her literary circle* (Chicago, IL: University of Chicago Press, 2006), which includes a description (pp. 70–71) and also a partial edition of poems. Nevertheless, the manuscript remains unpublished in its entirety.

[49]   On the structure of Magno's *Rime*, see Giuseppina Stella Galbiati, 'Epilogo sacro e libro: alcune considerazioni sulle Rime di Celio Magno', in Antonio Corsaro, Harald Hendrix and Paolo Procaccioli (eds), *Autorità, modelli e antimodelli nella cultura artistica*

edition. Among the *Rime* of Michelangelo Buonarroti (according to the modern, chronological order given to them by Girardi's critical edition), it is possible select a small group of poems from the final section of the book (corresponding to numbers 280–302). This sequence, characterized by themes of repentance and prayer, consists of ten sonnets (285, 288, 289, 290, 293, 294, 295, 296, 298, 300) and eleven fragments (280, 281, 282, 283, 284, 286, 287, 291, 292, 301, 302), and all the poems can be dated after 1550. These late poems confirm Michelangelo's sincere inclination towards spiritual sonnets, as well as his indifference to any idea of the collection or public dissemination of his poems. By the end of the century, only three sonnets had appeared in print: 285 ('Giunto è già 'l corso della vita mia') in Vasari's *Vite*; and 290 and 294 ('Scarco d'un'importuna e greve salma' and 'Mentre m'attrista, et duol, parte m'è caro'), included in 1565 by Dionigi Atanagi in the second book of the *Rime di diversi nobili poeti toscani*. Readers had no access to perhaps the most interesting episode in this poetic selection, that is, the brief spiritual exchange with Lodovico Beccadelli, to whom Michelangelo addressed two sonnets which are now among the most famous of his entire *oeuvre*: 288, 'Le favole del mondo m'hanno tolto', and 300, 'Per croce e grazia e per diverse pene'. This lack of a public presence can be easily explained if we look at the parallel behaviour of the recipient. Beccadelli was also a poet, and by the end of his life he had prepared his own *canzoniere* of 110 poems (plus several others received from correspondents, including Michelangelo's sonnets). Obeying a fairly traditional scheme, Beccadelli's collection included a large section of poetical correspondence, followed by a spiritual section (a translation of the last extracanonical psalm 151, sixteen sonnets and a *canzone*).[50] The collection is known to us from three manuscript copies kept in the Biblioteca Palatina in Parma, ms. 972 (1–3), but was never sent to press. The order of the poems, together with the external features of the manuscripts (three good copies), have led some scholars to think that Beccadelli intended to have the collection printed. I am personally unaware of any documentary evidence concerning this project, and think that such assumptions still derive from the old prejudice that in the age of printing every complete and ordered collection of verses must be understood as *ready to be printed*. (The same, for example, has

---

e letteraria tra Riforma e Controriforma, Atti del Seminario internazionale di studi Urbino-Sassocorvaro, 9–11 novembre 2006 (Manziana: Vecchiarelli, 2007), pp. 369–85.

[50]   The collection is based essentially on poems of correspondence, a sort of 'contrappunto epigrafico a una vita fittamente intessuta di incontri, di rapporti umani, di amicizie fedeli': Claudio Scarpati, 'Intorno alle Rime di Ludovico Beccadelli', in *Dire la verità al principe. Ricerche sulla letteratura del Rinascimento* (Milano, Vita e Pensiero, 1987), pp. 45–126 (p. 72). There is also a description of the three manuscripts and a transcription of a group of poems. The entire collection nevertheless remains unpublished.

been said of the famous selection on which Michelangelo worked in 1546, whereas it is actually doubtful that he really intended to publish it.)

In conclusion, therefore, the exchange between Beccadelli and Michelangelo, although limited to a few poems, allows us to appreciate their deliberate choice to resort to a private means of circulation for their poetic production. Neither of them was a professional poet. They belonged, in addition, to the 'old' generation that cultivated a humanistic cult of Petrarch, and spiritual verse was for them an answer to inner needs, rather than representing surrender to current fashions. For Beccadelli, Petrarch was not just a master of style, he was the

> ... *philosophus moralis* ... simultaneously drawn to the classics and the Church Fathers, working towards a *renovatio Ecclesiae* demanded in parallel with the *renovatio Romae*. If in Petrarch such writers seek the guidelines for their linguistic and stylistic approach, they also see him as the protagonist of a cultural circle that is still relevant, and finds within the *Ecclesia reformanda* one of its most striking themes.[51]

For Michelangelo, on the other hand, spiritual poetry appears to have been a means of self-expression that was subordinate to and part of a broader investigation into humanity. His famous devotion to Vittoria Colonna led him to enter into a poetic dialogue with her, but it never induced him to imitate her approach to poetry. On the contrary, in their lyric exchanges, Michelangelo seems not to accept, nor even to understand, Colonna's proposals, and he continued to produce poems in which the matter of human love and the matter of art are inextricably tied to spiritual attitudes. Finally, both Michelangelo and Beccadelli belonged to a culture that was still indifferent to the fame deriving from print publication. The fact of being inclined to spiritual writing, and the urgent need that they felt to answer the questions posed by faith with meditation and prayer, could never induce them to turn their poetry into some sort of indoctrination or religious propaganda.

---

[51]   '[P]*hilosophus moralis* ... teso simultaneamente verso i classici e verso i Padri, proteso ... ad una *renovatio Ecclesiae* reclamata parallelamente alla *renovatio Romae*. Se in Petrarca questi letterati cercano le direttive per un comportamento linguistico e stilistico, ancora lo sentono come protagonista di un ciclo culturale non esauritosi, che trova nell'*Ecclesia reformanda* uno dei suoi temi più pungenti': Scarpati, 'Intorno alle Rime di Ludovico Beccadelli', p. 64.

CHAPTER 3

Literary Production in the Florentine Academy Under the First Medici Dukes: Reform, Censorship, Conformity?

Abigail Brundin

Scholarly interest in the impact on Florentine culture and society of the reign of Duke Cosimo I de' Medici has resulted in a number of interesting publications in recent years, focusing on Cosimo's aptly named 'cultural politics' and the effect of his programme of reforms on various important institutions in the city.[1] In particular, attention to the constitution and output of the Florentine Academy in the 1540s and 1550s has revealed a picture of both capitulation and resistance, as academicians ceded to the increasingly close control of the academic environment by their duke, no doubt recognizing the very real benefits of his patronage, while simultaneously working to define the limits of their intellectual, religious and creative freedoms within the privileged academic space.[2] One recent study by Domenico Zanrè has underlined the failure by Duke Cosimo to impose cultural hegemony upon Florence (if indeed that was ever his intention), the Academy in particular serving to exemplify the continued co-existence of more mainstream and alternative modes of intellectual and literary self-expression in the mid-century.[3]

One of the manifestations of heterodox ideas within the Florentine Academy in its first decade was an expressed interest in religious reform

---

[1] See in particular, Michel Plaisance, *L'Accademia e il suo principe. Cultura e politica a Firenze al tempo di Cosimo I e di Francesco de' Medici* (Manziana (Rome): Vecchiarelli Editore, 2004); the various essays in Konrad Eisenbichler (ed.), *The Cultural Politics of Duke Cosimo I de' Medici* (Aldershot: Ashgate, 2001), and Henk Th. van Veen, *Cosimo I de' Medici and his self-representation in Florentine art and culture*, trans. by Andrew P. McCormick (Cambridge: Cambridge University Press, 2006).

[2] On tensions within the Academy and the rival factions that operated in the early years, see Plaisance, 'Culture e politique à Florence de 1542 à 1551. Lasca et les "Humidi" aux prises avec l'Académie Florentine', in *L'Accademia e il suo principe*, pp. 123–234.

[3] See on this topic, Domenico Zanrè, *Cultural Non-Conformity in Early Modern Florence* (Aldershot: Ashgate, 2004).

among a number of its members, including an explicit interest in the need for vernacular translations of biblical works, and a consideration of the importance of the form that this vernacular language should assume. Debates about the *questione della lingua* were intimately tied to questions of religious authenticity, and poetry in particular played a central role in the attempts to express and disseminate a renewed faith both within the Academy itself, and to a wider audience who came to listen to the weekly public lectures. A number of prominent Florentine academicians expressed an interest in a reform-flavoured faith in the 1540s, while at the same time placing poetry at the centre of their intellectual and academic activities. The reading of poetry, its composition, as well as the public and private lectures on Dante and Petrarch alongside a number of contemporary vernacular poets, allowed for the establishment of poetic discourse within the Academy as a vehicle for debates that went well beyond matters of lyricism to engage with some of the most crucial issues of the age.[4] Vernacular poetry, in other words, in the Florentine context as elsewhere in this period, had the capacity to speak on a number of different levels – literary, philosophical, political and spiritual – to wide audiences, and to engage with questions of religious reform in subtle but important ways.[5]

A clear example of the use of poetic analysis as a means to engage with significant religious debates of the period can be found in the lectures delivered before the Florentine Academy at the very end of the 1540s by Giambattista Gelli (1498–1563). Gelli was by trade a shoemaker, and began his studies in adulthood. He went on to become a well-respected academician, delivering a number of lectures on poetic topics before public and academic audiences.[6] In 1553, he was appointed, together with Benedetto Varchi (1503–65), as one of the first salaried lecturers under a newly regularized academic system, and paid a stipend by the duke to deliver

---

[4]   On the nature of these weekly lectures, see Michel Plaisance, 'Les leçons publiques et privées de l'Académie Florentine (1541–1552)', in *Les commentaries et la naissance de la critique littéraire. France/Italie (XIVe–XVIe siècles)*. Actes du colloque international sue le commentaire, Paris, mai 1988, ed. by Gisèle Mathieu-Castellani and Michel Plaisance (Paris: Aux Amateurs de Livres, 1990), pp. 113–21. See also Judith Bryce, 'The oral world of the early Accademia Fiorentina', *Renaissance Studies*, 9 (1995), 77–103, and more broadly, Richard S. Samuels, 'Benedetto Varchi, the Accademia degli Infiammati, and the Origins of the Italian Academic Movement', *Renaissance Quarterly*, 29 (1976), 599–634.

[5]   On the use of lyric poetry as a vehicle for the expression of religious reform in the work of Vittoria Colonna, see Abigail Brundin, *Vittoria Colonna and the Spiritual Poetics of the Italian Reformation* (Aldershot: Ashgate, 2008).

[6]   On Gelli's life and works, see Armand L. De Gaetano, *Giambattista Gelli and the Florentine Academy: The Rebellion Against Latin* (Florence: Olschki, 1976). Also more recently, Chiara Cassiani, *Metamorfosi e Conoscenza: I dialoghi e le commedia di Giovan Battista Gelli* (Rome: Bulzoni, 2006).

the weekly orations on Dante in Santa Maria Novella.[7] The texts of Gelli's public lectures on Petrarch and Dante were published, as were many such texts by academicians, by Torrentino for the first time in 1551, and display a keen awareness of the status of poetry as a vehicle for encapsulating and conveying the profoundest of theological truths:

> These things that I tell you about Petrarch should not seem novel to you, since even the ancient poets such as Museus, Orpheus and many others in the guise of love lyrics wrote of the wondrous and profound mysteries of their sacred theology.[8]

In line with this view, Gelli reads Petrarch and Dante holistically as sources for religious illumination, eschewing the kind of fragmentary linguistic analysis that characterizes other poetic commentaries of the period.[9] In addition, he makes evident as he progresses in his analysis of both poets that his understanding of faith has a distinctly reformed flavour, including frequent references to 'fra Girolamo' (Savonarola), to St Paul, and to contentious issues of faith and election, which he touches on frequently while clearly wishing to avoid a full and possibly compromising exposition of his views:

> But this light, as the Apostle tells us, is a gift from God given by him alone to whomever he wishes (and you will find in the holy gospel that he said to his disciple, I have elected you and not you me), and it does not derive from the natural power of our souls, so that man as mere man cannot receive it, but only as elect and servant of God; yet of all of this I do not wish to speak.[10]

---

[7]   See Plaisance, 'Les leçons publiques et privées', p. 115.

[8]   'Et non vi paia cosa nuova questo che io vi dico del Petrarcha, conciosia che anchora i Poeti antichi come furon Museo, Orpheo, & molti altri sotto concetti amorosi scrissero gl'occulti & profondi misterii della loro sacra Teologia': *Tutte le lettioni di Giovam Battista Gelli, Fatte da lui nella Accademia Fiorentina* (Florence: [Torrentino?], 1551), p. 57. (All translations my own unless otherwise stated.)

[9]   See for an example of a more 'traditional' kind of poetic lecture, *Giovanni Cervoni da Colle sopra il sonetto del Petrarca Amor, fortuna, & la mia mente schiva, letto publicamente nell'Accademia Fiorentina* (Florence: Torrentino, 1550). On poetic commentaries more generally in the sixteenth century, see Bernard Weinberg, *A History of Literary Criticism in the Italian Renaissance*, 2 vols (Chicago, IL: University of Chicago Press, 1961).

[10]   'Ma perche questo lume secondo che dice l'Apostolo, è un dono di Dio dato da lui solamente à chi e vuole (e però voi havete nel sacr'Evangelio, che ei disse a suo Discepoli, Io ho eletto voi & non voi me) & non è potenza naturale dell'anima nostra, onde non si conviene all'huomo come huomo, ma come eletto & servo di Dio, io non ne voglio parlare': *Tutte le lettioni di Giovam Battista Gelli*, p. 63.

Of particular note is Gelli's tendency, when lecturing on poetry, to cite all biblical passages in vernacular translation, putting his concern for clarity and understanding on the part of his audience before adherence to the new strictures on the diffusion of vernacular translations of the Bible.[11] At the centre of his cultural project is the concern for wide dissemination of theological truths via a philologically pure poetic language.

Gelli was not alone in fomenting an interest in reformed ideas in the Florentine Academy in the 1540s and 1550s. The Academy's first *console* and Gelli's co-appointee to a salaried lecture post in the Academy in 1553, Benedetto Varchi, was also personally concerned with a reformed spirituality and expressed this in his own poetry and prose works, as well as through his academic lectures.[12] Various other leading intellectuals and public figures cultivated an interest in reform, including Cosimo I's *Maggiordomo*, Pierfrancesco Riccio; Varchi's successor as *console*, Bartolomeo Panciatichi (1507–82); and notably Pietro Carnesecchi (1508–67), later sentenced to death for heresy.[13] At the same time, the primary vernacular text promoting the tenets of a reformed faith, the *Beneficio di Cristo*, was circulating among groups in the city and attracting a good deal

---

[11]   On Gelli's concern with the use of the vernacular and particularly with the Church's duty to communicate clearly with its congregations, see De Gaetano, *Giambattista Gelli*, pp. 248–61. On the status of the vernacular Bible and its subsequent banning in the sixteenth century, see the two important works by Gigliola Fragnito: *La Bibbia al rogo. La censura ecclesiastica e i volgarizzamenti della Scrittura (1471–1605)* (Bologna: Il Mulino, 1997); *Proibito capire. La Chiesa e il volgare nella prima età moderna* (Bologna: Il Mulino, 2005).

[12]   A highly reform-flavoured Good Friday sermon by Varchi was published by Torrentino in 1549, and subsequently together with prose works by Vittoria Colonna and an anonymous author thought to be Marcantonio Flaminio in a collection of 1557: the sermon is reproduced in Paolo Simoncelli, *Evangelismo italiano del cinquecento: questione religiosa e nicodemismo politico* (Rome: Istituto storico italiano per l'età moderna e contemporanea, 1979), pp. 445–51. More broadly on Varchi's writings, see *Benedetto Varchi 1503–1565*, Atti del Convegno (Florence, 16–17 December 2003), ed. by Vanni Bramanti (Rome: Edizioni di Storia e Letteratura, 2007).

[13]   On the culture of reform in Florence in this period and the religious tendencies of various academicians, see Massimo Firpo, *Gli affreschi di Pontormo a San Lorenzo. Eresia, politica e cultura nella Firenze di Cosimo I* (Turin: Einaudi, 1997). Bartolomeo Panciatichi was ultimately accused of heresy by Sant'Ufficio in Rome in 1551 according to Michel Plaisance ('Culture et politique à Florence', p. 147 n. 68), or 1555 according to Massimo Firpo (*Gli affreschi di Pontormo*, p. 359). On Carnesecchi's three heresy trials, see *I processi inquisitoriali di Pietro Carnesecchi (1557–1567). Edizione critica, I : Il processo sotto Paolo IV e Pio IV (1557–1561) ; II : Il processo sotto Pio V (1566–1567), I : Giugno 1566–ottobre 1566; II : Novembre 1566–gennaio 1567 ; III : Gennaio 1567–agosto 1567*, ed. by Massimo Firpo and Dario Marcatto. Collectanea Archivi Vaticani, 43 (Vatican City: Archivio Segreto Vaticano, 1998).

of interest and approval.[14] Within this context, it seems appropriate that one of the few contemporary vernacular poets chosen as the subject of a number of public lectures by Florentine academicians should have been Vittoria Colonna (1490–1547), the celebrated and highly reform-minded Petrarchist who had close connections to members of the Florentine Academy (notably Carnesecchi), as well as to the *Beneficio di Cristo* through her friendships with Marcantonio Flaminio and Reginald Pole.[15]

On three occasions between 1542 and 1550, members of the Florentine Academy delivered public lectures analysing sonnets by Vittoria Colonna. The first occasion was in January 1542, when Bernardo Canigiani (1524–1604) spoke on the sonnet 'D'ogni sua Gloria fu largo al mio sole'.[16] Subsequently, in November 1545, Francesco di Niccolò Bottegari offered a reading of the sonnet 'Perché dal tauro l'infiammato corno'; finally, in July 1550 Pierfrancesco di Tommaso Ginori spoke on an unspecified poem.[17] These occasions are highly significant as an indication of Vittoria Colonna's status as a member of the small cohort of vernacular 'greats' whose work came under discussion at the Florentine gatherings alongside the regular, bi-weekly expositions on the poetry of Dante and Petrarch. The interest in the work of Vittoria Colonna should also be connected to the reform-minded sympathies of Florentine academicians, and the recognition of her status as the primary reformed Petrarchist of her generation.

Two of the three public speakers who lectured on Colonna in the period, Bottegari and Ginori, had been proposed for membership of the Florentine Academy by Nicolò Martelli (1498–1555), an individual who had established direct relations with Colonna through their mutual interest in the composition of spiritual lyrics and in a reform-minded spirituality. In 1544, Martelli sent Colonna a manuscript of around fifty sonnets 'in

---

[14] On the circulation of the Beneficio di Cristo in Florence, see Simoncelli, *Evangelismo italiano*. More generally on the Beneficio, see Benedetto da Mantova, *Il Beneficio di Cristo con le versioni del secolo XVI, documenti e testimonianze*, ed. by Salvatore Caponetto (Florence: Sansoni, 1972).

[15] On Vittoria Colonna's association with Carnesecchi and with the *Beneficio di Cristo* prior to its publication in 1543, see Brundin, *Vittoria Colonna*, pp. 47–50.

[16] The manuscript of Canigiani's lecture on Colonna can be found in the Biblioteca Nazionale di Firenze, cod. XLII, Cl. IX. It is reproduced by Domenico Tordi in *Bricciche letterarie* (Rome: Tip. Pallotta, 1889); I have not yet been able to consult this volume. On Bernardo Canigiani, see *Dizionario Biografico degli Italiani*, 18 (Rome: Istituto dell'Enciclopedia Italiana, 1975), pp. 86–9. Colonna's poem, in a slightly different version, is reproduced in Vittoria Colonna, *Rime*, ed. by Alan Bullock (Rome: Laterza, 1982), p. 65.

[17] The poem discussed by Bottegari can be found in Colonna, *Rime*, p. 61. For more information on the lectures, see Plaisance, 'La diffusione a Firenze delle "Rime" di Vittoria Colonna', in *L'Accademia e il suo principe*, pp. 281–9. See also, on Bottegari's lecture, Bryce, 'The oral world', p. 81.

praise of Christ' and asked for her comments and response.[18] Martelli, who appears to have modelled himself on his idol Pietro Aretino in seeking financial gain and fame from his literary endeavours through the widest possible campaign of self-promotion, also corresponded with Marguerite de Navarre, Pietro Bembo, Michelangelo Buonarroti and others in Colonna's circle, in each case supplying numerous unsolicited examples of his poetry on religious topics, and asking repeatedly for responses and support.[19]

What is particularly notable about Martelli's letter to Colonna is the fact that he stage-manages his approach to the noblewoman through careful references both to poetry and to piety. First, he alludes to Colonna's cordial relations with his cousin Lodovico di Lorenzo Martelli, whose sonnets to Colonna on the death of her husband were published in Venice in 1533.[20] Secondly, he recalls the memory of an earlier meeting in Florence in 1538, when Colonna was in that city in order to hear a sermon delivered by her close friend, the Capuchin preacher Bernardino Ochino (1487–1564):[21]

> The affection and service that my poor cousin Lodovico Martelli bore for your singular goodness and unique virtue (with good reason), most humane lady, together with the fact that you graciously received me when I visited you on the occasion when that rare and more than human friar Bernardino of Siena was preaching in this land, give me the courage, since you already know of my devotion to you, to write you these twenty-five words and beg you to accept the enclosed sonnets in praise of Christ, limited to only around fifty in total, since they treat of a subject which the grace of your goodness has spread and diffused throughout your whole beauteous being, and not according to the merit of their rough form.[22]

---

[18]   Martelli's letter to Colonna, dated 22 June 1544, is cited in *Supplemento al carteggio di Vittoria Colonna*, ed. by Domenico Tordi (Turin: Ermanno Loescher, 1892), pp. 87–90.

[19]   A snapshot of Martelli's concerted programme of self-promotion is provided by his first, self-published book of letters (the 'secondo libro' never made it to press): *Il primo libro delle lettere di Nicolo Martelli* (Florence: Nicolo Martelli, 1546). The letter to Colonna was included in this volume, at p. 47r. Martelli's admiration for Aretino extended to his recommending his friend for membership of the Florentine Academy in 1545, although Aretino was excluded again following reforms in 1547: see Plaisance, 'Une première affirmation de la politique culturelle de Côme Ier: la transformation de l'Académie des "Humidi" en Académie Florentine (1540–1542)', in *L'Accademia e il suo Principe*, pp. 29–122 (pp. 140, 185–6).

[20]   'Stanze di Lodovico Martelli a la Illustriss. Sig. la S. Vittoria Marchesa di Pescara in morte de lo Illustriss. Marchese suo Consorte' in Lodovico Martelli, *Rime volgari* (Venice: Marchio Sessa, 1533), pp. 96–116.

[21]   Colonna's presence in Florence to hear Ochino preach is recorded in a sonnet by Anton Francesco Grazzini: see Plaisance, 'La diffusione a Firenze delle "Rime" di Vittoria Colonna', p. 281.

[22]   'L'affettione et la servitù (a gran ragione) che portava quel poverin di Lodovico Martelli mio cugino, alla singular bontà et unica virtù vostra, humanissima Signora, insieme con l'havermi dato grata udienza, nel visitare quella nel tempo che il raro et più c'huomo fra

Martelli is careful to refer to the 'more than human' Ochino in the most flattering terms, an interesting choice given the friar's apostasy over charges of heresy two years previously and Colonna's subsequent public embarrassment at her link to him.[23] It appears as if Martelli is deliberately using the friar's name in order to establish a subtext to his letter, one that links him to Colonna through his shared interest in evangelical ideas. The remainder of the letter supports this hypothesis in its deliberately obscure language and cloaked references to reformed concepts. Martelli expresses his confidence that Colonna will read the verses he has sent her, not because of their own merit but through her grace (a clear reference to the important arguments over grace and merit that were concerning reformers at the time), and he refers to his state of unhappy oscillation between two opposing 'styles' and his desire to choose the right one with guidance from God:

> If your humanity causes you to offer me any praise it will be due to your pity alone, for offering you a treatment in one style and the other, I derive comfort from following this one and not the other one, for God wished that I should do so, so that I might no longer be so unsettled and confused.[24]

Niccolo Martelli's courting of Colonna in 1544 reveals clearly his recognition of her status as a writer of reformed spiritual Petrarchism, made explicit in his sympathetic citing of Bernardino Ochino. The fact that the two men whom he sponsored into the Florentine Academy also chose Colonna as the subject of public lectures gestures towards a wider appreciation of the poet's particular reformed spiritual and poetic approach within the Florentine environment.[25]

The examples of Giambattista Gelli, Benedetto Varchi and Vittoria Colonna illustrate that the literary activities of the Florentine Academy

---

Bernardino da Siena predicava in questa Terra, mi danno ardire, poi che l'hà della servitù mia anchor conoscenza, di scriverle queste XXV parole et pregarla, che li presenti Sonetti in lode di *Christo*, scemati à un numero di forse cinquanta, gli accetti, per ragionar di quell soggetto, di che la gratia della bontà sua, vi ha sparso et difuso tutto il bello dell'anima vostra, et non pei meriti del loro rozzo fabbro … .'

[23]   On Ochino's apostasy, see Gigliola Fragnito, 'Gli "Spirituali" e la fuga di Bernardino Ochino', *Rivista storica italiana*, 84 (1972), 777–813.

[24]   '[E]t se lode alcuna nel cospetto dell'humanità vostra me n'averrà, sera solo per mercè di quella, che presentandole un saggio de l'uno stile et de l'altro, mi confortaste a seguitar questo, et non quellom che Dio il volesse che io l'avesse fatto, ch'io non viveria hora si inquieto, et in stato si confuso.'

[25]   Further evidence of the general esteem for Colonna in Florence is provided by the text of an anonymous lecture on a poem commemorating her death, from early 1547. See Plaisance, 'Vittoria Colonna et l'Académie Florentine: un commentaire en forme d'oraison funèbre', in *L'Accademia e il suo principe*, pp. 291–309.

in the late 1540s and 1550s had a resonance that went beyond the mere literary appreciation of vernacular poetry to the heart of some of the key debates of the period, specifically on the interrelated topics of language and spirituality, the search for a 'pure' form of both, and the important status of vernacular poetry as a vehicle for conveying religious truths. The apparent freedom to express heterodox views in front of an audience of academicians and members of the public at this time would seem to be at odds with the traditional view of Cosmian Florence, and particularly of the reconstituted Accademia Fiorentina, as a tightly organized and carefully managed environment in which Medicean political interests took precedence over all else, to the detriment of individual creativity.[26] It is notable that contemporaries record that the Academy's public lectures in Santa Maria Novella were always very well attended, drawing crowds of people of all classes and seemingly both sexes, including political figures close to the Duke himself.[27] That the views expressed by lecturers in this environment could be as unorthodox as Gelli's or Varchi's were suggests that heterodoxy was not only tolerated, but perhaps even encouraged by the Duke. In addition, the admission to the Academy of men from diverse social backgrounds, as well as the continued existence of sources of cultural activity outside the officially sanctioned academic environment (through the production of the Giunti press, for example) provides a picture of a 'plurality of cultural production' within the city which is suggestive of an energetic and lively cultural scene, nurtured rather than stifled by the centralizing focus of the Accademia Fiorentina.[28]

Despite his megalomaniac reputation, evidence points to the fact that Cosimo I was very canny when it came to recognizing the need for tolerance in the sphere of cultural production. While he was concerned with the need to be seen to comply with Rome on issues concerning religious practice and expression, he was seemingly less keen to stamp on literary freedoms or to police the boundary where literature and religion overlapped. Thus, for example, when it came to the implementation of the increasingly stringent Roman Indexes, the Duke played a clever game, authorizing the burning of prohibited books on theological subjects with seeming vigour while turning a blind eye to the continued circulation of banned literary titles, pragmatically aware of the need to protect the

---

[26]   On the transformation of the Accademia degli Umidi into the Accademia Fiorentina, and the latter's organization after 1541 (including on Cosimo's cultural 'absolutism'), see Plaisance, 'Une première affirmation de la politique culturelle de Côme Ier'; Zanrè, *Cultural Non-Conformity*, pp. 15–21.

[27]   Plaisance, 'Les leçons publiques et privées', pp. 113–15.

[28]   The phrase is Zanrè's: see *Cultural Non-Conformity*, p. 27 (including the description of the Giunti press as an antidote to the Medici-sponsored Torrentino).

local book trade as far as possible.[29] In her chapter in this volume on the reformed Pontormo frescoes in Florence, Chrysa Damianaki draws attention to the political motivations that probably led Cosimo to wish to promote tolerance of reform in the city, namely his desire to position himself in opposition to the curia and the Farnese.[30] In addition, his keen understanding of the importance of a broad programme of patronage led to his active promotion of cultural protagonism across different spheres and classes, including the admission to the Academy of men such as Gelli, a shoemaker, or Agnolo Bronzino (1503–72), a painter of humble origins, as well as the close participation in the cultural sphere of women like the poets Laura Battiferra degli Ammannati (1523–89) and Tullia D'Aragona (c.1510–56), never formally admitted to the Academy but benefiting from its patronage.[31] While this kind of cultural empowerment of more marginal classes and groups might have concerned the Church authorities and underpinned much of the substance of sixteenth-century indexes, Cosimo clearly saw its wider benefits for the intellectual health of his Duchy.[32]

The Later Sixteenth Century: Resistance or Capitulation?

From the preceding analysis, a picture emerges of mid-century Florence, in and around the Florentine Academy, as a lively and energetic cultural environment. This environment was one in which reform-minded religion played an important role, despite or perhaps thanks to ducal control and protection, and academicians and others were regularly drawn into debates on poetry, piety and language. Given the broader shifts in the religious climate of the time, the question of periodization arises. For how long did the period of relative cultural and religious freedom and innovation continue within the Academy and city of Florence? Was it simply a brief flowering before the Tridentine reforms, the increasing anxiety about vernacular print censorship, and the stifling nature of monarchical rule

[29]   On Cosimo's unwillingness to comply fully with the Pauline Index of 1558, and his attempt to *seem* to be doing so, see Antonio Panella, 'L'introduzione in Firenze dell'"Indice" di Paolo IV', *Rivista storica degli archivi toscani*, 1 (1929), 11–25.

[30]   See Chrysa Damianaki, 'Pontormo's lost frescoes in San Lorenzo, Florence: a reappraisal of their religious content', in this volume. On Cosimo's difficult political relations with the papacy, see Giorgio Spini, *Cosimo I e l'indipendenza del principato mediceo* (Florence: Vallecchi, 1980), pp. 168–94.

[31]   On this aspect of the academic environment, see Deborah Parker, *Bronzino: Renaissance Painter as Poet* (Cambridge: Cambridge University Press, 2000), pp. 15–18.

[32]   On the Church's anxiety concerning the need to protect 'i semplici', including especially women, from texts and ideas that they would certainly misinterpret, see Fragnito, *Proibito capire*, esp. pp. 9–10.

began to take effect and limit the potential for free expression? Certainly the long-standing reputation of late sixteenth-century Florence, albeit one that is increasingly challenged in more recent scholarship, is of a city sunk into a slough of political stability and cultural complacency, with a resultant 'general shrinking of cultural horizons'.[33] How far, though, is this 'shrinkage' actually apparent if one examines the cultural sphere in the later century in more detail?

An examination of print culture in Florence in the later years of the sixteenth century might offer a useful clue as to the literary energy of the city and its Academy. The ultimate fate of the Torrentino press, officially sanctioned and subsidized by Cosimo I, would seem to suggest that the period of cultural and literary renewal engendered by the Duke and the Academia Fiorentina in the 1540s was in fact short-lived. After an initial flurry of activity between 1548 (the first full year in which the press was operational in the city) and 1551, the Torrentino's print production declined dramatically, to only eight editions in 1554, and only four in 1557. Crippled by debt and having effectively swamped Florentine readers with volumes with a limited readership (primarily the printed 'lezioni' of academicians, as required by his ducal contract), Torrentino was also badly affected, as were all printers, by the increasingly stringent censorship laws imposed from Rome.[34] Conversely, however, and no doubt thanks in part to Torrentino's financial crisis, the Giunti press expanded in the 1550s, suggesting that it was not the book trade within Florence that was the problem, but rather the very unfavourable terms imposed on Torrentino by Cosimo I. In fact, in the 1560s, the productivity of the Giunti press was at its height, with 114 new editions published in that decade, including religious works (notably a vernacular translation of the gospels for use by those untutored in Latin), poetry and drama.[35]

Other indicators might seem to suggest an increasingly rigid academic system being imposed from the 1550s. From 1553, for example, when Gelli and Varchi were appointed as the first stipendiary lecturers to the

---

[33]   This view is expressed in Peter M. Brown, *Lionardo Salviati: A Critical Biography* (Oxford: Oxford University Press, 1974), p. vii. It is convincingly countered by Eric Cochrane in *Florence in the Forgotten Centuries 1527–1800. A History of Florence and the Florentines in the Age of the Grand Dukes* (Chicago, IL and London: University of Chicago Press, 1973), esp. pp. 73–91. The invaluable archival work of Michel Plaisance in particular has made a significant contribution to the rethinking of late-century Florentine academic culture.

[34]   See Antonio Ricci, 'Lorenzo Torrentino and the Cultural Programme of Cosimo I de' Medici', in *The Cultural Politics of Duke Cosimo I de' Medici*, pp. 103–19.

[35]   See William A. Pettas, *The Giunti of Florence, Merchant Publishers of the Sixteenth Century* (San Francisco, CA: Bernard M. Rosenthal, Inc., 1980), pp. 96–9, although the author is very dismissive of the literary production of this period, deeming it to be largely 'cant and hyperbole' (p. 98).

Academy, paid to ensure the delivery of the weekly lectures on, respectively, Dante and Petrarch, the potential to hear other voices and other points of view at these public sessions was dramatically reduced.[36] The fact that both Gelli's and Varchi's voices were notably unorthodox, however, casts a slightly different light on this development.[37] Similarly, in 1550, the Academy instructed its members that public lecturing on authors other than Dante and Petrarch was only permitted if the name of the author in question was included in the list of acceptable names compiled by Cosimo's secretary, Lelio Torelli. It was still possible to seek permission to lecture on other authors, but the permission of all four academic censors had to be obtained in advance.[38] Again, the net result of this ruling seems to have been the inevitable reduction in occasions when the work of contemporary vernacular poets could be analysed in public lectures. The initiative appears to have been undertaken in the interests of preserving quality, however, rather than due to any anxieties about orthodoxy, so that in fact the desire to limit consideration to only the best and purest examples of vernacular poetry remains absolutely in line with the broader literary, philological and religious concerns of the academy described above.

Other evidence runs counter to a picture of increasingly careful control, pointing instead to the continued vitality of Florence and its academic culture. A period of particularly vigorous activity can be detected around the marriage of the newly appointed regent, Francesco I, for example, when he wed Johanna d'Austria in 1565. At this time, forty-eight new academicians were elected, and two notably unorthodox figures – Agnolo Bronzino and Anton Francesco Grazzini, who had been excluded in reforms of 1547 – were readmitted. The system of public lectures and other academic activities also enjoyed a period of renewed interest and input.[39] What is more, although the Accademia Fiorentina continued to be the largest and most influential organization, two new literary academies were founded in Florence in the following decades, both with ducal approval and support. In 1569, the Accademia degli Alterati was founded by individuals, most of whom were already members of the Accademia Fiorentina. The Medici sanction of the Alterati is confirmed by the involvement of Eleonora di Toledo de' Medici, Duke Francesco's sister-in-law, as well as of Giovanni de' Medici,

[36]   See Plaisance, 'L'Académie Florentine de 1541 à 1583: permanence et changement', in *L'Accademia e il suo Principe*, pp. 325–37 (p. 327).

[37]   On Benedetto Varchi and his tempestuous relationship with the Florentine authorities, see as a starting-point, Umberto Pirotti, *Benedetto Varchi e la cultura del suo tempo* (Florence: Olschki, 1971).

[38]   Plaisance, 'Les leçons publiques et privées', p. 116.

[39]   Plaisance, 'L'Académie Florentine de 1541 à 1583', p. 328.

his half-brother.[40] In 1582, the Accademia della Crusca was founded, again by individuals who were members of the Fiorentina (notably Grazzini).[41] All three institutions seemingly co-existed with reasonable equanimity from this point, cross-fertilizing and complimenting one another while maintaining their own particular specializations, and contributing to a picture of cultural growth and innovation within the city that continued until the end of the sixteenth century.[42]

There is also evidence to suggest that Francesco I de' Medici carried on his father's practice of quiet but stubborn resistance to the Roman curia. A number of examples from the later part of the century demonstrate ducal support of printing initiatives that did not meet the approval of the Florentine Inquisition and were subsequently blocked. Unlike Cosimo, however, Francesco seems to have been less able by the 1580s to override or ignore the demands of the inquisitors. A case in point is the proposed publication of Anton Francesco Grazzini's poetry, fully supported by the Duke, and carefully managed by the members of the Accademia della Crusca, who carried out a pre-emptive programme of censorship in an effort to get the work passed for publication by the censors. The project never gained inquisitorial approval, however, and ultimately the Academy was forced to abandon altogether its interest in the burlesque mode, and even distance itself from its founder in public.[43] Francesco's continued support of such projects is indicative of the tension that existed between the two 'official' voices of late-century Florence, state and religious, which often failed to work in harmony.

An interesting example of the continued success in later sixteenth-century Florence of innovative and unusual literary voices nurtured in the environment of the Accademia Fiorentina is the case of Laura Battiferra degli Ammannati, recently uncovered in two modern editions and an impressive study by Victoria Kirkham.[44] Although she was not herself an academician (the Fiorentina remained notably conservative about the

---

[40]   For information on the bi-weekly meetings of the Accademia degli Alterati in this period, see Bernard Weinberg, 'Argomenti di discussione letteraria nell'Accademia degli Alterati (1570–1600)', *Giornale storico della letteratura italiana*, 131 (1954), 175–94.

[41]   On the Accademia della Crusca, see Severina Parodi, *Quattro secoli di Crusca: 1583–1983* (Florence: Accademia della Crusca, 1983).

[42]   On the coexistence of the three Academies in Florence in the late sixteenth century, see Plaisance, 'L'Académie Florentine de 1541 à 1583', especially pp. 330–31.

[43]   See on this, Plaisance, 'Le Accademie fiorentine negli anni ottanta del cinquecento', in *L'Accademia e il suo Principe*, pp. 363–74 (p. 369).

[44]   The two modern editions are: Laura Battiferra degli Ammannati, *Il primo libro delle opere toscane*, ed. by Enrico Maria Guidi (Urbino: Accademia Raffaello, 2000); and *idem*, *I sette salmi penitenziali di David con alcuni sonetti spirituali*, ed. by Enrico Maria Guidi (Urbino: Accademia Raffaello, 2005). See also Laura Battiferra degli Ammannati,

admission of women to its ranks), Laura Battiferra was directly supported in her literary endeavours by her mentor Benedetto Varchi, and clearly benefited greatly from the cultural patronage of the Medici Dukes together with her second husband, the sculptor Bartolomeo Ammannati (1511–92). Under Cosimo's benign eye, Battiferra, a middle-class writer and a woman, received the encouragement and support of the Academy and its members, and achieved a high level of literary acclaim in Florence and further afield. She was a prolific writer, amassing a corpus of nearly five hundred and fifty poems over the course of her lifetime, including a large amount of work left unpublished on her death in 1589.

Battiferra's poetry shows clear evidence of an interest in a reformed spirituality that no doubt reflects the Florentine academic climate in which she moved and wrote. In a sonnet addressed to Vincenzo Grotti, included in her first publication, the 1560 *Primo libro delle opere toscane*, she writes of her longing to be back in the company of a group presided over by the well-known reformer Caterina Cibo (1501–57), where it is not the beautiful natural setting but the uplifting talk of Christ that has nourished her soul:[45]

GROTTI, né 'l temperato aer sereno,
né le vaghe campagne e i verdi prati,
né le fresch'erbe e i dolci colli amati,
né della loggia il ricco albergo ameno,
  ma il parlar saggio e d'eloquenza pieno,
il dir di Cristo in stili alti e ornate,
sgombrare il cor de' van pensier gelati,
e d'amor caldo e fede empiere il seno,
  son la cagion perch'io sospiro e bramo
esser dell'onorata vostra schiera,
ov'alberga onestate e cortesia,
  e dove la gran donna, ch'io tant'amo,
di dolce Cibo, anzi di manna vera,
l'alma nodre e al ciel la scorge e 'nvia.[46]

Laura Battiferra and her Literary Circle, ed. and trans. by Victoria Kirkham (Chicago, IL: University of Chicago Press, 2006).

[45] Laura Battiferra degli Ammannati, *Il primo libro delle opere toscane di Madonna Laura Battiferra degli Ammannati* (Florence: Giunti, 1560).

[46] 'GROTTI, neither the temperate air serene, / nor winsome countryside and green meadows, nor /fresh grasses and sweet beloved hills, nor the rich / delightful abode beside the loggia, / but wise conversing, filled with eloquence, / speaking of Christ in styles lofty and embellished, / disencumbering my heart of vain frozen thoughts, and / replenishing my breast with warm love and faith / are the reason why I sigh and long to be in / your honoured

It is notable that Battiferra makes mention of the style and eloquence with which 'il dir di Cristo' is conducted among this group of friends, alluding to the link between reformed spirituality and elegant vernacular language which was one of the central concerns of the Accademia Fiorentina. The mention of the 'stili alti e ornate' that characterize the interlocutors' discussions is a clever double manoeuvre by the poet. While she demonstrates her poetic skill through a beautifully modulated description of the *locus amoenus* of Petrarchan versifying, she simultaneously rejects the poetic context that she clearly inhabits so effortlessly. Instead, the poet longs to embrace a spiritual end by turning her high style to the service of Christ. Cibo's 'onorata schiera', the in-crowd of like-minded companions that the poet wishes she might join, represents an idealized, spiritual academic gathering of the first order, and one of notable gender equality, which women may join and over which a woman presides.

In 1564, Battiferra published her second volume of poetry, *I sette salmi penitentiali*.[47] In this later work, while still relying fundamentally on Petrarchan language and imagery, she moved beyond the Petrarchan and epistolary framework of the *Primo libro delle opere toscane* into more overtly spiritual territory through a verse translation of the Psalms. Once again, it is possible to detect a reformed flavour to the work, for example, through occasional references to the unmerited gift of God's grace, as well as through the controversial choice of genre. The composition of vernacular translations of sacred texts was a problematic genre in the latter half of the sixteenth century, and some attempts were made at the Council of Trent to codify and limit this potentially risky practice, with an outright ban of vernacular translations in 1559 (aimed particularly at women readers), that was subsequently lifted in the Tridentine Index of 1564, the year of the first publication of Battiferra's *Sette salmi*.[48] The style in which Battiferra presented her work, that is, as verse translation with initial prose explanations, was a particularly concerning format for the authorities: verse translations and paraphrases allowed for a freedom of interpretation that was not considered desirable. What is more, Battiferra explicitly dedicates her work, as well as each individual psalm translation, to women, those who most need to be protected from heterodoxy. It is no doubt for this combination of reasons that in the early seventeenth century,

---

troop, where abide honesty and courtesy, / and where the great lady, whom I so love, / with sweet Food, nay with true manna, nourishes / the soul and guides and sends it heavenward': Battiferra degli Ammannati, *Laura Battiferra and her Literary Circle*, pp. 130–31. The translation is by Victoria Kirkham as are all others cited from this edition.

[47]   Laura Battiferra degli Ammannati, *I sette salmi penitenziali di David con alcuni sonetti spirituali* (Florence: Giunti, 1564). The work was reissued in 1566 and 1570.

[48]   See for details of the Tridentine decrees, Fragnito, *La Bibba al rogo*, pp. 75–109. See also the editor's introduction in Battiferra, *I sette salmi penitenziali* (2005), p. 13.

after the outright ban in the Clementine Index of 1596 of vernacular texts containing the words of the Scripture in any form, copies of Battiferra's *Sette salmi* were handed in to the Church authorities as suspect texts in Rome, Perugia, Foligno and Spoleto.[49] Although at the time of publication her text was not illegal (and notably it was reissued twice in the following few years), the decision to compose such a work none the less looks like a bold move on Battiferra's part, allying her with other forward-thinking, reform-minded writers in Florence, such as Giambattista Gelli for example, writers who refused to relinquish their precious access to vernacular biblical texts.

Although she remained outside the Florentine Academy by dint of her sex, Battiferra in her published work clearly draws on the same literary and religious currents as academicians such as Gelli and Varchi, expressing her interest in fundamental questions of language, literary self-expression and religious faith with notable freedom and distinction.[50] Her fame and acclaim in Florence until her death in the 1580s are indicators of the continued receptiveness of that context to novel and challenging literary voices well into the late century, although the question remains whether by the later decades of the sixteenth century such voices were necessarily confined to the outskirts of the official Academy. It is also interesting to note that the publication of indexes of prohibited books which included increasing numbers of literary works in their lists of banned material seems not to have dissuaded Battiferra from expressing in poetic form her particular religious beliefs, including a first-person 'interpretation' of biblical texts in a period when this was a particularly contentious genre. A further mode of assessing the cultural and literary energy of the later-century Florentine context, therefore, may be through the lens of the papal indexes, and their impact on literary culture in a city that continued stubbornly to resist control by Rome.

The Impact of the Indexes

In her wide-ranging study of the Italian indexes of the sixteenth century, Gigliola Fragnito points out the inevitable wider cultural impact of developments that were intended to reassert the primacy of Latin in

---

49   See Fragnito, *La Bibbia al rogo*, p. 305.

50   Florence was clearly not as forward thinking as Siena regarding the election of women to Academies: in 1560, Battiferra was inducted into the Accademia degli Intronati with the academic name 'La Sgraziata'. See Battiferra degli Ammannati, *Laura Battiferra and her Literary Circle*, p. 23.

religious practice, thus by association assuring the incomprehension of the masses as well as impeding their access to texts:

> With the excuse of protecting the 'simple people' from dangerous heterodox currents and from moral transgressions, the censors extended their control to literary and devotional works which enjoyed widespread success: chivalric romances and poems on religious topics were targeted by the hostility of the ecclesiastical hierarchies towards the 'impertinence' of poets and the commingling of sacred and profane ... Such censorship practices – whose effect on literacy levels and on the linguistic unification of the Italian peninsula have still to be fully assessed – were part of a much broader attack on Italian, which aimed at its ultimate removal from the daily practice of religion.[51]

Given that one of the fundamental aims of the Florentine Academy from its founding was the elaboration and defence of Florentine Italian as the definitive *lingua parlata e scritta*, via textual analysis and philological and linguistic debates, it is not surprising that the promulgation of the indexes would meet considerable resistance within Florentine academe. Although Florentines may have been concerned about the spread of heresy, opposition to the inclusion on the list of banned books of material not directly concerned with theology was a necessary politically charged and patriotic stance for them to adopt. Cosimo's own resistance to the Pauline Index in 1559 betrays clearly its political motivations that superseded any theological concerns.[52] In fact, as Fragnito points out, with or without Cosimo's opposition, so broad was the scope of the Pauline Index that it was seemingly more or less unenforceable, and it was swiftly modified through a *Moderatio indicis* in 1561.[53]

The Tridentine Index of 1564 was a document that was considerably more realistic in scope than its predecessor. This time, in recognition of the manner in which Paul IV's index had overreached itself and in an attempt by Pius IV to curb the growing power of the *Inquisitor Maior*, Cardinal Ghislieri, a number of significant u-turns were made. Expurgation was

---

[51]   'Con il pretesto di salvaguardare i "semplici" da pericolose derive eterodossee da trasgressioni morali, i censori estesero il loro controllo anche su opere letterarie e devozionali, che godevano di larghissima fortuna: romanzi cavallereschi e versificazioni di argomento religioso vennero colpiti dall'ostilità della gerarchia ecclesiastica verso la "petulantia" dei poeti e la commistione di sacro e profano ... Queste eclusioni – le cui ripercussioni sul processo di alfabetizzazione e di unificazione linguistica della penisola attendono di essere compiutamente misurate – si iscrivono in un'offensiva di più vasta portata contro l'italiano, che puntava alla sua rimozione dalla pratica religiosa quotidiana': Fragnito, *Proibito capire*, pp. 9–10.

[52]   See Panella, 'L'introduzione in Firenze dell'"Indice" di Paolo IV'.

[53]   See Fragnito, *Proibito capire*, pp. 29–32.

officially introduced as a viable means of preserving works for future readers; only those works dealing with religion were banned, so the secular works of certain heretical writers were re-legitimated. The sixty printers whose entire output had been placed on the Pauline Index were reinstated, and biblical translations were once again permitted. The era of pragmatic realism lasted only until the pontificate of Pius V (Cardinal Ghislieri) in 1566, when work began on a new, and newly stringent index, to be published finally under Pope Clement VIII in 1596. In the meantime, and for the next twenty-five years, a compromise situation continued in which the official Tridentine Index remained in force, yet papal representatives regularly sent out to the Italian states increasingly long supplementary lists of other banned works and authors.[54]

The period of hiatus and uncertainty between the indexes of 1564 and 1596 (as well as ongoing and profound disagreements between the various Vatican institutions responsible for censorship and expurgation) preserves a welcome space for literary activity in Florence as in other states not under direct Vatican control.[55] While the ecclesiastical authorities continued to contradict one another, and the messages transmitted to the Italian states remained confusing and continuously in flux, the potential still existed for a significant degree of freedom of expression. Thus, while the overall and long-term negative effect of the indexes on literary productivity cannot of course be ignored, one can argue that in the later decades of the sixteenth century their real impact was yet to be felt. It is in this context of uncertainty that we must read the work of a writer like Laura Battiferra, a deeply pious woman who interested herself directly in issues of faith, and ultimately refused to relinquish her access to the vernacular Bible, highlighting her defiance in her published work.

Conclusion

From the 1570s, when Laura Battiferra's works were published for the final time, until the end of the sixteenth century, when we might assume that the effects of the new Clementine Index began to be felt, the practice of regular discussion of poetry continued within the Florentine Academy, as the useful records kept by the eighteenth-century *consolo*, Salvini Salvini,

---

[54]   Ibid., pp. 41–3.

[55]   It is notable that Cosimo asked his advisers to let him know the response of Venice to the Pauline Index as he pondered his own tactics, indicating his awareness of a shared oppositional stance between the two states: see Panella, 'L'introduzione in Firenze dell'"Indice" di Paolo IV'.

attest.[56] In addition, in the newer Accademia degli Alterati, about which a good deal of documentary evidence exists, the discussion of poetry and the critique of contemporary works remained lively and energetic throughout the closing decades of the century.[57] Meanwhile, within the Accademia della Crusca, the important work of regularization and purification of the Florentine language had begun in earnest by the 1580s.[58] Alongside the more traditional, Aristotelian, discussion of poetics and practice of poetry writing, the lyric also moved in new and innovative directions at this time, through the development of new genres such as pastoral, for example, or in the meetings of the Florentine *Camerata*, where discussions of poetry and *calcio* were intermingled with those of music.[59]

Within the context of continued cultural endeavour in Florence in the closing years of the sixteenth century, the work of tracing a persistent strain of reform-inflected, spiritual lyricism remains to be done.[60] An initial survey of studies of the period (although few exist that pay attention to literary production in a historically sensitive manner) suggests rather that the city's cultural institutions turned increasingly to regularization and codification, and that it was only on the margins of such institutions that one can unearth alternative perspectives and currents of unorthodox intellectual expression.[61] In the environment of the Florentine Academy, where the reform-minded views of men such as Gelli and Varchi were so prominent in the 1550s, however, it seems problematic to assume that all traces of their influence had disappeared by the 1580s. The Academy, as a privileged space in which educated men could express their views freely, remained at the centre of the city's cultural life and it is difficult to imagine that its essential freedoms were easily relinquished. Likewise, the crucial

[56]   Salvino Salvini, *Fasti consolari dell'accademia fiorentina* (Florence: Nella stamperia di S.A.R, per Gio. Gaetano Tartini e Santi Franchi, 1717).

[57]   See Bernard Weinberg, 'The Accademia degli Alterati and Literary Taste from 1570 to 1600', *Italica*, 31 (1954), 207–14.

[58]   On this process and the key role played by Salviati, see Brown, *Lionardo Salviati*, pp. 183–204.

[59]   On the development of the pastoral genre, see Lisa Sampson, *Pastoral Drama in Early Modern Italy: the Making of a new Genre* (Oxford: Legenda, 2006). On the Camerata, see Claude V. Palisca, *The Florentine Camerata: Documentary Studies and Translations* (New Haven, CT: Yale University Press, 1989), and Tim Carter, *Music, Patronage and Printing in Late-Renaissance Florence* (Aldershot: Ashgate, 2000).

[60]   See Plaisance, 'L'Académie Florentine de 1541 à 1583', p. 337.

[61]   See for example, Brown, *Lionardo Salviati*; as well as the general remarks about the intellectual tendencies of the period in J.R. Woodhouse, 'Borghini and the Foundation of the Accademia della Crusca', in *Italian Academies of the Sixteenth Century*, ed. by D.S. Chambers and F. Quiviger (London: The Warburg Institute, University of London, 1995), pp. 165–73.

discussions about vernacular language and its wider political and religious implications continued in the late century, in particular in the work of the Accademia della Crusca. What is more, the role of the first Medici Grand Dukes in supporting and cultivating literary freedoms for primarily political ends, in opposition to curial attempts at censorship, must inform and underpin any reassessment of the late century's literary endeavours.

I would like to suggest, therefore, as the title of this chapter indicates, that the traditional picture of literary activity in Florence under the first Medici Dukes – the progression from an interest in religious reform in the city and its Academy, to increased censorship and ultimately to conformity with the 'Counter-Reformation' aesthetic promulgated by Rome – does not adequately describe the reality experienced by Florentine writers and academicians of the late sixteenth century and requires reassessment. On closer examination of the period after 1550, one finds a picture of cultural heterodoxy resulting in a lively and energetic literary scene, a scene that gave birth to varied and unusual literary voices as well as to new academies. Rather than dampening cultural activity in the city, the centralization of power in Florence allowed creative individuals to benefit from newly invigorated cultural institutions and a relatively benign yet generous mode of patronage. In addition, it would seem that the impact of the Council of Trent and its religious reforms in the later century has been overstated in traditional historiography, particularly given the uncertainties about the exact content of the official Roman index until the very end of the century, and the continued regional resistance to papal initiatives across the Italian peninsula. Perhaps, in fact, it was precisely the centralization of power in Florence that gave Florentines a new certainty of their status and the resultant ability to resist papal demands with increased confidence.

By locating this study within Florence, where Cosimo and his heirs have traditionally been viewed as cultural despots who worked to narrow the channels for creative expression available within the city, I hope to have gone some way to demonstrating the opportunities offered by this increased centralization, rather than its supposed limitations. The Florentine Academy, as the locus of cultural energy and heterodox literary and religious activity from the 1540s, provides a useful starting-point and focus for a study that asks to be expanded in future to look at other Italian centres, as well as being extended temporally to take account of the period following the publication of the Clementine Index in 1596. My broader aim, extending beyond the confines of this initial investigation, is to begin the process of chipping away at the many unhelpful assumptions about the 'post-Renaissance' period in Italy, and to revive interest in its literary production and its various cultural protagonists, including, significantly, a far larger number of women than in any other European centre.[62] The dramatic increase in the number of published women writers in Italy in the later sixteenth and early seventeenth centuries, as well as the innovative range of genres in which they wrote, cannot be comfortably accommodated within a view of the period as one of shrinking cultural horizons. Rather, it suggests that academic and literary culture remained open to strikingly new voices and perspectives precisely in the period when we traditionally view it as most closed. The process of re-evaluation promises to be a considerable task, not least because there is seemingly no available term with which to designate this period in Italian literary history that does not carry with it a host of negative associations.[63] By divesting such terms of their traditional meanings through a more nuanced examination of cultural production, it may be possible to come to a better understanding of the real interest of this neglected area of Italian literary history, including the key role played by academies and other vernacular cultural institutions in resisting the pull of the so-called 'mental stagnation' of the Counter-Reformation.[64]

---

[62]   See for an initial survey of writers, Axel Erdmann, *My Gracious Silence: Women in the Mirror of Sixteenth-Century Printing in Western Europe* (Luzern: Gilhofer and Rauschberg, 1999).

[63]   On the pressing problem of terminology, see in the first instance, John W. O'Malley, *Trent and All That: Renaming Catholicism in the Early Modern Era* (Cambridge, MA and London: Harvard University Press, 2000).

[64]   Geoffrey Elton is responsible for designating the later sixteenth century as a period of 'mental stagnation': see G.R. Elton, *Reformation Europe 1517–1559*, 2nd edn (Oxford: Blackwell, 1999), p. 134. It was the obedient citing of his view in an essay by a final-year undergraduate that set this entire research project in motion.

CHAPTER 4

Pontormo's Lost Frescoes in San Lorenzo, Florence: A Reappraisal of their Religious Content

Chrysa Damianaki

The History of the Frescoes

The greatest art work of the Protestant Reformation in the Florence of Cosimo I (1519–74) is Pontormo's series of frescoes in the Medicean Basilica of San Lorenzo, completed after his death (1557) by his most competent collaborator, Bronzino.[1] In this late work, Pontormo had pushed the theoretical, philosophical and religious prerequisites of his art, and of early Mannerism, to their furthest limits. No contract for Pontormo's frescoes in the choir of San Lorenzo has so far come to light; but according to documentation recently examined by Elizabeth Pilliod, preparatory work in the choir started early in 1545. In that year Pontormo is recorded, amongst other artists and artisans, in the account book of the 'Capitani di Parte Guelfa' (a Florentine magistracy in charge of public works) as having received his annual *provvisione* 'for works at San Lorenzo'.[2] This documentation dates the beginning of the work in San Lorenzo back to

---

[1] Giorgio Vasari offers an account of the circumstances of the frescoes' composition: see *Le vite de' più eccellenti pittori scultori ed architettori*, ed. by Gaetano Milanesi, 9 vols (Florence: Sansoni, 1973), VI, pp. 245–95, especially pp. 284–8. In his 'Vita' of Bronzino, Vasari informs us that Bronzino finished the frescoes of the lower range of the choir, namely the *Deluge*, the *Resurrection of the Dead* and the *Martydom of St Lawrence* (VII, p. 602).

[2] See Elizabeth Pilliod, *Pontormo, Bronzino, Allori. A Genealogy of Florentine Art* (New Haven, CT and London: Yale University Press, 2001), pp. 22, 33, 213–14. Pilliod investigated the documents registered in the ledger book of the 'Capitani di Parte Guelfa'; she states that Pontormo's earliest salary instalment in this account book dated 7 March 1545 probably marks his embarking upon the project of painting in fresco the choir of San Lorenzo. According to Pilliod, this is further proved by the following entries in the same account book of the year 1545, which registers payments made to the woodworker Girolamo, for work done in San Lorenzo, as well as to the mason Mariano di Simone for work done specifically for the chapel at San Lorenzo.

1545, and it therefore suggests that earlier theories, dating the beginning of the project to later on, need to be revised.[3]

A court artist and official painter in Florence during the rule of Alessandro de' Medici, and the early years of that of Cosimo I, Pontormo had produced works in the most prestigious and monumental medium of the time, fresco painting, for the Medici villas of Poggio a Caiano, Careggi and in the Loggia of Castello, in collaboration with artists like Bronzino and Salviati.[4] He had also executed portraits of the Medici family (such as those of Maria Salviati and Duke Cosimo I) and had designed tapestries for the Medici. It must be emphasized that for Pontormo – a fresco rather than decorative court painter, as has been observed[5] – the San Lorenzo fresco series was the most important and demanding project he had undertaken; this is why he abandoned the commission for tapestry designs, also assigned by Cosimo, in order to concentrate on it.[6] Pontormo worked on the San Lorenzo frescoes for more than ten years. Vasari wrote that Pontormo had isolated himself in the choir of San Lorenzo for eleven years to execute the frescoes,[7] and Agostino Lapini mentioned that the artist dedicated the final eleven years of his life to this great project.[8]

---

[3]   Frederick Mortimer Clapp recorded payments to an assistant of Pontormo made in the period between 1 March 1554 and 28 February 1557 (*Jacopo Carucci da Pontormo. His life and Work* (New Haven, CT and London: Yale University Press, 1916), Appendix II, doc. 27); Janet Cox-Rearick, *The Drawings of Pontormo*, 2 vols (Cambridge MA: Harvard University Press, 1964), I, p. 319 mentions documents referring to Pontormo's purchase of colours for the San Lorenzo choir in 1549; Philippe Costamagna suggests that Pontormo was chosen to execute the San Lorenzo frescoes in 1546 (*Pontormo* (Milan: Electa, 1994), pp. 253–66, especially pp. 252–3). This view was supported by Massimo Firpo, *Gli affreschi di Pontormo a San Lorenzo. Eresia, politica e cultura nella Firenze di Cosimo I* (Turin: Einaudi, 1997), pp. 155–7; whereas Francesco Mozzetti, reviewing Firpo's book (in *Venezia Cinquecento, Studi di Storia dell'arte e della cultura*, 8 (1998): 181–9, especially pp. 184–5), argued (in my view unreasonably) that Pontormo started work in San Lorenzo in 1548.

[4]   The important issue of Pontormo as an artist for and against the Medici has been thoroughly examined by Pilliod (*Pontormo, Bronzino, Allori*, pp. 11–42) in relation to the tapestry designs, and the San Lorenzo frescoes. On the same subject, also covering Bronzino, see Carl Brandon Strehlke's introduction, 'Pontormo and Bronzino, for and against the Medici' in *Pontormo, Bronzino, and the Medici. The transformation of the Renaissance Portrait in Florence*, ed. by Carl Brandon Strehlke (Philadelphia, PA: Philadelphia Museum of Art, 2004), pp. xi–xiii.

[5]   Pilliod, *Pontormo, Bronzino, Allori*, p. 41.

[6]   I should note here Pilliod's intention that her next monograph will discuss the complex questions raised by the San Lorenzo frescoes, their iconography and the importance of the commission to Duke Cosimo de' Medici (*Pontormo, Bronzino, Allori*, p. 237, n. 27).

[7]   Vasari, *Vite*, VI, pp. 285, 287.

[8]   Agostino Lapini, *Diario Fiorentino dal 252 al 1596* (1596), ed. by Giuseppe O. Corazzini (Florence: Sansoni, 1900), pp. 121–2.

By the late 1540s, the work was well advanced, as testified by an eyewitness account, that of the Florentine academic Anton Francesco Doni. In his *Disegno*, written and printed in Venice in 1549, Doni advised, with some irony, his readers wishing to visit the city of Florence, to go and see Pontormo's frescoes in the Medicean Basilica, even if they were not yet completed.[9] Although this advice could hardly be followed (Vasari claimed that Pontormo kept the Medici chapel of San Lorenzo closed from view for eleven years), it nevertheless may well indicate that by 1549 a number of the scenes were on their way to completion.[10] Besides, Doni's assertion may hint at certain socio-political aspects of Duke Cosimo I's commission of the San Lorenzo frescoes; I shall attempt to demonstrate the importance of these considerations later in this essay.

The frescoes had been commissioned by Cosimo, as Vasari reports,[11] but the choice of Pontormo as artist is probably down to the Duke's major-domo and the prior of San Lorenzo, Pierfrancesco Riccio (or Ricci), a friend of Pontormo and a man strongly connected to Reform circles.[12] It has long been accepted in the scholarship that Riccio had a strong influence on Cosimo's cultural policies in the 1540s,[13] and that he convinced the Duke to entrust the decoration of the choir to Pontormo rather than to

---

[9]   *Disegno del Doni, partito in più ragionamenti, ne quali si tratta della scoltura et pittura; de colori, de getti, de modegli, con molte cose appartenenti a quest'arti, et si termina la nobiltà* (Venice, 1549), p. 48: '… ma se per sorte saranno finite le pitture del choro del Pontormo, vi raccomando a Dio che sarà mezza notte tanto havrete che fare insieme con Rosso'.

[10]   Vasari, *Vite*, VI, p. 285.

[11]   Ibid., p. 284. Pilliod rightly argues that Vasari's account of the commission of the work is not completely accurate, and that his suppression of the official Ducal assistant minimized the level of commitment Cosimo invested in both Pontormo and in the San Lorenzo paintings (*Pontormo, Bronzino, Allori*, p. 51). On the whole, Vasari's account of Pontormo was considered by Pilliod to be unreliable and sometimes dishonest (pp. 1–42).

[12]   Riccio's commission of the work was fully demonstrated by Raffaella Corti, 'Pontormo a San Lorenzo. Un episodio figurativo dello "Spiritualismo" italiano', *Ricerche di Storia dell'Arte*, 6 (1977), 5–64 (especially pp. 10–14), and subsequently by Costamagna (*Pontormo*, pp. 252–3), Firpo (*Gli affreschi di Pontormo*, pp. 82, 155–67), and other critics. See also Paolo Simoncelli, 'Jacopo da Pontormo e Pierfrancesco Riccio. Due Appunti', *Critica Storica*, 17 (1980), 331–48. On Riccio's place in the broader religious culture, see Gigliola Fragnito, 'Un pratese alla corte di Cosimo I. Riflessioni e materiali per un profilo di Pierfrancesco Riccio', *Archivio Storico Pratese*, 62 (1986), 31–83. On the implications of the relationship between Vasari and Riccio, see Antonio Pinelli, *La bella maniera. Artisti del Cinquecento tra regola e licenza* (Turin: Einaudi, 1993), pp. 13, 26. I would add here that Vasari's antipathy to Riccio is revealed not in the *Vita* of Pontormo, but in that of Agnolo Montorsoli (Vasari, *Vite*, VI, pp. 640–41). Recounting the unpleasant events of Montorsoli's life, Vasari criticizes Riccio's cultural policy by saying that he favoured Pontormo, Bandinelli and Tribolo, and detested Montorsoli, who was then forced to leave Florence.

[13]   Alessandro Cecchi, 'Il Maggiordomo Ducale Pierfrancesco Riccio e gli Artisti della Corte Medicea', *Mitteilungen des Kunsthistorischen Institutes in Florenz*, 42 (1998): 115–43.

Salviati or any other artist of the period, despite the fact that Pontormo's fresco paintings at the villa of Castello had not fully satisfied the Duke.[14] Indeed, the decision to award the commission to Pontormo (and not to Salviati, who had greatly aspired to it, and – according to Vasari – hoped to win it back from Pontormo),[15] was probably due to Riccio's Protestant sympathies. Riccio chose Pontormo not only because he was held in great esteem by the Duke and the Florentines, being thought to have produced the most beautiful paintings in Florence in the 1530s, but also, and particularly, because Pontormo was the only artist of his generation deeply concerned with the content of his images, as shown in works like the frescoes in the Certosa of Galluzzo (1523–27), and the panel of the *Deposition* (1526).[16] Moreover, Pontormo was the painter most aware of the relationship between early Mannerism in Tuscany and the Reform movement,[17] and this characteristic would have appealed to Riccio.

Vasari's claim that Pontormo did not permit anyone to enter the San Lorenzo choir for eleven years[18] – an argument that led some scholars to suppose that Cosimo did not know what Pontormo was painting in the choir of San Lorenzo – has been rightly refuted by Pilliod's argument that Cosimo was a notoriously controlling patron who supervised even minute details of the commissions he awarded to artists.[19] It therefore seems unlikely that the Duke did not closely follow the progress of Pontormo's frescoes in San Lorenzo. Some new evidence, which will be discussed later in this essay, may further strengthen the hypothesis that Cosimo was aware of the fact that in the choir of his parish church (which was under Medici patronage), religious subjects which presented a pro-Lutheran rather than Catholic doctrine of salvation were being painted.

Even though the frescoes were destroyed in the eighteenth century,[20] visual memory of them nevertheless reached us thanks to an anonymous

---

[14]   Pilliod, *Pontormo, Bronzino, Allori*, p. 20.

[15]   Vasari, *Vite*, VI, p. 284. Following Vasari, Pilliod writes that Salviati hoped to win the commission from Pontormo in 1548 (*Pontormo, Bronzino, Allori*, p. 31). However, this date can hardly be accurate if one considers Doni's testimony of 1549, mentioned earlier.

[16]   Cf. Maria Calì, 'Arte e Controriforma' in *La Storia. I grandi problemi dal Medioevo all'età contemporanea*, IV, *L'Età Moderna 2. La Vita religiosa e la cultura*, ed. by Nicola Tranfagli and Massimo Firpo (Turin: UTET, 1986), pp. 283–314, especially p. 288. On the iconography and meaning of these works, see Costamagna, *Pontormo*, pp. 189–90.

[17]   This idea was first put forward by Luciano Berti, *Pontormo* (Florence: Il Fiorino, 1964), p. 24.

[18]   Vasari, *Vite*, VI, p. 285.

[19]   Pilliod, *Pontormo, Bronzino, Allori*, pp. 20–21.

[20]   The frescoes were destroyed in 1742 when the walls of the Medici chapel collapsed on account of restoration work carried out in the chapel. The central and lateral walls of the chapel with Pontormo's thirteen scenes, barely discernible in the Albertina engraving, were then

engraving, dated 1598, that was first published by Charles de Tolnay in 1950 (see Figure 4.1).[21] The print shows the choir of the San Lorenzo chapel decorated for the funeral of King Philip II of Spain in 1598 and reproduces Pontormo's frescoes of the upper central section while those of the lateral walls cannot be made out, owing to the viewpoint adopted. For the scenes of the side walls and their placement on the choir, critics have resorted not only to the descriptions of Giorgio Vasari (1568) and Raffaello Borghini (1584),[22] but also to Francesco Bocchi (1591),[23] Antonfrancesco Cirri (eighteenth century)[24] and Giuseppe Richa (1757),[25] who wrote about the interior of San Lorenzo. The most important source of information on the San Lorenzo iconography, however, is Pontormo's twenty-seven preparatory drawings (and likewise copies of them by Bronzino and Alessandro Allori, and probably also by Bastiano del Gestra and Ottavio Vannini), which were thoroughly examined by Cox-Rearick,[26] and more

destroyed. The events of the reconstruction of the chapel are reported by Domenico Moreni, *Continuazione delle Memorie istoriche dell'Ambrosiana Imperiale Basilica di San Lorenzo di Firenze dalla erezione della chiesa presente a tutto il regno medico*, 2 vols (Florence: Ciardetti, 1816–17), I, pp. 112, 115–21; Piero Ginori Conti, *La Basilica di S. Lorenzo di Firenze e la famiglia Ginori* (Florence: Fondazione Ginori Conti, 1940), pp. 144–6. For a detailed discussion and bibliography, see Firpo, *Gli affreschi di Pontormo*, pp. 14–21.

[21]   'Les fresques de Pontormo dans le choeur de S. Lorenzo à Florence', *La Critica d'Arte*, IX (1950), 38–52, especially p. 39, fig. 37. A copy of the drawing is kept in the École Nationale Superiour des Beaux-Arts, Paris (inv. 489r): see Costamagna, *Pontormo*, p. 265.

[22]   *Il Riposo di Raffaello Borghini*, ed. by Antonmmaria Biscioni (Florence: Nestenus and Moucke, 1730), pp. 59–62.

[23]   *Le Bellezze della città di Fiorenza* (Florence, 1571); edition of 1591, pp. 253–5, especially p. 254: 'Adam and Eve can be seen high up ... when, with sweat on their faces, they must secure their own livelihoods by tilling the earth. The figure of Abraham is most beautiful, when he sacrifices his son; and the posture of Isaac is widely praised ... The pride of Cain is shown, when he kills his brother, depicted with most beautiful artifice; and Abel, who tries to escape from such rage, cannot be more singular, nor more rare' [Si vede in alto Adamo, ed Eva ... e quando col sudore del volto zappando deono procacciarsi la vita. Bellissima è la figura di Abraam, quando sacrifica il figliulo; e l'attitudine d'Isaac molto è lodata ... Si mostra la fierezza di Cain, quando uccide il fratello, di bellissimo artifizio, ed Abel, che da tanto furore si vuol fuggire, esser non puote più singulare, ne più raro]. See also, Lapini, *Diario Fiorentino*, p. 122; and *Trattati d'arte del Cinquecento fra Manierismo e Controriforma*, ed. by Paola Barocchi, 3 vols (Bari: Laterza, 1960–62), III (1962).

[24]   *Le chiese di Firenze e Dintorni: Sepoltuario*, V, Biblioteca Nazionale, Florence, MS. 2368, fol. 42; see Cox-Rearick, *The Drawings of Pontormo*, vol. 1, p. 323, note 26.

[25]   *Notizie istoriche delle Chiese fiorentine divise ne' suoi quartieri*, 10 vols (Florence, 1754–62), V (1757), p. 29. He mentions the destruction of the frescoes during reconstruction work in the chapel. An analytical plan of all literary sources cited here is offered by Firpo, *Gli affreschi di Pontormo*, pp. 21–31.

[26]   *The Drawings of Pontormo*, I, p. 327–42, catal. entries 350–82; II, figs 336, 338–71 (the author discusses the stylistic similarities between Pontormo's tapestry designs and the San Lorenzo figures).

Fig. 4.1   Anon., *Choir of San Lorenzo, decorated for the funeral of King Philip II in 1598*, engraving.

recently by Philippe Costamagna,[27] Carlo Falciani,[28] and Elizabeth Pilliod.[29] We may emphasize here that these magnificent figure studies are a testament to Pontormo's consummate draughtsmanship. As such, they fully reveal his highly personal style, which is influenced by Michelangelo, although Pontormo was also inspired by Northern art, especially the prints of Dürer and Lucas van Leyden.[30] It should also be recalled that to Pontormo, *disegno* was the art that most favoured experimentation, and best fulfilled an artist's need to surpass nature. These concepts were fundamental to Pontormo's artistic thinking – highlighted in his letter on the *Paragone delle arti* – and to Mannerism itself.[31]

Scholars have argued that the frescoes provoked uncertainty and criticism from their inauguration on 23 July 1558.[32] Vasari made disparaging comments in his *Vita* of Pontormo, proclaiming that Pontormo's scenes had not followed 'the order of the scene, measure, time, variety ... nor any rule or proportion', and that despite having been a friend of the painter,

---

[27]   *Pontormo*, pp. 260–66, catal. entry 85; especially p. 262, provides reproductions of copies by Alessandro Allori, Ottavio Vannini, as well as drawings by unknown artists.

[28]   *Pontormo. Disegni degli Ufizzi* (Florence: Gabinetto Disegni e Stampe degli Uffizi, 1996), pp. 163–210.

[29]   Pilliod, *Pontormo, Bronzino, Allori*, pp. 34–41. The close stylistic affinities of some drawings for San Lorenzo (pp. 47–51) with tapestry drawings, examined by the author, resulted in the more accurate dating of the former. Pilliod also traced Bastiano del Gestra's contribution to the lost frescoes in San Lorenzo (figs 43, 45). In her study of 2003, Pilliod discusses Michelangelo's influences on Pontormo's draughtsmanship: see 'The Influence of Michelangelo: Pontormo, Bronzino and Allori' in *Reactions to the Master: Michelangelo's Effect on Art and Artists in the Sixteenth Century*, ed. by Francis Ames-Lewis and Paul Joannides (Aldershot: Ashgate, 2003), pp. 31–52, especially pp. 48–9. See also Emil Maurer, *Manierismus, Figura serpentinata und andere Figurenideale* (Zürich: Neue Zürcher Zeitung, 2001), pp. 170–71.

[30]   Vasari criticized Pontormo's influence by Dürer (Vasari, *Vite*, VI, pp. 266–7). However, the impact which Dürer's religious art had on Pontormo is an important aspect of the latter's art and is best exemplified in the panel of the *Supper at Emmaus* (Uffizi, Florence, 1525), inspired by Dürer's same subject ('Small Passion': Bartsch 48). A reappraisal of the religious aspect of Pontormo's art is attempted in my essay 'La Cappella Capponi di Jacopo Pontormo in Santa Felicita a Firenze: per un riesame dei contenuti iconografici e religiosi', in *Officine del nuovo. Sodalizi fra letterati, artisti ed editori nella cultura italiana fra Riforma e Controriforma* (Manziana: Vecchiarelli, 2008), pp. 309–48; and in the entry 'Jacopo Pontormo' in the *Dizionario Storico dell'Inquisizione*, directed by Adriano Prosperi with the assistance of Vinzenzo Lavenia and John Tedeschi, 4 vols (Pisa: Edizioni della Normale, 2009), III (forthcoming).

[31]   Benedetto Varchi, *Lezzione nella quale si disputa della maggioranza delle arti e qual sia più nobile, la scultura o la pittura* (Florence, 1549); Pontormo's letter is included in Paola Barocchi (ed.), *Trattati d'arte del Cinquecento fra Manierismo e Controriforma*, 3 vols (Bari: Laterza, 1960–61), I, pp. 67–9. This letter is also published in Pontormo, *Il libro mio*, ed. by Salvatore Nigro (Genova: Costa & Nola, 1991), pp. 39–43.

[32]   See Lapini's comments in *Diario Fiorentino dal 252 al 1596*, pp. 121–2: the paintings pleased some, and displeased others ('a chi piacque a chi no': p. 122). See Costamagna, *Pontormo*, pp. 255–6, and Firpo, *Gli affreschi di Pontormo*, pp. 146–54.

he had not ever been able to understand the meaning of the scene.[33] I shall argue in this essay that Vasari wanted to conceal his knowledge about the pro-Lutheran content of the images; such a desire would explain why he confined himself to discussing the aesthetic aspects of the work. Vasari's negative aesthetic assessment also conditioned later critics, such as Bocchi and Raffaello Borghini. The latter, inspired by the moral principles of the Counter-Reformation, fiercely protested in his *Riposo* not against the nudity of Pontormo's figures in itself, but against their unpleasing postures, judging them 'improper' and 'a filthy thing to behold'.[34] Borghini was also alarmed by the scant correspondence between the images portrayed and the episodes described in the Bible.[35] These comments located the conflict over Pontormo's frescoes at an aesthetic rather than a religious level, and may have been responsible for their survival up to the mid-eighteenth century despite their reputation as being heterodox.

In modern scholarship, the Reformed foundation of the iconography of Pontormo's frescoes was identified by Charles de Tolnay,[36] and was then specifically labelled Valdesian by Kurt W. Forster, who recognized a strong relationship between the doctrines of Juan de Valdés and the movement of

---

[33]   'Nè ordine di storia, nè misura, nè tempo, nè varietà ... non alcuna regola nè proporzione ... ': Vasari, *Vite*, VI, p. 286.

[34]   *Il Riposo* [1584] (*Il Riposo di Raffaello Borghini* (Florence: Nestenius, 1730), pp. 61, 62. See his discussion on Pontormo's scene of the *Resurrection of the Dead*: 'Then in an instant, and in an indivisible moment, will occur the wondrous mystery of the Resurrection, and all of the dead will come back to life naked, as they were born (for the Resurrection does not take place clothed) and just as our Lord came back to life naked' [Allora in un subito, ed in un tempo indivisibile, si farà il maraviglioso misterio della Resurrezione, e tutti i morti risusciterano ignudi, come nacquero (perchè la Resurrezione non si fa per li vestimenti) e come nudo risuscitò il nostro Signore] (p. 61). He goes on to speak of 'how far from the truth Pontormo has depicted [the scene]; as you know, he has made a great mountain of horrible bodies, a filthy thing to behold, where some are shown coming back to life, others are already revived, and other dead people are lying in improper poses' [quanto lontano dal vero abbia dipinto il Puntormo, il quale, come sapete, ha fatto un gran monte di corpacci, sporca cosa a vedere, dove alcuni mostrano di risuscitare, altri sono risuscitati, ed altri morti in disoneste attitudini si giacciono] (p. 62). It is worth recalling here the Jesuit priest Giuseppe Richa, who looked at the frescoes with disdain on account of their nude figures, and expressed his satisfaction upon their destruction in 1742: see Antonio Paolucci, 'Jacopo Pontormo a San Lorenzo: la melanconia e il nudo' in *Il Settimo Splendore. La modernità della malinconia*, ed. by Giorgio Cortenova (Venice: Marsilio, 2007), pp. 270–73, especially pp. 271–2.

[35]   I should also like to mention here a little-known source, Baccio Bandinelli's letter of 1559 to Cosimo I in which the sculptor writes about his carving of a 'gigante' (related to the *Neptune* fountain) and he also makes the proposal to the Duke to carve two large figures of Angels with candlesticks for the altar of the Medici chapel in S. Lorenzo. Furthermore, Bandinelli says that he promises to impart a truly religious character to his Angels, as they shall be public works, unlike Pontormo's 'dishonest' figures in the same church which have a very bad reputation.

[36]   'Les fresques de Pontormo', pp. 49–50.

Valdesian spiritualists, such as Benedetto Varchi and Vincenzo Borghini, to whose ideas Pontormo would have directly or indirectly adhered. Examining Varchi's spiritual sonnets, Forster indicated that Varchi and Borghini were instigators of the iconographic programme.[37] In his monograph on Pontormo, Forster further stressed that the principal Protestant doctrine of justification by faith, contained in Benedetto da Mantova's *Beneficio di Cristo*,[38] and in the writings of Valdés, should be considered the basis of Pontormo's religious concepts in San Lorenzo.[39] In her development of Forster's thesis, Raffaella Corti claimed that the frescoes interpreted the pro-Lutheran doctrines of Benedetto da Mantova's *Beneficio di Cristo*, a book that had a very wide circulation and was included on the Index as early as 1549.[40] Furthermore, Corti identified in the person of Duke Cosimo's major-domo Riccio the adviser for the iconographic programme of the frescoes.[41] Riccio, a figure with well-known Protestant sympathies, had in his library the only surviving manuscript copy of the *Beneficio di Cristo*, as part of a collection of writings on the doctrine of justification by faith which also included Valdés's *Sadoletis Cardinalis Epistola* (Florence, Biblioteca Riccardiana, MS 1785).

More recently, the historian of the Reformation Salvatore Caponetto identified the source of Pontormo's frescoes in Juan de Valdés's *Catechismo* which were probably inspired by Martin Luther's *Small* and *Large Catechisms*.[42] This inspiration was mediated through Valdés's celebrated reforming book, *Alfabeto cristiano*. Valdés's book, written in Naples in 1536 and printed in Venice in 1545, had been translated into Italian from Spanish by one of Valdés's most fervent followers, Marcantonio Flaminio. Its broad circulation resulted in two reprints, which appeared in Venice

---

[37]   'Pontormo, Michelangelo and the Valdesian Movement' in *Stil und Überlieferung in der Kunst des Abendlandes*, 2 vols, ed. by Florens Deuchler (Berlin: Mann, 1967), I, pp. 181–5.

[38]   *Trattato utilissimo del beneficio di Giesu Christo Crocifisso verso i christiani* (Venice, 1543). I have used the modern critical edition: Benedetto da Mantova, *Il Beneficio di Cristo con le versioni del secolo XVI. Documenti e Testimonianze*, ed. by Salvatore Caponetto (Florence: Sansoni, 1972).

[39]   Kurt W. Forster, *Pontormo. Monographie mit kritichem Katalog* (Munich: Bruckmann, 1966), pp. 93–122.

[40]   Corti's thesis was also accepted by Philippe Costamagna (*Pontormo*, p. 260). The author stated that the iconography of San Lorenzo was intended both to illustrate the doctrines of the *Beneficio* and also to celebrate Duke Cosimo I and his family; for this latter issue, see also n. 114.

[41]   'Pontormo a San Lorenzo', pp. 11–14.

[42]   Salvatore Caponetto, *La Riforma Protestante nell'Italia del Cinquecento* (Turin: Claudiana, 1992), pp. 109–14.

only a year after the *princeps* of 1545.[43] Caponetto argued that the ideology of Pontormo's frescoes adhered to the first eighteen articles of Valdés's brief *Catechismo*, entitled 'The Way in which one should instruct the children of Christians, from infancy, of matters of religion' [*Qual maniera si devrebbe tenere a informare insino dalla fanciullezza i figliuoli de' christiani delle cose della religione*], which was at the heart of Valdés's evangelical doctrine.[44] Furthermore, Caponetto affirmed that Florence's Valdesian circles encouraged policies aimed at rendering in art, for the citizens of Florence, the biblical message in ways which were consistent with Lutheran and Valdesian interpretations. Such reasoning was sharpened by the historian Massimo Firpo, who claimed that the adoption of the Valdesian doctrines in Pontormo's work in San Lorenzo was due less to the transmission of the message of the much-debated argument of justification by faith, than to the diffusion of Valdés's *Catechismo*.[45] This would have been especially true after the collapsed Diet of Regensburg in 1541, which marked the failure of the Catholics to reach doctrinal agreement with the Protestants.[46]

---

[43]   *Alphabeto Christiano, che insegna la vera via d'acquistare il lume dello spirito santo* (Venice, 1546). Significantly, the two reprints of it did not bear the names of the publishers. I have used the modern, critical edition: Juan de Valdés, *Alfabeto cristiano. Domande e risposte della Predestinazione. Catechismo*, ed. by M. Firpo (Turin: Einaudi, 1994).

[44]   *Alfabeto cristiano*, pp. 185–201.

[45]   *Gli affreschi di Pontormo*, pp. 92–144; see also pp. 73–92, in which the author summarizes all the earlier theories on the frescoes' interpretation. On the whole, Firpo's book is framed as an interpretation and explanation of the subject discussed, in search of causes and conditions. In a recent article, Firpo developed further his thesis that the San Lorenzo frescoes provided evidence of Valdés's doctrines ('Storia religiosa e documenti dell'arte. I casi di Iacopo Pontormo e Lorenzo Lotto', *Belfagor*, 59 (2004), 571–90, especially p. 579, note 8).

[46]   I should mention here some alternative interpretations offered by Victor Stoichita, 'La sigla del Pontormo: il programma iconografico della decorazione del Coro di San Lorenzo', *Storia dell'Arte*, 38/40 (1980), 241–56, figs 1–18, and Eva Petrová, 'Pontormovy Fresky v chóru san Lorenza. Rekonstrukcezniceného díla', *Umêní*, 14 (1971), 321–57. Stoichita rejected de Tolnay's and Forster's ideas about the influence on Pontormo of the Reformation, Juan de Valdés and the Florentine *spirituali*, and argued instead that Pontormo was a follower of Paracelsus and of Hermetic theories, and that, therefore, the key to the analysis of the San Lorenzo frescoes would be the artist's 'stile alchemico'. According to Stoichita, Pontormo formulated this style under the influence of the hermetic theories and Paracelsus, which were known to the Florentine Neoplatonic philosophers Pico della Mirandola and Marsilio Ficino. However, neither the iconography of the frescoes, nor the testimonies we have about them can support such a theory. Costamagna (*Pontormo*, p. 257) argued convincingly against Stoichita's theories. Petrová's reconstruction of the scenes on the choir is based on Cox-Rearick, while her analysis of the work's ideology focuses on Dante's poetry. Nevertheless, she does not discuss the religious and doctrinal content of the scenes. For further analysis of her views, as well as of Stoichita's argument, see Firpo, *Gli affreschi di Pontormo*, pp. 78–9 and 82–7 respectively.

It has been established that a reformer, a member of either the Medicean court or the Florentine Academy, provided Pontormo with Valdés's *Catechismo* and probably also with Benedetto da Mantova's *Beneficio di Cristo*. It is highly probable that this was either Pierfrancesco Riccio or Benedetto Varchi. Varchi's pro-Lutheran and Valdesian ideas had been clearly expressed in a sermon entitled *Sermone fatto alla Croce e recitato il Venerdì Santo nella compagnia di San Domenico*, which he read to the members of the confraternity of San Domenico of Florence. The text, printed in Florence by Torrentino in 1549, reveals strong Lutheran and Valdesian sympathies, such as those expressed more openly in the *Beneficio di Cristo*.[47] Salvatore Lo Re compared Varchi's *Sermone* with Pontormo's scenes in San Lorenzo and argued that Varchi's doctrines constituted the principal source of the frescoes of San Lorenzo.[48] On the other hand, it was shown by Firpo that the *proemio* of Varchi's *Sermone* derived both from the *Beneficio di Cristo* and the *Catechismo*; and that this text had many affinities with the heterodox texts written by members of the Florentine confraternity of San Domenico, notably Antonfrancesco Grazzini (known as 'il Lasca'), Giambattista Gelli and Giacomo Mazzuoli (known as 'lo Stradino'). Furthermore, Firpo justly remarked that the confraternity itself would have been a reference point for heretical ideas and of Nicodemite groups in Florence. In the light of these ideas, I would suggest that whether or not Pontormo was asked to follow the *Catechismo*, the *Beneficio di Cristo*, or the *Sermone*, we should accept the hypothesis that Varchi contributed greatly to the iconographic programme of the San Lorenzo cycle.[49] The anti-Medicean Varchi was probably amongst those 'learned and lettered persons', as Vasari says, with whom Pontormo was in touch;[50] it would also appear that Varchi and Bronzino (another friend of Varchi), were the only people close to the obstinately solitary Pontormo

---

[47]   Varchi's *Sermone* is reproduced in Paolo Simoncelli, *Evangelismo italiano del Cinquecento: questione religiosa e nicodemismo politico* (Rome: Istituto storico italiano per l'età moderna e contemporanea, 1979), pp. 445–51. Some passages of the work's *proemio* were published by Firpo (*Gli affreschi di Pontormo*, pp. 218–27) who compares them with Benedetto da Mantova's and Valdés's texts.

[48]   Salvatore Lo Re, 'Jacopo da Pontormo e Benedetto Varchi: una postilla', *Archivio Storico Italiano. Deputazione di Storia Patria per la Toscana*, 150, I (1992), 139–62, especially pp. 147–62. The relationship between Varchi and Pontormo is analysed in greater depth by Firpo, *Gli affreschi di Pontormo*, pp. 144–54 (Varchi and Pontormo); pp. 218–27 (Varchi's *Sermone*).

[49]   Costamagna, *Pontormo*, p. 260 argues that the iconographic programme was determined by Riccio with the help of his friends Gelli and Giambullari, and with contributions by Varchi and Vincenzo Borghini. Firpo maintains that Varchi was the instigator of the work's iconographic programme ('Storia religiosa e documenti', p. 575). Marco Collareta's recent article does not treat Varchi's relation with Pontormo: see 'Varchi e le arti figurative' in *Benedetto Varchi 1503–1565* (Rome: Edizioni di Storia e Letteratura, 2007), pp. 173–84.

[50]   'Persone dotte e letterate', *Vite*, VI, p. 286.

in the final years of his life.[51] Indeed, Varchi's friendship with Pontormo may have extended beyond their common interest in art, to spiritual matters. This issue, which has not been fully explored in modern scholarship, may be suggested by a beautiful sonnet written by Varchi for Pontormo in 1556. The fact that Pontormo recorded it in his *Diario* is indicative of the esteem in which the artist held the academic and probably also his affection for him.[52] Sent to Pontormo in March 1556, when the frescoes were almost complete, Varchi's sonnet celebrated the San Lorenzo frescoes as a highly spiritual achievement. Recent scholarship suggests that this sonnet is revealing of Varchi's veiled Nicodemitic tendencies.[53] Another reminder of Pontormo's close friendship with Varchi is one of Bronzino's sonnets written on his master's death, which refers to 'Varco tuo'. Significantly, Varchi is mentioned in it in relation to the San Lorenzo frescoes.[54]

Let us now turn to Pontormo's images themselves. By considering them alongside Protestant doctrines, we may confirm the direct influence of both the *Beneficio di Cristo* and the *Catechismo* on which Varchi's *Sermone* was grounded. The *Beneficio*, written in the vernacular, was the true epitome of Lutheran and Calvinist doctrines and to a lesser extent, of Valdés's spiritualism. Pontormo may have drawn inspiration from the forty-three articles of the *Catechismo*: not only from the first eighteen articles, as stated by Caponetto and Firpo, but also from articles 7, 9, 12, 23, 27–9, 32 and 41–2 for the scenes of the Old and New Testaments, and for the saving value of faith in Christ and in the Gospels.

Before we discuss Pontormo's biblical scenes, with their strong doctrinal content, we should stress that the diffusion of Protestant doctrines in Florence (both in the Medicean court and in the Academy) towards the middle of the sixteenth century was a historical determinant for Pontormo's work in San Lorenzo. It is therefore necessary, in order to understand better the significance of Pontormo's work, to illustrate the religious climate in Florence in the first half of the sixteenth century. Lutheranism had taken root in Florence even before the second dramatic reinstatement of the Medici family (1527–30): as Delio Cantimori wrote in 1939, the followers of Savonarola glimpsed in the actions of Luther a realization of their own

---

[51]   Elizabeth Cropper, 'Pontormo and Bronzino in Philadelphia: a double portrait', in *Pontormo Bronzino and the Medici*, pp. 1–33.

[52]   Pontormo, *Il libro mio*, pp. 55, 71, 77.

[53]   The sonnet claims that Pontormo has, through his painting, reached unseen glory [gloria non più vista mai]: 'by a secret Path, where no foot has trod, you have reached unseen glory' [per secreto calle,/ove orma ancor nonè segnata, solo/ven gite a gloria non più vista mai]. See Lo Re, 'Jacopo da Pontormo e Benedetto Varchi' (the full sonnet is reproduced at p. 150). I am grateful to Dr Lo Re for having read this paper, and for his interesting suggestions.

[54]   The sonnet is reproduced in Lo Re, 'Jacopo da Pontormo e Benedetto Varchi', p. 151.

hopes.[55] In fact, Lutheran theories were discussed and often well received in Florence, being viewed as a continuation of Savonarola's interrupted project.[56] In the 1540s and 1550s, the Reformation enjoyed great cultural and social support in Florence, especially in the Florentine Academy and the Medici court. The academics Benedetto Varchi, Vincenzo Borghini and Pierfrancesco Riccio, and the Florentine reformers Bartolomeo Panciatichi and Pietro Carnesecchi, were among the eminent personalities of the Italian Valdesian movement.

At the same time, Ludovico Domenichi's publishing activity also helped diffuse Protestant ideas in Florence: he translated and published Calvino's *Nicodemiana* in 1550.[57] Cosimo de' Medici himself tolerated such heterodoxy for political rather than religious reasons, this policy being part of his anti-curial and anti-Farnese plans.[58] Besides, in his court, there were pro-reformers, such as Riccio and Francesco Campana. Cosimo's pro-Lutheran position is confirmed by a little-known letter addressed to Ambrogio of Gumppenberg, in which the Duke wrote: 'I always have been, and always will be, a good Christian … ready to give to the Lutherans, too, all possible favours.'[59] Evidence of those leanings also emerges in a letter written by the ambassador of the Smalkaldic League in Venice, Baldassarre Altieri, to Heinrich Bullinger in 1549. In the letter, Altieri refers explicitly to the ambiguous behaviour of Cosimo (in particular to his 'piétas'), and to his many 'brothers' [fratelli] (as Altieri calls them) residing in Florence.[60]

The publishing choices of Doni in Florence in 1545–46 also reveal his intention to support Cosimo's cultural policy, and probably also his pro-Reform position. This was demonstrated in 1546 when Doni decided to print books by academics loyal to Cosimo, namely Giambattista Gelli[61] and Pier

[55]   See Delio Cantimori, *Eretici italiani del Cinquecento* (Florence: Sansoni, 1978), p. 21. Idem, *Umanesimo e religione nel Rinascimento* (Turin: Einaudi, 1975), pp. 117–19.

[56]   See Paolo Simoncelli, 'Pontormo e la cultura fiorentina', *Archivio Storico Italiano*', 153 (1995), 487–527, especially pp. 513–19.

[57]   Enrico Garavelli, *Ludovico Domenichi e i 'Nicodemiana' di Calvino. Storia di un libro perduto e ritrovato* (Manziana: Vecchiarelli, 2004), pp. 47–8, 59–66.

[58]   In 1549 the Vatican initiated an investigation to determine whether or not Cosimo I had supported Antonio Brucioli and Andrea da Voltera: see Gigliola Fragnito, 'Un pratese alla corte di Cosimo I', p. 47.

[59]   'Io sono stato e sarò sempre un buon christiano, disposto, tuttavia, fuor degli interessi della religione et fede christiana, di fare anche ai lutherani ogni piacere possibile': Cosimo I de' Medici, *Lettere*, ed. by Giorgio Spini (Florence: Vallecchi, 1940), p. 97.

[60]   Heinrich Bullinger, *Bullingers Korrespondenz mit den Graubündnern*, ed. by Traugott Schiess, 3 vols (Basel: Basler Buch-und Antiquariatshandlung, 1904–06), I (1904), p. 476.

[61]   *Capricci del Gello, col dialogo dell'invidia e con la tavola nuovamente aggiunti* (Florence: Torrentino, 1546).

Francesco Giambullari.[62] They were both fervent supporters of Cosimo's cultural policy, and perhaps also of his pro-Reform positions. Moreover, Doni had revealed his thinking through some letters included in the second volume of his *Epistolario*, published in 1547. Doni's provocatively heterodox letters advocated a strongly anti-theological brand of evangelism, and a return to the simplicity of the primitive Church. In the case of the *Disegno*, then, it would seem likely that Doni praised Pontormo's frescoes because he knew that these frescoes had been commissioned by Cosimo. In other words, Doni would have endorsed Cosimo's cultural policies, and consequently supported the commission of the frescoes of San Lorenzo, a soundbox of Protestant doctrine.

All of these factors point to the web of political and cultural ambitions stimulated by the policy of Cosimo and his court, which conditioned Vasari's writing of Pontormo's life. This would help to explain Vasari's significant reticence in Pontormo's life in the *Vite*, and his severe criticism of the San Lorenzo frescoes. This important issue about the history of the San Lorenzo frescoes has tended to be underestimated in scholarship. Cox-Rearick thought that Vasari ignored the importance of the doctrinal concepts embodied by the scenes and that the only level on which he could understand the iconography of San Lorenzo was the narrative one.[63] Modern scholars have argued that Vasari was fully aware of the frescoes' heterodox content, and have tried to find reasons why he failed to mention it. Paolo Simoncelli claimed that Vasari's motivation in criticizing Pontormo's work sprang from his hidden anti-Medicean feelings, in view of the fact that he considered Pontormo a court artist. This can be inferred, in Simoncelli's opinion, from the fact that when in Rome for a long period, Vasari stayed in the house of the notorious anti-Medicean Florentine, Bindo Altoviti.[64] Firpo largely concurs, but he also points out that Vasari's controversial opinions on Pontormo's panel and fresco paintings – his admiration and envy of them – can be attributed to the undisputed high quality of Pontormo's art.[65] In support of this latter statement, I would draw attention to Vasari's comments in the *Vita* of Bronzino, in which he did not conceal his disdain for Pontormo's work in San Lorenzo.[66] As to the question which most concerns us here – whether or

[62]   *Il Gello di m. Pierfrancesco Giambullari accademico fiorentino* (Florence: Torrentino, 1546).

[63]   *The Drawings of Pontormo*, I, p. 323.

[64]   'Pontormo e la cultura fiorentina': 518–21. See also Anna Forlani Tempesti's and Alessandra Giovannetti's view in *Pontormo* (Florence: Octavo, 1994), that Vasari expressed his disapproval about the San Lorenzo frescoes in aesthetic terms alone in the sense of obedience to the Tridentine regulations on religious images (p. 18).

[65]   *Gli affreschi di Pontormo*, pp. 148–54.

[66]   *Vite*, VII, p. 602.

not Vasari recognized the pro-Lutheran content of the San Lorenzo frescoes – I would argue that if we consider not only the political and social situation in the Florence of Cosimo I, as has tended to be the case in previous scholarship on this question, but also the period's literary production and the Duke's cultural policy highlighted here, it becomes clear that the heterodoxy of the religious discourse encoded in the choir frescoes of San Lorenzo would not have escaped Vasari. In attributing Pontormo's failure in this late work to his intellectual and spiritual regression, and to his exhaustion owing to hard work, Vasari found a way of protecting both Pontormo and Cosimo from later accusations of complicity with Protestant heresy.[67]

The Content of the Images

The drawings for the choir of San Lorenzo depict figures and scenes from the Old and New Testaments, while their placement on the choir walls reveals a layout of symbolic synthesis in keeping with Protestant doctrine. This Protestant inspiration can be inferred by three principal elements. First of these is the central role of Christ the Saviour in the iconography and, in general, the Christocentric content of the cycle. A second indication of the Protestant inspiration for the frescoes is the presence of the scene of the Resurrection of the Dead, which takes the place of the more traditional scene of the Last Judgement, which would have been likely to show Purgatory. Finally, the figure of the Virgin Mary is absent. The heterodox character of Pontormo's frescoes is, therefore, primarily suggested by the iconography and the content of the images; I shall argue below, moreover, that it is also enhanced by their arrangement on the choir's walls.

Furthermore, the biblical stories, as shown in the Pontormo drawings, are completely stripped of any descriptive or narrative feature, and the space is independent of the rules of perspective. Two fundamental values of Florentine painting – its celebrated depiction of narrative, and the study of perspective – are therefore absent here. These absences, which are very unusual in Florentine mannerist painting, are generally considered as the very elements betraying the work's heterodox character. Indeed, Pontormo's figures and scenes convey the religious message in a very direct, clear and effective way. It is my opinion that these indisputable qualities are to be associated with the principal characteristics of Lutheran art. Joseph Leo Koerner highlighted the importance of direct communication in artistic Lutheran propaganda, mixed with a symbolic, visual system suitable for the illustration of evangelical truths.[68] The composition of Pontormo's

---

67   *Vite*, VI, pp. 287–8.

68   *The Reformation of the Image* (London: Reaktion Books, 2003).

Fig. 4.2   Lucas Cranach the Elder, *Allegory of the Law and of the New Testament*, etching, c.1530.

frescoes corresponds to a plan of comparisons and contrasts of profound theological meaning conveyed through Old and New Testament scenes. This visual model would associate Pontormo's work not just with historical and religious sources, explored by critics to date,[69] but also with the iconography of the Protestant Reformation. It is widely known that the illustration of Lutheran doctrines through the visual arts was a very powerful instrument of Protestant propaganda. Lucas Cranach the Elder was a great exponent of it: a representative example of his Protestant imagery is the woodcut of the *Allegory of the Law and of the New Testament* with letterpress (*c*.1530) (see Figure 4.2), and an oil panel, *The Law and the Gospels* from the Schneeberg altarpiece (1539, S. Wolfgangskirche, Schneeberg). These works illustrate the distinction between Moses' Ten Commandments and Christ's Gospel, which was a fundamental dialectic in Luther's thought.[70] In Cranach's print, a tree in the centre divides the sheet into two halves in order to clarify the difference between man's condition of slavery under Moses' Law (Old Testament) and of freedom under the grace of Jesus Christ (New Testament). On the left, the image of Fallen Man, alienated from God, is pursued by Death and the Devil. This represents man under Moses' Law (I Corinthians 15:56: 'Now the sting of death is sin; and the strength of sin is the law'). On the right, the crucified and resurrected Christ, the focal point of Luther's preaching, redeems man through His suffering. Cranach's Moses on the left points out the Law to Adam in an emphatic fashion, just as God indicates the Law to Moses in Pontormo's drawing of *Moses Receiving the Tablets of Law* (see Figure 4.3). Cranach's print stresses, therefore, the distinction between the Old and the New Testament by introducing a communicative action between the religious image and the observer, which excluded narrative elements. This is also the case in Pontormo's San Lorenzo cycle, in which the doctrinal distinction between Moses' Law and the Gospel is illustrated in the symbolic frescoes of *Moses Receiving the Tablets of the Law* and the *Four Evangelists*.

One more example of the visual model of comparisons and contrasts between Old and New Testament precepts may be provided by the story of the Sacrifice of Isaac as portrayed by Pontormo in San Lorenzo and Lucas Cranach the Elder in the Wittenberg altarpiece (1547, Wittenberg Cathedral, oil on panels), at the back of which the scene is shown on the left wing, while the right wing is occupied by the Crucifixion scene.[71] In Pontormo's scheme, the Sacrifice of Isaac, which is examined later in this chapter, was probably related to another Old Testament scene, Noah

---

[69]   Corti, 'Pontormo a San Lorenzo', pp. 22–3; Firpo, *Gli affreschi di Pontormo*, pp. 64–154, 408–23.

[70]   Koerner, *The Reformation of the Image*, pp. 201–2, 246–8.

[71]   Koerner, *The Reformation of the Image*, fig. 129.

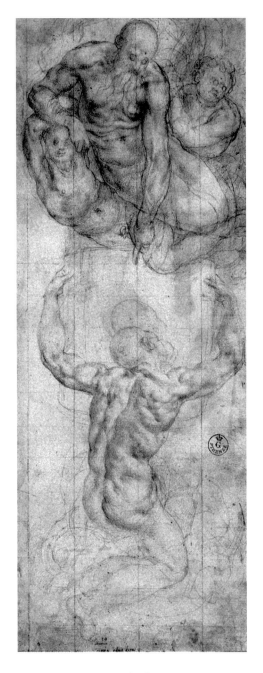

Fig. 4.3   Jacopo Pontormo, study for *Moses receiving the Tablets of the Law*, 385 x 148, black chalk squared.

designing the Ark, both probably alluding to the loyalty and faith in God of the biblical figures of Abraham and Noah. The juxtaposition of the Old and New Testament scenes in the Wittenberg altarpiece was probably meant to stress both Abraham's loyalty and faith to God, and the principal doctrine of Christ's redemption leading to freedom from the consequences of sin and evil – a central precept of Luther's theology of the Cross and his thinking on justification by faith. The iconographic similarities of the San Lorenzo frescoes to these Lutheran engravings and pictures may well suggest that in San Lorenzo Pontormo described a route to salvation that appears more Lutheran than Valdesian.

Before turning to the images' content, it is essential to address the question of the reconstruction of Pontormo's scenes. The reconstruction proposed by Clapp and de Tolnay was further elaborated by Cox-Rearick, primarily on the basis of Pontormo's drawings, but also drawing on the testimonies of Vasari, Cirri and Bocchi, as well as the anonymous engraving of 1596.[72] Cox-Rearick's reconstruction has been accepted by recent scholars, including Costamagna and Firpo.[73] I too accept this reconstruction; but what I believe is needed is a different model for reading the images, a revised interpretive 'key' based on the content of the images. This may clarify the visual model that renders effective the correspondence, or the marked difference, between theological concepts of the Old and New Testaments, a feature we have already noted in Northern Protestant prints. The generally accepted distribution of the scenes on the upper and lower ranges of the choir is as follows: in the central wall of the upper range, the most significant fresco shows *Christ in Glory and The Creation of Eve* (two subjects in one fresco, with the *Creation of Eve* portrayed on the lower part of the central image) (see Figure 4.4).[74] This central scene was flanked by the scenes of the *Temptation of Adam and Eve* (Cox-Rearick, I, p. 327), and the *Expulsion from Eden* (Figure 4.5; Cox-Rearick, I, pp. 330–31). On the left-hand wall, from the outer edge inwards, was the double scene of the *Sacrifice of Cain* and *the Death of Abel* (Figure 4.6; Cox-Rearick, I, pp. 327–9), while in the space between the windows was depicted the scene of *Noah Designing the Ark*.[75] The frescoes of the left wall

---

72   Cox-Rearick, *The Drawings of Pontormo*, I, pp. 321–7.

73   Costamagna, *Pontormo*, pp. 253–5 (diagram on p. 253) records all the earlier versions of the frescoes' reconstruction and presents his own version, which is similar to that of Cox-Rearick with the exception of the episode of the *Benediction of the Seed of Noah* (which Costamagna locates on the upper part of the fresco of the *Deluge*). Costamagna also published a drawing, which he identified as the *Benediction of the Seed of Noah*, and tentatively assigned it to Pontormo (p. 261). See also Firpo, *Gli affreschi di Pontormo*, pp. 64–73.

74   See Cox-Rearick, *The Drawings of Pontormo*, I, pp. 331–5.

75   No drawings of this scene have been found; it is only known through Vasari's account (*Vite*, VI, pp. 285–6).

Fig. 4.4   Jacopo Pontormo, final study for *Christ in Glory and the Creation of Eve*, 326 x 180, black chalk.

Fig. 4.5   Jacopo Pontormo, study for the *Expulsion from Earthly Paradise*, 385 x 14, black chalk squared.

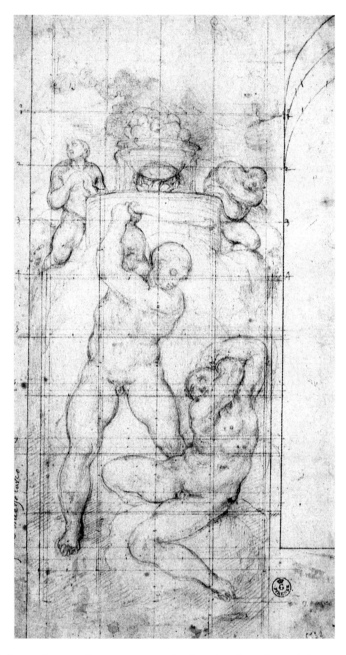

Fig. 4.6   Jacopo Pontormo, study for the *Sacrifice of Cain* and the *Death of Abel*, 405 x 218, black chalk, squared in black and red chalk.

culminated in the scene of *Moses receiving the Tablets of the Law* (Figure 4.3).[76] On the right-hand wall, reading from the outer edge inwards, the scene of the *Labour of Adam and Eve* (Figure 4.7; Cox-Rearick, I, pp. 338–9) was depicted. Adjacent was the scene of the *Sacrifice of Isaac* (Figure 4.8; Cox-Rearick I, pp. 335–6), and the series of scenes on the right-hand side ended with the New Testament scene of the *Four Evangelists* (Figure 4.9; Cox-Rearick, I, pp. 336–8). In the lower range, three major scenes from the Old and New Testaments were represented on the spaces of the back and central walls. These were the *Universal Deluge* on the left (Figure 4.10; Cox-Rearick, I, p. 340), the *Resurrection of the Dead* on the right (Figure 4.11; Cox-Rearick, I, p. 342),[77] and the *Ascension of the Souls* (Figure 4.12; Cox-Rearick, I, pp. 340–41) occupying the central wall facing the altar between the windows and in the side areas. Under the scene of the *Ascension*, the minor scene of the *Martyrdom of St Lawrence* was represented; this probably occupied the area beneath the windows and behind the altar and would, therefore, be barely visible to the observer (Uffizi, GDS, 17411F*v*, 17411Fr, 6560F, Florence; see Cox-Rearick, I, pp. 325, 324–43).[78]

How, then, should these images be read? This question has generally received less attention than that of the scenes' content. De Tolnay and Cox-Rearick made initial steps in analysing the reading order of the scenes. De Tolnay's arrangement is a narrative one that begins with the scenes on the end wall and then, starting with the field next to the arch on the left wall, progresses around the choir to the right in historical order skipping over the symbolic compositions showing Moses and the Evangelists.[79] Cox-Rearick observed that the order of Pontormo's San Lorenzo cycle was rather a reversion to medieval concepts. She pointed to the fact that the symbolic frescoes of Moses and the Evangelists interrupted the historical order, and that the remaining four scenes on the upper frescoes (*Cain and Abel*, *Noah designing the Ark*, the *Labour of Adam and Eve* and the *Sacrifice of Isaac*) could not make a narrative sequence. These observations led Cox-Rearick to the obvious conclusion that Pontormo's scheme is a symbolic one in which the sequence of events in time and their separation in space

---

[76]   This scene is not mentioned in the various descriptions of the choir but it is known through Pontormo's drawings in the Uffizi commented on by Cox-Rearick, *The Drawings of Pontormo*, I, pp. 329–30.

[77]   A design after the fresco of the *Resurrection* is preserved in the Victoria and Albert Museum in London (D. 2154–1885).

[78]   Cox-Rearick, *The Drawings of Pontormo*, I, pp. 325, 342–3. The fresco of the *Martyrdom of S. Lawrence* was evidently intended to celebrate the patron of the Medicean church. Its placement is recorded by Vasari, but there have been disagreements as to its exact location: cf. Costamagna, *Pontormo*, p. 255. In Vasari's 'vita' of Bronzino, we read that this fresco was finished by Bronzino (*Vite*, VII, p. 602).

[79]   'Les fresques de Pontormo', 49–51.

Fig. 4.7   Jacopo Pontormo, study for the *Labour of Adam and Eve*, 203 x 158, black chalk squared in black and red chalk.

Fig. 4.8   Jacopo Pontormo, study for the *Sacrifice of Isaac*, 230 x 165,
                black chalk squared in red chalk.

Fig. 4.9   Jacopo Pontormo, study for *Four Evangelists*, 413 x 177, black chalk squared.

Fig. 4.10   Jacopo Pontormo, study for the *Universal Deluge*, 156 x 244, black chalk.

Fig. 4.11   Jacopo Pontormo, study for the *Resurrection of the Dead*,
              243 x 184, black chalk.

Fig. 4.12   Jacopo Pontormo, study for the *Ascension of the Souls*, 288 x 190, black chalk squared in red chalk.

play no significant part.[80] Corti adopted this idea and further stressed that Pontormo's cycle was symbolic and, as such, was empty of narrative elements or narrative sequence, in order to conform with Protestant doctrines. I shall propose here an alternative reading of the frescoes, based on the scenes' doctrinal content (see Figure 4.13). This may substantiate both the thesis that the frescoes' disposition was intentionally extraneous to a logic of temporal progressive development,[81] and my own argument that the cycle was principally intended to illustrate with maximum clarity a synopsis of Christian doctrines by highlighting both the strong symbolic significance of the protagonists of the Biblical scenes, and of the doctrines suggested by the episodes. This symbolic visual system would have been in keeping with Lutheran modes of expression, in that it would communicate evangelical doctrine in a simple and direct way.

Reading from left to right (as was customary in the Renaissance), the first scene of *Cain and Abel* on the left hand wall is a pendant to the scene of the *Labour of Adam and Eve* on the opposite wall, across the chapel (see Figure 4.13: Diagram nos. 1, 9). These scenes have parallel meanings signifying man's moral condition after the Fall caused by his disobedience to God (Genesis 3:14–24). Protestant writers lay much stress on this doctrine, according to which Adam is shown as transmitting death with sin (Romans 5:12). Benedetto da Mantova defined the moral consequences of man's Fall by the term 'miseria'; he described them in the first chapter of the *Beneficio di Cristo*:

> There is no language that could express a thousandth part of our calamity, that we who were created by God's own hands, have lost that divine image and have become like the devil, acquiring his nature and identity, so that we want everything he does ... Because we have so abandoned ourselves to this evil spirit, each of us is ready to commit even the gravest sin, unless we are restrained by the grace of God.[82]

---

[80]   Cox-Rearick, *The Drawings of Pontormo*, I, pp. 326–7.

[81]   Corti, 'Pontormo a San Lorenzo: Un episodio figurativo dello 'spiritualismo' italiano', 14–23.

[82]   'Non è lingua che potesse esprimere la millesima parte della nostra calamità, perché, essendo noi stati creati da Dio con le sue proprie mani, abbiamo perduta quella divina imagine e siamo divenuti simili al diavolo, fatti connaturali e una medesima cosa con lui, volendo tutto quello che esso vuole ... e, per essere noi così dati in preda a così maligno spirito, non è peccato tanto grave, che ciascun di noi non sia pronto a farlo, quando dalla grazia di Dio non siamo impediti': *Beneficio*, pp. 14–15; translation by Ruth Prelowski, in *Italian Reformation Studies in Honour of Laelius Socinus*, ed. by John A. Tedeschi (Florence: Le Monnier, 1965), pp. 21–102 (p. 48).

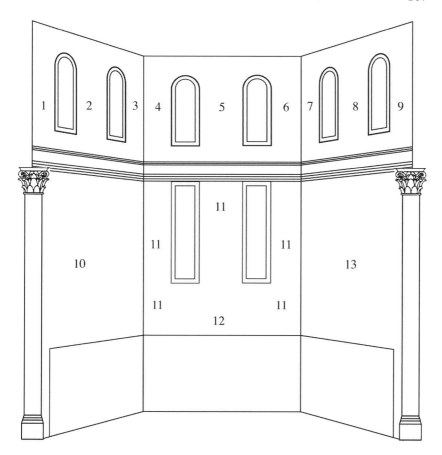

Fig. 4.13   Diagram in perspective of Pontormo's San Lorenzo cycle (author's own).

Valdés also admitted the dogma of original sin and he treated it, albeit summarily, in the first articles of the *Catechismo*.[83] So, too, did Varchi in his *Sermone alla croce*, in which the terms of discussion rely on both the *Beneficio* and *Catechismo*.[84]

---

[83] 'Che questo huomo disubidiendo a Dio perdet(t)e l'imagine di Dio et fu scacciato fuori del paradiso terrestre, et così rimase simile agli animali bruti nella passibilità et mortalità et rimase simile alli mali spiriti nella ingiustitia, impietà, malatia et malignità, et perché era così fatto fu scacciato fuori del paradiso ter(r)estre.' *Alfabeto*, p. 187, art. 7.

[84] 'L'huomo (...) cadde incontanente da tutte le perfezzione et felicità primiere et, perduta in un tratto la sembianza di Dio, divenne simile alle bestie et al dimonio: alle bestie in quanto al corpo, percioché diventò non solo *passibile et mortale* ma sottoposto a mille passioni ognhora, a mille morbi, a mille cure; al dimonio in quanto a l'animo, percioché si

Further on, the scene of *Noah designing the Ark* on the left-hand wall has its parallel to the scene of the *Sacrifice of Isaac* on the right-hand wall (Figure 4.13: Diagram nos. 2, 8), while the next scene showing *Moses receiving the Tablets of the Law* is juxtaposed to the scene of *Four Evangelists* on the opposite wall (both scenes in Figure 4.13: Diagram nos. 3, 7). In this Old Testament imagery, the real focus was, in my opinion, not the 'istoria' or narrative, but the personal qualities of Noah, Abraham and also of Moses prefiguring Christ. In both the *Beneficio di Cristo* and *Catechismo*, Noah, Abraham and also Moses are key figures being described as examples of obedience, faith and loyalty to God and, therefore, precursors of Christ, who, being Himself obedient to God 'and being found in appearance as a man, He humbled Himself and becoming obedient to death: even to the death of the cross' (Philippians 2:8).[85] In particular, Valdés praises Abraham and Noah as unequalled proof of faith and loyalty to God (*Catechismo*, articles 9, 23, 29), discussing the precept of the justification by faith:

> Because men's depravation in the world was increasing, God sent them a flood with which he submerged all of them, saving in an ark Noah, with his wife and his sons ... It was not the ark that saved Noah, but the faith with which he put himself in the ark. (art. 9)

> That all those who embrace this good news and hold themselves to be reconciled with God are children of Abraham, in that they imitate Abraham's faith: he believed in the promises of God. (art. 23)

> ... Just as Noah, placing trust in the word of God, placed himself in the ark and saved himself from the Flood, together with all that he placed in the ark, so too we, trusting in the word of God ... . (art. 29).[86]

Even greater emphasis is put on these qualities by Benedetto da Mantova, who takes Noah as an example of loyalty and faith in the sixth chapter of the *Beneficio*, dedicated to remedies against 'mistrust and incredulity'.

---

fece ingiusto, empio, infedele, malvagio, crudele, bugiardo et inimico di Dio.' Cf. Firpo, *Gli affreschi di Pontormo a San Lorenzo*, pp. 222–3.

[85]   *Alfabeto*, pp. 190–1, art. 17.

[86]   'Che crescendo nel mondo la depravatione degli huomini, li mandò Dio un diluvio col quale li sommerse tutti salvando in una arca Noè con sua moglie et suoi figliuoli ... non lo salvò l'arca, ma la fede con la quale si pose nell'arca'; 'Che tutti coloro che abbracciano questa buona nuova et si tengono per riconciliati con Dio sono figliuoli di Abraham in quanto imitano la fede di Abraham: egli credet(t)e alle promesse di Dio ... '; 'sì come confidando Noè nella parola di Dio si mise nell'arca et si salvò dal diluvio con tutto quello che mise nell'arca, così noi confidan-()-do nella parola di Dio la quale ci dice l'evangelio ... ': *Alfabeto*, pp. 188, 192, 194.

With the memory of baptism, we become more certain that we are reconciled with God, for St Peter says that Noah's ark was the symbol of baptism. Just as Noah believed in the promises of God and thus saved himself from the deluge in the ark, we save ourselves from God's wrath through faith, which is founded on the word of Christ, who says: 'Whoever believes and is baptised, will be saved.'[87]

Benedetto da Mantova's and Valdés's doctrines derive from Scripture; but they also echo Luther's doctrines. In his *Open Letter on Translating* of 1530, Luther chose Abraham as an example of faith to prove that the main point of the Christian doctrine of the justification by faith is our faith in Christ without any works of the Law. Luther argues that Abraham was so justified without works that even the highest work, which had been commanded by God, namely circumcision, did not aid him in justification. Rather, Abraham was justified without circumcision and without any works, but by faith.[88]

The distinction between the doctrines conveyed by the scenes of *Moses receiving the Tablets of the Law* and the *Four Evangelists* merits special attention here as these engage directly tenets of Martin Luther's thought. Indeed for much of his career, Luther focused on deconstructing the idea of the Law as an avenue for salvation. Luther stressed that the Law convicts us of our sin and drives us to the Gospel, but it is not God's avenue for salvation; this is received only through Christ. This was the subject matter of the already examined print by Lucas Cranach the Elder (Figure 4.2). Pontormo's two scenes adhered, therefore, to Luther's concept also stressing the importance of the Gospels. In particular, they symbolized the basic Christian doctrine of the shift from the Old Covenant and the Law of Moses (*Moses receiving the Tablets of the Law*) to man's salvation through Christ's word, His crucifixion and resurrection (*Four Evangelists*). The importance of these scenes was undoubtedly vital to the cycle and it was also enhanced by their proximity to the central and most important fresco of *Christ in Glory and the Creation of Eve*.

It may be worth expanding upon this concept of the Law not only because of its link to the principal doctrine of Christ's redemption symbolized by Pontormo's central scene, but also because of its association with the doctrine of the justification by faith. Theologically speaking, the

---

[87]   'Con la memoria del battesimo ci confermeremo d'esser pacificati con Dio, perché san Pietro dice che l'arca di Noè fu figura del battesimo. Adunque, sì come, Noè, credendo alle promesse di Dio, si salvò nell'arca dal diluvio, così noi per la fede ci salviamo nel battesimo dall'ira di Dio, la qual fede è fondata nella parola di Cristo, il qual dice: "Chi crederà e sarà battezzato, sarà salvo"': *Beneficio*, pp. 59–60 (trans. pp. 78–9).

[88]   *D. Martin Luthers Werke: Kritische Gesamtausgabe*, 60 vols, ed. by Otto von Albrecht, O. Brenner, Georg Buchwald and Karl Drescher (Weimar: Hermann Boehlaus Nachfolger 1883–), XXX, ii (1909), pp. 632–46.

notion that 'the law was given through Moses, grace and truth came by
Jesus Christ' (John 1:17), was discussed by Paul and was inextricably linked
to the doctrine of the justification by faith:

> Now we know that what things soever the law speaks, it speaks to those that
> are in the law: that every mouth may be stopped, and all the world may be made
> subject to God. Because by the works of the law no flesh shall be justified before
> him. For by the law is the knowledge of sin. But now without the law the justice
> of God made manifest, being witnessed by the Law and the Prophets. Even the
> justice of God by faith in Jesus Christ, unto all and upon all who believe in him:
> for there is no distinction. For all have sinned; and do need the glory of God, being
> justified freely by His grace through the redemption that is in Jesus Christ, whom
> God has proposed as a propitiation, through faith in His blood, to the showing
> of his justice, for the remission of former sins, through the forbearance of God,
> for the showing of his justice in this time, that he himself may be just, and the
> justifier of him who is of the faith of Jesus Christ. Where is then thy boasting? It is
> excluded. By what law? Of works? No, but by the law of faith. For we account a
> man to be justified by faith without the works of the law. (Romans 3:19–28)

This central tenet of Christianity was Luther's most fundamental doctrine.
As is well known, Luther came to understand justification as entirely the
work of God, as His act of declaring a sinner righteous by faith alone. Luther
argued that salvation or redemption is a gift of God's grace, attainable only
through faith in Jesus as the Messiah. Against the teaching of his day that
the righteous acts of believers are performed in cooperation with God,
he wrote that Christians receive such righteousness entirely from outside
themselves; that righteousness not only comes from Christ but actually *is*
the righteousness of Christ, imputed to Christians (rather than infused into
them) through faith. He explained this concept of justification by faith in
the *Smalcald Articles* (1537).[89] Luther's reformed views were spread by
Benedetto da Mantova, who largely treated this doctrine in the second and
third chapters of the *Beneficio di Cristo*. Commenting on Romans 3:20
('by the works of the law no flesh shall be justified before him'), Benedetto
writes: 'the Law was given to make sin known; but let us recognize that sin
is not as powerful as the justice of Christ, through which we are justified in
the presence of God.'[90] The same doctrine is summarily treated by Juan de
Valdés in the twelfth article of the *Catechismo*.

---

[89]   The first and chief article was 'Jesus Christ, our God and Lord, died for our sins and
was raised again for our justification' (Romans 3:24–5). On Luther's theology in general, see
Markus Wriedt, 'Luther's Moral Theology', in *The Cambridge Companion to Luther*, ed. by
Donald McKinn (Cambridge: Cambridge University Press, 2003), pp. 86–120.

[90]   'La Legge fu data acciocché 'l peccato fusse conosciuto, e insieme conoscemo ch'egli
non è di maggior efficacia che si sia la giustizia di Cristo, per la quale siamo giustificati

The intention of God in giving this Law was to keep [the Hebrews] in servitude, giving them the Law to teach them, until the coming of Christ. The purpose of this law was to show properly to those who were under it the depravation which is natural to all men because of the sin of the first man, whose depravation becomes known when it is prohibited, and when man is forced to do that which is its contrary.[91]

The other important meaning conveyed by the scene of the *Evangelists* represented by Pontormo (Figure 4.9) is faith in the Gospels. This is a principal Christian doctrine. Salvation comes to humanity through the 'Good News', the Gospel, Luther used to teach, and he explained that the essential content of the Gospel is 'the promise of God fulfilled in our midst, that is, in Jesus Christ'. Benedetto da Mantova followed Luther closely in declaring that Christians seeking for salvation ought to believe in Christ's Gospel, that is, the 'Good News' ('felicissima nuova') written by the apostles:

… This pardon is enjoyed by all those who believe in the Gospel, that is, in the most happy news which the Apostles published throughout the world, saying: 'We pray you, reconcile yourselves with God through Christ, because He who never knew sin has made Himself a sinner for us, so that we may become just in Him.'[92]

This doctrine of faith in the Gospels was, however, treated in detail and celebrated by the greatest exponent in Italy of the evangelical movement, de Valdés, in articles 27–29 of the *Catechismo*. These articles are fully consistent with his spiritualism: they constitute a distinct account of the existence of God's grace through the Gospels. The author puts special emphasis on Christians' acceptance of the Gospels through which Christ's salvation and redemption is offered to them as a gift of God's grace, writing 'that Christian faith is the acceptance of this grace of the Gospels of this remission of sins and reconciliation with God through the justice of God

---

appresso a Dio': *Beneficio*, p. 21 (trans., p. 52).

[91]   'Che l'intento di Dio in dar questa legge fu tener quel popolo [degli Ebrei] in servitù, dandoli la legge come pedagogo insino alla venuta di Cristo, et che l'offitio di questa legge era propriamente mostrare a coloro che stavano sotto di essa la depravatione che a tutti gli huomini è naturale per lo peccato del primo huomo, la quale depravatione alhora è conosciuta quando è prohibita l'essecutione di essa et quando l'huomo è sforzato a far quello che è contrario ad essa … ': *Alfabeto*, p. 189.

[92]   'Del quale [pardon] gode ognuno che crede all'Evangelio, cioè alla felicissima nuova che hanno pubblicata per il mondo gli apostoli, dicendo: "Vi preghiamo, per Cristo, riconciliatevi con Dio, percioché Colui, che non conobbe mai peccato, ha fatto esser peccato per noi, a fine che noi diventiamo giustizia in lui"': *Beneficio*, p. 22; trans. p. 53.

carried out in Christ.'[93] The importance of the Gospel is also underlined by Varchi in the *Sermone* in terms which emphasize the precepts put forward by de Valdés, who urges readers to be certain that 'if we believe without doubt in the Gospel, and place firm faith in its promises, we children of Adam will become children of God, and consequently brothers and coinheritors of the blessed Jesus Christ.'[94] In the light of these ideas, we may conclude that Pontormo's symbolic scenes of *Moses* and the *Evangelists* were meant to convey Lutheran and Valdesian interpretations of the main Christian doctrines of Moses' Law and Christ's Gospel.

Turning to the frescoes represented on the lower range of the choir, the symbolism of the scene of the *Deluge* (Figure 4.10)[95] to the left-hand side, may not have been directly related to that of *Moses' Law*, as Corti argued (Figure 4.3).[96] As was the case with the frescoes on the upper range, the meaning of this fresco could be symbolic and eschatological rather than historical. The story of Noah is, biblically, God's first intervention to save man. Therefore, the symbolism of the *Deluge* (notwithstanding the fact that its iconography complies with its Old Testament source [Figure 4.13: Diagram no. 10]) must relate to that of the eschatological scenes of the *Resurrection of the Dead* (Figure 4.13: Diagram no. 13) and the *Ascension of Souls* (also on the lower range) (Figure 4.13: Diagram no. 11), which are God's final acts for the salvation of mankind. A different interpretation of the symbolism of the *Deluge* scene has been presented by Cox-Rearick and Costamagna.[97] In their opinion, the Noah scene had a political meaning alluding to the glorification of Duke Cosimo and his family.

---

[93]   'Che la fede christiana è l'accettatione di questa gratia dell'evangelio di questa remissione de peccati et reconcilatione con Dio per la giustitia di Dio essequita in Christo'; see *Alfabeto*, p. 194, art 28; see also arts. 27 and 29.

[94]   'Se crederemo indubitatamente all'evangelo et daremo fede certa alle sue promesse, diventaremo di figliuoli d'Adamo figliuoli di Dio, et conseguentemente frategli e coeredi di Giesù Cristo benedetto': *Alfabeto*, p. 194.

[95]   According to Costamagna's reconstruction (*Pontormo*, pp. 254–5), this fresco showed the episodes of the *Blessing of the Seed of Noah* on the upper part and the *Deluge* on the lower part.

[96]   'Pontormo a San Lorenzo', pp. 22–3.

[97]   Janet Cox-Rearick, *Bronzino's Chapel of Eleonora in the Palazzo Vecchio* (Los Angeles: University of California Press, 1993), p. 290. The scene of the *Blessing of the Seed of Noah* is suggested by Borghini in his description of the *Deluge*: 'the ark is seen above the mountain, and Noah with his sons and nephews, who are speaking reverently to God' [l'arca si vegga sopra il monte, e Noè co' suoi figliuoli e nipoti, che riverentemente parlano a Dio]. For Castamagna's view on this, see *Pontormo*, pp. 259–60, where he expands Cox-Rearick's argument by pointed out Gelli's association of Noah with Duke Cosimo I, as a founder of a dynasty. Gelli first expressed this association in an *Ecloga* praising Cosimo (*c*.1539) and he then fully developed it in his book *Dell'origine di Firenze* (Florence, 1544).

Aesthetically speaking, the scene of the *Deluge* was considered by Pontormo's contemporaries as the most indecent, even provocative.[98] Vasari expressed his disdain of the stark realism with which the bodies were portrayed in the lower part of the scene, and described them as 'a mass of dead and drowned bodies'.[99] Raffaello Borghini's criticism of the scene in the *Riposo* (1584) was much more severe. He criticized the scene for its extreme realism, saying that it lacked 'onestà' and 'riverenza' and declared that it did not conform with the doctrines and sense of decorum of the Counter-Reformation with regard to religious images.[100] Pontormo's complex scene, however, seems to raise a theological rather than aesthetic matter. According to the Bible, God saw the wickedness of men and determined to destroy them, with the exception of Noah and his family, by a great flood. The relevant sections of Genesis (6:5–7, 17; 7:4, 10–12, 17–23) suggest that the bodies which appeared on the earth when the waters subsided and the earth dried up were the bodies of the sinful. In the light of these passages, I would suggest that Pontormo's swollen bodies, piled up and stretched out on the ground, as shown in the three remarkable drawings in the Uffizi made for the *Deluge*, would have been purposefully rendered realistic, so as to enable the viewer to form a mental picture of the sinful men's bodies, thus alluding to the Fall of mankind discussed in the *Beneficio*, the *Catechismo* and the *Sermone*.[101] They would therefore contrast dramatically with the souls of the righteous and the saved, gracefully rising vertically towards the heavens in the next scene of the *Ascension* (Figure 4.13).

If we accept this idea, then one may affirm that Pontormo interpreted the *Deluge* from a moral and philosophical, rather than historical, point of view. The artist's representations of the sinners (in the scene of the *Deluge*), as well as those of the righteous and children of God (in the scene of the *Ascension of the Souls*), could presumably derive from the Epistles of St Paul – the central source for the Protestants – and from Romans in particular. Paul makes a strong argument about those who are 'dead because they lived according to sin' and stresses that 'if you live according to the flesh, you shall die; but if by the Spirit, you mortify the misdeeds of the flesh, you will

---

[98]   Bocchi in his *Le Bellezze della città di Fiorenza* narrates a macabre story related to Pontormo's drawing human bodies from real corpses, writing that Pontormo attempted to depict realistically the bodies of those drowned in the flood by experimenting with keeping corpses under water, so that they would swell up (see Paolucci, 'Jacopo Pontormo a San Lorenzo', p. 271).

[99]   Vasari, *Vite*, VI, p. 286.

[100]   *Il Riposo*, pp. 59–61. Such ideas about *decorum* in visual arts had earlier been expressed by Ludovico Dolce in his *Dialogo della pittura intitolato l'Aretino*, published in Venice in 1557, anticipating the regulations of the Counter-Reformation which were subsequently imposed on art works.

[101]   *Beneficio*, pp. 13–15; *Alfabeto*, pp. 187–8.

live, for whosoever are led by the Spirit of God, are sons of God' (Romans 8:12–14).[102] The metaphysical meaning of the human body alluded to here may make a reference to Ficino's Neoplatonic ideas, which had influenced Pontormo.[103] This is suggested by his mature work on the whole, and also by his letter on the *Paragone delle arti* sent to Varchi. The assessment of intellect and spirituality as regards the bodily senses, and also the intimate and immediate relationship with the divinity, are some of Ficino's principal Neoplatonic notions, which were developed later in Florentine evangelical circles, not independently of the Valdesian 'alumbradismo', or illumination.

The scenes of the *Resurrection of the Dead* (Figure 4.13: Diagram no. 13) and the *Ascension of the Souls* (Figure 4.13: Diagram no. 11) are logically tied to the central scene of *Christ in Glory* (Figure 4.13: Diagram no. 5) on the upper range. These are not spoken of in detail either in the *Catechismo* or in the *Beneficio*, apart from a brief mention by Valdés:

> At the appointed time ... Christ will come, glorious and triumphant, to judge the living and the dead once God has revived all the dead. In this universal judgment, those who have not accepted the grace of the Gospels, so that faith is not efficacious in them, will be condemned to eternal punishment ... those who have accepted the grace of the Gospels, and placed themselves in the baptismal waters, as Noah placed himself in the ark, will gain eternal, glorious and happy life.[104]

The principal source for the fresco of the *Resurrection of the Dead* (shown in the preparatory drawings in the Uffizi) (Figure 4.11) would not be the Gospels but again, in this case, the epistles of St Paul.[105] It should be recalled

---

[102]   For discussion of the resurrection body in contemporary theology, see Kallistos Ware, *Inner Kingdom* (Crestwood, NY: St Vladimir's Seminary Press, 2000), pp. 37–41.

[103]   See Corti, 'Pontormo a San Lorenzo', pp. 9–10. According to Corti, the forms of Pontormo's human bodies (not their postures) were ideologically based on Marsilio Ficino's Neoplatonic concepts of the 'incorporeal eye' and, to quote Corti's words, the 'abandonment not only of the body, but also of the senses and of the imagination'.

[104]   'Nel tempo determinato ... verrà Cristo glorioso et triomphante a giudicare li vivi et li morti havendo Dio risuscitato tutti li morti, et che in questo giudicio universale coloro che non haveranno accettato la gratia dell'evangelio di tal maniera che la fede non sia stata efficace in loro saranno condannati a pena eterna ... et coloro che havranno accettato la gratia dell'evangelio et postitsi nell'acqua del battesimo come Noè si pose nell'arca, acquisteranno vita eterna, gloriosissima et felicissima': *Alfabeto*, pp. 199–200.

[105]   A comparison of this scene (as known through the Uffizi drawings, 17411Fr and 6528Fr) with the panel of the *Legend of the Eleven Thousand Martyrs* of 1530 in the Palazzo Pitti, Florence (inv. 1912 no.1821529) showing the nude bodies of the martyrs may be revealing of Pontormo's unique ability to create forms of great dramatic force. Detailed photos of the scenes of martyrdom in this panel can be seen in Doris Krystof, *Jacopo Carrucci detto il Pontormo 1494–1557* (Köln: Könemann, 2000), figs 98, 99.

that Paul himself solemnly proclaimed his faith in Christ and the resurrection of the dead when he was brought before the Tribunal of the Governor of Caesarea (Acts 24:15). In addition, in his first Letter to the Corinthians, Paul describes how the resurrection of the dead will occur, and makes a distinction between the 'carnal body' on the one hand, and the 'spiritual body', which only the righteous will have, on the other (15:42–4, 48–54; see also Philippians 3:21). He continues with the emblematic concept of the first man created by God, the carnal Adam made of clay, and of the new spiritual Adam full of the Holy Spirit, Jesus Christ (I Corinthians 15:45–7), a precept current in Lutheran and Valdesian theology.

Paul's key words constitute the doctrinal passage from the last examined scene of the *Resurrection of the Dead* to the scene of the *Ascension of the Souls* (Figure 4.13: Diagram no. 11).[106] Before its destruction, this scene was portrayed in the central section of the lower range, therefore linked directly, vertically, to the central scene of *Christ in Glory* (Figure 4.13: Diagram no. 5). Based on Vasari's description and also on the drawing preserved in the Gallerie dell'Accademia in Venice (inv. 550), we can assume that the scene of the *Ascension of the Souls* represented knots of bodies ascending to heaven (Figure 4.12). Firpo maintains that the scenes of the *Resurrection of the Dead* and the *Ascension of the Souls* in some way reflect the eschatological doctrine – that the righteous and elected souls will gain eternal life, whereas the damned souls will suffer the torments of hell for all eternity – which was current in the circles of the Anabaptists of the Veneto in the 1540s, and which also became widespread in various parts of Italy, including Florence, through reformers already linked to Valdesianism.[107]

The scene of *Christ in Glory* was central to the choir's iconography and religious symbolism. Indeed, this scene was the focus of the theology of the whole cycle. The characterization of the figure of the blessing Christ is highly significant (Figure 4.4). He is not portrayed as a wrathful judge

---

[106]   *Alfabeto*, p. 196. Articles 32, 41 and 42 of the *Catechismo* deal with eschatological precepts of Christian faith, stressing the importance of the dogma of the eternal life announced in the Gospels.

[107]   Firpo writes that Anabaptist doctrines had been accepted by the followers of Valdesianism (*Gli affreschi di Pontormo*, pp. 125–57). According to Firpo, these precepts could be encountered in the works of Florentine academics of the period, notably, in Giambattista Gelli's *Capricci del bottaio* (Florence, 1548). This work manifests the author's introspection in a surprisingly modern way. Gelli is in search here of spiritual freedom and of those conditions in life which lead man to his preparation for receiving illumination by God through intellectual and cultural development. These ideas reflect Gelli's influence of de Valdés's and Luther's inner belief and inner illumination. The book was inserted in the Index of 1562 on account of the author's views of the Catholic Church. See *Opere di Giovan Battista Gelli*, ed. by Delmo Maestri (Turin: UTET, 1976), pp. 9–27, especially pp. 13–19. See also Davide Dalmas, *Dante nella crisi religiosa del Cinquecento italiano. Da Trifon Gabriele a Lodovico Castelvetro* (Rome: Vecchiarelli, 2005), pp. 115–16.

over mankind (as in Michelangelo's *Last Judgement*) but as the *Resurrected Son of God* (my emphasis)[108] who has trampled Death and is now blessing the elected souls. A comparison with Lucas Cranach the Elder's Resurrected and Blessing Christ in the *Resurrection* triptych with St Barbara and St Catherine (1508–09, oil on panels, Staatliche Museen, Kassel, inv. Nr GK 116) may be revealing. Evidently, the iconography of the scene diverts from the traditional Catholic iconography of the Last Judgement, owing to the absence of the figures of the Virgin Mary and St John the Baptist, who are usually depicted seeking to intervene on behalf of the souls. This diversion from Catholic tradition constitutes the Christocentric character of the cycle and manifests its inspiration by Martin Luther's theology. Luther's central belief was that Christ was the sole mediator between God and man; forgiveness of sin and salvation are effected by God's grace alone, and are received on the part of man by faith alone. That the cycle focused on the notion of salvation through Christ is further confirmed by the scenes of *Original Sin* (on the right), and the *Expulsion from Eden* (on the left), which were represented to the sides of the depiction of *Christ in Glory* (Figure 4.13: Diagram no. 5): they were intended to stress man's Fall, from which he was saved through Christ's redemptive sacrifice. With this concept was also associated the Old Testament episode of the *Creation of Eve* depicted beneath the feet of Christ the Redeemer in the fresco of *Christ in Glory*, as can be seen in the definitive study held in the Uffizi (Figure 4.4). This episode must have complicated Vasari's reading of the frescoes, who thought it to be a paradox.[109] Undoubtedly, Pontormo wanted to emphasize, with a symbolic synthesis, the link between the acts of Creation by God and the New Creation performed as a consequence of the regenerative sacrifice of Christ, defined by Benedetto da Mantova as 'mediator of the New Testament' (*Beneficio*, vi).

Furthermore, the scene *Christ in Glory* may have also had an eschatological character, being visually connected to the scene of the Ascension of Souls. This was clear to Vasari, who described it as follows: 'In the middle he did Christ in majesty surrounded by nude angels, and raising the dead for judgment.'[110] I suggest that the scene's eschatological aspect might have been denoted by the seated position of the figure of Christ: it corresponds to the vision of Christ in the Last Judgement as described in the Apocalypse: 'Then I saw a great white throne, and one sitting upon it' (20:11). Accordingly, the solemn scene of *Christ in Glory* was intended as the glorification of Christ the Redeemer, to whom the instruments of the Passion, held up by

---

108   'Christ whom God the Father raised from the Dead': *Alfabeto*, pp. 190–1, art. 17.

109   Vasari, *Vite*, VI, p. 286.

110   '[Pontormo] fece nel mezzo in alto Cristo nella sua maestà, il quale circondato da molti Angeli tutti nudi fa resuscitare que' morti per giudicare': Vasari, *Vite*, VI, p. 286.

the Angels, allude (Figure 4.4). They form a *mandorla* around Him, a traditional iconographic theme which is also apparent in Lucas Cranach the Elder's magnificent *Trinity* panel of 1515–18 (Museum der Bildenden Künste, Gemäldesammlung, Leipzig) and his famous Wittenberg altarpiece of 1547 (rear panel). The figure of Christ crucified and resurrected, exalted by Paul (I Corinthians 1:18–24), was at the heart of Protestant theology, as the final page from the *Beneficio di Cristo* demonstrates:

> ...our principal aim has been to praise and exalt ... the stupendous benefit that the Christian has received from Jesus Christ crucified, and to demonstrate that faith of itself justifies, meaning that God receives as just all those who truly believe in Jesus Christ ... .[111]

Epilogue

The reappraisal of the religious content of the San Lorenzo iconography which I have attempted here may demonstrate that Pontormo's destroyed frescoes were inspired principally by Lutheran doctrines, and to a certain extent by Valdesian notions, presented by the *Beneficio di Cristo* and the *Catechismo* respectively. These books were widely known throughout Italy in Pontormo's day, and are regarded in modern scholarship as the source for the main dogmatic principles on which the reformed Church was to be based. Inspired by Luther, they relied heavily on the writings of St Paul. Their nature was highly instructive, and their discussion of fundamental Christian doctrines very effective, as it was based on a synthesis of parallel and juxtaposed precepts of the Old and New Testaments. The instigator of the iconographic cycle in San Lorenzo was not unaware of the highly didactic value of this way of communicating the Christian doctrines. Nor was Pontormo unconscious of the content of these doctrines or the visual image's potentiality to propagate them.[112] The outcome was a work

---

[111] ' ... [I]l nostro principale intento è stato di celebrare e magnificare ... il beneficio stupendo che ha ricevuto il cristiano da Iesù Cristo crocifisso, e dimostrare che la fede per se stessa giustifica, cioè che Dio riceve per giusti tutti quegli, che veramente credono Iesù Cristo ... ': *Beneficio*, p. 83; trans. p. 94.

[112] I do not share Paolucci's view that Pontormo was not religious, or was, as he puts it, an 'ateo devoto' ('Jacopo Pontormo a San Lorenzo', p. 273). This view is primarily contradicted by the content itself of Pontormo's religious images and possibly also by some events of his life (recounted by Vasari), and works of art. I should like to mention here a self-portrait painted on clay, a medium, the use of which might have had some religious connotation, perhaps alluding to the temporal nature of human life, a concept treated by Juan de Valdés: 'The Christian should live in this present life in continuous hope of life in eternity ... holding himself and judging himself to be a pilgrim and an outsider in this present

with significant spiritual resonances. He moved away from the narrative sequence typical of the Renaissance to one which conveyed the most important doctrines of the Christian belief through a series of scenes of a purely symbolic character: from the state of man's wretchedness after original sin (scenes of *Abel* and *Cain* in conjunction with the scene of the *Labour of Adam and Eve*) to the scenes of the main Old Testament figures, namely Noah and Abraham, representing their exemplary loyalty to God – hence prefiguring Christ – to the central Christian doctrine of man's salvation by Christ, whose sacrifice put an end to the Old Covenant and offered man God's promised blessings of the New Covenant testified in the Gospels (scenes of *Moses* and the *Evangelists*). The lower range affirmed the spiritual significance of the whole pictorial work, symbolizing in the scene of the *Deluge* God's first act to save the righteous. The whole cycle culminated in the eschatological events of the *Resurrection of the Dead*, and finally, the *Ascension of the Souls*, depicting the elected souls rising to heaven, towards their Saviour, represented in the cycle by the magnificent scene of *Christ in Glory* surrounded by the Angels. The figure of the blessing Christ in this scene would have certainly been a marvel of Florentine religious painting. Undoubtedly, Pontormo's San Lorenzo cycle was the most important statement in mid-sixteenth-century Florentine art of Luther's new notion of inner belief. As such, it might have been the painter's own response to Michelangelo's *Last Judgement* in the Sistine Chapel (1536–41).[113]

---

life' [Che al christiano appertiene vivere nella presente vita in una continua speranza della vita nella eterna ... tenendosi et giudicandosi pellegrino et forestiere nella presente vita]: *Alfabeto*, p. 196. Pontormo's self-portrait in question is kept in the Museo Amedeo Lia, Spezia (inv. 375, 51.5 x 37 cm.) and is registered in the museum's catalogue: *Museo Civico Amedeo Lia. Dipinti*, ed. by Federico Zeri and Andrea G. De Marchi (Spezia, 1997), pp. 276–8, entry 121. Also, there are two notes in his diary dating from the last months of his life, which I find very significant: the first records his day-long visit to a church while the second refers to a trip to his beloved Certosa di Val d'Ema in Galluzzo, where he had stayed during difficult periods of his life and in which he had depicted the famous series of Christ's Passion: see Pontormo, *Il libro mio*, pp. 77–8.

[113]   I am convinced that Pontormo's response to Michelangelo was on the level of the content of his images, rather than, as Costamagna suggests, on the aesthetic level (*Pontormo*, p. 253). Costamagna's argument is based on Vasari's incorrect idea that Pontormo tried to surpass Michelangelo in the San Lorenzo frescoes solely in terms of draughtsmanship (*Vite*, VI, p. 285).

CHAPTER 5

Defining Genres: The Survival of Mythological Painting in Counter-Reformation Venice

Tom Nichols

From its very inception early in the sixteenth century, the Venetian Renaissance mythological cabinet painting was defined by its distinction from the visual mode familiar in the sacred art of the city. One only needs to recall pioneering examples such as Giorgione's *Sleeping Venus* (*c*.1510, Dresden, Gemäldegalerie), featuring a female nude sensuously reclining in a lush landscape, or Titian's multi-figured *Bacchanals* for the court in Ferrara (1518–24), in order to establish this point.[1] These works employ a horizontal 'landscape' format, which supports their emphasis on idyllic rural settings, and have an insistent emphasis on the fleshy corporeality of nude or semi-nude figures placed close to the picture surface. Many of the forms either recall specific antique sculptures, or make more generic reference to classical relief composition in the planar arrangement of their figure groups. The approach to the classical subject-matter typically asserts a generic association with the nostalgic sensuality of classical and Renaissance pastoral poetry, in spite of the fact that the poetic sources are not typically drawn from this literary genre.[2] But while the classical forms and meanings recovered in this tradition were quickly fed back into the mainstream tradition of Christian art (Titian's early religious paintings, for example, have neatly been described as a form of 'Christian

---

[1]   See Jaynie Anderson, *Giorgione: The Painter of 'Poetic Brevity'* (Paris: Flammarion, 1997), pp. 307–8; Harold Wethey, *The Paintings of Titian III: The Mythological and Historical Paintings* (London: Phaidon, 1975), nos. 12, 13, 14, 15.

[2]   Sources such as Philostratus's *Imagines*, Ovid's *Fasti* and Catullus's *Carmina* were used to provide the subject-matter for the 'pastoral' Bacchanals: see Paul Holberton, 'The Choice of Texts for the Camerino Pictures', in *Bacchanals by Titian and Rubens*, ed. by Görel Cavalli-Björkmann (Stockholm: Nationalmuseum Stockhom, 1987), pp. 57–66. For a useful overview of depictions of classical subjects in Venice, see Charles Hope, 'Classical Antiquity and Venetian Renaissance Subject-Matter', in *New Interpretations of Venetian Renaissance Painting*, ed. by Francis Ames-Lewis (London: Birkbeck College, 1994), pp. 51–62.

pastoral'), influence did not so readily flow in the other direction.[3] The new secular genre proved almost impervious to influence from a tradition of monumental religious art in the city that was vigorously developing in the same period, and which increasingly emphasized sudden movement and heightened narrative drama, subjecting its Christian protagonists to intense emotional suffering and physical violence.[4] The unidirectional nature of formal and semantic interaction between sacred and profane in this regard indicates that mythological art in Venice owed its very definition to its perceived separateness, a quality that was probably a result of its minority status within a dominant Christian culture.[5]

Sacred and Secular Modes in Titian's *Poesie*

It is the extent to which mythological painting is penetrated by the formal and semantic modes of sacred art that marks out Titian's cycle of paintings known as the *poesie* (1550–62) as so different from previous works of this type.[6] This admission of elements from the separate domain of religious painting can only be understood in general terms, and is certainly not a matter of borrowing from specific formal or iconographic sources. Titian's cycle is, though, permeated by the kind of physical and emotional dynamism, with frequent intimations of violence and bodily desecration, which is more typical of the presentation of Christian subjects in sixteenth-

[3]   For Titian's 'Christian pastoral' (and its origins in contemporary Renaissance literature reconciling religious and pagan literary modes), see Una Roman d'Elia, *The Poetics of Titian's Religious Paintings* (Cambridge: Cambridge University Press, 2005), pp. 9–26.

[4]   The most telling example of this new conception is Titian's lost *St Peter Martyr* altarpiece of 1528–30; see Patricia Meilman, *Titian and the Altarpiece in Renaissance Venice* (Cambridge: Cambridge University Press, 2000).

[5]   Carlo Ginzburg noted that Venetian imagery of the sixteenth century served two essentially separate 'iconic circuits' defined above all by their distinct audiences: 'the public and the private: the first, broad and socially undifferentiated; the second restricted and socially of high rank'. The fact that 'public' religious art readily adapted socially elite mythological modes, while the latter remained impervious or resistant to popular 'Christian' modes, may reflect this kind of hierarchical distinction in the social domain. See Carlo Ginzburg, 'Titian, Ovid and Sixteenth Century Codes of Erotic Illustration', in *Myths, Emblems, Clues* (London: Radius Books, 1990), pp. 77–94, a translation of 'Tiziano, Ovidio e i codici della figurazione erotica del Cinquecento', *Paragone*, 339 (1978), 125–35.

[6]   Titian described his new paintings as 'poesie' in a letter to Philip II of September 1554, using a word that had been used (by Jacopo de' Barbari) to describe mythological works in Venice as early as 1501. He might thereby have sought to establish the continuity of his new paintings with earlier examples of the genre: see Hope, 'Classical Antiquity', p. 52. For Titian's cycle see Wethey, *Paintings of Titian*, nos. 6, 9, 10, 30, 32. The London *Death of Actaeon* (n. 8) clearly has an important connection to the other paintings (especially to *Diana and Actaeon*) but it was never sent to Philip II.

century art.[7] As has often been noted, the *poesie* typically possess a level of seriousness that runs counter to the bucolic tone that had rapidly come to be an expectation of mythological painting in Venice. If the pagan gods were generally allowed to occupy a timeless realm of sensual desire, pleasure and invitation, then in Titian's new cycle the Ovidian myths are set in a fragile moment that is radically contingent and non-discrete, its meaning made dependent on the wider temporal continuum with frequent intimations of the dark consequences of present actions. This approach is realized in formal terms by the expressive enlargement in scale (and thus significance) of the main protagonists, as well as by the opening of spatial depth.[8] In technical terms, it is realized by the 'intervention' of Titian's radically loose brushwork, which means that form never quite achieves the defined outline characteristic of classicizing art in the sixteenth century.

Emphasizing the significance of these generalized adaptations from sacred art does not entail reading the *poesie* as Christian allegories, as some scholars have attempted to do. It also sets a limit on the more recent tendency to understand the cycle simply as a vehicle for the presentation of the erotic female nude in a manner that merely extends the approach taken in earlier Venetian mythological paintings.[9] Stress on the expressive doubleness of the *poesie* allows us to highlight instead the way in which recognizable sacred and secular pictorial modes are brought into a new proximity that destabilizes and complicates the meanings of both. This approach certainly necessitates the presence of identifying links to the more expected mythological type. So it is true that the erotic female nude remains a fundamental marker in each painting, a kind of core condition, even if the impassioned responses it generates can now have unhappy or violent consequences.[10] Many of the nudes featured are based on well-known

---

[7]   The integrity of the body might be taken as paradigmatic in classicizing art and culture, as opposed to Christian corporeal violation.

[8]   The distinction between plane and depth is increasingly felt as a tension in the *poesie*. If the earliest works, such as the *Danaë* and the *Venus and Adonis* (Figures 5.2 and 5.3) maintain something of the typical planarity of Venetian mythologies, then *Perseus and Andromeda*, *Diana and Actaeon*, *Diana and Callisto* and the *Rape of Europa* (Figure 5.6) are all characterized by a new spatial instability, their fast-moving and partially foreshortened forms typically placed in an ambiguous relationship to the picture surface.

[9]   For the 'erotic' reading of the cycle, see Charles Hope, 'Problems of Interpretation in Titian's Erotic Paintings' in *Tiziano e Venezia* (Vicenza: Neri Pozza, 1980), pp. 111–24; Ginzburg, 'Titian, Ovid and Sixteenth Century Codes', pp. 77–94. Their secular interpretation replaced the Christian/allegorical one proposed by Harald Keller, *Tizians Poesie für König Philipp II. Von Spanien* (Wiesbaden: Franz Steiner Verlag, 1969) and Jane C. Nash, *Veiled Images: Titian's Mythological Images for Philip II* (London: Associated University Presses, 1985).

[10]   These darker consequences are strongly hinted at in the *Venus and Adonis* (Figure 5.3) and in the two *Diana* paintings, and (more arguably) in the *Rape of Europa* (Figure 5.6).

antique sculptures, an established practice in Renaissance mythological painting.[11] Such insistent quotations served to suggest that Titian's new inventions were authentic recreations of the antique paintings sometimes described in classical texts. They also engaged the still fashionable *paragone* debate in a manner that has precedents in earlier mythologies. In a number of the *poesie*, Titian forces his nudes into extreme physical torsions, increasing to the very limits of plausibility the view of the given body, and thereby offering a kind of visual riposte to the common criticism (in favour of sculpture) that painting is limited by its necessary assumption of a static observer.[12]

There is a further way in which the *poesie* reflect the kind of amalgam of Christian and classicizing modes of expression discussed above. This particular point needs to be carefully nuanced, as it is dependent on Titian's utilization of *both* aspects, even if it appears to further define the cycle as distinctly secular. In each work, the careful elaboration of narrative does not end with a meaning conforming to the Christian redemptive schema of moral cause and effect.[13] While it is true that in earlier mythological paintings the pagan protagonists were typically released from the contingencies of Christian morality, in the *poesie* the predominance of implacable *fortuna* is mostly registered less as a freedom than as a lack, engendering a sense of sometimes terrifying fragility[14] The often precarious and unprotected situation of Titian's pagan protagonists was, in a sense, truer to the dark spirit of the *Metamorphoses* than the more typical pictorial treatment of the myths as if they were a form of benign pastoral poetry. It is not surprising that Titian's new conception in the *poesie* has recently been linked to

---

[11]   See, for example, the antique sources cited in David Rosand, 'Titian and the "Bed of Polyclitus"', *Burlington Magazine*, 117:865 (April, 1975), 242–5, and Cecil Gould, 'The "Death of Actaeon" and Titian's Mythologies', *Apollo*, 95 (June, 1972), 464–9.

[12]   Benedetto Varchi's question regarding the relative value of painting and sculpture of 1547 indicates continuing interest in the *paragone* question into the mid-Cinquecento: see Leatrice Mendelsohn, *Paragone: Benedetto Varchi's Due Lezzioni and Cinquecento Art Theory* (Ann Arbor, MI: UMI Research Press, 1982). For the idea that Titian engaged in a form of ongoing and self-defining *paragone* in his paintings against the sculpture of Michelangelo, see Rona Goffen, *Renaissance Rivals: Michelangelo, Leonardo, Raphael, Titian* (New Haven, CT and London: Yale University Press, 2002). The multiplication of temporal indicators within the paintings in a manner that threatens to displace the primacy of present view might also reflect Titian's deeper engagement with the question of the *paragone*.

[13]   It is this point that most clearly reveals the shortcomings of the attempt by Keller (*Tizians Poesie*) and Nash (*Veiled Images*) to understand the series in terms of Christian allegory.

[14]   This is most clearly the case in the two *Diana* paintings, in which the indiscretions of the 'victims' Actaeon and Callisto do not seem to merit the harsh retributive justice of the goddess. In the *Rape of Europa* (Figure 5.6), the Jupiter-bull's treatment of the princess is similarly rough and overpowering.

the sixteenth-century rediscovery of texts such as Aristotle's *Poetics*. Remembering the harsh, non-redemptive schema of pre-Christian tragic drama, and the popularity of Seneca and others in contemporary Italian theatre, Thomas Puttfarken has argued that the *poesie* should be regarded as 'painted tragedies'.[15] Yet it is necessary to reiterate that Titian's paintings engage a mode of expression that owes more to traditions of Christian art than to classical literary forms. Narrative expression, dramatic pathos and an acute rendering of the effects of physical and psychological suffering had, after all, a long provenance in the religious art of the Renaissance. And it was above all to this *visual* tradition that Titian turned in his new transformation of mythological painting.

Jacopo Tintoretto's 'Anti-*poesie*' of the 1550s

The peculiarity of the *poesie* might be understood as the cause of a temporary hiatus in mythological painting in mid-sixteenth-century Venice, particularly in earlier works of this type by Jacopo Tintoretto. Despite his conflicts with Titian, Tintoretto seems to have had an entrée to Titian's workshop in the 1550s and was clearly aware of the developing cycle for Philip.[16] Certain of his mythologies from the period engage the older master's incorporation of 'Christian' elements, but with very different results. For, unlike in the *poesie*, perspectives from beyond the closed purview of mythological art are used in a parodic manner, as if to challenge the very validity of the pagan image as a visual genre. In his *Rape of Arsinoë* (*c*.1555–56, Dresden, Gemäldegalerie) (Figure 5.1), it may be that Tintoretto's irreverent approach remains within the established bounds of erotic mythological art. There were, after all, good precedents for the use of comedy (as opposed to tragedy) in Venetian depictions of mythological subjects.[17] Tintoretto's subject-matter, from a rarely depicted passage in Lucan's *Pharsalia* relating Ganymede's liberation of Cleopatra's

---

15   Thomas Puttfarken, *Titian and Tragic Painting: Painting Aristotle's Poetics and the Rise of the Modern Artist* (New Haven, CT and London: Yale University Press, 2005). Closer analysis of individual paintings reveals, however, that Puttfarken overestimated the impact of the concept of 'tragedy' on the paintings. It is very hard indeed to see exactly how works such as the *Danaë* (Figure 5.2) and *Perseus and Andromeda* bear any meaningful relationship to Aristotelian notions of tragedy.

16   Tom Nichols, *Tintoretto, Tradition and Identity* (London: Reaktion Books, 1999), pp. 29–48.

17   See the discussion in Paul Barolsky, *Infinite Jest: Wit and Humor in Italian Renaissance Art* (University Park: Pennsylvania University Press, 1975), pp. 158–81. For Tintoretto's painting, see *Jacopo Tintoretto: l'opera completa*, ed. by Rodolfo Pallucchini and Paola Rossi, 3 vols (Milan: Alfieri, 1982), II, *Le opera sacre e profane*, n. 203.

Fig. 5.1   Tintoretto, *Rape of Arsinoë*, c.1555–56, Dresden, Gemaldegalerie.

sister from a tower in Alexandria, was inherently humorous and erotic: in the vernacular edition followed by Tintoretto, the heroine and her helper conveniently had to take off their clothes in order to escape through a narrow window. This textual addition provided the opportunity to depict female nudes, shown in studied front and back views that recall (at least in terms of their *contrapposto*) the contrasting nudes in Titian's first pair of *poesie* (Figures 5.2 and 5.3).[18] Tintoretto's *Arsinoë* was, though, closer in a formal sense to one of the works from Titian's second pairing, namely the Wallace *Perseus and Andromeda*. But response is simultaneous with alteration in meaning away from the elevated or poetic, the dramatic quality of Titian's painting subtly undermined by the intrusion of elements of debunking realism and humour: in this case, an insistence on the quotidian (for Venetians!) physical exigencies and effects of getting into a rocky boat. The sudden entry of the princess into the vessel (depicted as a Venetian gondola) threatens to up-end it, throwing the *gondoliere* to the right forward, and in the process reversing the expected male-dominated romantic clinch of the two lovers. Arsinoë towers (or rather flops) over a surprised Ganymede who topples backwards supported only by his phallic oar.

The same kind of bathetic anti-poetic literalism of interpretation is evident in other Tintoretto mythologies from the 1550s, such as the much-disputed *Danaë*, which may be a response to Titian's earliest *poesia* (Figure 5.2), now in Madrid.[19] In this example, the supernatural presence of Jupiter indicated in Titian's explosion of coloured light, and thus the act of sexual union, is downplayed, the fall of carefully defined coins becoming the governing motif. While these coins serve to express a formal and thematic *contrapposto* in Titian's work, between the 'high' sensual abandonment of Danaë and the 'low' material concerns of her maid-servant, in the Lyon painting they bind the two young women together in a vulgar moment of common (and commonplace) economic interest. Their particular fall

---

[18]   In an often quoted letter of September 1554, which evokes the *paragone* debate, Titian drew attention to the complementary positions of the female protagonists in his *Danaë* (Figure 5.2) and *Venus and Adonis* (Figure 5.3): 'because the figure of Danaë ... is seen entirely from the front, I have chosen in this other *poesia* to ... show the opposite side', quoted in Charles Hope, *Titian* (London: Jupiter Books, 1980), p. 125. For Tintoretto's literary source, see Roland Krischel, *Jacopo Tintoretto 1519–1594* (Cologne: Konemann, 2000), p. 46.

[19]   See Pallucchini and Rossi, *L'opera*, II, n. 378 (with a date of 1577–78). In a recent catalogue, the painting is dated *c*.1583–85, and is seen as executed by Domenico Tintoretto following a design by his father: see *Tintoretto*, ed. by Miguel Falomir (Madrid: Museo Nacional del Prado, 2007), n. 46. But given the formal and conceptual similarities with other Tintoretto depictions of reclining nudes from the 1550s, for example, the *Susanna and the Elders* in the ceiling painting now in the Prado (ed. Falomir, n. 19, dated 1552–55) or the *Leda and the Swan* composition discussed below, there seems no need to date the *Danaë* to the painter's late period.

Fig. 5.2   Titian, *Danaë*, *c.*1551–54, Madrid, Museo del Prado.

Fig. 5.3   Titian, *Venus and Adonis*, 1554–55, Madrid, Museo del Prado.

into Danaë's genital region euphemistically makes the connection between money and sex clear, while the upturned phallic lute and faithful dog with his back pointedly turned make sure that we read the scene, not as one of liberating union between mortal and God, but rather as an image of venal prostitution.[20]

This interpretation renders the viewer's relation to the nude problematic, undermining the usual invitation to gaze with impunity at a display of naked female flesh. In a further composition, extant in two versions now in Florence, Tintoretto tackled the erotic subject of 'Leda and the Swan'

[20]   Though Titian's erotic depiction is admittedly very different from the depictions of Danaë as a Christianized model of chastity, it is equally distinct from the increasingly popular visual tradition, based on the discussion in Horace's *Carminum* (III, xvi. 1–8) that makes her an example of corruption by gold. This latter tradition, often evoked in later sixteenth- and seventeenth-century emblems, is the one to which Tintoretto refers. See Madlyn Millner Kahr, 'Danaë: Virtuous, Voluptuous, Venal Woman', *Art Bulletin*, 60 (1978), 43–55.

(Figure 5.4).[21] In doing so, he ignored versions of this subject by Leonardo da Vinci and Giulio Romano, who showed Leda in an upright position embracing the swan. In a copy after a painting by Michelangelo brought to Venice by Giorgio Vasari in 1540, Leda reclines on a bed but, as in the other Central Italian versions, bird and woman are still shown in the midst of the sexual act.[22] The use of explicit eroticism for the subject was thus well known in Venice: indeed, in the triumph of Leda observed by Polifilo in Francesco Colonna's *Hypnerotomachia polifili* (Venice, 1499) and recorded in a woodcut, the heroine is imagined 'lying comfortably on two cushions' and 'in amorous embrace ... the two of them united in their delectable sport, with the godlike swan positioned between her delicate, snow-white thighs'.[23]

Tintoretto also shows Leda lying on a bed, his heroine presented in the manner of a reclining Venus in the Venetian tradition going back to Giorgione's Dresden painting. But focus on the explicit moment of union is avoided in favour of a slightly earlier one, with the result that the solely erotic meaning of the scene is dislodged. This thematic displacement is supported in a formal sense by the retraction from Titianesque engagement with texture and substance. Tintoretto's treatment of Leda's flesh is schematic, as if his viewer is not permitted to dwell on the physical reality of her body.[24] As is so often the case in Tintoretto's art, human form functions, rather, as a visual pointer in a narrative or symbolic presentation: a carefully shaped directional structure through which the eye moves in order to arrive at a semantically loaded target. Undisturbed absorption in the soft flesh of the young woman on the bed, an expectation of the picture type, is

---

[21]   Pallucchini and Rossi, *L'opera*, II, 158 and 384 with contrasting dates for the smaller and larger painting (1551–55 and 1578). Both are likely to date from Tintoretto's earlier period as is pointed out in *Jacopo Tintoretto 1519–1594. Il grande collezionismo mediceo*, ed. by Marco Chiarini, Sergio Marinelli and Angelo Tartuferi (Florence: Centro Di, 1995), nos. 12 and 13.

[22]   Michelangelo's original painting, made for the Duke of Ferrara in 1530, is known through a number of copies, the best known of which is now in London: see Paul F. Watson, 'Titian and Michelangelo: The "Danaë" of 1545–1546' in *Collaboration in Italian Renaissance Art*, ed. by W.S. Sheard and J.T. Paoletti (New Haven, CT and London: Yale University Press, 1978), pp. 245–60 (p. 246).

[23]   'Commodamente sedeva sopra due Puluini'; 'negli amorosi amplexi ... istavano delectabilmente iucundissimi ambi connexi, et el divino Olore tra le delicate e nivee coxe collocato': Facsimile edition of *Hypnerotomachia Poliphili* (New York and London: Garland Publishing, 1976), trans. by Joscelyn Godwin, *Hypnerotomachia Poliphili: The Strife of Love in a Dream* (London: Thames and Hudson, 1999), p. 166.

[24]   This may reflect the fact that Tintoretto did not work directly from live models. It is likely that the generic and expressionless female nudes featured in his mythologies were based on wooden mannequins and wax models mentioned in early sources such as Carlo Ridolfi, rather than real bodies. See the discussion of *Venus, Vulcan and Mars* below.

Fig. 5.4   Tintoretto, *Leda and the Swan*, c.1550–55, Galleria degli'Uffizi, Florence.

further undermined by the admission of quotidian secondary episodes that encourage us to see the incipient sex between swan and woman as (at least) absurd, and perhaps even morally perverse. Though Leda reclines toward the swan, who in turn wiggles his phallic neck in her direction, her body (and perhaps also her gaze) point downwards towards the bottom left where a beak-to-nose stand-off between an outsized caged duck and a small cat offers a kind of parodic commentary on the unnaturalness of the immanent coupling on the bed.

Tintoretto takes an aggressively generic approach to form in his earlier mythologies, de-individualizing the reality of bodies, faces and postures in reductive fashion, and this is evident too in his non-specific approach to the classical subject-matter itself. Arsinoë and Leda are presented as mere types of Venus, goddess of love, as if a single semantic category were adequate to circumscribe the entire genre of pagan tales featuring beautiful young heroines in erotic situations.[25] At the same time, Tintoretto's disturbances to the exclusive secularity of the genre of mythological painting, exacted above all through displacement of its leading principle of eroticism, reveals a perspective that is both ideologically more pointed than Titian's, and emotionally more detached. If Tintoretto follows Titian in so far as he opens the genre of mythological cabinet painting to perspectives drawn from sacred art, in his hands these are deployed as a potentially hostile form of ironic moralism. The tendency to offer a satire of the sexual mores of the classical gods may reflect Tintoretto's close association with writers such as Anton Francesco Doni and Alessandro Caravia in Venice in this period, men who often proclaimed the virtues of a simple reformed Erasmian-style religion, while demonstrating a Rabelaisian propensity to mock the kind of elevated and learned classicism prevalent in aristocratic circles.[26]

---

[25]   This generic kind of treatment was to some extent typical of many mythological paintings prior to the *poesie*, which are unusual in the extent of their individuation of the protagonists. Thus, Primaticcio and Titian himself drew on Michelangelo's design for 'Leda and the Swan' in their depictions of 'Danaë': see Erwin Panofsky, *Problems in Titian, Mostly Iconographic* (London: Phaidon, 1969), p. 146.

[26]   Tintoretto, to this extent, confused the two 'iconic circuits' separating public/popular religious and private/elite mythological painting: see Ginzburg, 'Titian, Ovid and Sixteenth Century Codes', pp. 23–36. Tintoretto painted portraits of the *poligrafo* Doni and the goldsmith/writer Caravia. In *Il sogno di Caravia* (Venice, 1541), Caravia particularly attacked the flamboyant style of classicism in the architecture on the new Scuola di San Rocco, mocking the 'columns carved in the newest manner ... in order to build and not out of devotion / Columns that jut into the piazza': quoted in Manfredo Tafuri, *Venice and the Renaissance* (Cambridge, MA and London: MIT Press, 1989), pp. 81–101. For more on Tintoretto's relations with popularizing literary culture of the period see Tom Nichols, 'Tintoretto, *prestezza* and the poligrafi: a study in the literary and visual culture of Cinquecento Venice', *Renaissance Studies*, 10:1 (1996), 72–100.

It may be that some of Tintoretto's mythologies were made for lesser patrons among non-noble *cittadini* circles in Venice itself, whose lack of access to the kind of 'elite iconic circuits' described by Ginzburg meant that they remained at a sceptical distance from the socially elevated erotics of mythological art. However, the painting in which Tintoretto's debunking approach in his early career reached its apogee, the *Venus, Vulcan and Mars* (c.1550–55, Munich, Alte Pinakothek) (Figure 5.5), is likely to have been a foreign courtly commission from the Gonzaga at Mantua.[27] As in the paintings discussed above, the more typical moment in the story, showing Venus and Mars making love on a bed while Vulcan works on unwittingly in his forge, is avoided, in a manner that downplays erotic impact. Instead, we are shown a later point in the narrative when Vulcan returns and attempts to catch the lovers. The god of war cowers in terror under a bed, Venus failingly attempts to cover her naked body, while Vulcan limps toward the bed to peer at his wife's genitals. The actions of all three are rendered absurd by this choice of dramatic moment, as is suggested again by Tintoretto's use of formal sources. Rather than the Enea Vico engraving after Parmigianino recently adduced, the formal presentation of Venus and Vulcan recalls a woodcut in Colonna's *Hypnerotomachia* in which a libidinous satyr approaches from behind the reclining goddess lying in the foreground. This illustration had already been adapted by Giorgione for the figure of Venus in the pioneering painting mentioned earlier. Tintoretto's particular use of the print is, however, a telling one: he focuses on the approach of the excited satyr toward the female nude rather than the nude itself. Like the satyr in the print, Vulcan stands as a proxy for the viewer, a mocking mirror image of *our* approach to Venus from the front.[28]

Tintoretto's Munich painting may be very close in date to Titian's *poesia* of *Venus and Adonis* (Figure 5.3); a brief comparison of the two

---

[27]   Pallucchini and Rossi, *Opera completa*, II, n. 155. For the possible Mantuan provenance, see Beverly L. Brown, 'Mars's Hot Minion or Tintoretto's Fractured Fable' in *Jacopo Tintoretto nel quarto centenario della morte*, ed. by Paola Rossi and Lionello Puppi (Padua: Il Poligrafo, 1996), pp. 199–205.

[28]   For the putative influence of Vico's engraving, see Brown, 'Mars's Hot Minion', p. 202 followed in Falomir, *Tintoretto*, n. 5. For the woodcut adduced here: Colonna, *Hypnerotomachia*, p. 73. Its influence on Giorgione's *Venus* has recently been noted by Paul Hills, 'Titian's Veils', *Art History*, 29:5 (2006), 771–95 (pp. 787–8). The burlesque elements of the *Hypnerotomachia* woodcut were repeated and developed in many other sixteenth-century prints for parodic effect: see, for example, Marco Dente's after Giulio Romano illustrated in Malcolm Bull, *The Mirror of the Gods* (London: Allen Lane, 2005), p. 210. Though the satyr's strange erect phallus in the woodcut is not present in Tintoretto's painting, it remains possible that he sought to suggest Vulcan's sexual arousal on approaching his wife's body. The rent drapery serves to emphasize that Venus has been split open by Mars' recent attentions, a point reiterated by her parted legs.

Fig. 5.5   Tintoretto, *Venus, Vulcan and Mars*, c.1550–55, Munich, Alte Pinakothek.

works demonstrates further the two painters' distinct approaches to erotic mythological painting in the early 1550s. There is a very broad link between the themes, in so far as both works feature narrative treatments of the loves of Venus, in which the goddess is not allowed the kind of timeless, iconic dignity commonly reserved for her in the tradition of Venetian reclining nudes. Venus is shown in the process of losing her authority and dignity, a loss symbolized in both works by the presence of sleeping cupids. In both, too, the popular Virgilian epithet 'Omnia vincit Amor', which may lie behind many sixteenth-century depictions of Venus, is reversed, 'Love' being shown as impotent (Titian) or false (Tintoretto), rather than all-conquering. But if Venus' predicament in Titian's painting is presented, as Puttfarken has argued, as a form of painted tragedy, in Tintoretto's she is reduced to a role more familiar in contemporary theatrical farces, where attractive but deceitful young wives are often shown cuckolding their ugly old husbands.[29]

Venus has no jurisdiction in the two paintings under discussion. But if, in the *poesia*, this lack of agency is shown as a consequence of Adonis' mortal blindness, in Tintoretto's painting, it is the sexual rapacity of the goddess herself that is at issue. Emphasizing the sexual appetites, and consequent jealousies and deceptions of the pagan gods, subjecting their unruly behaviour to moral scrutiny, Tintoretto in the process makes them serve as our surrogates. The position of Venus' convex mirror on the back wall of the bedroom reflects not only the unedifying scene in front of it, but (by extension) that of the real world of the viewer beyond the frame of the painting. If, as has been suggested, another mirror is glimpsed in *its* reflection, then the multiplication of this object (its circular shape also repeated in the windows and the floor tiles) only serves to intensify its wider illustrative significance in the painting.[30] In the 'Venus at her Toilet' tradition where the goddess peers directly into a mirror, it had no such ethical associations: the angled reflection in paintings on this theme by Titian and Veronese, for example, simply multiplies points of visual entry for a male viewer encouraged to observe the goddess's body with impunity.[31] In Tintoretto's *Venus, Vulcan and Mars*, the mirror is significantly detached from the goddess herself, meaning that her body

[29]   The painters' contrasting approaches recall Aristotle's distinction between comedy that 'aims at representing men as worse than they are nowadays and tragedy as better': Aristotle, 'Poetics' in *Classical Literary Criticism: Aristotle, Horace, Longinus*, trans. by Theodor S. Dorsch (Harmondsworth: Penguin, 1965), p. 33.

[30]   See Erasmus Weddigen, 'Nuovi percorsi di avvicinamento a Jacopo Tintoretto. Venere, Vulcano e Marte: l'inquisizione dell'informatica' in *Jacopo Tintoretto nel quarto centenario*, pp. 155–61.

[31]   See Wethey, *The Paintings of Titian: III*, n. 51; Terisio Pignatti, *Veronese*, 2 vols (Venice: Alfieri, 1976), II, n. 357.

is not reflected in it. Like another all-seeing eye, its reflection is, instead, largely given over to an unedifying rear view of the limping Vulcan, a potentially libidinous figure whose role as the viewer's proxy has already been mentioned.[32] If the mirror had often functioned as a metaphor for the act of painting in the Renaissance, in Tintoretto's work, its older moral functions are revived: it turns truth-teller, offering a still more banal reverse image of the degrading scene near the bed.

In a further moralizing mythological painting from the 1550s, sometimes seen as a pendant to the Vienna *Susanna and the Elders* discussed below, Tintoretto depicted Narcissus staring absorbedly at his own reflection.[33] Good reason for placing the Colonna painting among the others from the early to mid-1550s under discussion is that its theme is coherent with them: Leon Battista Alberti had, of course, named Narcissus the inventor of painting, but a self-reflexive celebration of the illusionistic power of painting seems less likely here than a ethical reflection on the destructive and isolating results of self-love.[34] The handsome protagonist, replete with the tightly curled hair and Roman profile familiar in antique statuary, peers intently down at a self-reflection we cannot see, his right arm reaching beyond the lower edge of the painting in a vain attempt to grasp it. Once again, the directionality of form is freighted with moral meaning: the powerful downward movement of Narcissus' head and thrusting arm indicate that his intense and fruitless self-absorption will end in death.

The mirror recurs as a prominent object in Tintoretto's Vienna *Susanna and the Elders*, though I am disinclined to see it, in this instance, as a reflection of the heroine's supposed *superbia*, as has recently been suggested.[35] It does, however, pointedly conflate the iconographies of Venus and Susanna in a manner that renders problematic the whole issue of men looking at eroticized female nudes in paintings. If the desirability of Susanna is intensified with reference to the established imagery of the goddess of love, then our usual unguarded sensual response is thrown into doubt, given that hers is the body of a virtuous wife. Perhaps the interchangeability between Venus and Susanna is imagined here as akin to the intellectual slippage that is a central aspect of sexual desire: it is telling

---

[32]   The 'eye' might also refer to that of Helios (Apollo) as the all-seeing sun who reported the lovers' affair to Vulcan: see Falomir, *Tintoretto*, p. 200.

[33]   Pallucchini and Rossi, *L'opera*, vol. 1, n. 201 reference the earlier scholars (beginning with Johannes Wilde), who noted the connection with the Vienna painting, particularly evident in the luminous treatment of the landscape.

[34]   Leon Battista Alberti, *On Painting* (1435), trans. Cecil Grayson (Harmondsworth: Penguin, 1991), p. 61.

[35]   For the (somewhat unlikely) idea that the Old Testament heroine is shown as a vain prostitute, see Krischel, *Tintoretto*, p. 46. See also Pallucchini and Rossi, *L'opera*, II, n. 200; Falomir, *Tintoretto*, n. 31.

in this regard that the lascivious Elders seem oddly unable to locate the object of their lust in visual terms, turning their gazes away from Susanna as if the substitution of goddess of love for chaste wife was dependent upon maintaining the interiority of their fantasy. As in the Munich painting, Tintoretto turned to contemporary prints picturing Venus spied on by lecherous satyrs in his conception of the Vienna 'Susanna'.[36] But in these sources, of course, the satyr's excitement has no other consequence than an erection. In the *Susanna*, on the contrary, the Elders' viewing is thematically illicit and forbidden. It is no accident that the foreground Elder is shown trying to take up a position close to the viewer's, his head turned into the composition, in order to arrive at a better view of the young woman. As we look at the painting, we all too readily take in the glistening naked body before us, but our enjoyment is compromised by the fact that our view from the front goes beyond that of the lecherous old men at the back and side, with the suggestion that it trumps theirs in terms of its voyeuristic violation.

Once again, Tintoretto responded to Titian in the careful spatial positioning of his figures, for the older painter had already introduced 'proxy' male viewers into his paintings of the reclining Venus of the late 1540s. Characteristically, though, these excitable surrogates, shown as organ-players or lutenists, do not so much challenge the viewer's own erotic response to the female nude depicted as intensify it.[37] And this approach was developed further in the *poesie* that followed. As was suggested long

---

[36]   While Susanna's form was undoubtedly based on sixteenth-century drawings and prints after an antique sculpture showing the *Crouching Venus* (see Falomir, *Tintoretto*, pp. 298–300), the more general conception of the painting, with concealed 'male' viewers watching the unaware goddess, was dependent on popular images of 'Venus Spied on by a Satyr'. As we have seen, Tintoretto had already drawn on this iconography in his *Venus, Vulcan and Mars*. But in the Vienna painting, his composition is closer to Marco Dente's engraving after Giulio Romano mentioned at note 28 above than to the equivalent woodcut from the *Hypnerotomachia*.

[37]   See Wethey, *The Paintings of Titian: III*, pp. 45–8. It may also be that the viewer's response is simultaneously elevated by the presence of these staring musicians with reference to the Neoplatonic connection between music (hearing) and the perception of beauty (sight) and their common sacred origin. In the Italian edition of Marcilio Ficino's *Commentary on Plato's Symposium on Love* published in 1544, sound and sight are jointly elevated as two means of perceiving beauty: 'Love is a great and wonderful god and also noble ... let us indulge in love in such a way as to be content with its own end, which is beauty ... we know it with the intellect, the sight and the hearing' ('Adunque confessiamo al tutto che Amore sia Iddio grande e mirabile: ancora nobile ... allo Amore opera diamo, che del suo fine, che è essa Bellezza rimanghiamo contenti ... Con la Mente, col vedere e con l'udire lo conosciamo' (Marsilio Ficino, *Sopra lo amore, o ver' Convito di Platone*, ed. by G. Ottaviano (Milan: CELUC, 1973), p. 19), trans. by Sears Jayne (Dallas: Spring Publications, 1985), p. 42). But such associations would have validated rather contradicted the primary erotic response indicated here.

ago, the anticipated male viewer in this series (probably King Philip II himself) is made to identify with the mythological male 'viewer' within the scene (disguised as he sometimes is): with Jupiter in the *Danaë* and the *Rape of Europa* (Figures 5.2 and 5.6), for example; or with the eponymous hero in the *Perseus and Andromeda*. In most of these paintings, however, this identification is not made thematically central, functioning rather as a means of heightening the 'real' viewer's sensual engagement with, and fantasized possession of, the depicted nudes. In the Edinburgh *Diana and Actaeon*, the act of looking at female nakedness becomes crucial to the narrative and has dire repercussions. Even in this painting, though, looking and the desire it engenders is not made a matter of blame, precisely because it is not shown as a condition of the will or as a result of moral choice. Remaining true to the pre-Christian spirit of Ovid's text, Titian depicts Actaeon's grim fate (he is transformed into a stag and hunted down by his own hounds) simply as a consequence of ill fortune. If, as Puttfarken would have it, the painting is conceived as a 'tragedy', then this is primarily because the consequent spilling of the young man's blood is 'fortune's fault and not any crime of his: for what crime has mere mischance?'[38]

In Tintoretto's contemporary works, on the contrary, such proxy figures mediate, deflect, or undermine erotic response: the emphasis falls less on the bodies themselves than on the consequence of observing them. When figures reminiscent of the erotic nudes of mythological art appear in Tintoretto's sacred paintings, our potentially impassioned response to them is similarly highlighted as part of the moral consequence of the painting. We have seen how the conflation of Venus with Susanna in the Vienna painting, the tension between pictorial presentation and moralizing theme, is set as a kind of visual snare for the unsuspecting viewer. Something similar is at play in the *Temptation of Adam* from the cycle showing scenes from Genesis which Tintoretto painted a few years earlier.[39] In this work, too, Tintoretto implicates the potentially impassioned viewer by suggesting identification between Venus, the pagan goddess, and the Old Testament figure of Eve. And here, also, he works in the device of the proxy male viewer by making Adam take up a position very similar to our own, as if he were looking into the painting from outside its frame. Again, Tintoretto chooses his narrative moment very carefully: Adam has not yet taken the offered apple. In contrast to Titian's innocent Actaeon, enslaved by antiquity's cruel *fortuna*, and for whom all is in the lap of the

---

[38] From Ovid's *Metamorphoses* (III, 138–42) quoted in Puttfarken, *Titian and Tragic Painting*, p. 175.

[39] For the Scuola della Trinitá (1550–53), see Pallucchini and Rossi, *L'opera*, II, n. 151.

Fig. 5.6   Titian, *Rape of Europa*, 1559–62, Boston, MA, Isabella Stewart Gardner Museum.

gods, Adam (and by extension *we* the Christian viewers) can still make a moral choice when confronted with the sexually alluring but sinful figure of an Eve/Venus before us. And even if Adam must, as the text of Genesis dictates, take the proffered fruit and fall from grace, we are granted a better view, privileged by the glimpse of the bleak future scenario of divine punishment in the landscape beyond.

Responses to the *Poesie* after 1560: Tintoretto and Veronese

Tintoretto's mocking and moralizing approach to mythological subjects was short-lived: from about 1560 onwards, he seems to have abandonedthe genre altogether, returning to it only after Titian's death in 1576. His manner in the series of four mythologies apparently commissioned by the Emperor Rudolf II of Prague around this time, as in the 'cabinet' paintings featuring the pagan gods for a room in the Ducal Palace of 1578, displays a more accommodating approach to the genre.[40] These mature works are essentially free of his earlier iconoclastic tendencies, a difference secured by the development of a mode for such secular subjects that is very distinct from the loosely handled, chiaroscuro-based style of his mature work in sacred painting, for example, at the Scuola di San Rocco. These later mythologies are characterized by soft and warm colouring, flattened space and closely interlinking forms, which generate complex patterns on the picture surface. This intensely artificial mode, with its formal drive toward decorative abstraction, and its semantic one towards allegory, allowed Tintoretto to recast the mythological genre in a manner that suppressed not only the comic and satirical aspects of his earlier work, but also Titian's free combination of the erotic and tragic. In works such as the *Tarquin and Lucretia* (Figure 5.7, *c.*1578–80, Art Institute of Chicago), something of the drama of Titian's late mythologies undoubtedly remains. But comparison with Titian's version of the subject in Cambridge of *c.*1570–71 reveals the extent to which Tintoretto has retreated from the older master's focus on the immediate realities of violent physical rape in favour of a more abstract and moralizing treatment supported by symbols such as the falling pearls of Lucretia's necklace, and a learnedly apposite formal allusion to the *Laocoön* in the complex arbitrary patterning of her body.[41]

Something surprisingly similar happens in Paolo Veronese's version of this subject (1580–85, Vienna, Kunsthistorisches Museum), where the struggle between man and woman is replaced by the later solitary moment of Lucretia's suicide.[42] In this painting, as in the *Death of Procris* (before 1582, Strasbourg, Musée des Beaux-Arts), Veronese remains true to the spirit of the subject, producing a non-Christian painting, which is perhaps more straightforwardly 'tragic', in the classical sense, than any of Titian's *poesie*. But this is primarily because Veronese studiously untangles the

---

[40]   Pallucchini and Rossi, *L'opera*, do not catalogue a single mythological painting by Tintoretto between 1560 and the year of Titian's death, 1576. For the paintings mentioned here see ibid., nos. 373–6, 390, 447.

[41]   For Tintoretto's painting, see Pallucchini and Rossi, *L'opera*, vol. 1, n. 450. For Titian's version, see Wethey, *The Mythological Paintings III*, n. 34. My contrast between the two works tends to contradict that offered in Falomir, *Tintoretto*, n. 42. Tintoretto's interest in the *Laocoön*, perhaps also present in the figure of Juno in the London *Origin of the Milky Way*, may paradoxically have been stimulated by Titian. In the very same period, Tintoretto modelled his *St Sebastian* (1578–81, Venice, Scuola di San Rocco) on the famous sculpture, though this figure is also a reference to Titian's Laocoön-based Sebastian figure in his Brescia altarpiece of 1519–22. For Titian's use of the sculpture in this latter painting, see Roman d'Elia, *The Poetics of Titian's Religious Paintings*, pp. 28–35.

[42]   Pignatti and Pedrocco, *Veronese*, vol. 2, n. 353. Veronese's painting pointedly departs from Titian's early painting of the subject at Hampton Court (London) of *c.*1520, in which Lucretia is shown as a full-bodied erotic nude: see Wethey, *The Mythological Paintings III*, n. 26.

Fig. 5.7   Tintoretto, *Tarquin and Lucretia*, *c.*1578–80, Chicago, Art
Institute of Chicago.

contrary inflections of Titian's uninhibited cycle. The 'tragic' tone of the
Strasbourg painting is achieved by the suppression of eroticism in the
mythological scene, a modulation that also allows it to provide a clear
thematic and visual *contrapposto* with the more sensual presentation of
Venus and Adonis in the pendant now in Madrid.[43] In other Veronese

---

43   Pignatti and Pedrocco, *Veronese*, II, nos. 311, 312.

mythologies of this period, however, such as the *Mars and Venus with Love* (Figure 5.8, 1575–80, Turin, Galleria Sabauda), eroticism provides the key in a manner that takes up once again the pictorial theme of the sensual female nude in mythological painting favoured in the first half of the century.[44] This is different from Tintoretto in so far as it reinstates, rather than displaces, the erotic, but in its suppression of the mixture of contrary elements co-existent in Titian's *poesie*, it reflects a similar impulse.[45] The erotic moment in the Turin painting is disturbed not by dark intimations of immanent loss or death, but only by the intrusion of Cupid leading Mars' horse by its bridle. The humorous narrative interlude characteristically leads back only to the underlying theme of the goddess of love's inevitable civilizing victory over coarser 'animal' instinct.

In place of the heightened narrative drama, complex psychological interaction and intimation of physical and mental suffering in the *poesie*, Veronese re-establishes the iconic centrality of the sensuously reclining female nude, whose domineering fleshy presence simultaneously resurrects the original hieratic separateness of the mythological genre. His more precise reaction to Titian's cycle can be established with reference to a number of paintings that pick up the subject-matter of the *poesie*. An example is the *Perseus and Andromeda* (1575–80, Rennes, Musée des Beaux-Arts), a respectful reworking of Titian's Wallace picture, which, while ignoring Tintoretto's bathetic response in the *Liberation of Arsinoë*, none the less recasts the drama of the *poesia* into a more decorative idiom.[46] A very similar reconception is evident in Veronese's *Rape of Europa* (Figure 5.9, *c*.1580, Venice, Ducal Palace), which carefully suppresses the violent drama of Titian's Boston *poesia* (Figure 5.6), relocating the scene to a pastoral landscape (albeit with a sea view) and placing the lavishly draped heroine in an elegant side-saddle posture atop a bull/Jupiter who sprawls obediently on the earth.[47] Surrounded by her fussing ladies-in-waiting, Europa readies herself for the departure shown in sequential fashion in the background. Her orderly retreat recalls Carpaccio's courtly paintings of public ceremonial departure of the late fifteenth century, rather than the isolating uncontrolled

---

44   Ibid, n. 252.

45   Veronese's reinstatement of the exclusively erotic is highlighted by a painting from his workshop of *Leda and the Swan* (*c*.1580, Ajaccio, Musée Fesch), which draws closely on Tintoretto's versions of the subject from the 1550s discussed above. But in Veronese's redaction, the sexuality of the scene becomes all dominant: the swan now lies on top of the woman and sticks his beak into her open mouth: see Pignatti and Pedrocco, *Veronese*, II, A 1. See also the exhibition catalogue *Splendeur de Venise 1500–1600; Peintures et dessins des collections publique francaises* (Paris, Bordeaux, Caen: Somogy, 2005), n. 118.

46   Pignatti and Pedrocco, *Veronese*, II, n. 256; *Splendeur de Venise*, n. 109.

47   Ibid., n. 244.

Fig. 5.8   Veronese, *Mars and Venus*, 1575–80, Turin, Galleria Sabauda.

bareback ride pictured in the *poesia*.[48] The significance of this modification lies in the reversal of gender roles, the victory of the feminine principle of Love indicated by the dozy passivity of the bull/Jupiter, as by the careful suppression of the idea that Europa's ride is in any way involuntary, or that it can be equated with a physical rape.[49]

---

[48]   Veronese's archaizing approach perhaps deliberately recalls, in a generic sense, works such as Carpaccio's *Leavetaking of the Betrothed Pair* from the St Ursula cycle of 1495, which itself extends the late medieval tradition of simultaneous narrative. See Patricia Fortini Brown, *Venetian Narrative Painting in the Age of Carpaccio* (New Haven, CT and London: Yale University Press, 1988), p. 281.

[49]   The involuntary nature of Europa's ride in Titian's *poesie* is stressed by the disequilibrium of her sprawling body, and this in its turn opens the possibility that her rape involves much more than the fact of her abduction.

Fig. 5.9   Veronese, *Rape of Europa*, *c*.1580, Venice, Ducal Palace.

In a furniture painting probably dating from the late 1560s, Veronese revisited the subject of Titian's *poesia* showing *Diana and Actaeon*, but in this work the young hunter simply reclines on a bank enjoying his view of Diana and her nymphs while his hounds drink at the fountain.[50] In place of Titian's fraught moment juxtaposing the contrary emotions of surprise and desire in the mortal Actaeon with fear and retributive anger in the goddess and her train, we are simply encouraged to follow the lolling Actaeon's gaze and enjoy with him a pleasing view of naked female flesh. Veronese made a similar kind of transposition to Titian's *poesia* showing *Venus and Adonis* (Figure 5.3) in his repeated versions of this subject, even if the Madrid painting remained his fundamental source (Figure 5.10). Titian's painting was also important for Veronese's depictions of 'Venus and Mars', such as the Turin painting mentioned above (Figure 5.8) and the versions now in New York and Edinburgh.[51] It is telling that the two subjects become almost interchangeable

---

[50]   Pignatti and Pedrocco, *Veronese*, II, n. 159.

[51]   For the paintings of Venus and Adonis in Seattle, Stockholm, Vienna and Madrid, see ibid., nos. 267, 268, 276 and 311. For those of 'Venus and Mars' mentioned here, see ibid., nos. 265 and 269.

Fig. 5.10   Veronese, *Venus and Adonis*, 1575–80, Vienna, Kunst-historisches Museum.

in Veronese's mythological oeuvre, sharing many formal elements: both typically feature a semi-naked couple holding or caressing one another, often in a pastoral landscape, while nearby cupids play with dogs, armour, or horses. In an earlier version of *Venus and Adonis* (*c*.1560–62, Augsburg, Staatliche Kunstsammlungen), a more direct response to Titian's *poesia* is evident.[52] Titian's original quotation from the *Bed of Polyclitus* is to some extent maintained, and Veronese also follows the older master's departure from Ovid's text to generate a dramatic moment of conflicting emotions between the two lovers. But Veronese's subsequent versions of this subject show that he steadily moved away from Titian's model, producing paintings in which the alarm of Venus over Adonis's desire to hunt is downplayed. In place of Titian's formal dynamism and reference to the dark future, Veronese offered increasingly static presentations of the lovers as non-narrative erotic tableaux, which effectively elide the subject matter with his contemporary depictions of 'Venus and Mars'.[53] If Titian's *poesia* of the earlier 1550s had reversed the epithet of 'Omnia vincit Amor' for tragic effect, Veronese gradually reasserted the centrality of this Virgilian trope in his mythologies of the 1570s and 80s, making Venus victorious over her mortal lover (as she is over the god of war) and in the process moving the tone back toward the comic.[54]

At the same time, Veronese's approach to classical subject-matter becomes more generic in kind, one subject tending to collapse into another in order to establish a single governing mode for the painting type based on the idea of the ultimate victory of 'Love'. We have seen how subjects such as 'Venus and Adonis' and 'Venus and Mars' were increasingly treated as interchangeable variations on the abstract theme of 'Love Conquers All'. Playful details typically included in this kind of work could also generate further thematically dependent paintings, such as the *Cupid and Two Dogs* (1580–85, Munich, Alte Pinakothek), which combines reference to the victory of Venus's son over Mars and his restraining role regarding Adonis's hunting dogs.[55] This elevating allegorical dimension, replete with generalized Neoplatonic associations, is largely missing in Titian's

---

[52]   Ibid., n. 136.

[53]   Compare the paintings noted at notes 44 and 51 above.

[54]   Pictorial cycles devoted to 'Omnia vincit Amor' were also very popular in Counter-Reformatory Rome where, for example, the ceiling of the patrician Corradino Orsini's Palazzo in Parione frescoed by the Cavaliere d'Arpino in 1594 illustrates the theme. See Roberto Zapperi, *Eros e Controriforma: preistoria della Galleria Farnese* (Turin: Bollati Boringhieri, 1994), pp. 110–30.

[55]   Pignatti and Pedrocco, *Veronese*, II, n. 358.

'Aristotelian' *poesie*.[56] It could, of course, serve as a kind of answer to more fastidious Counter-Reformatory patrons concerned about displays of naked flesh in paintings. And as if to demonstrate this point, Veronese was easily able to modify his erotic mythological mode in the direction of more overtly moralizing allegories in which 'Love' is featured as the guiding principle, for example, in four mythological paintings for the Prague court and in the so-called *Allegories of Love* now in London.[57]

In his mythological paintings, Veronese effectively unpicked the complex mode of the *poesie*, reasserting the original distinctness of the genre from the predominant tradition of Christian narrative art. Reference to Titian's cycle typically involved a simplifying return to a mode that has much in common with Venetian mythological paintings of the early decades of the century (including to works of this period by Titian himself).[58] Veronese's approach to form may not so directly reference classical relief composition, but his monumental, static and rotund forms are, none the less, placed close to the picture plane, their fleshy bodies typically supported by extended areas of drapery which flatten and expand form across the picture surface, discouraging the eye's movement into depth. In support of this decorative approach, Veronese typically avoids any reference to violence or retribution and reduces dramatic action to a minimum. The associational richness of the *poesie* is to this extent also replaced by a single quasi-allegorical focus on the pleasures, virtues and ultimate triumph of 'Love' reiterated through different mythological subject-matter. Veronese's mythologies offer a reforming purification of the genre that is deeply retrospective in nature, seeking to re-establish the simpler parameters of the Venetian tradition in the earlier part of the century. This is somewhat different to Tintoretto's approach in his later mythologies, which depart from both the *poesie and* the 'classical' mode that preceded Titian's cycle. But though it may be that, in Tintoretto's art, the classical world is never allowed to exist as a

---

[56]   The Neoplatonic tendencies evident in Veronese's mythologies may have been stimulated by the publication of the vernacular edition of Marcilio Ficino's *Commentary on Plato's Symposium on Love* in 1544, where 'Love' is imagined as a 'great and wonderful god and also noble, and very useful' and the reader is advised to 'indulge in Love in such a way as to be content with its own end, which is beauty': see Ficino, *Commentary on Plato's Symposium on Love*, p. 42 and note 37 above.

[57]   The overlap between erotic mythology and moral allegory is suggested by the fact that one of the Prague paintings (now in New York) features Mars and Venus. For this and the other paintings mentioned here, see Pignatti and Pedrocco, *Veronese*, II, nos. 247–50 and 263–66.

[58]   Something similar to this has been noted in Veronese's altarpieces, such as the early painting for Sansovino's San Francesco della Vigna, which 'reforms' the secularized Pesaro altarpiece on which it is modelled by omitting the patrons: see Peter Humfrey, 'Altarpieces and Altar Dedications in Counter-Reformation Venice and the Veneto', *Renaissance Studies*, 10:3 (1996), 371–87 (pp. 371–2).

hieratically sealed locus of preoccupied sensual pleasure, his later work in this genre shares with Veronese's both its sense of clean distinction from sacred painting and its tendencies toward the allegoric and the generic.

Conclusion

In his *Dialogo* of 1564, Giovanni Gilio da Fabriano cleverly turned Renaissance artistic principles against the representation of hybrid or metamorphic figures from pagan antiquity in visual art, claiming that they were unworthy of imitation because their forms could not be found in nature.[59] He was not alone among leading Counter-Reformation art theorists in voicing concerns over the established Renaissance taste for mythological art. By the end of the century, the post-Tridentine position had hardened still further: in *De Poesi et Pictura* of 1595, for example, the Jesuit Antonio Possevino proclaimed that the saints were appalled to see 'Jupiters, Venuses and other unclean beings recalled from the infernal regions'. His further description of such deities as 'false gods' was already something of a cliché in the writings of the Catholic reformers.[60] But it would be a mistake to take such admonitory and hostile comments as evidence that Christian values and mythological art were fundamentally at odds with one another in the late sixteenth century. As in other Italian cities, such as Rome, commissions for mythological works did not die out, or even dwindle, after 1580. In certain Venetian examples from these final 'Counter-Reformatory' decades, the traditional eroticism of the type was taken to a new level of explicitness.[61]

---

[59]   Among the monstrous hybrids quoted by Gilio are Actaeon and Callisto, depicted in Titian's *poesie* discussed earlier. See *Trattati d'arte del Cinquecento*, 2 vols, ed. by Paolo Barocchi (Bari: Laterza, 1961), II, p. 16. The passage is examined further in Bull, *Mirror of the Gods*, p. 392.

[60]   In the previous decade, Gabriele Paleotti, the reforming bishop of Bologna, had rounded on images of 'falsi dèi', describing the making of pictures of the classical gods as an 'abuse', and quoting Zechariah 13:2 'And it shall come to pass in that day ... that I will cut off the names of the idols out of the land, and they shall be no more remembered': *Discorso intorno alle imagini sacre e profane* (1582) in Barocchi, *Trattati d'arte del Cinquecento*, II, p. 289. Possevino is quoted in P. Janelle, *The Catholic Reformation* (Milwaukee, WI: Bruce, 1963), p. 162.

[61]   Witness, for example, the Veronese workshop painting of *c*.1580 mentioned at note 45 above, in which the swan inserts his beak into Leda's mouth. Another example is Palma Giovane's *Venus and Mars* (*c*.1590, London, National Gallery) which shows the lovers writhing with pleasure on a bed, with the naked goddess on top of Mars in a mouth-to-mouth embrace: see Stefania Mason Rinaldi, *Palma il Giovane, L'opera completa* (Milan: Electa, 1984), n. 132. Palma's later erotic mythologies are similarly explicit: see ibid., 228, 405, 485, 541.

The continuing demand for such works only in part reflects Titian's death in 1576, and the inevitable search for new providers of Venetian mythological cabinet paintings this generated among leading art patrons: it may also illustrate a wider point regarding the relationship between Christian reform and the classicizing culture reflected in the taste for mythological art. The contradiction that the continuing taste for erotic paintings seems to offer to the Church's expressions of moral disapprobation is only an apparent one. Religious reformers were typically more concerned with obedience to the decorum of place than with an attack on mythological art *per se*. It was the perceived invasion of the often naked forms that were the stock-in-trade of mythological art into religious imagery in Italian churches that most concerned reformist theologians such as Gilio and Possevino. Given that paintings featuring the pagan gods were self-evidently unreal from a Christian perspective, and were rarely displayed in places of public worship, they offered no immediate threat to public morality.[62] It has recently been suggested that the rise of mythological art from the fifteenth century onwards represents the lasting acceptance of a new category of falsity into the expanding domain of European Christian culture.[63] Paradoxically, it may have been the increasingly confident perception that such mythological imagery *was* 'false' that secured its continuing survival in Venice, as elsewhere in Catholic Europe. It is at least arguable that the elements of formal artificiality that predominate in mythological painting in the Counter-Reformation period reflect, at some level, this acceptance. The continuity and intensification of the type reflects a reinvigorated sense of its own identity based on a clean division from the tradition of sacred art which simultaneously reasserted *its* distinctness as legitimate Christian imagery. This polarizing (and at the same time archaizing) tendency is reflected in the cultural desire for conformity to type, necessitating a new level of attention to image specification and categorization that may be a cultural phenomenon common to many periods of religious reformation. The definition of a properly Christian artistic genre under the impact of the Counter-Reformation has often been noted. It is equally apparent in the redefinition of mythological art in the

---

[62]   Gilio (*Dialogo*, in Barocchi, *Trattati d'arte*, p. 20) stresses that paintings should always be 'suited … to the place' ('convenevoli … al luogo'), making the rather obvious point that erotic mythological subjects should not be shown in churches. But though 'one should not paint Vulcan who caught Venus and Mars in bed with an iron net, or Jove who in the form of a swan lay with Leda' in the sacred context, the clear implication is that such subjects (despite their subsequent scathing designation as 'impertinent histories') are permissible, perhaps even suitable, for other locations. For the wider theoretical context of the concept of 'convenevolenza' (or decorum), see Rensselaer W. Lee, *Ut Pictura Poesis: The Humanistic Theory of Painting* (New York: W.W. Norton, 1967), pp. 34–41.

[63]   See Bull, *The Mirror of the Gods*, pp. 380–95.

same period. The purifying separation of the sacred and secular modes served, in an important sense, to maintain both aspects of the dualistic Renaissance visual tradition against Protestant attacks on visual imagery. But if, in the case of mythological painting, this separation protected a category that had become especially vulnerable in an age of deepening religious values, it did so at the expense of the creative hybridity between sacred and profane modes so compellingly proposed in Titian's *poesie*.[64]

---

[64]   The inadmissible position of hybridity in religious reformatory thought is, of course, equally apparent in the passage mentioned above from Giglio (see note 59 above), who (wrongly) imagined pagan art as necessarily committed to such fluid and unstable forms.

CHAPTER 6

The Representation of Suffering and Religious Change in the Early Cinquecento

Harald Hendrix

During the early decades of the sixteenth century, particularly in the late 1520s, the 1530s and 1540s, in Italy both poets and artists started to experiment with radically new and audacious forms of expression, out of a combined desire to promote innovation and to gain personal success and admiration. These experiments are rooted in a background of growing competition between artists and poets, which in its turn was one of the results of what one might call the advent of the free market economy in the arts, that offered artists and poets many new opportunities to obtain commissions or to address different audiences. The most common strategy to gain maximum profit from these new opportunities was, as it is now, excellence, or simply the suggestion of it. The directions taken by this tendency to what one might call artistic or poetic self-promotion, were in great part determined by elements of contingency. Two such elements will be the subject of this essay: on the one hand, the inspiration that newly discovered elements of antique or ancient culture offered, and on the other hand, the ideological preoccupations that in these very years were offered to the dominant orthodox culture by the challenge of Protestantism.[1]

---

[1]   This essay presents some of the results of an ongoing research project on the representation of suffering in early modern Italian literature and the visual arts. Related issues have been presented in the following publications by Harald Hendrix: 'The Repulsive Body. Images of Torture in Seventeenth-Century Naples', in *Bodily Extremities. Preoccupations with the Human Body in Early Modern European Culture*, ed. by Florike Egmond and Robert Zwijnenberg (Aldershot: Ashgate, 2003), pp. 68–91; 'Pietro Aretino's *Humanità di Christo* and the Rhetoric of Horror', in *Il Rinascimento italiano di fronte alla riforma: letteratura e arte. Sixteenth-Century Italian Art and Literature and the Reformation*, ed. by Chrysa Damianaki, Paolo Procaccioli and Angelo Romano (Manziana: Vecchiarelli, 2005), pp. 89–114; 'Renaissance Roots of the Sublime. Ugliness, Horror and Pleasure in Early Modern Italian Debates on Literature and Art', in *Histories of the Sublime*, ed. by Christophe Madelein, Jürgen Pieters and Bart Vandenabeele (Brussels: Koninklijke Vlaamse Academie van België voor Wetenschappen en Kunsten, 2005), pp. 13–22; 'Orrore e diletto. Peripezie di un concetto 'sublime' fra Cinque e Seicento', *Aevum Antiquum*, (2003) [= 2007], 3, 173–86; 'Provoking Disgust as an Aesthetic Strategy. On the Representation of the Non-Beautiful in Aristotle's

The drive towards experimentation can be perceived particularly clearly in the Venetian context of the late 1520s, when in the wake of the Sack of Rome, Venice grew into the most productive and innovative cultural centre on the Italian peninsula, thanks to the many artists and poets finding refuge there and to the rapidly expanding influence of the newly established printing press. In this melting pot of talents, some strong allegiances between artists and poets, notably between Titian, Aretino and Sansovino, came into being, facilitating the transfer of innovative notions from one form of artistic expression to another; but also inviting these very friends to compete with each other and to demonstrate in this competition their own excellence and the superiority of their trade, be it painting, architecture, or poetry. It is this particular breeding ground, the Venice of the late 1520s and the 1530s, that I propose to examine, concentrating in particular on one of the most innovative techniques for promoting artistic distinctions that matured in this particular environment: the inclination to experiment with an art intended to shock audiences, because of an extremely realistic rendering of scenes of human suffering and of agony. By manipulating the emotions of their audiences, writers and artists such as Aretino and Titian experimented with an art that, as well as underpinning their own excellence, also touched upon a quite different and audaciously new aesthetics based on the concept of delightful horror, and anticipating what in the seventeenth century would become universally popular as the aesthetics of the *meraviglia*, and by the eighteenth century was to become one of the central elements of the aesthetics of the sublime.

In order to illustrate such a claim, in this chapter, I will first present a discussion of the concept of delightful horror, tracing its origins back from its well-known manifestation in sublime and Seicento aesthetics to what I consider its first modern reappearance in some particular corners of early Cinquecento art and poetry, both in theory and in practice. What will emerge from my discussion will be the suggestion that the change in artistic and literary sensibility that I address here first emerged as a kind of practical experiment by artists and poets eager to find new modes of expression able to meet new requirements, and that only subsequently was this new sensibility grounded in a more theoretical articulation. For this reason, in the second part of this chapter, I will concentrate on the duo of Titian and Aretino, examining some of their most daring productions of the late 1520s and early 1530s. In doing so, I intend to address some of the stimulating recent scholarship on Titian and to contextualize the experiments by Titian and Aretino, notably by trying to identify possible models or sources of

---

Poetics and in Art Theory of the Italian Renaissance and Baroque', in *Wie sich Gefühle Ausdruck verschaffen. Emotionen in Nahsicht*, ed. by Klaus Herding and Antje Krause-Wahl (Taunusstein: Driesen, 2007), pp. 119–31.

inspiration that might explain their motivations in choosing to embark upon such audacious innovations.

In order to illustrate the concept of delightful horror and its sources, we must first turn to a much later reaction by a prominent French art critic, Dezaillier d'Argenville, to the art of one of the most outstanding masters of the Neapolitan Baroque, Jusepe de Ribera, whose pictures of Christian martyrs and of mythological torture scenes astonished his audience for their crude realism. In his *Abrégé de la vie des plus fameux peintres*, compiled in the 1740s, Dezaillier d'Argenville found it difficult to account for the particular quality of this 'peinture atroce', as he called it, which is why he resorted to the traditional *ut pictura poesis* expedient and quoted a passage from Boileau's poetics:

> His natural genius led him to search for terrible and horrifying subjects. In the profane mode, it was Ixion, Tantalus, Prometheus; in the sacred mode, the martyrdom of Saint Bartholomew, of Saint Stephen, of Saint Laurence etc.: scenes which greatly pleased the Spanish and Neapolitan people. One must allow that these pieces are full of great truth, and their only fault is the ferocity of the subjects. Yet 'There is no snake, nor odious monster,/That when imitated in art, cannot please the eye;/With a delicate brushstroke the pleasing artifice/ Of the most horrendous object makes it agreeable' (Boileau).[2]

Apparently still unaware of the growing interest in Longinus's *Traité du sublime, ou du merveilleux*, circulated from 1674 in Boileau's famous translation, the French art critic here tries to explain a phenomenon close to what his successors a short while later would start to call the aesthetics of the sublime. What struck Dezaillier d'Argenville in the 'peinture atroce' of Ribera was in fact its capacity to give pleasure and disgust at the same time, and thus to produce a twofold and perhaps ambiguous but no doubt strong effect on an audience. In order to account for this highly appreciated though not undisputed quality, Dezaillier d'Argenville resorted to an ancient and authoritative aesthetic paradigm, Aristotle's concept of imitation as it was explained in a famous passage from his *Poetics*:

---

[2] 'Son génie naturel le portait à rechercher les sujets terribles et pleins d'horreur. Dans le profane c'était des Ixions, des Tantales, des Prométhées; dans le sacré, le martyre de saint Barthélémi, de saint Etienne, de saint Laurent, etc.; tableaux qui plaisaient infiniment à la nation Espagnole et Napolitaine. Il faut convenir que ces morceaux pleins d'une grande vérité, n'ont contre eux que la férocité des sujets. Mais 'Il n'est point de serpens (sic), ni de monstre odieux,/Qui, par l'art imité, ne puisse plaire aux yeux;/D'un pinceau délicat l'artifice agréable/ Du plus affreux objet fait un objet aimable (Boileau)': Antoine-Joseph Dezaillier D'Argenville, *Abrégé de la vie des plus fameux peintres* (Paris: De Bure, 1762), vol. II, p. 235.

For the process of imitation is natural from childhood on: man is differentiated from other animals because he is the most imitative of them, and he learns his first lessons through imitation, and we observe that all men find pleasure in imitations. The proof of this point is what actually happens in life. For there are some things that distress us when we see them in reality, but the most accurate representations of these same things we view with pleasure – as, for example, the forms of the most despised animals and of corpses.[3]

Aristotle's unrestrained appraisal of the power of imitation not only condones the representation of those elements that are considered ugly or even repellent, it also invites artists to show off their talents by making beautiful poems or pictures on subject matter that is by its nature ugly or horrible.

Aristotle's challenge was taken up by the most ambitious artists and poets of early modern Italy, who from the 1520s became involved in experiments with an audacious aesthetics that, while it tried to excite both pleasure and disgust, ultimately aimed to stimulate astonishment in an audience, and thus admiration for the artist or poet. Doubtless the most eloquent advocate of this technique, however, was the Neapolitan poet Giambattista Marino, who in 1620 dedicated one of his best-known poems on contemporary painting to a canvas by Guido Reni on the notoriously cruel subject of the Massacre of the Innocents:

> Che fai, Guido, che fai?
> La man, che forme angeliche dipigne,
> tratta or'opre sanguigne?
> Non vedi tu, che mentre il sanguinoso
> stuol dei fanciulli ravivando vai,
> nova morte gli dai?
> O ne la crudeltate ancor pietoso,
> fabro gentil, ben sai,
> ch'ancor tragico caso è caro oggetto,
> e che spesso l'orror va col diletto.[4]

By emphatically resorting to the oppositional scheme of Petrarchist poetry (forme angeliche/opre sanguigne; vita/morte; crudeltà/pietà) Marino underlines the central, paradoxical and therefore artful idea that pleasure can be produced by disgust: 'l'orror va col diletto'. This can be accomplished, however, only by a 'fabro gentil', an artist able to maintain the right balance between the different elements. By contrasting the various

---

[3]   Aristotle, *Poet.* 1448b. The English translation is Aristotle, *Poetics*, ed. by L. Golden and O.B. Harrison (Englewoods Cliffs, NJ: Prentice-Hall, 1968), p. 7.

[4]   Giambattista Marino, *La Galleria*, ed. by Marzio Pieri (Padua: Liviana, 1979), I, p. 56.

emotions (crudeltà/pietà; orrore/diletto), they become all the stronger, and poetry and painting gain in effectiveness. The final result is, of course, that the audience is astonished and experiences a sense of what Marino calls elsewhere 'meraviglia'.

The central concept of delightful horror is what unites this technique of the meraviglia and the idea of the sublime. Essential to both is the emphasis on the emotional and psychological aspects of art, rather than on its formal qualities. And within this emphasis on the pragmatics of the arts, and thus on the audiences involved, both methods advocate a technique based on a mixture of strong and often contrasting effects in order to accomplish an overall effect that is of yet another nature and is not easy to grasp or to direct. In developing this particular style, Marino not only turned for inspiration to late Antique oratory,[5] but also elaborated on an ongoing debate regarding the status of the non-beautiful, a debate that centred precisely on the dynamism between agreeable and disagreeable artistic effects.

This debate had dominated literary and art criticism during the second half of the sixteenth century, when Counter-Reformation ideology began to advocate an audience-oriented mode of artistic expression. It was unleashed, however, much earlier, in the 1540s, following the rediscovery of Aristotle's *Poetics*, and even as early as the late 1520s and early 1530s. The first traces of the debate did not occur in the context of a theoretical debate, however, but rather through the experiments of artists like Titian and authors like Aretino, and particularly in their religious works, in which they tried on the one hand, to demonstrate their own excellence, and on the other, to respond to contemporary preoccupations with religious matters, while also coming to terms with a newly discovered classical heritage, from texts such as Aristotle's *Poetics* to sculpture like the Laocoön.

In their 2005 books on *Titian and Tragic Painting* and *The Poetics of Titian's Religious Paintings*, both Thomas Puttfarken and Una Roman D'Elia concentrate on the intersections between art and literature, especially in the Venetian circles around Titian and Aretino, in order to better understand Titian's production of religious and mythological painting.[6] Both scholars are especially interested in those paintings where the master experiments with a fundamentally new kind of realism, clearly intended to shock his audience by presenting scenes of torture and agony with almost graphic detail, as in the *Marsyas* he painted at the end of his life, in the early 1570s (Figure 6.1). This is a period in which many art theorists had started to

---

   [5]   See Marc Fumaroli, *L'Age de l'éloquence: Réthorique et res literaria de la Renaissance au seuil de l'époque classique* (Geneva: Droz, 1980), pp. 213–15.

   [6]   Thomas Puttfarken, *Titian and Tragic Painting: Aristotle's* Poetics *and the Rise of the Modern Artist* (New Haven, CT: Yale University Press, 2005); Una Roman D'Elia, *The Poetics of Titian's Religious Paintings* (Cambridge: Cambridge University Press, 2005).

Fig. 6.1   Titian, *The Flaying of Marsyas*, *c.*1570–75, Kromeríz,
             Archbishop's palace.

reflect on such emotionally oriented painting, generally in the context of
Counter-Reformation ideology which advocated the use of realism in order
to stimulate piety and devotion. This is what we find in texts like Gilio's *Due
Dialoghi* (1564) and even in Dolce's *Dialogo della pittura* (1556), including
statements like this one:

> Finally the painter needs a further quality, and painting which lacks this
> remains cold and lifeless as a corpse that can do nothing. This is the need for
> the figures to move the souls of viewers, some disturbing them, others rendering
> them joyful, some inciting them to piety and others to scorn, according to the

manner of the narrative. Otherwise the painter is deemed to have achieved nothing, for this is the final touch to all his other virtues, just as is the case with poets, historians and orators; for if the words written or spoken lack this power, they also lack spirit and life. Nor can the painter move others if he does not himself feel in his own soul, when painting the figures, those passions or affects that he wishes to impress upon other people.[7]

Dolce relates naturalism to an emotional impact on the audience, but also to decorum: the representation of a particular scene must be in accordance with the nature of its subject matter. Most significantly, he relates naturalism to the excellence of the artist: only through naturalistic imitation, in line with decorum, can artists and poets gain excellence. This fundamentally Aristotelian notion, based as it is on the passage from the *Poetics* cited above, is most prevalent in the second half of the Cinquecento and in the early Seicento. It is clearly evident, for example, in a text such as Giulio Camillo's *Idee* dating from 1594:

> It is easy to find delight in things that sensitive people naturally delight in, such as when one speaks of beauty, of plants, flowers, springs of water or other such things. But when one offers up subject matter so serious, that for its very severity it seems far from any delight, in treating such subjects the genius of the Poet is revealed.[8]

Both Puttfarken and D'Elia try to explain Titian's dramatic realism, as in his *Tarquin and Lucretia* painted around 1570 (Figure 6.2), as a reflection of the debates on Aristotle's *Poetics*, and particularly on the nature of tragedy, which is the main subject of the treatise. This is certainly plausible, although neither author can convincingly document Titian's position on this fundamentally literary debate, not only due to the lack of such

---

7 'Finalmente ricerca al pittore un'altra parte, della quale la pittura ch'è priva, riman, come si dice, fredda et è a guisa di corpo morto, che non opera cosa veruna. Questo è, che bisogna che le figure movano gli animi de' riguardanti, alcune turbandogli, altre rallegrandogli, altre sospingendogli a pietà et altre a sdegno, secondo la qualità della istoria. Altrimenti reputi il pittore di non aver fatto nulla, perché questo è il condimento di tutte le sue virtù, come aviene parimente al poeta, all'istorico et all'oratore; ché se le cose scritte o recitate mancano di questa forza, mancano elle ancora di spirito e di vita. Né può movere il pittore, se prima nel far delle figure non sente nel suo animo quelle passioni, o diciamo affetti, che vuole imprimere in quello d'altrui': Ludovico Dolce, *Dialogo della pittura* (Venice, 1557); reproduced in *Trattati d'arte del Cinquecento*, 3 vols (Bari: Laterza, 1960–62), vol. I, pp. 141–206 (pp. 185–6).

8 'Et la dilettatione è facile a trovare nelle cose, che li sensibili naturalmente dilettano, come quando si parla di bellezza, di herbe, di fiori, di fonti, ò di cose simili. Ma quando si offeriscono materie sì gravi, che per la loro severitate da ogni dilettatione lontane siano, d'intorno à quelle si conosce l'ingegno del Poeta': Giulio Camillo, *Le Idee, overo forme della oratione da Hermogene considerate, & ridotte in questa lingua* (Udine: Natolini, 1594), c.86v.

Fig. 6.2   Titian, *Tarquin and Lucretia*, *c.*1570, Cambridge, Fitzwilliam Museum.

documentation on Titian's life, but also because the painter was not an intellectual or a scholar. Leaving this argument to one side, much more captivating is the suggestion found in both books that Titian embarked upon his experimental journey long before the debate on Aristotle's *Poetics* was unleashed.

Although rediscovered at the end of the fifteenth century, Aristotle's treatise only started to become the focus of a heated intellectual debate in the late 1540s, following its translation into Latin and Italian by Alessandro Pazzi (1536) and Bernardo Segni (1549). But it was not until the translation and commentary by Castelvetro, published in 1570, that the work came to occupy the centre of poetic and artistic debates. In Bernardo Daniello's *Poetica* from 1536, we already find indications of a reaction to Aristotle's idea of imitation, but only much later, from the 1560s onwards, can one find systematic references to this key concept in the many treatises on literature and art that were produced in the second half of the Cinquecento. So while Puttfarken and D'Elia may have a good point in relating Titian's later production to this debate, in the case of his earlier production, preceding the 1550s, one must look for other explanations.

Perhaps the first instance in which we can pinpoint Titian's preference for realism and relate it to Aristotelian ideas on imitation and excellence is the series of the *Four Great Sinners*, executed by Titian for Mary of Hungary's summer residence near Brussels between 1548 and 1549 (Figure 6.3). Puttfarken explicitly relates this horror-aesthetics to the debates following the reappraisal of Aristotle's *Poetics*, from the 1540s onwards, and to the production of Seneca-inspired tragedies full of shocking horror-scenes, such as the ones by Giraldi Cinzio: Cinzio's notorious drama on *Orbecche* was first staged in 1541. The effect of these paintings certainly was what Aristotle had in mind, because as we know from contemporary eyewitness accounts, they were not considered too audacious, but were on the contrary admired like 'maravillosa pintura', to quote the courtier Calvete de Estrella who saw the canvases when they were first exhibited.[9] The paintings must have been intended for a specific purpose other than simply for the demonstration of Titian's excellence, placed as they were in a highly significant context: the room where Mary of Hungary orchestrated the official presentation of the heir to the throne, the future Philip II of Spain, in the presence of her brother, Emperor Charles V himself (Figure 6.4). Puttfarken suggests that the punishment of the giants refers to the continuation of the battle against Protestantism, but one might also think of other options. Given the specific context of the *rite-de-passage* of a new monarch, I would tend to read the iconography of the punished giants as

---

[9]   Quoted in Puttfarken, *Titian and Tragic Painting*, p. 87.

Fig. 6.3   Titian, *Tityus*, *c*.1548, Madrid, Museo del Prado.

an allegory of the punishment of bad monarchs, and thus as an invitation
to good government.

What is most interesting in the discussions presented by Puttfarken
and D'Elia concerns Titian's production of realistic scenes of suffering and
agony dating from well before the moment in which Aristotle's concept
of imitation was being reappraised, that is, prior to the 1540s. A fine
example is the *Sebastian* included in Titian's *Resurrection* altarpiece in
Brescia (Figure 6.5), painted in 1522, and significantly reproduced on the
cover of D'Elia's book. This iconography of suffering is clearly inspired

Fig. 6.4   Anon., *The Great Hall at Mary of Hungary's Summer Residence at Binche*, 1548, Brussels, Royal Library.

by the Laocoön, which after its discovery in 1506 unleashed a continuous flow of imitations, of poetry and of commentaries, as has been very well documented by Salvatore Settis and Sonia Maffei.[10] Although we have no documentation concerning the way Titian came into contact with this model, and perhaps intermediate works such as Michelangelo's *Schiavo ribelle* (1513) must be considered here, the parallel is so obvious that we may certainly conclude that Titian's *Sebastian* reflects his ambition to

---

[10]   Salvatore Settis, *Laocoonte. Fama e stile*, ed. by Sonia Maffei (Rome: Donzelli, 1999).

Fig. 6.5   Titian, *Resurrection Altarpiece*, 1522, Brescia, Santi Nazzaro
e Celso.

experiment with audacious representations of dramatic suffering inspired
by newly discovered ancient prototypes. So even in this case we can explain
the preference for an emotionally oriented realistic rendering of agony on
the basis of antique models: not in this case a text, Aristotle's *Poetics*, but
an artefact, the Laocoön.

This is no longer the case when we consider Titian's religious painting
of the late 1520s, and particularly his altarpiece of *S. Pietro Martire*,
executed shortly before 1530 for the church of Santi Giovanni e Paolo.
Though destroyed in a fire of 1867, the painting is very well documented,
since many copies were made from its first appearance until its loss, such
as the one by Géricault from 1812 (Figure 6.6); it was widely considered
to be Titian's religious masterpiece, celebrated by contemporaries and

Fig. 6.6   Géricault, *Martyrdom of St Peter Martyr*, *c*.1812, copy of
an altarpiece by Titian of *c*.1526–30, Basel, Öffentliche
Kunstsammlung.

later generations of admirers. A comment by Titian's close friend Aretino
demonstrates why the work was so highly regarded:

> In gazing upon it, both you and Benvenuto were changed into visions of
> amazement; fixing your eyes and minds upon the work, you understood all
> the vivid terrors of death and all the deep pains of life marked on the face and

in the flesh of the fallen man, marvelling over the cold and livid bruises on the end of his nose and the extremities of his body, and unable to keep quiet you exclaimed aloud, upon contemplating his companion who flees the scene, when you saw upon his face the whiteness of cowardice and the paleness of fear.[11]

Aretino admires Titian's capacity to draw his audience into the painting, to make them relive the dramatic action and cause them to be emotionally disturbed, exactly the way the saint must have felt. Titian's painting, in Aretino's view, is not just a representation of suffering; it is a re-enactment of suffering, and a projection of that agony upon an audience. Aretino's comment is highly significant, because it helps explain at the same time his own religious production of these very same years, to which I will turn in the remainder of this essay.

In his pioneering book on Aretino, Christopher Cairns has made it clear that the author's early religious works, notably his *Humanità di Christo* published in 1535, are to be regarded as an expression of the intense religious debate Venetian intellectuals were engaged in during this particular moment, the years between 1530 and 1540, which preceded a period of ever-increasing religious orthodoxy.[12] One of the main issues in this debate was the call for a simple and open religion based on the Bible, a religion accessible to as many as possible. This led of course to the demand for popularization of the Scriptures, something Aretino himself supported warm-heartedly, as he states in the introduction to the *Humanità*:

The simplicty and purity of Christ demanded pure and simple writers who illustrated his truth purely and simply. One can find nothing other than simplicity and purity in his faith ... Blessed are those who live in native purity and simplicity, and in believing allow that true faith to sustain them.[13]

---

[11] 'Nel guardarlo converse e voi e Benvenuto ne l'imagine de lo stupore; e, fermati gli occhi del viso e le luci de l'intelletto in cotal opra, comprendeste tutti i vivi terrori de la morte e tutti i veri dolori della vita ne la fronte e ne le carni del caduto in terra, maravigliandovi del freddo e del livido che gli appare ne la punta del naso e ne l'estremità del corpo, né potendo ritener la voce, lasciaste esclamarla, quando nel contemplar del compagno che fugge, gli scorgeste ne la sembianza il bianco de la viltà e il pallido de la paura': Pietro Aretino, *Lettere sull'arte*, ed. by Ettore Camesasca and Fidenzio Pertile, 3 vols (Milan: Edizioni del Milione, 1957), I, p. 73.

[12] Christopher Cairns, *Pietro Aretino and the Republic of Venice. Researches on Aretino and his circle in Venice 1527–1556* (Florence: Olschki, 1985), especially pp. 69–124; see also Élise Boillet, *L'Arétin et la Bible* (Geneva: Droz, 2007).

[13] 'La semplicità e la purità di Christo ha voluto puri e semplici scrittori i quali hanno ritratto il suo vero puramente e semplicemente. E già non si comprende altro che semplicitade e puritade nella fede sua ... E beati coloro che vivono nella purità e nella semplicità natia, e credendo si contentano in quella credenza verace': Pietro Aretino, *Humanità di Christo* (Venezia: Marcolini, 1535), f. 22r.

On several occasions, Aretino expressed his enthusiasm for a 'simple religion of belief' and emphasized the usefulness of the popularization of Scripture and the legends and figures of Christian history in the *volgare*, in terms and in a language that all could understand. What is surprising in this context, however, is the fact that in his paraphrase of the Bible Aretino himself by no means adopts a simple language, but instead chooses a deliberately complex and difficult style, abundant with rich vocabulary and extravagant rhetorical ornamentation. Cairns considers this an outright failure: 'Most critics would agree that as a *stylistic achievement*, rather than *intention*, this was one of Aretino's conspicuous failures.'[14]

One of the best-known and most influential examples of this style is Aretino's description of the horrors of the Massacre of the Innocents, a passage that in the 1590s would inspire Giambattista Marino to write his poem on the *Strage degli Innocenti*, which in its turn was to alter fundamentally the representation of this scene in Baroque imagery:[15]

> Here are the rogues elected to this horrible office and hateful act. Alas the daggers are held high: and falling they wound the heads, slit the breasts, pierce the throats, open the kidneys, slash the thighs, tear the bellies, chop off the hands, and gouge out the eyes. Already the ground is soaked with blood: it is covered with entrails and cut limbs: the famished wolves have crept into the sheep pens, and are slaughtering the lambs; mothers are bleating, shepherds are shouting; the executors of royal impiety have turned their attention elsewhere. Here is one who murders an infant lying between his mother and father in bed, who turns to him laughing. Here is another who drags a baby from the arms of she who loves him more than life itself, and tossing him from a balcony he curses her as she laments. There they are thrown in the fire in their infants' swaddling; burning and wailing they writhe and thrash in their bonds until death. These ones are plucked from the breasts of their fleeing defenceless mothers, and slaughtered without delay. As they hurl themselves downstairs clutching the cradles, at every step they spew forth blood, limbs, gore. They smash into the walls. They plummet from the roofs. They plunge into the roiling waters. They are throttled with cords. Strangled by hand. Kicked, punched, thrown into the sewers. They are torn apart, ripped to pieces.[16]

---

[14]   Cairns, *Pietro Aretino*, pp. 118–19. A similar comment can be found in Paul Larivaille, *Pietro Aretino fra Rinascimento e Manierismo* (Rome: Bulzoni, 1980), p. 237.

[15]   See Giuseppe Scopa, *Le fonti della Strage degli Innocenti di G.B. Marino* (Naples: Michele D'Auria, 1905); Elisabeth Cropper, 'Marino's 'Strage degli Innocenti', Poussin, Rubens, and Guido Reni', *Studi Secenteschi*, 23 (1992), pp. 137–66.

[16]   'Ecco i manigoldi eletti all'officio horribile, & all'opra detestabile. Oime i coltelli sono in alto: e pionbando [*sic*] giuso feriscono le teste, rompono i seni, forano le gole, aprono le reni, tagliano le coscie, sdruisciono i ventri, mozzano le mani, e cavano gli occhi. Già la terra si bagna di sangue: si copre di viscere, si sparge di membra: i lupi famelici sono entrati ne gli ovili, e fanno strage de gl'agnelli; e madri belano, e i pastori esclamano; gli esecutori

Here we are confronted with the paradox of a complex and ornamental stylistics full of pathos being applied in order to communicate in a supposedly 'simple' manner. This stylistics, and therefore this aesthetics, must in a way be considered 'popular', since Aretino applies them in order to bring the simple message of Christian faith to the people. But why did he choose as instruments of popularization such extreme devices and not more plain linguistic choices, more in accordance with the simple message he aims to divulge amongst those who live 'nella purità e nella semplicità natia'? To consider this choice as a mistake or a 'conspicuous failure' does not seem very satisfactory in the light of the huge significance this issue undoubtedly has. A more promising strategy to untangle this paradox is to look for possible models Aretino made use of, since they might clarify the context and background that motivated this apparently surprising choice.

To date little research has been done to identify possible sources for Aretino's religious production. Scholars have at most suggested links with three related but nevertheless distinct traditions: religious poetry stemming from humanistic roots, of which Sannazaro's *De partu Virginis* is no doubt the finest example; digressive paraphrases of Scripture, such as Teofilo Folengo's *Umanità del Figliuolo di Dio*, and contemporary oratory as manifested in the sermons of popular preachers like Bernardino Ochino. The comparison with Sannazaro's highly regarded sacred poem does not seem very convincing, since it is in Latin and in verse, and therefore in no way devised as a means to make the Bible accessible to a larger audience of people who have retained their simplicity. Folengo's text, however, is evidently much closer to Aretino's book: although in verse, it is written in Italian, it presents a more or less identical subject, and it was published in 1533 in Venice, only one year before Aretino began work in that same city on his version of the life of Christ. Moreover, Folengo justifies his paraphrasing of Scripture in much the same way as Aretino would do: as being a process of dissemination aimed at ending the elite's monopoly on knowledge of God's word.

---

della impietà reale sono per l'altrui case. Ecco quello tra il padre, e la madre giacenti in letto uccide il figliuolo, il quale scherzando gli rallegra. Ecco quell'altro, che lo trahe di braccio à colei, che più che sè lo ama, e gittandolo da un balcone la proverbia, mentre ella se ne rammarica. Eccone là nel fuoco con i legami, che ci fasciano ne i primi giorni; onde ardendo, e piangendo si torcono, e dibattendo l'una, e l'altra spalla si muoiono. Questi sono rapiti da i petti fuggendo i vasi materni, e scannati senza indugio. E quelli avventati insieme con le culle giù per le scale danno ad ogni grado tributo di sangue, di membra, di cerebri. Ne sono rotti nel muro. Se ne scagliano da i tetti. Se ne tuffano nelle acque, che bollono. Se ne affoga con lacci. Se ne strangola con le mani. Se ne traffige co i piedi. Se ne schiaccia co i pugni, se ne gitta nelle latrine. Se ne sbranano, e se ne tagliano in pezzi': Pietro Aretino [= Partenio Etiro], *Dell'Humanità del figliuolo di Dio libri tre* (Venice: Marco Ginammi, 1645), pp. 77–9.

Voglion non so quai saggi che 'l Vangelo
non mai debbiasi esporre al volgo in carte
con stil volgar, però ch'a lui già il velo
del tempio ascose la più santa parte.
Rispondo che, morendo, il Re del Cielo
squarciollo d'alto a basso acciò che sparte
sian or sue grazie al nobil, al plebeo,
Tartaro, Indo, Latin, Greco, Afro, Ebreo.[17]

Folengo's text is the product of an ideology of religious innovation and reform very close to the one adopted by Aretino. Significantly, here we find, as slightly later in Aretino, a detailed and lengthy presentation of the Massacre of the Innocents, an episode that Sannazaro had evoked in only a few lines. In its objective to establish a popular kind of Christian literature ('esporre al volgo in carte con stil volgar'), Folengo's *Umanità del Figliuolo di Dio* must therefore clearly be considered a prototype that more or less directly inspired the *Umanità di Cristo*, conceived very shortly afterwards and in the same cultural context. This correspondence underlines once more the pragmatic nature of Aretino's religious production and its popular orientation. It does not offer, however, a better understanding of the particular style and imagery adopted by Aretino. In fact, Folengo's text exhibits a quite different stylistics, characterized by simplicity and a lack of fantasy rather than by the hyperbolic depiction of scenes stemming entirely from the author's imagination, with which Aretino's *Humanità* abounds.

Equally disappointing is the hypothesis that contemporary oratory supplied Aretino with some of the material he used in the ornamentation of his religious narratives. In several of his letters, Aretino expresses his enthusiasm for some of the more popular preachers of his day, in particular, the unorthodox Sienese Capuchin Bernardino Ochino. Although this might suggest a link between his own devotional works and the oratorical production in the *volgare* of the period, equally oriented to the popularization of Scripture, a closer examination of Ochino's sermons reveals that on a stylistic level there is no correspondence whatsoever. In comparison to Aretino's, Ochino's writing is syntactically rather plain and not at all inclined to complex ornamentation and elaborate narrative digressions. And although to date very little research has been done on this topic, there are no indications that the works of other contemporary vernacular preachers offer elements that would allow one to establish a

---

[17] Teofilo Folengo, *La Umanità del figiuolo di Dio* (Venice: Pincio, 1533), partially reprinted in *idem*, *Opere*, ed. by Carlo Cordié (Milan-Naples: Ricciardi, 1977), pp. 913–50 (pp. 917–18).

link between early sixteenth-century oratory and the stylistic and aesthetic innovations introduced in Aretino's devotional production.

There is, however, one clear parallel, which, although it raises many questions, offers a surprising new perspective on this debate. In a sermon on the Massacre of the Innocents, Basil of Seleucia (Silifke), a Byzantine bishop living in the fifth century, operates in quite a similar manner to Aretino some 1100 years later.[18] Basil exploits both the emotional and the pictorial potential of the episode. He imagines himself to be a personal witness to the scene, and thus heightens the effect of his report. Concentrating moreover not on the children, but on the mothers and soldiers, he is able to represent the scene as a highly dramatic battle between desperate women and cruel men. But what interests us most is the fact that Basil uses a particular rhetorical technique very similar to the one to be found in Aretino's *Humanità*. In order to make the audience relive the despair of the mothers, he gives, in three different passages of his sermon, a particularly detailed account of the way the mothers react to the slaughtering of their babies. This produces a very rich and varied image of the scene, which closely resembles the enumerative syntax we have detected in Aretino's version of the Massacre.

In his discussion of this sermon, Henry Maguire has demonstrated that this particular technique, a recurrent feature of Byzantine oratory, springs from the *ekphrasis* figure recommended by antique authorities to be used in descriptions of war.[19] In Basil's sermon, this origin is indeed clearly in evidence. Not only is the scene represented as a battle between mothers and soldiers, there is also much attention paid to the figure of Herod, who is represented as a warlord: when urging his men to kill the infants, he delivers an address that is clearly inspired by classical examples of speeches famous commanders were thought to have given to their troops when entering the battlefield. Basil's sermon thus might be seen as a compound text that adopts the antique rhetoric of war in the context of an emotionally oriented early Christian oratory. But what is the relationship between this sermon and Aretino's *Humanità*?

There certainly is no direct intertextual connection between the two. Although similar in rhetorical structure, there are no precise analogies. Aretino does not present the scene of the Massacre as a battle, and instead of concentrating principally on the mothers, he gives ample attention to the children being slaughtered. Some of the actions described by Basil

---

[18]   Basilius Seleuciae, 'De infantibus ab Herode occisis', in *Patrologiae cursus completus. Series graeca prior*, ed. by J.P. Migne (Paris: Excudebat Migne, 1864), vol. 85, columns 387–400.

[19]   Henry Maguire, *Art and Eloquence in Byzantium* (Princeton, NJ: Princeton University Press, 1981), pp. 22–34, 118–21.

might nevertheless have served in a rudimentary manner as a model for Aretino, but the details given in the *Humanità* are much more elaborate and indeed more disturbing. Basil, for instance, includes in his account the well-known motif of the babies' blood being mixed with the milk of the mothers. But he presents it as part of Herod's speech rather than as an actual event, thus tempering its distressing effect. Aretino, on the other hand, exploits this detail much more effectively, transforming it into a highly dramatic scene of pitiful maternal love: 'Some of them showed great compassion in feeding the dying with their milk, mixed with blood from the wounds that they had received in defending them.'[20]

The similarities on a technical level are, on the other hand, striking. Aretino makes extensive use of the technique of *ekphrasis*, pushing it to new and unexpected heights. But he also adopts other, less conspicuous techniques already introduced in the Greek prototype. He presents, for instance, the Massacre initially in the form of a vision, suggested by a repeated use of 'Ecco', and gradually lapses into plain narrative with an alternation of direct, reported and impersonal speech, in exactly the way the Byzantine bishop did before him. There is nevertheless no cause to consider this a direct derivation, since Aretino's vision is made up of an *ekphrasis* centred on the murdering of the infants, whereas Basil's vision is dedicated to an *ekphrasis* on the mothers' despair.

On the basis of this evidence, we can conclude that Aretino did not model his description of the Massacre of the Innocents on Basil's sermon as such but that he must have been aware of the tradition to which it gave rise. Maguire in fact has demonstrated that this particular sermon was highly influential. It not only set the standard for all later Byzantine writers on this specific subject, it also caused a gradual but drastic alteration of the iconography of the Massacre in Byzantine art. As late as the twelfth and thirteenth centuries, the sermon was still in use in Greek liturgy as the reading for the Feast of the Innocents, and other preachers, such as the southern Italian Philagathus, used it extensively when preparing their own sermons for that feast day. Although we have no conclusive evidence concerning the means by which Aretino came into contact with the tradition of Byzantine oratory, and particularly with Basil's homilies, the evident correspondence between his *Humanità di Cristo* and Basil's sermon on the Innocents suggests that Aretino turned for inspiration to certain models from antique culture when he embarked upon his project to invent a new kind of religious prose.

---

[20]   'Gran pietade dimostravano alcune nel dare i morenti il latte mescolato co'l sangue uscito dalle ferite, che loro erano date difendendogli': Aretino, *Dell'Humanità del figliuolo di Dio libri tre*, p. 90.

This was actually a standard procedure during this period of religious turmoil, not only for Aretino but for all intellectuals who were interested in finding new ways of thinking about devotion that were able to mediate between the extremes of orthodoxy and Protestantism. From the Quattrocento humanists to Erasmus himself, one of the most successful expedients of mediation had been the reappraisal of the early Church fathers, including Byzantine authorities like Saint Basil (the other Basil, not of Silifke but of Caesarea). In 1532, Erasmus had published a modern edition of Basil's homilies and of his work on education, which rapidly became an important source of inspiration for reformist intellectuals, as the well-known portrait of Melanchthon reading Basil's treatise by Lucas Cranach the Younger illustrates (Figure 6.7).

In digging up and reapplying stylistic techniques that were highly reminiscent of ancient oratory, Aretino had a clear goal in mind, that of rendering the Gospels accessible to a large audience. Perhaps simply as a result of the strong literary intuition which is one of the most striking features of his personality, in order to attain this goal he used exactly those techniques that theorists both before and after him deemed appropriate: the introduction of an emphatic kind of realism by which to move the audience to emotion. In the context of his personal aesthetic and literary environment, this was certainly a bold choice. The hyperbolic style and imagery of works like the *Humanità* were unprecedented in Italian literature. Aretino introduced a literary model that conspicuously deviated from the models offered by contemporary literature in the *volgare*. Although departing from the same premises, that is, the desire to popularize Scripture, he did not follow the example of writers such as Folengo or preachers such as Ochino in matters of style. The particular style adopted in his religious narratives must therefore be considered the result of a conscious and deliberate choice, based on an innate understanding of Byzantine rhetorical traditions.

This argument serves to shed a new light on the problem we confronted earlier. In order to communicate in a simple way, Aretino deliberately adopted a highly ornamental and complex style. This was not a mistake. The awareness that his stylistic and aesthetic experiment was a conscious and deliberate one makes it easier to account for the inherent paradox. The key to the problem is the (mis)interpretation of the concept of 'communicating in a simple manner'. This does not necessarily imply an art that communicates by way of simple modes of expression; it indicates an art that communicates to the 'simple', regardless of the means of expression. The key factor is not the means but the goal: to reach the uneducated, via whatever kind of expression is required. Aretino chose not to write in a simple way, but to experiment with a complex and difficult style, abundant with rich vocabulary and extreme rhetorical ornamentation.

Fig. 6.7   Lucas Cranach the Younger, *Philip Melanchthon*, 1559, Frankfurt a.M., Städelsches Kunstinstitut.

This particular stylistics he apparently considered capable of captivating and involving the audience he had in mind. In his opinion, the uneducated, humble people to whom the Gospel had to be communicated would be attracted by a highly rhetorical language and by exaggerated narrative, not by simple stories and plain vocabulary.

Conclusion

The case of Titian and Aretino illustrates that in early modern Italian culture the representation of suffering is one of the most cherished instances of experimentation, both for painters and for poets. It offers them the opportunity to investigate the emotional potential of their trades, particularly when it comes to applying various degrees of realism to the portrayal of human pain and agony. These experiments are grounded in and stimulated by three different motivations and contexts that moreover are active in successive chronological phases. In late Cinquecento and Seicento art and poetry, these experiments with realism are fostered by a Counter-Reformation ideology interested in creating piety and devotion. Prior to this, however, experimentation is encouraged and legitimized on the basis of antique models: on the one hand, texts like Aristotle's *Poetics* and Basil's homilies; on the other, artefacts like the Laocoön, that seem to call for both a more audience-oriented, realistic imitation, and competition with antiquity. This development coincides with and is favoured by a new sense of excellence and of self-promotion fostered by the increasingly competitive organization of art and poetry. The experimental drive fostered by both Aretino and Titian in the 1520s and 1530s is one of the finest and earliest examples of such a complex disposition (one that I would not hesitate to call typical of modernity). It also demonstrates that the initial impetus to innovate does not necessarily originate from ideologically inspired regulations or even sensibilities, religious or otherwise, or from models or prototypes that invite imitation. The case of these two artists suggests that they were inspired by a fundamentally personal motivation to gain excellence and admiration, driven by ambition and competition, while integrating into their formal experiments both the incentives they perceived in antique models and sensibilities deriving from contemporary debates on religious reform.

CHAPTER 7

Aretino, Titian, and 'La Humanità di Cristo'

Raymond B. Waddington

In October 1549, Pietro Aretino wrote two urgent letters, very probably on the same day. One, addressed to Giovan Giacomo Passeri, general of the Order of Friars Minor Conventual, protests against the imprisonment of Fra Curado, of San Nicolò della Lattuga on the Campo dei Frari, who is suspected, it emerges, of being a Lutheran.[1] Aretino assures the general that this 'modest priest and most humble man' is the innocent victim of envy and calumny.[2] Fra Curado, he testifies, has been his confessor for sixteen years, a relationship giving him complete knowledge of the man's character. Presenting himself as a religious moderate, Aretino makes an emotional appeal for the release of 'my spiritual father, my Catholic father, my religious father'.[3]

The second letter warns Titian that 'our Confessor is in prison', explains the charges against him, and offers a plan of action: as soon as the papal legate returns, Titian should seek his intercession.[4] The letter is curious in several ways. There is an avoidance of proper names; other than 'Vecellio' and 'Reverendo Curado' (which, since *curado* or *curato* simply means a parish priest, is hardly distinctive), Passeri is referred to as 'sua Signoria Reverendissima' and Giovanni Della Casa as 'il Legato'. Written in a style of strained jocularity with much word-play, at one point it dismisses what has gone before as idle chit-chat ('ciancie'), almost as if encoded against possible interception. None the less, the two complaints against Curado are clearly stated and explained away. First, trying to create the impression of being a very learned man, by chance he thoughtlessly stated

---

[2] 'Sacerdote modesto e uomo umilissimo'.

[3] 'Il mio padre spirituale, il mio padre catolico, il mio padre religioso.' Presumably, Curado is the 'Spirital Padre' who inspires Aretino's 1545 sonnet on confession. See *Lettere*, III, no. 307 (to Girolama Beltrama). On a possible portrait of Curado, see Jaynie Anderson, 'Titian's *Franciscan Friar* in Melbourne: A Portrait of the Confessor to Titian and Aretino?', in *Titian: Materiality, Likeness, Istoria*, ed. by Joanna Woods-Marsden (Turnhout: Brepols, 2007), pp. 71–81.

[4] 'Il Confessor nostro è in prigione.'

that confession is not '*de iure divino*'.[5] Secondly, instead of confirming the vows of a young woman to enter the convent, he urged her to get married. If one allows that the priest has erred without erring ('ho non errando errato'), in the first offence he has imitated 'il predicator de la Carità'; with the second, recognizing that the girl was more devoted to the flesh than the spirit, he has advised her according to Luther's rule and not Chieti's law – that is, the stern conservatism of Aretino's enemy Gianpietro Carafa, Bishop of Chieti and future Pope Paul IV. Perhaps significantly, as early as 1532, Carafa had traced a major source of Venetian heresy to the Conventual Franciscans, denouncing them as 'that cursed nest of conventual friars minor'.[6]

With his defence, Aretino rather daringly grasps the nettle of the Lutheran charge. The reformer had issued his declaration 'On Monastic Vows' in 1521; four years later, he married Catherine von Bora, a former nun, in defiance of the vows of chastity both had made, and fathered six children. Fra Curado, Aretino implies, simply acted as any good confessor would; perceiving that the girl's commitment to the spiritual life was superficial, he advised her appropriately and thus 'erred without erring', an apparent mistake only in the eyes of rule-bound reactionaries. None the less, anyone who had read the account of orgies in the convent, which opens the *Ragionamento de la Nanna e de la Antonia* (1534), would realize that Aretino's scepticism about the efficacy of vows of chastity was fully as deep as Luther's.

Equally, the dismissal of confession – presumably auricular confession in private – would have set off alarm bells for heresy. Hostility towards

---

[5]   For the origins of this controversy, see Henry Charles Lea, *A History of Auricular Confession and Indulgences in the Latin Church*, 3 vols (Philadelphia, PA: Lea, 1896), I, pp. 168–71. Thomas Tentler, *Sin and Confession on the Eve of the Reformation* (Princeton, NJ: Princeton University Press, 1977), pp. 57–133, discusses the practice of auricular confession; and briefly, pp. 349–63, reformation attacks. For the sixteenth century, see Silvana Seidel Menchi, *Erasmo in Italia, 1520–1580*, 2nd edn (Turin: Bollati Boring Ghieri, 1990), pp. 168–75; W. David Myers, 'Humanism and Confession in Northern Europe in the Age of Clement VII', in *The Pontificate of Clement VII: History, Politics, Culture*, ed. by Kenneth Gouwens and Sheryl F. Reiss (Aldershot: Ashgate, 2005), pp. 363–83; and Wietse de Boer, *The Conquest of the Soul: Confession, Discipline, and Public Order in Counter-Reformation Milan* (Leiden: Brill, 2001).

[6]   Cited in John Martin, *Venice's Hidden Enemies: Italian Heretics in a Renaissance City* (Berkeley and Los Angeles: University of California Press, 1993), p. 39; see also Stephen D. Bowd, *Reform before the Reformation: Vincenzo Querini and the Religious Renaissance in Italy* (Leiden: Brill, 2002), pp. 222–3. On the recent schism between Observant and Conventual Franciscans, see for example Rona Goffen, *Piety and Patronage in Renaissance Venice: Bellini, Titian, and the Franciscans* (New Haven, CT: Yale University Press, 1986), pp. 79–82.

auricular confession was particularly strong among Venetian artisans.[7] Although Luther had conceded that secret confession was useful, Protestants generally followed Calvin's belief that it was not only lacking in biblical authority but, with its pretence of giving absolution, a diminution of baptism. In its rebuttal, the Council of Trent affirmed that Jesus instituted the sacrament of Penance with the words, 'Receive ye the Holy Ghost: whosoever sins you shall forgive, they are forgiven them' (John 20:22–3). Aretino's claim that his unfortunate confessor has only imitated Jesus, the preacher of *carita*s, implicitly calls attention to the Saviour's practice of forgiving sins without confession (for example, Matt. 9:2–6; Mark 2:5–10; Luke 5:20–24; 8:47–8). Fra Curado has erred without erring, offended against the institutional regulations but spoken with a more accurate perception of Christ's example.

Aretino's tactic of lobbying both by himself petitioning the general of the order and by arranging for the intercession of an important person was not new. Only a month earlier, he had written an appeal on behalf of another priest, Bonaventura of Aste, and urged a patron, Raimondo di Cardona, to do the same.[8] In the case of Fra Curado, his instructing Titian to approach the papal nuncio for support acknowledges the artist's closer relationship. When Della Casa assumed his post in 1544, Aretino had written him letters full of courtesies and compliments, praised him to others, and been rewarded with a gift; earlier in this year, he had acknowledged Della Casa's assistance in the matter of his daughter Adria's marriage and rewarded the legate with a laudatory sonnet. Yet Della Casa commissioned paintings from Titian, and seems to have developed a friendship with the artist.[9] We do not know whether Aretino's plan succeeded; the confessor's name does not appear in the *Lettere* again. The absence may indicate a satisfactory outcome – or not; however well disposed toward Titian, the constraints of his office may not have allowed Della Casa to grant the request.

---

[7]   See Richard Mackenney, *Tradesmen and Traders: The World of the Guilds in Venice and Europe, c. 1250–1650* (London: Croom Helm, 1987), p. 179.

[8]   See *Lettere* V, nos. 317 (to Cardona), 325 (Passeri), 326 (Giovan Domenico Molcetto); for Cardona's reply, see *Lettere scritte a Pietro Aretino*, II, no. 299.

[9]   See *Lettere*, III, nos. 8 and 116 (to Della Casa); for the gift, 189 (to Cosimo Pallavicino); for his role in the marriage arrangements, see V, no. 202 (to Cosimo de' Medici) and the sonnet, no. 209 (to the Legate). For Della Casa's connections with Titian, see the summary in Una Roman D'Elia, *The Poetics of Titian's Religious Paintings* (Cambridge: Cambridge University Press, 2005), p. 171. J.A. Crowe and G.B. Cavalcaselle, *Titian: His Life and Times*, 2 vols (London: Murray, 1877), II, pp. 216–17, mistakenly assume that the plan was to appeal to Della Casa's successor, Lodovico Beccadelli. Della Casa, however, was not recalled until after the pope's death in November; and his replacement arrived the following year. Aretino's scheme for Titian to act on the legate's return may refer to a journey or even simply Della Casa's residence on Murano, rather than in Venice.

In January 1543, the preceding nuncio, Fabio Mignanelli, had urged the Senate to stop the circulation of Ochino's *Prediche* and Celio Secondo Curione's *Pasquino in estasi*. Within the next month, he was able to notify Rome that two men had been imprisoned for selling *Pasquino in estasi*. Curione's dialogue delivers a stinging attack on auricular confession, denying that it has scriptural authority and scorning the Pope's declaration that the practice is *de jure divino*.[10] The current Inquisitor, Fra Marino da Venezia, was himself a Conventual Franciscan, another possible complication; moreover, Della Casa had been urging confessors to elicit denunciations of heretics.[11] This apparent violation of the Seal of Confession (or, at least, the slippery distinction between confession proper and confidential revelation) also may have been at issue in Fra Curado's attitude toward the sacrament.

Aretino's religious attitudes in the 1530s, it now seems firmly established, were Erasmian and fully consonant with the values of Venetian *spirituali*; the shift from the biblical paraphrases of 1534–38 to the hagiography of 1539–43 has been seen as his conforming to the rising tide of conservative orthodoxy.[12] This inference omits another possibility: Nicodemism. In a recent study, I pointed to the consistency of Aretino's core religious beliefs, his attachment and continued loyalty to such suspect figures as Ochino, Vergerio, Antonio Brucioli and the otherwise forgotten Fra Curado, raising the possibility that he may have been a Nicodemite, remaining faithful to beliefs he formed in the 1530s.[13] I wish here to both refine and complicate that argument, as well as extending it to consider Titian. A question I ignored, for example, is the paradoxical notion of a public Nicodemite, a man whose life was an open book or, more precisely, six books of letters. Even allowing that the time-lag between the dates that letters were written and their publication afforded a degree of self-protection, the epistolaries

[10] See Paul F. Grendler, *The Roman Inquisition and the Venetian Press, 1540–1605* (Princeton, NJ: Princeton University Press, 1977), pp. 77–8.

[11] See Martin, *Venice's Hidden Enemies*, pp. 66–7; for Fra Marino, p. 55, and Anne Jacobson Schutte, 'Un inquisitore al lavoro: Fra Marino da Venezia e l'Inquisizione veneziana', in *I Francescani in Europa tra Riforma e Controriforma*, Atti del XIII Convegno internazionale (Perugia: Università degli Studi di Perugia, 1987), pp. 167–96.

[12] See Christopher Cairns, *Pietro Aretino and the Republic of Venice: Researches on Aretino and his Circle in Venice, 1527–1556* (Florence: Olschki, 1985), p. 124. In a very thorough study, Paolo Procaccoli has reconfirmed this view. See '1542: Pietro Aretino sulla via di Damasco', in *Il Rinascimento italiano di fronte alla riforma: letteratura e arte / Sixteenth-century Italian art and literature and the Reformation*, ed. by Chrysa Damianaki, Paolo Procaccioli and Angelo Romano (Rome: Vecchiarelli, 2005), pp. 129–58.

[13] See R.B. Waddington, 'Pietro Aretino, religious writer', *Renaissance Studies*, 20 (2006), 277–92.

are conscious literary constructs of a persona, and a persona who is sometimes prudent, sometimes not.

Aretino published over 3,200 letters to hundreds of people; the subjects, levels of formality, tone and style present an infinite variety. Any discussion necessarily draws on a selection; it would be disingenuous not to admit that one can find evidence to support an entire range of interpretations. One conservative count arrives at a total of thirty-two correspondents whose religious orthodoxy came into question; these range from a single letter to an extensive correspondence over a period of years or decades.[14] With a few notable exceptions – the 1537 letters to Vittoria Colonna and to Brucioli, the praises of Ochino's preaching, his comments on his own religious writings – the letters do not often discuss religion. Discounting the persons addressed solely for advantage – patrons, intermediaries, those in a position to grant some favour – the choice of addressees, none the less, can be revealing; correspondence with various close friends is especially interesting for our purposes. These include, for example, the *poligrafo* Lodovico Domenichi, probable Erasmian and suspected Nicodemite, who edited Book III of the *Lettere*;[15] Francesco Coccio, translator of Erasmus's *Institutio principis christiani* (1539) for Aretino's printer, Marcolini,[16] and Lodovico Dolce, to whom we shall return.

Aside from the evidence of the correspondence, the shift from biblical paraphrase to hagiography can bear more than one explanation of motive. Aretino was both a good story-teller and judge of market trends; it may be that, after the life of Jesus, Genesis, and stories of Noah, Moses and David, Aretino felt that he had cast his net over enough biblical narratives. Conversely, as the unending popularity of the *Golden Legend* would indicate, the lives of saints were a source of pure romance, page-turning stories of wonderment, miracles, danger and happy endings. This is true of the Virgin Mary and Catherine of Alexandria; if less spectacular, the life of Thomas Aquinas, once mocked as the 'dumb ox,' follows the pattern of the Horatio Alger story, the boy making good against adversity. Venice enjoyed what has been called a 'Cult of the Madonna', which, for prospective sales, would have made the Virgin an attractive subject.[17] Catherine, beyond the

---

[14]   Procaccioli, '1542', pp. 139–40.

[15]   See Enrico Garavelli, *Lodovico Domenichi e i 'Nicodemiana' di Calvino. Storia di un libro perduto e ritrovato* (Rome: Vecchiarelli, 2004), and 'Lodovico Domenichi Nicodemista?', in *Il Rinascimento italiano*, pp. 159–75.

[16]   See Cairns, *Pietro Aretino*, pp. 76–83, and Paolo Procaccioli, 'Note e testi per Francesco Angelo Coccio', *La Cultura*, 27 (1989), 387–417.

[17]   See Goffen, *Piety and Patronage*, pp. 138–54; also, Edward Muir, 'The Virgin on the Street Corner: The Place of the Sacred in Italian Cities', in *Religion and Culture in the Renaissance and Reformation*, ed. by Steven Ozment (Kirksville, MO: Sixteenth Century Journal Publishers, 1989), pp. 25–40.

popular appeal of a princess who suffers martyrdom, is most interesting as a proto-reformist icon, a patron of education and learning who obviously could read the Bible for herself, and who, in the mystical marriage vision, appealed to a Christocentric religious sensibility.[18] This may account for her popularity as a subject in paintings by, for example, Correggio, Titian and Lorenzo Lotto. Vittoria Colonna proposed Catherine as a model for virtuous women to emulate;[19] it may not be simply coincidental that her kinsman, Alfonso d'Avalos, the marchese of Pescara and Vasto, sponsored these works.[20] The lives of St Catherine and St Thomas were commissioned by Avalos to whom they are dedicated, whereas the life of Mary, the first in the sequence, is dedicated to her namesake, Alfonso's wife, Maria of Aragon. It seems likely that Aretino wrote this as a speculation, hoping to arouse interest; if so, the plan certainly succeeded. A writer who lived by the sweat of his ink and was always in need of money did not have the luxury of ignoring a patron's taste and interests; sometimes, however, those interests coincided with the writer's.

Perceptively discussing Aretino's biblical paraphrases as 'a popular counterpart to the learned discussions of Justification by Faith and Works' among the *spirituali*, Christopher Cairns observed, 'Of course the works are unorthodox, but orthodoxy was negotiable up to Ratisbon.'[21] The tendency to accept a paradigm shift with the years 1541–42 perhaps indicates the still-powerful hold of Delio Cantimori's 'Crisis' thesis, despite the extent to which his chronology has been questioned by more recent historians. Silvana Seidel Menchi, commenting on the 1542 reorganization of the Inquisition, asserts, 'Rather than precipitating the decline of the movement, as historians of the previous generation believed, it ushered in the most vibrant phase of the Italian Reformation.' Seidel Menchi defines this phase, 1542–55, as a period of 'spontaneous diffusion', which because of the prominence of artisans, merchants and professionals, she calls the 'people's Reformation'.[22] For La Serenissima herself, another scholar

---

[18]   For useful background, see Katherine J. Lewis, *The Cult of St. Katherine of Alexandria in Late Medieval England* (Woodbridge, Suffolk: Boydell, 2000).

[19]   See Abigail Brundin, 'Vittoria Colonna and the Virgin Mary', *Modern Language Review*, 96 (2001), 79–80.

[20]   See *Lettere*, II, nos. 124, 143, 204, 209, 212, 224, 238, 293, 312, 329, 354, which extensively document Avalos's connection with the three biographies.

[21]   Cairns, *Pietro Aretino*, p. 122.

[22]   Silvana Seidel Menchi, 'Italy', in *The Reformation in National Context*, ed. by Bob Scribner, Roy Porter and Mikuláš Teich (Cambridge: Cambridge University Press, 1994), pp. 181–201 (pp. 189 and 191). See further, Anne Jacobson Schutte, 'Periodization of Sixteenth-Century Italian Religious History: The Post-Cantimori Paradigm Shift', *Journal of Modern History*, 61 (1989), 269–84, especially pp. 269–73. Pointing to the 1542 appointment of three *spirituali* cardinals, Elizabeth G. Gleason insists, 'there was no sudden change of

concludes, 'In Venice the turning point was 1547. Before then, she kept an ambiguous attitude.'[23] Moreover, as John O'Malley once remarked, 'after several decades of research, it is still not altogether clear where heresy begins or where orthodoxy ends.'[24] Nor was it altogether clear to those Italians living through the 1540s. Consider the example of Cardinal Giovanni Morone, bishop of Modena, friend and ally of Contarini at Regensburg and early admirer of the *Beneficio di Cristo*. When Carafa became Paul IV, he ordered Morone's arrest for heresy; the suspect plaintively remarked to his inquisitors that things then were not as they are now. After two years in prison, Morone was released within days of the pope's death and declared innocent by the Holy Office.[25] Pius IV restored Morone to his position and, as papal legate, he presided over the last and most productive session of the Council of Trent.

Or consider the example of Aretino. The Colloquy of Regensburg had collapsed in July 1541; a year later, possibly needing to placate Carafa's faction of hardliners after the elevation of three *spirituali* to cardinal, the pope ordered the reorganization of the Roman Inquisition. Gasparo Contarini died in August 1542, the same month that Ochino and Vermigli both fled to Switzerland, and, coincidentally, the month in which Francesco Marcolini issued Aretino's *Secondo libro de lettere* with, astonishingly, a dedication to Henry VIII. The dedicatory letter praises Henry for bearing 'the stamp of a priestly minister', who 'always fulfil[s] the duties of Christian worship' and 'the laws'. When Henry takes up his pen, he 'disperses the rabble of heretics, and in the generosity of faith reassures the minds of the doubters'.[26] A full decade after Henry's marriage to Anne Boleyn, when this reached Rome it must have seemed tantamount

---

attitude at the papal court toward the *spirituali*, nor did they abruptly fall from favour': *Gasparo Contarini: Venice, Rome, and Reform* (Berkeley and Los Angeles: University of California Press, 1993), p. 300; also Bowd, *Reform before the Reformation*, pp. 219–20. For a thoughtful review article on this and other relevant topics, see William V. Hudon, 'Religion and Society in Early Modern Italy – Old Questions, New Insights', *American Historical Review*, 101 (1996), 783–804.

[23]   See Antonio Santosuosso, 'Religious Orthodoxy, Dissent and Suppression in Venice in the 1540s', *Church History*, 42 (1973), 476–85; quotation, p. 476. For an analysis by occupation of accused heretics, 1547–86, see Martin's valuable appendix in *Venice's Hidden Enemies*, pp. 235–47.

[24]   O'Malley, 'Catholic Reform', in *Reformation Europe: A Guide to Research*, ed. by Steven Ozment (St Louis, MO: Center for Reformation Research, 1982), p. 305.

[25]   See Massimo Firpo and Dario Marcatto (eds), *Il processo inquisitoriale del cardinal Giovanni Morone*, 5 vols (Rome: Istituto Storico Italiano per l'Eta Moderna e Contemporanea, 1981–89), and Firpo, *Inquisizione romana e Controriforma: Studi sul cardinal Giovanni Morone (1509–1580) e il suo processo d'eresia* (Brescia: Morcelliana, 2005).

[26]   Trans. by George Bull, *Aretino: Selected Letters* (Harmondsworth: Penguin, 1976), pp. 163, 164.

to placing Antichrist on the pope's throne. What could Aretino have been thinking? Despite the political acuteness with which everyone credits him, he certainly displays no anxiety about religious conformity. Whether foolhardy or merely insouciant, the gesture suggests that he, like others in the Venetian community, did not perceive Regensburg and the loss of Contarini as a death knell for the *spirituali*.

Indeed, the year 1543 saw the publication by a Venetian printer, Bernardino Bindoni, of the *Beneficio di Cristo*, a book that, Vergerio claimed, sold 40,000 copies in Venice alone before the end of the decade.[27] The reconstituted Roman Inquisition at first made little impact in Venice; the thin edge of the wedge appeared in 1544 with Giovanni Della Casa, the newly appointed papal nuncio who had 'the specific charge to serve as the official representative of the Holy Office of the Inquisition in Venetian territory and to obtain the republic's cooperation in the repression of heresy'.[28] Aretino's cordial reception may have been founded on Della Casa's literary inclinations; a poet, he would write an enormously popular guide to good manners, the *Galatea*, and, ironically enough, his poems were banned along with Aretino's works in the 1559 Pauline Index. If so, although he continued to praise the nuncio, Aretino was to be disappointed in both large and small ways. In January 1545, Della Casa received permission to bring the Bishop of Capodistria, Aretino's friend Vergerio, to trial; this sorry business dragged on until 1549 when Vergerio, deposed of his office and now converted to Protestantism, fled north.[29] In January 1546, Aretino wrote to the ex-friar Francesco Strozzi, praising his mastery of Greek in translating Xenophon (*Lettere* III, no. 627). Three months later, Della Casa was instructed to arrest and extradite Strozzi for being the author of a Protestant book; Venetian authorities permitted the arrest but blocked the extradition and Strozzi eventually was released.[30]

Della Casa was thwarted in this instance; however, his success rate improved when, responding to changing political conditions, in 1547 the government created a body of three laymen, senators – the 'Tre Savii sopra eresia '– to act in conjunction with the Holy Office. The increase in numbers of heresy trials is striking: from 1544–46, seven trials; in 1547,

[27]   Grendler, *The Roman Inquisition*, p. 82, n. 58, suggests 10,000 as a more reasonable (but still impressive) figure.

[28]   Martin, *Venice's Hidden Enemies*, p. 53.

[29]   The most comprehensive account is that by Anne Jacobson Schutte, *Pier Paolo Vergerio: The Making of an Italian Reformer* (Geneva: Droz, 1977).

[30]   For this episode, see Antonio Santosuosso, 'The Moderate Inquisitor: Giovanni della Casa's Venetian Nunciature, 1544–1549', *Studi veneziani*, n.s. 2 (1978), 159–64.

twenty-five; 1548, fifty-one; 1549, forty-one trials.[31] In 1548, Della Casa commenced to stage public burnings of confiscated books in the Piazza San Marco; in 1549, an index of books prohibited in Venice was issued.[32] In July 1548, Antonio Brucioli had his first encounter with the Inquisition when the authorities seized three bales of contraband books that he owned; the books were burned in public, Brucioli was fined fifty ducats and exiled from the city for two years. Like Vergerio, Brucioli was Aretino's *compare*, a long-time, close friend, who wrote Titian into one of his dialogues. His vernacular Bible and Protestant-based scriptural commentaries had enabled Aretino's own biblical paraphrases; Aretino had vehemently protested 'la calunnia di Lutherano' when it was first directed against Brucioli's works (*Lettere* I, no. 220, to Brucioli, 7 November 1537). Yet that ancient charge proved to have teeth when Brucioli was again tried in 1555, this time for heretical writings; in 1558, he was imprisoned for three years before the sentence was commuted to house arrest.[33]

Aretino was no fool. Della Casa's harassment of Brucioli, the exhausting trial against Vergerio, and the arrest of his confessor must have given him a sharp sense of the changing times. Indeed, his 1545 letter to Paolo Giovio, complaining that three cardinals have recommended burning his religious writings and defending the value of those works, indicates his awareness of his own vulnerability.[34] The letter none the less stoutly maintains his claim to be a religious moderate, rejecting the extremism of Luther and Carafa at their opposite poles. Alessandro Caravia, the jeweller and amateur poet, has attracted considerable scholarly attention for his poems *Il sogno di Caravia* (1541) and *La verra antiga de castellani, canaruoli e gnatti, con la morte di Giurco e Gnagni* ('The ancient war of the Castellani, Canaregioti, and Nicolotti, with the deaths of Giurco and Gnagni') printed in 1550. Whereas the *Sogno*, which attacks the confraternities for their lack of

---

[31]   See Santosuosso, 'Religious Orthodoxy', p. 481. The archival records, he notes, are less than complete.

[32]   See Grendler, *The Roman Inquisition*, pp. 85–9. Epitomizing the still transitional state of orthodoxy with a fine irony, the *Catalogo* was printed 'in the Erasmus workshop of Vincenzo Valgrisi' [alla bottega d'Erasmo di Vincenzo Valgrisi] (see title-page illustration, p. 88). In 1559, the year of Paul IV's Index, Valgrisi found it prudent to drop that designation (see p. 122).

[33]   See Andrea del Col, 'Il controllo della stampa a Venezia e i processi di Antonio Brucioli (1548–1559),' *Critica storica*, 17 (1980), 457–510; Appendix 6 gives an enumeration of Brucioli's 'errors'. For a recent review of vernacular Bible publication and Brucioli's case, see Michael Douglas-Scott, 'Prohibition of Text and license of Images: Painters and the vernacular Bible in Counter-Reformation Venice', in *Il Rinascimento italiano*, pp. 234–8.

[34]   On this letter (*Lettere*, III, no. 152, February 1545), see Cairns, *Pietro Aretino*, pp. 112–16; Procaccioli, '1542', pp. 130–31, 142–4. Concern may have been aroused at the Curia by a spike in the popularity of Aretino's religious writings. For the number of editions printed in 1545, see Procaccioli, ibid., Tables I and II.

true charity, calls for a return to the pure Gospel and to the humility of Christ, has been described as popular evangelism, the last part of *La verra antiga*, modelled on the Erasmian colloquy *Funus* has a noticeably Protestant spokesman. This work caused Caravia to be questioned by the Holy Office in 1557–59.[35] *La verra antiga* is dedicated to Aretino, 'patron honorandissimo', whose letter of acknowledgement shows no obvious sign of discomfort at this connection.[36]

Aretino would continue to encourage and, where possible, aid his threatened friends, all the while printing the record in successive volumes of letters.[37] His repeated affirmations that he is middle-of-the-road in his religion may well have been, not just a rhetorical ploy, but sincere belief. After all, at the simplest level, what is heresy other than an opinion different from one's own? To invoke an English heretic writing a century later, John Milton asserted:

> He then who to his best apprehension follows the scripture, though against any point of doctrine by the whole church received, is not the heretic; but he who follows the church against his conscience and perswasion grounded on scripture.[38]

Brucioli and Vergerio certainly would have applauded, quite possibly Aretino as well. Retrospectively, Aretino's strenuous campaign for a cardinalate following the election of his compatriot, Julius III, has seemed the height of folly to many scholars.[39] It may appear less so when one

---

[35] See Martin, *Venice's Hidden Enemies*, pp. 156–8; Seidel Menchi, *Erasmo in Italia*, pp. 223–5, identifies the source in Erasmus; Massimo Firpo, *Artisti, gioiellieri, eretici: il mondo di Lorenzo Lotto tra Riforma e Controriforma* (Rome: Laterza, 2001), pp. 180–212, discusses the Aretino connection and provides full bibliography. The *Sogno* helped to form the beliefs of Domenico Scandella, who was burned at the stake for heresy in 1599. See Carlo Ginzburg, *The Cheese and the Worms: The Cosmos of a Sixteenth-Century Miller*, trans. by John and Anne Tedeschi (1980; repr. New York: Dorset Press, 1989), pp. 22–7.

[36] Augusto Gentili describes the letter as 'alquanto fredda, dal tono acido e scostante' and suggests that Aretino tries to distance himself from Caravia's heretical work. If so, simply omitting the letter (V, no. 468) from the volume would have been a more effective tactic. See Gentili, 'Tiziano e Aretino tra politica e religione', in *Pietro Aretino nel Cinquecentenario della nascita*, 2 vols (Rome: Salerno, 1995), I, 292–6; quotation, p. 293.

[37] For another petition to Della Casa, see *Lettere* V, no. 100 (to Francesco Coccio, July 1546).

[38] *A Treatise of Civil Power* (1659), quoted from *Complete Prose Works of John Milton*, gen. ed. Don M. Wolfe, 8 vols (New Haven, CT: Yale University Press, 1953–82); VII (1980), ed. by Robert W. Ayers, p. 248.

[39] For a full and judicious account, see Paolo Procaccioli, 'Un cappello per il divino. Note sul miraggio cardinalesco di Pietro Aretino', in *Studi sul Rinascimento italiano/Italian Renaissance Studies. In memoria di Giovanni Aquilecchia*, ed. by Angelo Romano and

reflects that Cardinal Reginald Pole, *de facto* leader of the *spirituali* after Contarini's death and a suspected Nicodemite, came within a single vote of being elected pope in 1549.[40]

In contrast to Aretino, Titian's hundred-and-some surviving letters are largely pragmatic, matters of business and patronage, warming to individuality occasionally with family or friends, notably with Aretino, his *compare* of three decades.[41] They tell us nothing about his religious beliefs, which only can be inferred from contexts and from the visual evidence of his paintings – a process requiring tact, judgement and plausible conjecture, but still fraught with peril. One scholar asserts, 'There is no evidence that Titian had any contact with known heretics after they had declared heretical beliefs', but immediately must acknowledge the glaring exception.[42] Andrea di Ugoni, an author from Brescia, ran afoul of the Inquisition there and moved to Venice, where he rented rooms from Titian; his contact with the artist may have been Vergerio, who referred to Titian as 'compar' and 'mio caro' and with whom Ugoni once lodged. In 1565, Ugoni was questioned by the Venetian Holy Office, to whom he admitted, among other errors, denying Purgatory, believing in justification *sola fide*, and that Christ was the only intercessor. Upon recanting, he was released and again took up residence with Titian. Marion Kuntz, who rescued this incident from the archives, remarks appositely, 'Although Titian did not want prostitutes on the floor below his quarters, he apparently did not mind having there one suspected of various heresies.'[43] More generally, the proposition that lack of contact with 'known heretics' somehow exonerates Titian from suspicion really does not help. Known heretics were either in another country, imprisoned, or dead; moreover, it ignores the entire grey area of Nicodemism and of those persons who came under suspicion without undergoing trial or simply escaped the attention of the Holy Office – for example, Coccio, Dolce, Sebastiano Serlio, Jacopo and

---

Paolo Procaccioli (Rome: Vecchiarelli, 2005), pp. 189–226. Ironically, Giovanni Della Casa's ambitions to become a cardinal were thwarted by the death of Paul III. See Santosuosso, 'The Moderate Inquisitor', 206–9.

[40]   See Dermot Fenlon, *Heresy and Obedience in Tridentine Italy: Cardinal Pole and the Counter Reformation* (Cambridge: Cambridge University Press, 1972), pp. 226–32.

[41]   For a helpful survey, see Giorgio Padoan, 'Titian's Letters', in the exhibition catalogue, *Titian, Prince of Painters*, ed. by Susanna Biadene (Venice: Marsilio, 1990), pp. 43–52. Norbert Wolf states that Titian first met Aretino in February 1523 at the Gonzaga court. See *I, Titian*, trans. Ishbel Flett (Munich: Prestel, 2006), p. 70. On the question of religion, Wolf is cautiously non-committal: 'Just where the artist stood in the battlefield between orthodoxy and hereticism remains a moot point' (p. 104).

[42]   D'Elia, *Poetics*, p. 4.

[43]   See Marion Leathers Kuntz, 'Voices from a Venetian Prison in the Cinquecento: Francesco Spinola and Dionisio Gallo', *Studi veneziani*, 27 (1994), 85–8 (p. 86).

Francesco Sansovino.[44] Instead, it is more productive to turn to Aretino's opinions – as Mina Gregori once sensibly concluded, 'the writings of Aretino are the most important path in attempting to know what Titian thought'[45] – and to the inner circle of their associates.

I wish to focus now on the pivotal figure of Lodovico Dolce, who addressed both Aretino and Titian as *compare*. The busiest of the Venetian *poligrafi* entered Aretino's printed record in the 1534 *Marescalco* (V.iii), where he is praised as a coming man; possibly his initial contact was through a mutual friend, Giulio Camillo (Delminio), creator of the famous memory theatre, of whom Titian did a now-lost portrait.[46] Dolce made himself valuable to Aretino both as a translator and editor of the letters; he was rewarded by becoming a speaker in a dialogue, which favour he returned in a dialogue of his own. Dolce dedicated his 1538 vernacular paraphrase of Juvenal's satires to Titian; the dedication indicates they were sufficiently close that he could tease the artist about his lack of classical languages. Dolce's poem, *Il primo libro di Sacripante* (Francesco Bindoni, 1536), offers praise to both Philipp Melanchthon and Erasmus. Attention has been focused on his role as a source of Erasmian texts and ideas; however, equally interesting is his involvement in the mid-1540s with a suspect group: Caravia's friend, Paolo Crivelli; the printer (and publisher of Aretino's *Lettere* IV and V), Andrea Arrivabene, 'at least a Protestant sympathizer and probably a heretic', who was 'deeply involved in the clandestine trade in prohibited books', and Arrivabene's friend, the heretic doctor Orazio Brunetto whose letters Dolce edited. In 1545, Dolce wrote to Paolo Manuzio, enclosing a poem: 'I am sending you a spiritual sonnet as a sign of my conversion.'[47] He printed eighteen of his *sonetti*

---

[44]   For Serlio and for Francesco Sansovino, see Firpo, *Artisti, gioiellieri, eretici*, pp. 90–94.

[45]   Gregori, 'Tiziano e l'Aretino', in *Tiziano e il manierismo europeo*, ed. by Rodolfo Pallucchini (Florence: Olschki, 1978), pp. 271–306; trans. by Padoan, 'Titian's Letters', p. 45.

[46]   There are two 1532 letters from Camillo to Aretino; Camillo praises the portrait in a treatise of *c*.1537. On this see Luba Freedman, *Titian's Portraits through Aretino's Lens* (University Park: Pennsylvania State University Press, 1995), p. 29. Dolce begins the *Dialogo della pittura* with a reference to Camillo. Dolce's letter to Gasparo Ballini concludes with a teasing greeting to Camillo, a puzzle since Camillo died in 1544 and the letter has been dated 'from 1550 or later'. See Mark W. Roskill, *Dolce's Aretino and Venetian Art Theory of the Cinquecento* (1968; repr. Toronto: University of Toronto Press, 2000), pp. 84–5, 210–11; and, on the letter date, p. 36.

[47]   'Vi mando un sonetto spirituale per segno della mia conversione.' See Ronnie H. Terpening, *Lodovico Dolce: Renaissance Man of Letters* (Toronto: University of Toronto Press, 1997), pp. 20–22; for Arrivabene, see Grendler, *The Roman Inquisition*, pp. 105–22; quotations, pp. 111–12. The Aretino volumes, both 1550, bear Arrivabene's mark 'al segno del Pozzo'; see Procaccioli's textual notes on them. For Paolo Crivelli, see Firpo, *Artisti, gioiellieri, eretici*, pp. 212–26, who comments on Dolce's connection. On Brunetto, see

spirituali in *Rime di diverse illustri signori ... Libro secondo* (Giolito, 1547), a volume containing a number of suspect authors. Other examples of Dolce's editorial choices may further reveal his religious sympathies: the 1554 *Lettere* anthology, which contains explicit comments on justification by faith alone or the two editions, 1552 and 1559, of Colonna's *Rime*.[48] Dolce was called before the Holy Office twice: in 1558, for approving publication of a heretical book; and in 1565, for questioning about books during the trial of his employer, Gabriele Giolito, who was caught up in a widening net of inquiries regarding Francesco Spinola.[49] Dolce was released on both occasions. Ten months after the death of Aretino, Dolce published the *Dialogo della pittura*, subtitled *l'Aretino* (Giolito, 1557); this was a dual tribute, on the one hand, to the artistic and literary judgement of his dead friend while, on the other, to the complete painterly achievement of his living friend, Titian. The claim that Dolce's account of Titian's life and works betrays a lack of intimacy with the artist has been refuted by Charles Hope, who notes that Dolce published five recent Titian letters in 1554 and that two of his own letters, printed in 1555, demonstrate his access to Titian's studio.[50] Dolce has been credited with designing Titian's *impresa* of the bear cub being licked into shape and the motto 'NATURA POTENTIOR ARS'.[51] He is buried in the church of San Luca, by some accounts beside Aretino. Given the two-decade record of contacts and friendship, it seems inherently improbable that Titian would not have known or at least guessed Dolce's religious views, nor those circulating amongst their inner circle of friends.

Nor is it likely that Titian was unaware of his fellow artist Lorenzo Lotto's intense religious struggles. The title-page of Brucioli's *Bibbia* (Venice, 1532), has a woodcut frame, Evangelical and Pauline in its emphasis, with seven vignettes ranging from the creation of Eve to the resurrection of Jesus

---

Andrea Del Col, 'Note sull'eterodossia di fra Sisto da Siena e i suoi rapporti con Orazio Brunetto e un gruppo veneziano di "spirituali"', *Collectanea franciscana*, 47 (1977), 27–64. For discussion of his 1548 *Lettere*, see Anne Jacobson Schutte, 'The *Lettere Volgari* and the Crisis of Evangelism in Italy', *Renaissance Quarterly*, 28 (1975), 667–8.

[48]   For some discussion of Dolce's editorial work, see Firpo, *Artisti, gioiellieri, eretici*, pp. 216–17, 223–4; Brian Richardson, *Print Culture in Renaissance Italy: The Editor and the Vernacular Text, 1470–1600* (Cambridge: Cambridge University Press, 1994), pp. 112–22. His letter anthology is analysed by Schutte, 'The *Lettere Volgari*', pp. 639–88.

[49]   For this sorry affair, which concluded with Spinola's execution by drowning, see Kuntz, 'Voices from a Venetian Prison', pp. 79–126.

[50]   See Hope, 'The Early Biographies of Titian', in *Titian 500*, ed. by Joseph Manca, Studies in the History of Art, 45 (Washington, DC: National Gallery of Art, 1993), pp. 174–5.

[51]   See Freedman, *Titian's Portraits*, p. 89 and n. 93. The device appears in Dolce's *Imprese di diversi prencipi, duchi, signori* (1562); see Harold E. Wethey, *The Paintings of Titian: Complete Edition*, 3 vols (London: Phaidon, 1969–75), III (1975), p. 249, and pl. 240.

and two larger panels, Moses receiving the Law and St Paul preaching. The designs for the woodcuts have been attributed reasonably securely to Lotto; the panel of the nativity, for example, pairs interestingly with Lotto's Nativity painting in Siena, both set at night, almost as if he conceived them through a Nicodemist vision.[52] In October 1540, Lotto painted small portraits, presumably copied from woodcuts, of Martin Luther and his wife for a young relative, Mario d'Armano, who later was denounced to the Inquisition.[53] He was a close friend of Bartolomeo Carpan, the Nicodemite jeweller, who was implicated in 1547 and arrested in 1568.[54] A reader who owned the *Imitation of Christ* and vernacular commentaries on the Psalms, Lotto, none the less, made his peace within the Church, specifying in his last will that he be buried in a Dominican habit. Titian had known Lotto at least since 1531, when they both were appointed to a committee by the painters' guild. In April 1548, Aretino wrote to Lotto, conveying greetings from Titian, then in Augsburg, who expressed the wish that Lotto, with his unerring eye, were able to judge and approve his current work for the emperor. Aretino elaborates on Titian's message, stating that, because he is completely lacking in envy, Lotto delights in seeing artistic qualities that he does not have in his own brush, although it performs miracles beyond many who think they have technical skill. In his conclusion, Aretino asserts that to be surpassed as a painter ('nel mestiero del dipingere') is nothing compared to his superiority in religious devotion ('l'offizio de la religione'), for which Lotto will be recompensed with heavenly glory exceeding all earthly praise (*Lettere* IV, no. 500). The letter has excited a full spectrum of response from art historians, who have found it, on the one hand, scornful, sarcastic, or condescending, while on the other, judicious or even flattering. Condescending it may be; however, for Aretino, who held that only Raphael, Titian, and in a more restricted way Michelangelo were absolute masters, second rank was not bad, the same level he assigned, say, to his friend Sebastiano del Piombo.[55] In particular, the assumption that praising Lotto more highly for his religiosity than for his professional achievement is a put-down strikes me

---

[52]   On the *Bibbia* and the title-page, see Firpo, *Artisti, gioiellieri, eretici*, pp. 100–16. 'Evangelical' and 'Pauline' are Peter Humfrey's assessment; see *Lorenzo Lotto* (New Haven, CT: Yale University Press, 1997), p. 114.

[53]   See Firpo, *Artisti, gioiellieri, eretici*, pp. 37–46; Martin, *Venice's Hidden Enemies*, p. 132, describes Armano as a Nicodemite. Humfrey, *Lorenzo Lotto*, p. 177, translates Lotto's record: '17 October, two little pictures with portraits of Martin Luther and his wife, which Mario gave to Tristan with gilt frames, a bargain at 6 ducats'.

[54]   See Firpo, *Artisti, gioiellieri, eretici*, pp. 148–52 and passim.

[55]   In Dolce's dialogue, when Fabrini criticizes Lotto's use of colour, 'Aretino' does not reply directly, but in effect explains that many painters are worse offenders. See Dolce's *Aretino*, pp. 154, 155.

as anachronistic tunnel vision. I do not doubt that Titian and Aretino both believed heavenly glory was more important than worldly, regardless of the high valuation they placed on the latter.

As archival scholarship continues to add to the roll-call of confirmed or suspected Nicodemites, it is only fair to acknowledge that they remain a small minority of Venetians during the 1540s and 1550s, but with the further caveat that no one knows how many escaped notice entirely. The ready acceptance of dissimulation in matters of religious conformity was greatly facilitated by the assumption that one's identity consists of an exterior, public or social, persona and an interior being, probably called a soul. The consequence was often 'the experience of a divided self, of a person who was frequently forced to wear a façade in public that disguised his or her convictions, beliefs, or feelings'. The prudential course of concealing one's interior identity was itself complicated by the fluidity or mutability of the interior self, which could cause individual belief to constantly evolve to more radical positions or, conversely, to vacillate between heresy and orthodoxy.[56] Moreover, the fluidity of the boundary between the two further complicated the question of where one's allegiance lay during the 1540s and early 1550s. Only with the election of Paul IV and the charges against the living – Morone, Pole and Pietro Carnesecchi (with whom both Aretino and Dolce had corresponded) – as well as the dead – Marcantonio Flaminio, Vittoria Colonna – was the dividing line unmistakably drawn.[57] Calvin's condemnation of Nicodemism was quite wrong.[58] It may have taken more courage, and certainly optimism, for such people to stay in the Church than to declare their beliefs as apostates.

---

[56]   I summarize the argument of John Martin, 'Spiritual Journeys and the Fashioning of Religious Identity in Renaissance Venice', *Renaissance Studies*, 10 (1996), 358–70; revised as Chapter 3 of his *Myths of Renaissance Individualism* (New York: Palgrave Macmillan, 2004) (quotation, p. 48). I make a similar distinction between interior identity and social presentation in *Aretino's Satyr: Sexuality, Satire, and Self-Projection in Sixteenth-Century Literature and Art* (Toronto: University of Toronto Press, 2004), pp. xvii–xviii. Martin's emphasis on the changeability and vulnerability of the interior identity is well taken, as the phenomenon of demonic possession dramatically witnesses.

[57]   See Fenlon, *Heresy and Obedience*, pp. 269–81; for the attention to Colonna, see p. 279, n. 2. For Carnesecchi, see Massimo Firpo and Dario Marcatto, *I processi inquisitoriali di Pietro Carnesecchi (1557–1567). Edizione critica*, 2 vols (Vatican City: Archivio Segreto Vaticano, 1998–2000). Aretino sent Carnesecchi a copy of a poem praising the queen of France (*Lettere*, VI, no. 27, March 1551); he also stated that Carnesecchi had read one of his religious books in his official capacity (V, no. 455). Dolce's correspondence with Carnesecchi is mentioned by Terpening, *Lodovico Dolce*, p. 189, n. 56.

[58]   For Calvin's pronouncements on Nicodemism, which he roundly condemned as an unacceptable compromise, see Martin, *Venice's Hidden Enemies*, pp. 126–7. The term was introduced in Protestant writings as early as 1521.

Artists, however, had a means of wordlessly revealing a commitment to heterodox belief that was not available to their language-bound fellows. Michelangelo's Florence *Pietà* presents the dominant living figure of a hooded man towering over the two Marys; that figure was identified by Vasari and Condivi as Nicodemus. Vasari also informs us that the group was intended for the artist's own tomb and that the face of Nicodemus is his self-portrait. The design of the sculptural group has a clear relationship to the *Pietà* drawing that Michelangelo gave to Vittoria Colonna, suggestively since he apparently began the work in the year of her death. The sculpture thus seems to pay tribute to the spiritual beliefs that animated their intimate friendship.[59] Far less attention has been given to Titian's parallel representation of himself as Nicodemus in the 1559 painting of the Entombment (Madrid). It is accepted that the figure at the head of Christ's body is a self-portrait of the artist; the biblical prototype, whether Joseph of Arimathea or Nicodemus, is a matter of dispute.[60] Joseph usually is described as the figure at the head of the body with Nicodemus at the feet; in religious art, however, the positions are more variable.[61] Here, as Augusto Gentili has noted, Titian appears to have followed the guidance of Aretino, whose *Humanità di Christo* specifically places Joseph at the feet and Nicodemus at the head of Christ's body.[62] In this he duplicates the design of Michelangelo's *Pietà*; one might say that the rival artists in both instances represent themselves mourning the demise of their Christocentric faiths, with little hope of a resurrection.[63]

---

[59]   The argument that the self-portrait alludes to the artist's Nicodemism was made in two articles, published virtually simultaneously. See Jane Kristof, 'Michelangelo as Nicodemus: The Florence *Pietà*', *Sixteenth Century Journal*, 20 (1989), 163–82; Valerie Shrimplin-Evangelidis, 'Michelangelo and Nicodemism: The Florentine *Pietà*', *Art Bulletin*, 71 (1989), 58–66. See also John Dillenberger, *Images and Relics: Theological Perceptions and Visual Images in Sixteenth-Century Europe* (New York: Oxford University Press, 1999), pp. 143–8. On the drawing for Colonna, see Kristof, pp. 178–80, and particularly, Alexander Nagel, *Michelangelo and the Reform of Art* (Cambridge: Cambridge University Press, 2000), pp. 163–9, 202–5.

[60]   The catalogue entry by Jesus Urrea in *Titian, Prince of Painters*, no. 70, states, 'Titian himself is portrayed as Joseph of Arimathea.'

[61]   See Kristof, 'Michelangelo as Nicodemus,' pp. 167–71, and Wolfgang Stechow, 'Joseph of Arimathea or Nicodemus?', in *Studien zur Toskanischen Kunst*, ed. by Wolfgang Lotz and Lise Lotte Moller (Munich: Prestel, 1964), pp. 289–302. Since both men were secret disciples of Jesus before his death (John 19:38–9), the meaning remains the same, regardless of the specific identification.

[62]   See Gentili, 'Tiziano e la religione', in *Titian 500*, pp. 148–52.

[63]   Various conjectures have been made concerning Michelangelo's attempt in 1555 to destroy the *Pietà*. One is that, in the year of Paul IV's election, he came to feel that religious beliefs unacceptable to the Church were too candidly revealed. See Kristof, 'Michelangelo as Nicodemus', pp. 181–2; also, Nagel, *Michelangelo and the Reform of Art*, pp. 202–12.

In fascinating symmetry, not only did the two men use their art during the 1550s to confess silently religious views of a previous decade; earlier they had used that art to project those convictions. From 1536–41 – the period in which Colonna had become his spiritual mentor and, through Colonna, Ochino[64] – Michelangelo was engaged with the execution of the *Last Judgment*. The rampant nudity in the crowded scene, which offended Carafa's Theatines, has been explained convincingly as representing the resurrection of the body.[65] Illuminatingly, if more controversially, Leo Steinberg interpreted the fresco as a 'merciful heresy', omitting Purgatory, minimizing Hell, and celebrating the possibility of a near-universal salvation through faith alone.[66]

Two years after the completion of the *Last Judgment*, Titian produced his *Ecce Homo* (Vienna, Kunsthistoriches), a large (nearly 8' x 12'), complex work itself full of puzzles (Figure 7.1). We know from Vasari that it was commissioned by Giovanni d'Anna, son of Martino d'Anna (originally van Haanen, 1475–1553), one of the wealthiest Flemish merchants in the Venetian foreign community. Well connected with the Habsburgs, in 1529, he was ennobled by Ferdinand of Austria; in 1538, he purchased the Palazzo Talenti on the Grand Canal, then celebrated for the façade painted by Pordenone, and in 1545, was granted Venetian citizenship. His two sons, Daniele and Giovanni, were thoroughly assimilated; Giovanni became a patron of Titian, commissioning religious paintings and a portrait.[67]

---

[64]   See Massimo Firpo, 'Vittoria Colonna, Giovanni Morone e gli "spirituali"', *Rivista di storia e letteratura religiosa*, 24 (1988), 211–61; Colonna, *Sonnets for Michelangelo*, ed. and trans. by Abigail Brundin (Chicago, IL: University of Chicago Press, 2005), 'Introduction,' pp. 11–18, 26–33; and Nagel, *Michelangelo and the Reform of Art*, pp. 170–87.

[65]   See Marcia B. Hall, 'Michelangelo's *Last Judgment*: Resurrection of the Body and Predestination', *Art Bulletin*, 58 (1976), pp. 85–92. For the Theatine reaction, see the letter of 19 November 1541, quoted by Bernadine Barnes, *Michelangelo's* Last Judgment: *The Renaissance Response* (Berkeley and Los Angeles: University of California Press, 1998), p. 78.

[66]   See Steinberg's articles, 'Michelangelo's "Last Judgment" as Merciful Heresy', *Art in America*, 63:6 (1975), 49–63; and 'A Corner of the *Last Judgment*', *Daedalus*, 109 (Spring 1980), 207–73.

[67]   Although it was long thought that Martino commissioned the frescoes, Blake De Maria has proven that the artist completed this work before d'Anna bought the house from Lodovico Talenti. See 'The patron for Pordenone's frescos on Palazzo Talenti d'Anna, Venice', *Burlington Magazine* 146 (August 2004), 548–9. The error originates with Giorgio Vasari, *Lives of the Painters, Sculptors and Architects*, trans. by Gaston du C. de Vere, intro. by David Ekserdjian, Everyman's Library, 2 vols (New York: Knopf, 1996), I, 876; for Giovanni and Titian, see II, 782, 797. On the d'Anna family, see further Wethey, *Paintings of Titian*, II, 79; Piero Voltolina, *La storia di Venezia attraverso le medaglie*, 3 vols (Venice: Voltolina, 1998), 1, 393–5, and Philip Attwood in *The Currency of Fame: Portrait Medals of the Renaissance*, ed. by Stephen K. Scher (New York: Abrams, 1994), pp. 151–2.

Fig. 7.1   Titian, *Ecce Homo*, 1543, Vienna, Kunsthistorisches Museum.

In 1544, Leone Leoni, shortly to become Charles V's court medallist, was in Venice and created portrait medals of the male d'Annas – Martino, his two sons, and his grandson, Paolo. The medal of Martino has a reverse with a personification of Hope, looking toward rays of light emanating from Heaven, and the legend SPES MEA IN DEO EST. This is suggestively similar to the formula 'viva fede et speranza' ('living faith and hope') which, as Massimo Firpo remarks, recurs in the *Beneficio di Cristo* and in Valdesian and Flaminian writings.[68] A medal of Giovanni (Figure 7.2), sponsor of the *Ecce Homo*, bears a reverse with a female personification, possibly Prudence, holding a sceptre with an eye (*oculus divini*); the inscription states NVMINA CVNCTA EGO (I am all that is divine). Prudence was a watchword of Nicodemite behaviour.[69] Both mottoes provide some sense of their subjects' religious beliefs. Representations of the *Ecce Homo* type in which Pilate presents Jesus to the crowd for judgement originated and remained almost exclusively a subject in northern art: 'In cinquecento Italy, Titian was likely the only painter who depicted this scene on a monumental scale (or on any scale).' This causes Luba Freedman to conclude that it reflects the taste of the family and that the interpretation of the scene 'may have been requested' by d'Anna.[70] Martin van Haanen migrated to Venice from Brussels, where Erasmus had served as councillor to Prince Charles (later Charles V). It seems reasonable to speculate that he remained well connected in Erasmian territory.

Titian's design for the *Ecce Homo* places the actors on two pictorial planes. Above left, Pilate stands on a landing with his back to the rusticated exterior wall; he gestures toward Jesus, who emerges from a portal with a guard partly visible behind. Below, in contemporary dress is a milling crowd with several identifiable figures in the foreground. Leone's portrait of Giovanni d'Anna supports the supposition that Titian represented his patron in the bearded man talking earnestly to the bulky, bald man in the red robe. Although the latter has been identified as Doge Pietro Lando, this beardless and bareheaded man looks nothing like Lando, nor does he wear the doge's biretta; the suggestion that he is modelled on Dürer's figure of

[68] See Firpo, *Artisti, gioiellieri, eretici*, pp. 179–81; quotation, p. 180.

[69] On prudence, see Martin, *Myths of Renaissance Individualism*, pp. 48–56. Although the date is disputed, Titian's *Allegory of Prudence* (London, National Gallery) may be relevant here. In *Titian, Prince of Painters*, no. 67, Lionello Puppi follows Panofsky's argument for 1565; however, in the recent exhibition catalogue *Titian* (London: National Gallery of Art, 2003), no. 34, Nicholas Penny states 'about 1550–60'.

[70] See Freedman, *Titian's Portraits*, pp. 48–62; quotations, pp. 52, 53. D'Elia, *Poetics*, p. 148, condemns scholars who have argued for the signs of Nicodemism in Titian's work: 'There is no evidence for such a view, and it makes those who praised, collected, and imitated Titian's art during the Counter-Reformation into pathetic dupes.' Apparently the possibility that collectors and patrons might share such views has not occurred to her.

Fig. 7.2   Leone Leoni, medal of Giovanni d'Anna, c.1544–46, London, British Museum, Dept of Coins and Medals.

the high priest Caiaphas may be well taken.[71] The most securely identified of the cameo portraits are those of the two men on horseback at the far right: Sultan Suleyman the Magnificent and Alfonso d'Avalos.

For his part, the Marchese del Vasto's career was entwined with the Ottoman Empire, which the historian Paolo Giovio acknowledged in composing his *Discorso dell' impresa contro al Turco* as a letter to Avalos. He commanded the infantry in the 1535 expedition to capture Tunis, a triumph in publicity if not in substance; and he was appointed governor of Milan in 1538. In December 1539, hoping to forestall the Republic's negotiations for a separate peace treaty with Suleyman, Charles V sent Avalos to Venice as his emissary; and the marchese brought his friend Giovio in his entourage. The Senate was not impressed by Avalos's offer to personally assume a sea command in an effort to defeat the corsair Barbarossa, Suleyman's admiral, and the embassy failed.[72] Avalos and Giovio consoled themselves with visiting Aretino; it is entirely possible that, after the October publication of the Virgin Mary's life, the scheme to commission the biographies of Catherine and Thomas Aquinas was broached at this meeting. Titian's first portrait of Alfonso (Paris, Louvre) may date about 1533, which would be consistent with Aretino's effusive praise in the *Marescalco* (1534); more certain is the *Allocution of Alfonso d'Avalos* (Madrid, Prado), which was commissioned in 1539 and completed in 1541.[73]

During the late 1530s and the early 1540s, Aretino's entire circle were making a dead set at Alfonso d'Avalos. The three biographies are crucial, but there also are Titian's two paintings; Sansovino contributed a small bronze sculpture of St Catherine, while Coccio dedicated his Erasmus

---

[71]   Wethey, *Paintings of Titian*, I, no. 21, says 'in all likelihood Giovanni' of the first figure, and that the second 'can only be' Lando. Flavia Polignano is persuasive on Lando/Caiaphas, but her assertion that the bearded man is Bernardino Ochino, not d'Anna, fails to convince, nor does her identification of the terrified youth with his dog as Judas Iscariot. See Polignano, 'I ritratti dei volti e i registri dei fatti. L' *Ecce Homo* di Tiziano per Giovanni d'Anna', *Venezia Cinquecento: Studi di storia dell'arte e della cultura*, 2:4 (1992), 7–54. For the woodcut portrait on which Polignano bases the Ochino identification, see Bernardino Ochino, I *'Dialogi Setti' e altri scritti del tempo della fuga*, ed. by Ugo Rosso, Collana 'Testi della Riforma', 14 (Turin: Claudiana, 1985), pl. 3 and Rosso's appendix, 'Per un'iconografia Ochiniana', pp. 153–7.

[72]   On this episode, see T.C. Price Zimmermann, *Paolo Giovio: The Historian and the Crisis of Sixteenth-Century Italy* (Princeton, NJ: Princeton University Press, 1995), pp. 168–70; also Aretino's letter to Charles V (*Lettere*, II, no. 144, 25 December 1539). Augusto Gentili also discusses Avalos's role in the painting through Giovio's and Aretino's writings. See 'Tiziano e Aretino tra politica e religione', pp. 276–86.

[73]   See Titian, *Prince of Painters*, 'Supplement to the Catalogue', for dating of these works. The *Allocution* may commemorate an event in the 1532 Hungarian campaign against the Turks and contains a cameo of Aretino. See Freedman, *Titian's Portraits*, pp. 44–5.

translation, *Institutione del principe chistiano* (Education of a Christian Prince), to Alfonso's son. Dolce did his bit, grinding out a tercet praising the marchesa, Maria of Aragon, for her beauty and Vittoria Colonna for her learning; and, perhaps coincidentally, Alfonso became fascinated by Giulio Camillo.[74] Patronage rewards aside, one inference might be that they sought to gain Colonna's attention through Alfonso, to whom she was close; another might be that they thought Alfonso shared something of Vittoria's spiritual convictions. In March 1542, Gasparo Contarini wrote a letter to Avalos, praising the marchese for having 'the true interior reformations which only God can bring about, and not merely the exterior reformations which men can suffer. Blessed be God, and Jesus Christ be thanked without end.'[75] John Martin has argued that Contarini's prudential sense of an interior, spiritual identity that was not to be compromised by his public life paralleled closely the situation of the Nicodemite.[76] Contarini's admiration of the real inner reformation ('vere riformatione interiore') that Avalos has achieved might be understood as a tribute to a like-minded spirit.

The Habsburg inflection of the *Ecce Homo*, foregrounded by the double-headed eagle on the sentinel's shield, is, if anything, hyper-determined: by the mercantile allegiance of the d'Anna family, the patronage commitments of Aretino and Titian, the military duty of Avalos. It is noticeable, therefore, that the two horsemen are not presented as antagonists. Literally above the arm-waving mob in the background, they are posed in an amity figured by the converging muzzles of their horses. Avalos points in a gesture replicating Pilate's, presumably explaining the meaning of the tableau to the sultan who cocks his head attentively. Not only was the Ottoman Empire generally tolerant of other religions and races, Suleyman himself

[74] See *Lettere*, II, no. 233 (to Avalos, 22 December 1540); also Aretino's two sonnets on St Catherine, no. 235 (to Luigi Anichini, 30 December 1540) and no. 236 (to Sansovino, 13 January 1541). For Dolce's tercet – 'One wife alone I would have, but a dear one; as beautiful as Maria d'Alfonso, and as learned as the Marchesa di Pescara' (Una moglie haverai sola, ma cara; / Bella, com' e Maria d' Alfonso, e dotta / Si come è la Marchesa di Pescara) – in Francesco Marcolini's *Le sorti, intitolate gardino d' i pensieri* (1540), see Lodovico Dolce, *Terzetti per le 'Sorti'*, ed. by Paolo Procaccioli (Traviso: Fondazione Benetton; Rome: Viella, 2006), p. 119, st. 24. On Avalos's response to Camillo, see the charming anecdote in Lina Bolzoni, *The Gallery of Memory: Literary and Iconographic Models in the Age of the Printing Press*, trans. by Jeremy Parzen (Toronto: University of Toronto Press, 2001), pp. xiii–xiv.

[75] 'Queste sono le vere riformatione interiore, quale solo Dio puole fare, et non solamente exteriore, quale possono fare li homeni. Sia benedetto Iddio, et senza fine ringratio Iesu Christo': trans. quoted from Gleason, *Garparo Contarini*, p. 279, Italian, n. 85. Avalos employed Giambattista Salis Grisone, whom Aretino salutes as 'un discepolo di quello Erasmo che ha islargati i confini de l' umano ingegno': *Lettere*, II, no. 69, 13 August 1538.

[76] See Martin, *Myths of Renaissance Individualism*, pp. 53–6. On Contarini's spiritual vacillations, see Gleason, *Gasparo Contarini*, pp. 10–26.

was known in the Christian world to be a sensitive and decent ruler. Giovio admiringly informed Charles V:

> He has marvellous intuition. Not only is he adorned with many virtues, he lacks the salient vices of cruelty, avarice, and treachery which marred his predecessors ... Above all, he is religious and liberal, and with those two qualities one flies to heaven.[77]

How, then, to reconcile this character with his policy of ruthless expansionism? Erasmus and Luther were not the only ones to declare that the Turks were an unavoidable divine scourge, Aretino's explanation also for Pilate's inability to move the Jews to release Jesus. The painting juxtaposes the inscrutable, often terrible, workings of divine providence on two temporal planes.

It has become a critical commonplace to observe that the heavily rusticated wall of the judgement hall evokes Serlian architecture; the same might be said for Titian's handling of the stairs and for the polished marble column, which is echoed in Avalos's burnished armour. Whether the inspiration comes directly from Serlio's theories or from Jacopo Sansovino's interpretation of them is a moot question.[78] The nexus of friendships among Sansovino, Serlio, Lorenzo Lotto and Giulio Camillo has been traced by Manfredo Tafuri, who argues that Sansovino's simple and unostentatious style of church architecture should be understood within a reformist context.[79] Needless to say, this group of associates intersects in numerous ways with the Aretino-Titian circle. Titian's painting of the *Crowning with Thorns* (1540?, Paris, Louvre) similarly presents a massively rusticated hall of judgement. It may be that the architectural backdrops represent not just an order appropriate to a more primitive age, but for those with the necessary 'inner reformation' the awareness to interpret the New Testament events by the light of that reformation.

Behold the man. From the beginning of the Cinquecento, religious art took on a new focus, 'a return to the figure of Christ as the main subject of Christian art, a trend ... requiring the removal of the accretions of

---

[77]   Trans. quoted from Zimmermann, *Paolo Giovio*, p. 122. Eric R. Dursteler, *Venetians in Constantinople: Nation, Identity, and Coexistence in the Early Modern Mediterranean* (Baltimore, MD: Johns Hopkins University Press, 2006) comments on 'the relatively tolerant attitude of the Ottoman state toward its minority populations' (p. 7).

[78]   For Serlio on the rustic order, see John Onians, *Bearers of Meaning: The Classical Orders in Antiquity, the Middle Ages, and the Renaissance* (Princeton, NJ: Princeton University Press, 1988), pp. 171–3 and fig. 156; for Sansovino and Titian, pp. 287–304. Onians, p. 304, makes the suggestion about the column and armour.

[79]   See Tafuri, *Venice and the Renaissance*, trans. by Jessica Levine (Cambridge, MA: MIT Press, 1985), pp. 51–78.

hagiographic piety that had accumulated throughout the late Middle Ages'. Thus, the figure of Christ displaced the Virgin Mary from the altarpiece, as in Titian's Averoldi altarpiece (1519–22, Brescia). The subject of 'the man of sorrows' was purified of late Gothic excesses; and, responding to the impetus of the humanist recovery of classical antiquity and of Neoplatonic aesthetics, Christ was given an idealized, heroic body, as in Michelangelo's sculpture of the *Risen Christ* in Santa Maria sopra Minerva (1519–21, Rome) and in the figure of the beardless, Apollonian Christ in the *Last Judgement*.[80] Yet, as Leo Steinberg demonstrated in *The Sexuality of Christ*, even earlier had begun a development, sometimes contradictory, sometimes complementary, that would have significant consequences for Christ-centred art. Briefly, he maintains that the theology of the Incarnation, demanding the Son's assumption of human nature in its totality, also requires his human sexuality with its potential liability to sinfulness, an emphasis that artists symbolized by genital display. Michelangelo's *Risen Christ*, for example, may be seen not just as a sculptural realization of a timeless antique mode, but for Steinberg an assertion of the one greater man's exemption from 'genital shame'.[81]

Nowhere was the artistic response to the belief in Christ's complete humanity more pronounced than in Venice. Since Steinberg attributes the representational emphasis to 'the spread of Franciscan piety with its stress on Christ's human nature' (p. 33), some credit may go to the Franciscans for their powerful influence on Venetian religious art.[82] Undoubtedly a larger factor, however, was Venice's situation as an incubator of heterodox opinion. The Venetian convocation of Anabaptist ministers in 1550 was the logical outcome of a dialogue continuing over two decades: 'Whereas both Catholics and evangelicals accepted the received tradition that Christ was God and made man, the Venetian Anabaptists argued instead that Christ was a man just like all others.' John Martin comments that this 'was not altogether surprising in a Renaissance culture that had come to

---

[80] Primarily I rely here on Alexander Nagel, 'Experiments in Art and Reform in Italy in the Early Sixteenth Century', in *The Pontificate of Clement VII*, pp. 385–409; quotation, p. 396, and his book, *Michelangelo and the Reform of Art*.

[81] See Steinberg, *The Sexuality of Christ in Renaissance Art and in Modern Oblivion*, 2nd edn (Chicago, IL: University of Chicago Press, 1996). On the *Risen Christ*, see pp. 19–22, 146–7. In a detailed study, William E. Wallace, 'Michelangelo's *Risen Christ*', *Sixteenth Century Journal*, 28 (1997), 1251–80, concludes that the 'life-size marble statue' was 'audacious, but it was also theologically appropriate'. See also the Eucharistic interpretation by Timothy Verdon, 'Michelangelo and the Body of Christ: Religious Meaning in the Florence *Pietà*', in Jack Wasserman, *Michelangelo's Florence* Pietà (Princeton, NJ: Princeton University Press, 2003), pp. 127–48.

[82] For the role of the Franciscans, see Goffen, *Piety and Patronage in Renaissance Venice*.

emphasize the humanity of Christ in its devotions, its art, and the stories it told about the life of Jesus'.[83]

Preceded by the *Passione di Gesú* (1534), Aretino's *La Humanità di Christo* was published in three books in 1535 and expanded to four in 1538; the two versions accounted for seven editions before Titian entered the conversation in 1543. With Titian's Christ (Figure 7.4), one registers first the absence of divine attributes – no nimbus, radiant light, attendant angels, or hovering Father. Although his body is muscular, even athletic, his slumping posture, bowed head and downcast eyes project despair. The purple robe is slewed to the left side, exposing his body in three-quarters; visible on his face and chest are rivulets of blood from the scourging and crowning. The prominent knot with which the loincloth is tied over his genitals signifies his vulnerable humanity in another way. As Titian's nineteenth-century biographers, Crowe and Cavalcaselle, wrote disapprovingly but exactly, the artist transforms 'the sublime sacrifice of Christ into a display of ordinary suffering'.[84] This man endures a humiliation. Any successful meditation on the life of Christ is a process of symbolic simultaneity; an event in the past is evoked and re-enacted in the present. This pictorial meditation reminds us that, more often than he is imitated, Christ continues to be betrayed and denied.

Titian's identification of Pontius Pilate with Aretino, although not asserted in print until 1648 by Carlo Ridolfi, must have been obvious to anyone in contemporary Venice (cf. Figure 7.3). I believe that Philipp Fehl was the first scholar to connect the choice with Aretino's *Humanità* and call attention to his amplification of the sympathetic elements in the Gospel accounts of Pilate's dilemma: 'he showed them Christ in the hope that the sight would appease their wrath, crying out: Behold the man! Do you not see that heaven and earth shout forth the injustice which your iniquity makes him suffer! Let your soul be moved by the testimony they hear!'[85] In contrast to the other contemporaries who are in modern dress, Pilate is in pseudo-classical, Roman costume, itself a recognition of the extent to which the writer had fused imaginatively with the psychology of the procurator. He stands in a posture revelatory of his internal conflict: his *controposto* body turns toward both Jesus and the crowd below; one hand

83   Martin, *Venice's Hidden Enemies*, p. 111.

84   *Titian: His Life and Times*, II, 93.

85   'Ecco huomo ... Non udite voi, che la terra e il Cielo esclama del torto, che gli fa la vostra nequitia? Deh rimettete gli ogni ingiuria, e acquetate gli animi mossi per debil cagione': *I tre libri della Humanità di Christo* (Venice, 1535); translation by Helen Wells Magnifico, quoted from Fehl, 'Tintoretto's Homage to Titian and Pietro Aretino', in his *Decorum and Wit: The Poetry of Venetian Painting* (Vienna: IRSA, 1992), p. 176. This essay, pp. 167–80, was first presented as a 1980 conference paper. For discussion of the *Humanità*, see pp. 157–62, 175–6, 178–9, 264–7, 271–4, 276–9.

Fig. 7.3   Titian, *Ecce Homo*, 1543, Christ and Pilate (detail), Vienna, Kunsthistorisches Museum.

Fig. 7.4   Anon., medal of Pietro Aretino (private collection).

gestures toward Jesus in advocacy and the other hand, downward with open palm, proclaims his neutrality. In Aretino's words, 'Veremente Pilato era tra il sacro e il sasso': Pilate was truly between the sacred and the stone. Here 'stone', or 'sasso', may mean the stony-hearted mob, the sepulchre, even the rock of the Church. Shortly after Fehl, Augusto Gentili made a signal contribution, stating what now seems obvious: that the position of Pilate in Aretino's work 'corresponds in contemporary reality to a precise Nicodemitic attitude', a position that was Aretino's own in the 1540s.[86] As yet, one significant detail in the *Humanità* has escaped proper attention. In all four Gospel accounts of the crucifixion, the cross bears the title 'King of

---

[86]   'La posizione di Pilato nell' opera dell'Aretino corrisponde nella realtà contemporanea ad un preciso atteggiamento nicodemitico, come scelta definita di pacificazione': Gentili, 'Tiziano e la religione', p. 148, repeated with slight variation in 'Tiziano e Aretino tra politica e religione', p. 287. He was not aware of Fehl's study. See also Polignano, 'I ritratti dei volti', pp. 10–12.

the Jews'. Only in John is the superscription attributed to Pilate: 'And Pilate wrote a title also, and he put it on the cross. And the writing was JESUS OF NAZARETH THE KING OF THE JEWS' (John 19:19). The high priests ask Pilate to change the inscription to 'he said, I am King of the Jews.' Pilate refuses to change it, only responding, 'What I have written, I have written' (John 19:21–2). Like Nicodemus at the Deposition (John 19:39), Pilate emerges from the protective night to act openly for his belief. Here, unmistakably, Aretino follows John's account:

> Pilate in great state could be seen in the midst of his soldiers and the multitude. They obeyed him in the name of Caesar. He ordered his men to place an inscription over his head which read: 'Jesus of Nazareth, King of the Jews.' This was written in Hebrew, Greek, and Latin letters. Now the leaders among the priests, with twisted faces, said to Pilate: Write not 'King of the Jews' but rather 'He who pretended to be King of the Jews.' But Pilate answered, 'What I have written, I have written.'[87]

Titian's portrayal of Aretino as Pilate is not simply an homage (from Lt. *homo*), a tribute to his achievement in transposing the story of Jesus to vernacular Italian, or an oblique confession of their Nicodemite beliefs. It also is a declaration of principle and, anticipating the turbulent times to come, a plan of action. Aretino, the religious writer, will not recant; like Nicodemus and Pilate, he will make his belief known: 'What I have written, I have written.'

---

[87]   'Pilato, che con altera pompa si stava immezzo delle sue armi, e della moltitudine che gli ubidiva in nome di Cesare, fece porre sopra il capo di Christ oil titolo, in cui era scritto; GIESU NAZZARENO RE DE I GIUDEI. E cotali parole si scrissero di caratteri Hebrei, Greci, e Latini. Onde i prencipi de i sacerdoti torcedo il vilo dissero a Pontio: Scrivi non Re de I Giudei; ma quello, che si faceva Re loro. Et egli, Quel che ho scritto, sia scritto': *Humanità di Christo*, trans. by Magnifico, in Fehl, *Decorum and Wit*, p. 178. Pilate's inscription may have had a particular significance for Venetians. In 1492, Girolamo Donato brought a fragment of the *titulus* from Rome; he donated it to the church of Santa Maria dei Servi, commissioning an elaborate reliquary, tabernacle and altar as a setting for the relic. See Patricia Fortini Brown, *Venice and Antiquity: The Venetian Sense of the Past* (New Haven, CT: Yale University Press, 1996), p. 243; also Claudio Franzoni, 'Girolamo Donato: collezionismo e instauratio dell' antico', in *Venezia e l' archeologia*, ed. by Gustavo Traversari, *Rivista di Archeologia*, supplementi 7 (Rome, 1990), pp. 27–31. I am grateful to Alexander Nagel for calling the *titulus* to my attention. Concerning a related relic, in the judgement of Nicholas Penny, Titian's *The Vendramin Family venerating a Relic of the True Cross* (that is, splinters of wood preserved in a reliquary owned by the Scuola di San Giovanni Evangelista), 'must have been made, or at least begun, between 1540 and 1542'. Quoted from the exhibition catalogue *Titian*, no. 29, p. 146. The commission may have stimulated thought relevant to the *Ecce Homo*.

CHAPTER 8

Varieties of Experience: Music and Reform in Renaissance Italy

Iain Fenlon

It was originally Leopold von Ranke who, in his *Geschichte der Päpste*, which began to appear in 1834, arrived at the notion of a general movement of Catholic reform and resistance to Protestantism.[1] Essentially conceived as a series of reflex defensive actions, Ranke's *Gegenreformationen* brought into a grand synthesis such phenomena as the foundation of the Jesuits, the Council of Trent and the activities of the later sixteenth-century popes, events that had previously been treated only in an isolated fashion. With Ranke, the concept of the Counter-Reformation was introduced into the language of periodization, and by the second half of the nineteenth century, it had been established as an historical development of European significance. Other scholars came to argue that rather than being merely a direct consequence of Protestantism, the Catholic Reformation (as some preferred to call it) had deep historical roots. In place of the simple model of action and reaction, the question was now raised of the double character of the Counter-Reformation, with Protestantism on one side and reformed Catholicism on the other. In this process, the idea of an independent and ultimately successful Catholic Reformation gained increasing acceptance. For Ludwig Pastor, as for Ranke, the importance of Trent was central, and that position has been further consolidated, above all by Hubert Jedin's conviction, argued throughout his *Geschichte des Konzils von Trient*, that a whole period of the history of the Church was fashioned by the Council.[2]

In view of this historiographical background, it is hardly surprising that for musicologists, whose discipline was largely fashioned by nineteenth-century German historians and philologists, the question of the Council of Trent and its effect on the composition of polyphonic sacred music

---

[1]   Leopold von Ranke, *Die römischen Päpste: ihre Kirche und ihr Staat im sechszehnten und siebzehnten Jahrhundert*, 3 vols (Berlin: Duncker und Humblot, 1834–36).

[2]   Hubert Jedin, *Geschichte des Konzils von Trient*, 2 vols (Freiburg: Herder, 1949–57); see also Ludwig Freiherr von Pastor, *Geschichte der Päpste seit dem Ausgang des Mittelalters: mit Benutzung des päpstlichen Geheim-archives und vieler anderer Archive* (Freiburg im Breisgau and St. Louis, MO: Herder, 1891–1933).

has long been an accepted concern. The framework within which most subsequent discussions have taken place was established as long ago as 1919 by Karl Weinmann, and most later historians have been happy to expand it despite the comparatively small number of musical works than can be drawn into the debate.[3] The traditional starting-point, though not a particularly instructive one, is the Council's own *Canon on Music to be used in the Mass*, approved in September 1562, which then formed the basis for the abbreviated and imprecisely worded statement on the subject that subsequently became an official part of the Council's decrees.[4] Its main conclusion was that music must serve to uplift the faithful, that the words should be intelligible, and that secular elements should be excluded. In this rather general way, the decree attempted to respond to a body of complaint about the complex and inappropriate character of much elaborate liturgical polyphony that had been growing among churchmen during the previous decades. Yet on the subject of what an appropriate sacred musical style should actually sound like, the Council was characteristically inarticulate. This has been interpreted as an essentially negative approach, more concerned with reiterating common abuses than with recommending alternatives, but this is to misunderstand the relationship of the Council to the reformed institutions of diocesan Church government which were envisaged as the instruments of many aspects of its policies. In common with some of its other pronouncements, such as the decree relating to painting and images, the Council's statement about music, which was in any case a rather peripheral aspect of the question of Church reform which Pius IV had determined to place at the centre of the final session of the Council, was never intended to be anything more than a series of general guidelines to be entrusted to diocesan synods for clarification.

In this, as in other matters, it has become increasingly apparent that the reformation and revitalization of the Italian Church was not wholly dependent upon papal initiatives. It is true that after 1560, the papacy willingly assumed the responsibilities of leadership that it had shirked before the pontificate of Paul III. A seemingly unending stream of special instructions were issued, nuncios and apostolic visitors were appointed to see that those instructions were carried out, reports were required from bishops during their visits, and a certain degree of uniformity was achieved by demanding compliance with the Tridentine decrees. The papal visitors in the decades after Trent did their utmost to enforce the decrees to the letter. Nevertheless, the striving for uniformity did not preclude diversity in practice, due to differences in the backgrounds and inclinations of the leading reformers. In addition, there

---

[3]   Karl Weinmann, *Das Konzil von Trient und die Kirchenmusik: Eine historisch-kritische Untersuchung* (Leipzig: Breitkopf & Härtel, 1919).

[4]   For the latest discussion see Craig Monson, 'The Council of Trent Revisited', *Journal of the American Musicological Society* 55 (2002), 1–37.

was considerable latitude in some areas, of which music and liturgy was just one and ecclesiology the most important, about which the Council itself had been vague.

To meet the challenge of reform, the years immediately after the conclusion of the Council of Trent were ones of profound change in the structure of the Church, particularly at diocesan level. On the one hand, old institutions were revitalized and renewed to enable them to discharge the functions for which they were originally designed, while on the other, new bodies were created to further the aims of reform. But beyond this general pattern, there was no uniformity of approach, and it cannot be assumed that the most famous *exemplum* of ecclesiastical reorganization, that of Carlo Borromeo in Milan, was a model that was widely adopted. This is not to deny the enormous contemporary prestige of 'that acknowledged model bishop for the whole Catholic world, zealous, efficient, ascetic, tireless, charitable, selfless, uncompromising', but rather to emphasize the variety of styles and forms which reform initiatives took in various parts of Italy;[5] this was a reflection of the temperaments and personalities of the different churchmen charged with instituting reform at a local level. This is as true of individual reactions to the decree on music as it is of other aspects of institutionalized reform, though it is also true that outside Rome itself the diocese of Milan provides the best-documented example of a local interpretation of the decree on music, largely because the matter was so actively pursued by Borromeo himself. His tight control of reform in the diocese was all-encompassing; it aimed not merely at improved clerical behaviour and correct liturgical observance, but at the complete moral and spiritual submission of both clergy and laity alike.

It was as part of his reorganization of the liturgy that Borromeo promoted the revision of the Ambrosian rite, despite some opposition from Rome where the trend was towards the abolition of local liturgies. As for polyphonic music, the first Provincial Council, convoked in Milan in the autumn of 1565, issued guidelines covering four main points. First, no secular melodies were to be used in the Divine Office, a reference to the common practice among composers of using motifs from madrigals or chansons as the basis for sacred pieces. Next, music was to be used in church 'so that simultaneously the words shall be understood and the listeners aroused to piety'.[6] Both these concerns are commonplace in the literature of complaint against contemporary church polyphony, and appear in the Council of Trent's decree from which the Milan statement is clearly derived. Following these two major resolutions, the Council

---

[5]   H.O. Evenett, 'The Counter-Reformation', *The Reformation Crisis*, ed. by Joel Hurstfield (London: Edward Arnold, 1965), p. 70.

[6]   Cited in Lewis Lockwood, *The Counter-Reformation and the Masses of Vincenzo Ruffo* (Venice: Universal, 1970), p. 110.

went on to stipulate that where possible singers should be clerics, and that instruments other than the organ were to be banned in church. These more specific requirements typify Borromeo's strict views about the suppression of secular elements in worship.

In practical terms, these resolutions took matters little beyond what Trent had stipulated, and Borromeo's real innovation was to promote composition of the type of polyphony that he believed to be in conformity with Trent's intentions. The principal agent in this was Vincenzo Ruffo, who had been in Milan as *maestro di cappella* at the cathedral since 1563. Ruffo's four-voiced Masses, published in Milan in 1570 are, in their adoption of a syllabic chordal style designed to make the words intelligible, a clear response to Tridentine thinking.[7] Their more direct relationship to Borromeo himself is clear from their title, and even clearer from the dedication, which explains

> ... that in accordance with the decrees of the Most Holy Council of Trent I was to compose some masses that should avoid everything of a profane and idle manner in worship ... Accordingly ... I composed one Mass in this way: so that the numbers of the syllables and the voices and notes together should be clearly and distinctly understood by the pious listeners ... later, imitating that example, I more readily and easily composed other Masses of the same type.[8]

Churchmen were not, of course, the only ones in a position to actively encourage and experiment with compositional styles. Among princely patrons, the most startling example of interest in the question of a suitable polyphonic style for the liturgy is provided by the example of the works commissioned for Duke Guglielmo Gonzaga's specially constituted basilica of Santa Barbara at Mantua. Here there is the added consideration that Gonzaga clearly conceived the project as a way of presenting and extending a particularly distinctive image of himself as the embodiment of the True Christian Prince. The new church was planned as a dynastic temple, a theatre for Gonzaga's politico-dynastic ceremonies, as well as a highly individual interpretation of Catholic reformist attitudes towards sacred art. Its special character, expressed through extraordinary papal privileges including a separate rite and prestigious positions for its clergy unprecedented outside Rome itself, automatically conferred a status upon the institution which made it the envy of other Italian princes. And since

---

[7]   Vincenzo Ruffo, *Missae Quatuor Concinate ad Ritum Concilii Mediolani* (Milan: Antonio Antoniano, 1570).

[8]   Vincenzo Ruffo, *Seven Masses*, ed. by Lewis Lockwood, 2 vols (Madison, WI: A.R. Editions, 1979), I, p. viii. For the original Latin text, see Lockwood, *The Counter-Reformation*, pp. 237–8.

the building, begun in 1562–63 when the last session of the Council was finally drawing to a close, was the particular brainchild of Gonzaga who was also an amateur composer, it is not surprising that the recruitment of musicians and the composition of polyphony to conform with the special requirements of the Santa Barbara rite played an important part in the initial conception and were a major preoccupation during the early stages of planning, construction and operation. More than that, it is clear from Guglielmo's correspondence with composers both in Mantua and elsewhere, from his own compositions, and from works commissioned for Santa Barbara by others (including Palestrina), that there is a common concern with issues of constraint, the use of material taken from plainsongs, a concern for clarity of text, an emphasis upon old-fashioned contrapuntal skills, and an avoidance of extravagant representational devices and adventurous effects. This is the best-documented example outside Milan of reformist ideas about music and liturgy being put into practice, for all that Gonzaga's motives were undoubtedly complex and embraced political as well as spiritual concerns.

The examples of Mantua and Milan are intriguing, but they are not representative. Now that a more comparative approach is possible, a picture of different initiatives taking place in different dioceses and at different times is emerging from the previous impression of a uniform response to most aspects of the Tridentine decrees. In this process, it has become clear that the aura of sanctity that surrounds the historiography of Borromeo has effectively disguised the extent to which there were considerable divergences, even among those churchmen who were in sympathy with his ideals, from the general model he so rigorously established. Both Domenico Bollani in Brescia and Gabriele Paleotti in Bologna provide examples of allies who shared some reaction to certain aspects of Borromeo's reforming method, feeling that a more practical approach was necessary for the reorganization of their own dioceses once the theory had been formulated at Trent. For them, Borromeo's initiatives often seemed too abstract, and the decrees of the Provincial Councils remote from local circumstances. By contrast, their own reforms were to be characterized by action. Neither Bollani nor Paleotti seem to have taken much interest in the question of music and liturgy, though Paleotti asked that sacred painting be historically accurate, naturalistic and comprehensible to the devout observer, while leaving the problem of how these objectives were to be realized to artists. Except for a handful of special cases, the Council of Trent had as little practical effect on the various styles of liturgical polyphony that continued to be composed and performed throughout Italy as it did on the other arts.

Nevertheless, the deliberation of Trent, and its alleged influence on the composition of sacred music, continue to occupy an exaggerated position in conventional histories of sixteenth-century music. Similarly, most musicological discussions of the more specific question of music and reform have placed an unjustifiably heavy emphasis on what might be described as the conciliar position. According to this interpretation, Trent itself is seen to be the culmination of a body of complaint about sacred polyphony that dates back at least as far as the late fifteenth century, despite the fact that these earlier pronouncements, which are usually of the most vague and unspecific kind, occur almost as a rhetorical gesture and seem to have had little practical effect, even less than Trent itself. Moreover, these pre-Tridentine statements about polyphony are sometimes thought of as a coherent tradition despite their very different origins, some of them monastic. And inevitably, in a subject which has produced so much of its history on the typological model, the main focus of attention has been on the major elaborations of the liturgy, the motet, and particularly the Mass, rather than simpler styles of music, whether polyphony or monophony. Thus Trent, or rather the provincial synods which were charged with enacting its decrees, have come to be regarded as marking the crucial point when criticisms of polyphony finally bore artistic fruit in the works of Ruffo in Milan and Palestrina in Rome, small in number and apparently slight in influence though such 'Tridentine' works might be.

In this process, insufficient attention has been paid to the impact of a different tradition of concern with the character of sacred music, a tradition whose roots lie in late medieval monasticism but whose effects in the second half of the sixteenth century were potent. This is not to suggest that this development, which found an effective, coherent political and ideological voice for the first time during the Savonarolan interlude in Florence between the years 1494 and 1498, did not interact with the polyphonic tradition which, initially at least, it set out to counterbalance. On the contrary, it was the bringing together, in the fertile soil of mid-century Rome, of a Savonarolan aesthetic and the skills of professional musicians attuned to that philosophy, that produced a more characteristic and influential body of 'reformist' music than Palestrina's *Missa Papae Marcelli*. Consideration of these two differently motivated and constituted attitudes, the one conciliar, the other monastic in origin, not only emphasizes that for music too there were different reactions, at different times and in different places, to the question of musical reform, but also underlines the unhelpfulness of some cherished distinctions between sacred and secular music and written and unwritten traditions. It also reveals the extent to which the importance of the musical aspects of more popular forms of devotion have been underestimated.

The circulation and performance of laude in Florence and Tuscany during the sixteenth century was not only a commemoration of Savonarola's life and works, but also an acknowledgement of the continued validity of his prophecies. And although the failure of the Last Republic in Florence in

1530 did not immediately extinguish the power of the Savonarolan revival, it did inaugurate a slow process of attrition. Florentine visions of religious renewal were inextricably intertwined with dreams of civic liberty; both were essential components of the myth of Florence, the notion of a free republic that would liberate, enrich and even redeem its citizens.[9] Perhaps it was the unique combination of a bourgeois society, a lay culture, and a fierce republicanism that created the atmosphere in which the Savonarolan movement could flourish.[10] During the Last Republic, the memory of Savonarola, which evoked resonances of republicanism, made a brief comeback, but with the slow death of the Savonarolan ideal at the hands of the Medici, the old complex of associations began to lose their potency. In 1545, the Dominicans were expelled from San Marco in Florence by Cosimo I on suspicion of advocating Savonarolan ideas.[11] A sustained campaign to eliminate the friar's memory was resisted by his followers, the Piagnoni, and as late as 1583, Alessandro de' Medici, Archbishop of Florence, wrote to the Grand Duke complaining about their activities.[12] Yet notwithstanding the fervour with which his memory was perpetuated and his cult consolidated, particularly in a handful of monasteries and convents in Tuscany, it was not so much in Florence but in Rome that the late medieval tendencies towards sectarianism and lay piety, which had received renewed impetus from Savonarola's teaching, were endowed with a fresh sense of purpose during the post-Trent period. It was there, in the hands of Filippo Neri and his followers, that the ideals of popular devotion and spirituality, as Savonarola had defined them, once more took root and flourished.[13]

Neri, the key figure in this development, was himself an expatriate Florentine, and the spiritual and musical traditions upon which he drew

---

[9]   For this idea, and its use by and absorption of Savonarola, see Donald Weinstein, 'The Myth of Florence', in *Florentine Studies: Politics and Society in Renaissance Florence*, ed. by Nicolai Rubinstein (London: Faber & Faber, 1968), pp. 15–44, and the first chapter of Weinstein, *Savonarola and Florence: Prophecy and Patriotism in the Renaissance* (Princeton, NJ: Princeton University Press, 1970).

[10]   Weinstein, *Savonarola and Florence*, p. 377.

[11]   Antonietta Amati, 'Cosimo I e i frati di San Marco', *Archivio storico italiano*, 81 (1923), 225–77 (pp. 242–6).

[12]   Lorenzo Polizzotto, *The Elect Nation: The Savonarolan Movement in Florence 1494–1545* (Oxford: Oxford University Press, 1994), pp. 432–3 and, for Alessandro de' Medici's assault, pp. 442–3.

[13]   For an overview, with a catalogue of the Roman Lauda repertory, see Giancarlo Rostirolla, 'La musica a Roma al tempo del Baronio: l'arte e la produzione laudistica in ambiente romano', in *Baronio e l'arte: atti del convegno internazionale di studi, Sora, 10–13 ottobre 1984*, ed. by Romeo de Maio et al. (Sora: Centro di studi sorani 'Vincenzo Patriarca', 1985), pp. 573–771.

have a distinctly Florentine if not specifically Savonarolan character.[14] Indeed, Neri's father Francesco was a great admirer of Savonarola, and part of Filippo's education had taken place at San Marco. There, veneration of Savonarola was still strong despite attempts to suppress the cult, and evidence from his later years suggests that Neri's devotion to Savonarola's memory was deep. Thus at an early age he was exposed, in an intimate way, to the quite specific Florentine Dominican traditions of popular music and prayer which were fostered by the community at San Marco, strongly influenced by Savonarola's teachings and by the memory of his charismatic personality. That memory became even more vivid during the period of the Last Republic, when San Marco itself became the focal point of the re-evocation of the Savonarolan past as part of the strategy of defence.[15] As for Neri, there can be little doubt of the impact that his connections with San Marco made on his formation during those years. Many of the practices later adopted in Rome by the Congregation of the Oratory and its precursors can be traced back to these experiences, and later Neri himself was to say to the Dominicans in Rome that '[a]ll that I have of good I owe to your fathers of San Marco.'[16] After the Oratory itself, the Dominican church of Santa Maria sopra Minerva also provided a focal point for Neri's activities and those of his sympathizers, and some of the most vivid accounts that have survived of the musical aspects of the Oratorians' early meetings record activities at the Minerva during the late 1550s and early 1560s.

From Florence, Neri moved briefly to San Germano near Montecassino, and then, around 1537, to Rome. Little is known of his first years there, which he spent living in the house of a Florentine customs official, acting as a tutor to his children, studying philosophy at the Sapienza and theology with the Augustinians. From the late 1540s, he was associated with the church and monastery of San Girolamo della Carità, not far from the new church of the Florentine community, San Giovanni dei Fiorentini.[17] There he reacquainted himself with the Florentine traditions of simple public devotion that he had first encountered during his youth. It seems clear that Neri's involvement with his fellow Florentines in Rome was a factor

---

[14]   See Antonio Cistellini, 'San Filippo Neri e la sua patria', *Rivista di storia della chiesa in Italia*, 23 (1969), 54–119.

[15]   Cecil Roth, *The Last Florentine Republic* (London: Methuen, 1925); J.N. Stephens, *The Fall of the Florentine Republic 1512–1530* (Oxford: Clarendon Press, 1983), pp. 203–55; Polizzotto, *The Elect Nation*, pp. 314–86.

[16]   Louis Ponnelle and Louis Bordet, *St. Philip Neri and the Roman Society of his Times, 1515–1595*, trans. by Ralph Francis Kerr (London: Sheed and Ward, 1932), p. 64, citing from P. Pietro Giacomo Bacci, *Vita di San Filippo Neri Fiorentino, Fondatore della congregazione dell'oratorio ...* (Rome: Bernabò e Lazzarini, 1745), p. 6.

[17]   For the details see ibid., pp. 257ff.

of considerable importance for the early practices, including musical ones, of the Congregation of the Oratory. Philosophical and theological continuities were no doubt strong, but they possessed geographical and cultural dimensions, and conceivably political ones as well.

The 'Nazione Fiorentina' had been particularly strong in Rome since the end of the fifteenth century, when the formation of the Compagnia della Pietà, composed entirely of Florentines, had given them some form of status in the city. Under the Medici popes, the number of resident Florentines increased dramatically, and during the pontificate of Leo X it seemed that they would monopolize everything – court and city, offices and wealth. The Venetian ambassador reported Cardinal San Giorgio's remark that in comparison with Pope Julius, who spent about 4,000 ducats a month on his *famiglia*, 'this pope needs eight or nine thousand, so many are the Florentines who come and claim to be his relatives, and come to live at his expense.'[18] By now, Rome had thirty Florentine banks, which formed the heart of a community for the people of all professions who came to the city from the banks of the Arno. Running through its centre was the Via Giulia which, apart from its deliberate evocation of the splendours of ancient Rome, had modernized the transport of goods coming to the Florentine warehouses along the Via dei Banchi and had consequently strengthened that part of the city as a commercial centre.[19] The Florentine area was also of some importance in the cultural life of the city: artists such as Raphael and Cellini lived there, as did important patrons.[20] In the midst of this culturally and topographically distinct area was the house and church of the Arciconfraternità della Carità, founded in 1518 by Cardinal Giulio de'Medici on the model of the Florentine charitable body of the same name. Neri took Holy Orders and moved to San Girolamo in 1551. There he promoted meetings of the laity for informal discussions of religious topics and for communal prayer; his congregation consisted almost entirely of young Tuscans.[21] In essence, this was the beginning of what later became the Congregation of the Oratory, and by 1554, when the number of adherents had become so great that

---

[18]   Eugenio Albèri, *Relazioni degli ambasciatori veneti al senato, raccolte, annotate, ed edite*, 15 vols (Florence: Soc. Ed. Fiorentina, 1839–63), 2nd ser., vol. III, p. 54: 'Questo papa ne vuole otto o novemila. La causa è, che vengono molti Fiorentini che si fanno parenti del papa, e vanno in tinello a mangiare … .' See also the similar remarks of Mario Equicola to Francesco Gonzaga: 'Tanti Fiorentini che e una compassione: tucto il palazzo, tucta Roma non e altro', reported in Luigi Salerno, Luigi Spezzaferro and Manfredo Tafuri, *Via Giulia: una utopia urbanistica del' 500* (Rome: Staderini, 1975), p. 78.

[19]   See Albèri, ibid., pp. 65–76

[20]   Details of Raphael's house are given in ibid., pp. 265–70.

[21]   Ponnelle and Bordet, *St. Philip Neri*, p. 171. For the confraternity at S. Girolamo della Carita, see Salerno, Spezzaferro and Tafuri, *Via Giulia*, pp. 469–72.

new accommodation had to be found, the Oratory may be said to have existed as an institution. Its early development had taken place in, and had drawn much of its inspiration from, the Florentine traditions of popular spirituality practised in the households along the Via Giulia.

The importance of these traditions in the devotions of the Oratorians became only greater as the community grew and its congregation increased. Some recognition of the place which the activities of the Oratory had come to hold in the life of Rome, and particularly of the Florentine community there, came in 1564, when Neri was invited to become the rector of San Giovanni dei Fiorentini, still uncompleted through lack of funds but nevertheless a focal point for the activities of the Florentine community. Sanctioned by Leo X's bull of 1519, San Giovanni had rapidly become established as the parish church for all the Florentines in the city, a symbol of the union between Florence and Rome, and a visible demonstration of the economic predominance of the Florentines, lying as it did in the heart of an area largely occupied by banks, warehouses and the houses of the aristocracy and merchant classes.[22] Neri's appointment underscores his associations with Florentine institutions and traditions, but it also benefited the Oratorians in a practical way, since six of his followers were now despatched to live at S. Giovanni as a religious community; it was this group that formed the nucleus of what later became the Congregation of the Oratory.[23] Neri himself preferred to remain at S. Girolamo. For a brief period, the Oratorians now operated from a hall attached to the church of Sant'Orsola, which had been presented to the Arciconfraternità della Pietà by Clement VII in 1526, but then in 1575 Gregory XIII officially recognized Neri and his followers as a religious community, and presented them with the old church, then in ruins, of Santa Maria in Vallicella. Within a short time, the church and some of the surrounding houses had been demolished, and the Chiesa Nuova, testimony in itself to the strength of Neri's following, had been begun on the site. Lying due east of S. Giovanni dei Fiorentini, the new complex was still within the confines of the Florentine area of the city.[24]

This topographical and cultural context helps to explain a number of specifically Florentine aspects of the early practices of the Oratorians, not least Neri's enthusiasm for the lauda. At a philosophical level, Neri recognized the power of music as a crucial element in the battle for the

[22]   Salerno, Spezzaferro, and Tafuri, ibid., p. 78.

[23]   Ponnelle and Bordet, *St. Philip Neri*, pp. 258 ff.

[24]   For the Chiesa Nuova, see Maria Teresa Bonadonna Russo, 'Il contributo della Congregazione dell'Oratorio alla topografia romana', *Studi romani*, 13 (1965), 21–43. The building history of the Oratory is treated in Joseph Connors, *Borromini and the Roman Oratory: Style and Society* (Cambridge, MA and London: MIT Press, 1980).

salvation of souls,[25] a fact neatly demonstrated by an anecdote concerning a musician from the Castel Sant'Angelo who reputedly died in Neri's arms singing the lauda 'Giesù, Giesù, ogn'un chiami Giesù'.[26] The image is powerfully Savonarolan.

From the first days in San Girolamo, Neri seems to have appreciated the value of music, and of singing, as a way of uniting his followers in their devotions. According to Cesare Baronio, whose *Annali* provide a rare and detailed account of one of Neri's gatherings of about 1557–58, a lauda was sung towards the end of the meeting. By the early 1570s, the Oratorians had developed several quite distinct types of 'spiritual exercises', and although these differed in structure according to the time of day and the season of the year, they nevertheless retained the basic components of readings, a sermon and music, which they believed to be a revival of an ancient Christian practice.

By incorporating the lauda into his daily 'spiritual exercises', Neri was clearly drawing upon his own experience of Florentine and specifically Savonarolan traditions, but from the early days of the Oratory the music that was performed there began to depart from the roots of those traditions in a number of significant ways. While simple monophonic laude continued to be sung congregationally, much as they had been in Florence during the Savonarolan period, more complex polyphony (of the kind that Savonarola so vehemently criticized) was also performed. And in addition to elaborations of traditional lauda melodies, specially composed pieces were also now performed. These developments, which took the lauda away from its late fifteenth-century social functions and stylistic simplicity, are largely to be explained, on the evidence of contemporary observers of the Oratory, by two important social factors: first, the involvement of professional musicians in the affairs of the Congregation, and secondly, the changing character of the congregation who flocked to the Oratory in ever-increasing numbers during the 1560s and 1570s. In effect, that process which was ultimately to take every aspect of the Oratory's activities away from the accent on austerity, which is such an essential feature of Neri's philosophy, had already begun in response to the tastes of the bourgeois and aristocratic congregations that now began to attend the Chiesa Nuova. The impact of these trends was to be seen

---

[25]   Federico Mompellio, 'San Filippo Neri e la musica "pescatrice di anime"', *Chigiana*, 12 (1956), 3–33.

[26]   Giovanni Incisa della Rocchetta, Nello Vian and D.C. Gasbarri (eds), *Il primo processo per San Filippo Neri nel codice Vaticano Latino 3798 e in altri esemplari dell'Archivio della Congregazione dell'Oratorio di Roma*, 4 vols (Vatican City: Biblioteca Apostolica Vaticana, 1957–63), I, pp. 239, 319, 320. The text of the lauda is by Belcari; a setting of it is in Razzi's *Libro primo* as well as in one of Animuccia's collections; see Rostirolla, 'La musica a Roma', for concordances.

above all in the architecture and decoration of the church and its attached oratory. The church, built between 1575 and 1593, represents the ideals of the first Oratorians, men who had known Neri personally; as such it was constructed along the severe lines characteristic of much institutional church building in Counter-Reformation Rome. But the Casa dei Filippini, built next to the church starting in 1637, breathes a different spirit in that interiors were often austere, but the exterior was now extravagantly ornamented.[27]

The daily 'spiritual exercise' was not the only activity of the Oratorians that involved music. More elaborate from the musical point of view was the *oratorio vespertino*, held after vespers on Sundays and other feast days during the period from Easter to All Saints Day. This took the form of a walk, usually to a high point on the Janiculum near the monastery of Sant'Onofrio, where a sequence of laude interspersed with sermons would take place. A notable feature of this exercise was that the sermons were often recited by young boys, a practice distinctly reminiscent of Savonarola's processions of adolescents, and for much the same reasons.[28]

Close in spirit to the *oratorio vespertino* were the famous walks to visit the seven principal churches of Rome, which Neri had instituted as early as 1552. The idea dates back to the early days of Christianity, but Neri's revival of it developed into a cult that reached a peak of popularity during the pontificate of Paul IV. These took place several times a year, but the most popular was held on *giovedì grasso* as an alternative to the excesses of carnival. In the early morning, a crowd gathered at San Paolo fuori le Mura and walked to San Sebastiano along the Via Ardeatina, the participants singing simple chants and laude. At San Sebastiano, Mass was celebrated to the accompaniment of vocal and instrumental music and afterwards refreshment was taken at the Villa Mattei to the accompaniment of music provided by the musicians of the Castel Sant'Angelo with professional singers. During the afternoon, the pilgrimage continued from basilica to basilica, the crowd still singing chants and laude with a sermon at each sanctuary and, between San Giovanni in Laterano and Santa Maria Maggiore, the devotion of the Scala Santa. The conclusion took place in

---

[27]   Connors, *Borromini and the Roman Oratory*, pp. 1–3.

[28]   For which see Richard C. Trexler, 'Ritual in Florence: Adolescence and Salvation in the Renaissance', in *The Pursuit of Holiness in Late Medieval and Renaissance Religion*, ed. by Charles Trinkaus and Heiko A. Oberman (Leiden: Brill, 1974), pp. 200–64; and the same author's *Public Life in Renaissance Florence* (New York: Academic Press, 1980), esp. pp. 367–87. As Trexler argues, the emergence of adolescents as male 'saviours' was a fifteenth-century phenomenon which was given a particularly strong inflection in Savonarolan Florence.

the Basilica of Santa Maria Maggiore in the evening, with a final sermon and a polyphonic motet.[29]

It is clear that both the older tradition of congregational singing of laude, and the newer tradition of polyphonic settings, were used by the Oratorians from the beginning of their activities. At the same time, the use of increasingly elaborate music in their services during the 1560s was not only a result of the involvement of professional musicians, but is also a reflection of a distinct change in the social composition of the congregations which those services attracted. The dedication of Animuccia's *Secondo libro* of 1570 makes this point explicitly:

> The Oratory having increased, by the grace of God, with the coming together of prelates and of most important gentlemen, it seemed to me fitting in this second book to increase the harmony and combination of parts, varying the music in diverse ways, now setting it to Latin words and now to the vernacular, sometimes with a greater number of voices and sometimes with fewer, with verses now of one kind and now of another, concerning myself as little as possible with imitations and complexities, in order not to obscure the understanding of the words.[30]

Music historians have developed a rather monolithic view of the whole question of the 'reform' of sacred music in the Cinquecento. This is partly because only one aspect of the discussion has occupied attention, the body of complaint voiced by humanists, musical theorists and churchmen in the decades before the Council of Trent.[31] The focus of enquiry has been their concerns with textual clarity, and with the formulation of a theory

---

[29]   The basic account of the devotion of the Seven Churches is that of Andrea Lazzarini and Carlo Gasbarri, *La spettacolarità del 'Gaudium' e la visita filippina delle sette chiese studiata in gran parte su fonti inedite ritrovate nell'Archivio dei Padri dell'Oratorio di Santa Maria in Vallicella in Roma* (Rome: Palombi, 1957). The quotations relating to music are taken from the Processo of Neri, as cited above.

[30]   'Ma essendosi poi tuttavia l'oratorio suddetto per gratia di Dio venuto accrescendo co'l concorso di prelati & gentil'huomini principalissimi, è parso anco a me conveniente di accrescere in questo Secondo libro l'harmonia & i concenti, variando la musica in diversi modi, facendola hora su parole latine, hora sopra vulgari, & hora con più numero di voci & hora con meno, & quando con rime d'una maniera & quando d'un altra, intrigandomi il manco ch'io ho potuto con le fughe & con le inventioni, per non oscurare l'intendimento delle parole, acciocché con la lor efficacia, aiutate dall'harmonia, potessero penetrare più dolcemente il cuore di che ascolta': Giovanni Animuccia, *Il secondo libro delle laudi* (Rome: Eredi di Antonio Blado, 1570), [2].

[31]   The most important are conveniently brought together in Lewis Lockwood's introduction to Giovanni Pierluigi da Palestrina, *Pope Marcellus Mass: An Authoritative Score, Backgrounds and Sources, History and Analysis, Views and Comments* (New York: W.W. Norton, 1975).

of decorum in which considerations such as the eradication of secular elements and the correct use of the modes were prominent. Much attention has been devoted to the practical application of these ideas through the institutions of the Church in cases where influential churchmen or secular patrons took a direct interest in polyphony. This can be followed to some degree in Rome, and with great clarity in the case of Carlo Borromeo's Milan, but it should be remembered that the outcome can be observed in the works of only a few composers: certain masses by Palestrina and his Roman contemporaries, and the works of Ruffo and one or two other north Italian contemporaries. Similarly, the example of Duke Guglielmo Gonzaga in Mantua is an extreme version of the appropriation of reformist ideas, whether for reasons of genuine piety or in the interests of statecraft; as such, it was clearly attractive to rulers both inside and outside Italy, but again the practical efforts were limited to a handful of compositions. To these should be added the taste for publishing contrafacta of secular pieces, a practice that was largely associated with reformist centres, but the instances are again few in number.[32]

Indeed, these developments, which begin in the 1560s, represent only one rather small aspect of the question. There may have been other ways in which the spirit of the Catholic Reformation was expressed in sacred polyphony,[33] but in contrast to this conciliar response, there was another tradition of interest in the subject of music and devotion. This was essentially monastic in origin and drew on traditional Italian popular religious feeling as expressed in simple chants and in the lauda. Its roots lay in late medieval piety, but it was only expressed for the first time with any coherence and force during the Savonarolan period in Florence. Here, there was a more relaxed attitude towards secular and popular elements, perhaps out of expediency, and probably because the melodies themselves were so firmly embedded in unwritten culture and hence an irreplaceable aspect of Florentine civic and religious ritual.

---

[32]   The continuing strength of this tradition is illustrated by Margaret Ann Rorke, 'Sacred Contrafacta of Monteverdi Madrigals and Cardinal Borromeo's Milan', *Music & Letters*, 65 (1984), 68–76. In Rome, the taste for contrafacta is shown by collections of madrigals with sacred texts such as MS O.91 in the Biblioteca Vallicelliana, and the copy of the printed collection *L'Amorosa Ero*, with a textual contrafactum by Ancina, in the same library; both were evidently used by the singers in the Oratory. See *The Madrigal Collection L'Amorosa Ero* (Brescia, 1588), ed. by Harry B. Lincoln (Binghamton, NY: State University of New York Press, 1968), pp. viii–xii.

[33]   See, for example, Harold S. Powers, 'Modal Representation in Polyphonic Offertories', *Early Music History*, 2 (1982), 43–86, which argues that 'Palestrina's modal offertory cycle for the winter season is the quintessential polyphonic manifestation of Counter-Reformation ideology' (p. 84), on account of its faithful adherence to predetermined texts and modal categories.

The incorporation of secular melodies into the lauda repertory, a characteristic of the genre that continued at least until the eighteenth century, is a reminder that neither the 'monastic' and 'conciliar' traditions of concern and complaint about sacred music, nor the music which these traditions fostered, were totally unrelated. The use of the Savonarolan chant 'Ecce quam bonum' in polyphonic compositions is something of a special case because of its political potency, but there are other examples of melodies from the lauda repertory being incorporated into liturgical and even secular polyphony.[34] In fact, traditional categories are clearly unhelpful in this context, and even the attitudes of reformers towards a broad distinction between 'sacred' and 'secular' seem to be ambiguous, if not actually contradictory. Similarly, the interpenetration of 'popular' and 'art' music, and of written and unwritten traditions, is widespread and complicated with influences travelling in both directions. These elements come together in the polyphonic laude written for Roman consumption in the second half of the century, most noticeably in the works of Animuccia and in the activities of Filippo Neri, both of whom were Florentine by birth and had been formed in the Florentine tradition. In this sense, they were the true inheritors of the Savonarolan practices of popular music, ritual, devotion and spirituality, which, relatively free from censure and the political overtones of republicanism, could be executed with greater freedom in Rome than in Medicean Florence.

---

[34]   For extensive treatment of the phenomenon of Savonarolan laude being incorporated into polyphonic compositions, see Patrick Macey, *Bonfire Songs: Savonarola's Musical Legacy* (Oxford: Clarendon Press, 1998), Part II. For some non-Savonarolan examples, see Agostino Ziino, 'Testi laudistici musicati da Palestrina', in *Atti del Convegno di studi palestriniani*, ed. by Francesco Luisi (Palestrina: Fondazione G.P. Da Palestrina, 1977), pp. 381–408.

CHAPTER 9

Church Reform and Devotional Music in Sixteenth-Century Rome: The Influence of Lay Confraternities

Noel O'Regan

For music historians, the effects of religious change on music in the Roman Catholic Church in the late sixteenth century have always been somewhat difficult to pin down.[1] While much discussion preceded and accompanied the deliberations of the Council of Trent's twenty-second session in 1562, the ensuing pronouncement was extremely short and dealt only with secular influence on music for the Mass: 'Let them keep away from the churches compositions in which there is an intermingling of the lascivious or impure, whether on the organ or in the voice.'[2] The twenty-fourth session in 1563 laid down that provincial synods should prescribe an established form for the proper direction of the divine offices, including singing and playing on instruments. As Craig Monson has pointed out, although there had been much deliberation surrounding the issue of the intelligibility of the words and an instruction covering this area had been discussed at the Council during the twenty-second session, it did not find its way into the final documents.[3] However, the strong views of churchmen such as Cardinals Borromeo and Paleotti, as well as subsequent instructions by provincial synods in Rome and Milan, meant that a need for comprehensibility of religious texts in musical settings quickly became identified in the minds of commentators, composers and their employers as having emanated from the Council.[4]

---

[1]   The most recent survey, particularly of the role of the Council of Trent, is Craig Monson, 'The Council of Trent Revisited', *Journal of the American Musicological Society*, 55 (2002), 1–37, which also contains a useful bibliography. The classic studies for music are: Karl Gustav Fellerer, 'Church Music and the Council of Trent', *Musical Quarterly*, 39 (1953), 578–80; Lewis H. Lockwood, *The Counter-Reformation and the Masses of Vincenzo Ruffo* (Studi di Musica Veneta, 2) ([Vienna]: Universal Edition, 1969).

[2]   Monson translates the word 'organo' in the Latin orginal as 'instrument': Monson, 'The Council of Trent Revisited', p. 11.

[3]   Ibid., pp. 1–19.

[4]   Ibid.

Iain Fenlon has suggested that traditional historiography of Catholic music reform has focused too narrowly on the Council of Trent and its decrees and on a relatively small number of works by composers such as Giovanni Pierluigi da Palestrina in Rome and Vincenzo Ruffo in Milan, ignoring the impact of more populist traditions, particularly that of the *lauda spirituale* given a new lease of life in the Florence of Girolamo Savanarola and transplanted to Rome by Filippo Neri.[5] Some years ago, the Italian historian Agostino Borromeo, also raised questions about the real effects of the guidelines issued by the Council of Trent on common musical practice.[6] Borromeo wondered, for instance, how much the so-called 'Tridentine' repertoire (that is, the reform masses of Palestrina, Giovanni Animuccia and Ruffo) was used in minor institutions. He also asked how much pre-Tridentine music continued in use after the 1560s. In the context of late-sixteenth-century Rome, the answer to his second question is: a considerable amount. For example, Palestrina's *First Book of Masses* of 1554, which contained some pretty uncompromisingly pre-Tridentine settings, was continually bought by Roman institutions and reprinted into the 1590s.[7] The *Masses* and *Magnificats* of Cristóbal de Morales, published in the early 1540s, continued to be popular in Rome. The *Magnificats* were reprinted in Venice in 1562 while the Council of Trent was in session and were copied into manuscript for the papal choir as late as 1576; they were supplanted only in the early 1580s by those of another Spanish composer, Tomás Luis de Victoria.[8] As far as Borromeo's first question is concerned, evidence is harder to come by. What he seems to be implying is that much of the Tridentine debate and subsequent experiments with style were somewhat esoteric, removed from the experience of the ordinary church-going public. It is doubtful if the average mid-sixteenth-century Mass-goer was aware that a setting of the

    [5]   Iain Fenlon, 'Music and reform: the Savonarolan legacy', in Iain Fenlon, *Music and Culture in Late Renaissance Italy* (Oxford: Oxford University Press, 2002), pp. 44–66.

    [6]   Agostino Borromeo, 'La storia delle cappelle musicali vista nella prospettiva della storia della chiesa', in Oscar Mischiati and Paolo Russo (eds), *La Cappella Musicale nell'Italia della Controriforma: Atti del Convegno internazionale di studi nel IV Centenario di fondazione della Cappella Musicale di S. Biagio di Cento, Cento, 13–15 ottobre 1989* (Florence: Olschki, 1993), pp. 229–37.

    [7]   I am currently preparing a book on Roman confraternities and their music, 1486–1650, which will give details of inventories and records of purchases of music by various confraternities. Among those which held Palestrina's 1554 Masses were S. Rocco, mentioned in an inventory of 1583 (Rome, Archivio di Stato, Fondo Ospedale di S. Rocco, 175, f. 31v) and S. Giovanni dei Fiorentini (purchased together with other music books in 1586: Rome, Archivio dell'Arciconfraternita di S. Giovanni dei Fiorentini, 198, non-foliated: 25 April 1586). The Masses were reprinted in 1572, 1581, 1591 and 1596.

    [8]   Both Morales' and Victoria's works are found in virtually all surviving inventories from Roman institutions in the sixteenth or seventeenth centuries.

Ordinary was based on a courtly secular song or was worried that the words were not clearly distinguishable. Of course, we do not know what the general public thought: the surviving documents are concerned with courtly or large church practice. The chances are, however, that the soul-searching left the man in the street largely untouched, with popular religious practices and devotions carrying on in their usual way. The music for such devotions had to be simple, capable of being sung during processions or by selected confraternity members in their oratories.

The contribution of such devotional music to stylistic change in the sixteenth century has been largely overlooked, the *lauda spirituale* excepted. Discussion of the effectiveness of Trent, with its focus on the pressure felt by musicians in Rome and Milan, and on the *Missa Papae Marcelli* of Palestrina, has tended to be concerned with settings of the Mass Ordinary. While significant, the Mass setting was only one genre among many, as Iain Fenlon has pointed out.[9] Within polyphonic sacred music, other genres were also important: psalms, hymns and Magnificats for Vespers; motets which were multivalent in their use; litanies for processions and oratory devotions; lamentation settings for the *Tenebrae* offices during Holy Week; the four Marian antiphons sung at the end of Compline or Vespers, above all the *Salve Regina*, which was also sung devotionally on Saturday evenings in front of images of the Virgin. Then there was a series of categories of devotional music in Italian: *laude spirituali*, *madrigali spirituali* and *canzonette spirituali*, as well as music for *sacre rapprasentationi*. In all of these, particularly those setting Italian texts, stylistic changes occurred over the course of the sixteenth century by a gradual process, dictated more from the ground up as a result of popular devotional requirements than by imposition from above. The simple direct musical style required, in which comprehension and expression of the text were paramount, was already in use for many of these genres throughout the sixteenth century and even before. In seeking to develop a new 'reformed' style, these models were to hand, as were the secular madrigals being composed alongside them.

The main vehicles for the commissioning and consumption of devotional music in Rome, as elsewhere, were lay confraternities. The first half of the sixteenth century saw a significant growth in their number in Rome, some coming from trade and artisan corporations, like S. Maria di Loreto dei Fornai or S. Eligio degli Orefici; others like S. Luigi dei Francesi or S. Giovanni dei Fiorentini, serving the various foreign nationalities (including those from other Italian states) in the city; others again were founded for devotional and charitable purposes like S. Spirito in Sassia or S. Gerolamo della Carità, running the city's hospitals, burying the dead, visiting

---

[9]   Fenlon, 'Music and reform: the Savonarolan legacy', p. 44.

prisons, or accompanying criminals to execution.[10] Among the oldest was the Gonfalone, refounded in the 1480s by amalgamating a number of existing groups of Racommandati della Beata Virgine, probably for the purposes of mounting a *sacra rappresentatione* of the Passion on Good Friday in the Colosseum.[11] This it did from 1490 until banned from doing so by Pope Paul III in 1534 because the anti-Semitic text led to violence against the city's Jewish population.[12] Other *sacre rappresentationi* were performed too, probably on other days. In the Jubilee Year of 1500, as well as the Passion, there were *rappresentationi* of the Resurrection and of the Gospel narrative from the death of Lazarus up to the expulsion of the money-changers from the Temple and the attempted stoning of Christ by the Pharisees.[13]

No music is extant from any of these *sacre rappresentationi*, but there are payments for the copying of music and for food for the singers, some of whom were in the regular employ of the confraternity's choir, so we know that sections of the text were sung.[14] As well as sections for individual characters, some sections of the text are marked 'chorus'; some are even marked for double chorus, something that sets them apart from other Italian Passion texts.[15] These commenting choruses, which come at the end of scenes like those of Greek tragedy, can be written for Prophets and Sibyls, Shepherds and Kings, Gentiles and Pharisees, the three Marys – or just labelled *primo*

---

[10]   For information on Roman confraternities, see Matizia Maroni Lumbroso and Antonio Martini, *Le confraternite romane nelle loro chiese* (Rome: Fondazione Marco Besso, 1963), and Luigi Fiorani et al., 'Repertorio degli archivi delle confraternite romane', in *Ricerche per la storia religiosa di Roma*, 6 (1985), 175–413. For a more general discussion of confraternities in Italy, see Christopher Black, *Italian Confraternities in the Sixteenth Century* (Cambridge: Cambridge University Press, 1989).

[11]   Luigi Ruggeri, *L'archiconfraternita del Gonfalone: Memorie del sacerdote Luigi Ruggeri* (Rome: Bernardo Morini, 1866); Anna Esposito, 'Le "confraternite" del Gonfalone (secoli XIV–XV)', *Ricerche per la storia religiosa di Roma*, 5 (1984), 91–136.

[12]   Nerida Newbiggin, 'The decorum of the Passion: The plays of the Confraternity of the Gonfalone in the Roman Colosseum, 1490–1539', in Barbara Wisch and Susan Munshower (eds), *Crossing the Boundaries: Christian Piety and the Arts in Medieval and Renaissance Confraternities*, Papers in Art History from The Pennsylvania State University, 6 (1990), pp. 172–202. Attempts to revive the play in the 1560s were unsuccessful.

[13]   Newbiggin, 'The decorum of the Passion', pp. 179–83.

[14]   The payments are found in the various *libri entrate-uscite* from 1490 onwards in the Fondo Arciconfraternita del Gonfalone in Rome, Archivio Segreto Vaticano (hereafter ASV). Full details will be included in my forthcoming book on Roman confraternities and their music.

[15]   Newbiggin, 'The decorum of the Passion', p. 180. Excerpts from the text, including the choruses, are given in Vincenzo di Bartholomaeis, *Laude drammatiche e rappresentazioni sacre*, vol. II (Florence: Felice L. Monnier 1943), and in Marco Vatasso, *Per la storia del dramma sacro in Italia*, Studi e Testi 10 (Rome, Vatican City: Tipografia Vaticana, 1903).

and *secondo coro*. We can only speculate about what the music might have been like. The characters must have used some sort of declamation akin to plainsong or the recitation formula of the liturgical singing of the passions during Holy Week. The choruses may have been more complex, or they might have been in *falsobordone*, a chordal harmonization of plainsong or plainsong-like melodies, which was often improvised and commonly used in Roman processions and liturgical celebrations. They might also have used the sort of formulaic three-part music found in contemporary *laude spirituali*; while none of the texts can be found in surviving *laude* collections, texts with a similar syllable and verse structure and with themes related to the Passion are commonly found in those collections. The Gonfalone text is known to have been largely the work of the Florentine Giuliano Dati, one of many Florentines who came to Rome during this period, bringing with them something of their tradition of popular singing of *laude*. In the Resurrection play, popular Latin texts such as the motet *Adoramus te, Christe* and the Marian antiphon *Regina Coeli* are instructed to be sung; these were probably performed in standard imitative polyphony since settings are relatively common from this and later periods. The rest of the music had to be simple and declamatory, appealing directly to ordinary people and easily sung from memory in the Colosseum.

The Passion play was not the only devotional activity engaged in by the Gonfalone. Its 1495 statutes include a chapter dealing with its five major processions. Two were general Roman processions, those of the Rogation days before the feast of St Mark (25 April) and before the Ascension, called the greater and lesser litanies.[16] The other three were specific to the confraternity: the feast of St Lucy (the patronal feast of its main church when dowries were handed out) and two feasts associated with the church of SS. Annunziata outside the walls near S. Sebastiano, the Annunciation (25 March) and the anniversary of the church's dedication (the first Sunday in May). Chapter 32 of the same statutes deals with the singers and their *maestro di canto figurato* and lists four further feast-days on which polyphony (*canto figurato*) was provided. These were the patronal feasts of the main component parts of the new confraternity: SS. Peter and Paul (the dedicatees of an old church which was to become the confraternity's oratory), St Mary Magdalene, St Lucy and the Forty Holy Martyrs. Two other feasts were also by long tradition celebrated by the confraternity with music: the Assumption and Candlemas. As well as all of these, there was also music during Mass on the first Sunday of each month when the confraternity gathered in their main church of St Lucy in order to take Communion together.

---

[16]   The statutes are given in full as an appendix to Esposito, 'Le "confraternite" del Gonfalone'.

Other confraternities had similar celebrations, though none had quite as many as the Gonfalone. One or two patronal feast-days were celebrated with processions which often included young girls to whom dowries were being given and prisoners which they had the privilege of having released. Virtually every day of the year saw at least one procession in some part of the city, all of them accompanied by singers and musicians.

What sort of music was performed during these processions? There is not much solid evidence, but the 1565 Statutes of the Archconfraternity of SS. Crocifisso specifically mention hymns and psalms, as well as some devout *laude* during the processions which accompanied their crucifix as it was carried around the outside of the church of S. Marcello on special feast-days.[17] In the Jubilee Year of 1550, the Gonfalone paid for the copying of five *madrigali* for four and five voices to sing in the Good Friday procession when singers from S. Giovanni in Laterano, S. Maria Maggiore and S. Spirito in Sassia were hired to take part.[18] The use of the word *madrigali* in this processional context is very unusual for this period in Rome but it presumably refers to pieces in the Italian language, most likely *laude spirituali*.[19] The word was used in this way in a description of a *sacra rapprasentatione* of the visit of the three Marys to the sepulchre during the Forty Hours devotion celebrated by the Compagnia del Arcangelo Raffaele on Easter Monday, 1593.[20] The singing of polyphonic motets in four and five parts was also common in processions, as evidenced by two surviving sets of partbooks for processional use that contain such a repertory.[21] Not surprisingly, eucharistic motets loom large, as well as the *Te Deum* and pieces for Holy Week and Easter. The style of these pieces is relatively simple and could have been sung while processing or during breaks in the actual procession. The Litany of the Saints was also commonly sung, particularly during Rogation Day processions, as well as the Litany of Loreto; various settings of both of these by Rome-based composers survive.

The banning of the Passion Play had two consequences for the Gonfalone's devotional life. One was the development of a Good Friday

---

[17]   *Statuti et ordini della Ven. Arciconfraternita del SS. Crocifisso in S. Marcello di Roma, con l'origine di essa* (Rome: Antonio Blado, 1585), Chapter 26.

[18]   Rome, ASV, 252, pp. 16–17. I am grateful to Barbara Wisch for drawing this payment to my attention.

[19]   It is also possible that spiritual madrigals are meant but the earliest Roman collection to use that word was not published until 1565 (see below).

[20]   John Walter Hill, 'Oratory Music in Florence, I: Recitar Cantando, 1583–1655', *Acta Musicologica*, 51 (1979), 108–36 (doc. 11, pp. 116, 134).

[21]   Noel O'Regan, 'Processions and their music in post-Tridentine Rome', *Recercare*, 4 (1992), 45–80.

procession to St Peter's basilica to be shown the relics of the Passion believed to be kept there (the veil of Veronica and the lance with which Longinus pierced Christ's side); this procession was also undertaken by SS. Crocifisso and eventually by many other confraternities. It was just one among a series of processions which accompanied virtually all confraternity activities: patronal feast-days with prisoners liberated by concession of the Pope, or with girls to whom dowries were given, Rogation Days, accompanying visiting groups of pilgrims around the four major basilicas, and so on. All processions had at least one group of musicians and often more than one: a small group at one end and a larger one at the other was a common practice. The musicians were placed near key elements such as crucifixes or floats, in order to draw attention to them. The music consisted of relatively simple motets, litanies, or *laude*, often for five voices.[22]

The other consequence of the banning of the Passion Play was the building of a purpose-built oratory in which devotional services took place during Lent and Holy Week. As the art historian Barbara Wisch has pointed out, the Gonfalone interiorized its devotion to the Passion in this private space, in which the walls were decorated with scenes of the Passion by the mannerist painters Federico Zuccari, Cesare de Nebbia and others.[23] The building of oratories and their housing of devotional services was probably the most significant development for confraternity music during the sixteenth century. They were designed primarily as meeting places but quickly also became the venue for the chanting of some of the divine offices once a week, or once a month, on the mornings of Sundays, or on special feast-days. The members gathered to chant the psalms and other items of Matins (just one nocturn), Lauds and Vespers, most commonly taken from the Office of the Blessed Virgin, but also from other offices appropriate to particular feasts. The model was the chanting of the mendicant orders, using the reciting tones appropriate to the different church modes; this became increasingly bound into the fabric of confraternity life as the sixteenth century progressed. The 1495 Statutes of the Gonfalone include among the duties of the *maestro di cappella* that of teaching singing ('canto') to those of the men of the confraternity and their sons who wished to learn; other confraternities preserve payments for a similar purpose. What sort of singing is not specified but, since these were not professional singers, the teaching would have concentrated on what they needed to know to chant the offices in the oratory and to sing in processions. Confraternity

---

[22]   Ibid.

[23]   Barbara Wolleson-Wisch, 'The Archiconfraternita del Gonfalone and its Oratory in Rome: Art and Counter-Reformation Spiritual Values', unpublished Ph.D. dissertation, University of California, Berkeley, 1985.

oratories like that of the Gonfalone needed a certain number of *coristati*, laymen experienced enough to lead the chanting of the offices.

As well as chant, some oratories encouraged the formation of small groups of more experienced singers to harmonize the chant in *falsobordone*. Some confraternities provided some training for these singers, who took part in the offices and in processions, SS. Crocifisso and S. Ambrogio dei Lombardi for example.[24] There was also the regular chanting of litanies, Marian antiphons – especially the ubiquitous *Salve Regina* – and psalms such as the *Miserere*. All of this meant that confraternity members, which included a majority of the city's population, became accustomed to psalm-singing and got to know the texts of the common psalms and other items of the liturgy. It also provided a ready market for simple and uncomplicated polyphonic settings of these items.

Oratories were, above all, associated with Lent and Holy Week activities. Lenten Friday devotions, including a sermon and psalm-singing, may have started at the Dominican church of S. Maria sopra Minerva, home to a number of confraternities, during the second quarter of the sixteenth century. In 1559, the confraternity of SS. Crocifisso decided that, instead of processing to that church, they would hold their own devotional exercises in their temporary oratory at S. Marcello, where they were based;[25] shortly afterwards, they began to build their own oratory, completed in 1568.[26] The earliest payment to musicians for their Friday devotions comes two years later, in 1561, when one *scudo* was paid to 'cantori per li sette salmi per tutta la quadragesima'.[27] These were the seven penitential psalms, regularly mentioned in connection with Lenten devotions: they included Vulgate Ps. 6 (*Domine ne in furore tuo*), Ps. 50 (*Miserere mei, Deus*) and Ps. 69 (*De Profundis*). The most significant was the *Miserere*, a particularly totemic psalm for Lenten and Holy Week devotions, of which many settings in decorated *falsobordone* survive.

Other oratories with Lenten devotions and music in the second half of the sixteenth and the early seventeenth centuries included SS. Trinita, S. Maria dell'Orto, S. Giovanni dei Fiorentini, S. Maria del Pianto and S. Maria dell'Orazione e Morte (which also had similar devotions with

---

[24]   Rome, ASV, Fondo SS. Crocifisso in S. Marcello, A XII 1573, A XII 1574, non-foliated: 24 March 1574: 'a il mastro che insegni cantare a Oratio di musica per il mese di Marzo ... baiocchi 60'; Archivio di SS. Ambrogio e Carlo al Corso, 89, non-foliated, 5 April 1574: 'a Maestro Giovanni Francese per la sua provisione d'imparare il falsobordone alli giovani del oratorio per Marzo passato ... scudo 1.'

[25]   ASV, Fondo SS. Crocifisso, P I 55, f. 376.

[26]   Josephine Von Henneberg, *L'oratorio dell'Archiconfraternita del Santissimo Crocifisso di San Marcello* (Rome: Bulzoni, 1974).

[27]   ASV, Fondo SS. Crocifisso, F XIX 23, non-foliated.

music during the octave of the dead in the first week of November), and there must have been more.[28] The music got rather more elaborate as the sixteenth century moved to a close, with aristocratic guardians paying out ever-increasing sums of money for hired-in singers and instrumentalists who sang more complex music. As well as the penitential psalms and Marian antiphons, Gospel dialogues were common and these were to grow into small-scale oratorios in the seventeenth century and ultimately into full-fledged oratorios by the middle of the seventeenth century.[29]

The oratories also played host to professional singers for the offices of *Tenebrae* on the last three days of Holy Week. These were more sombre settings, in contrast to the Lenten devotions, and consisted of the chanting of psalms, and the singing in polyphony of the first three lessons (taken from the lamentations of Jeremiah) and the nine responsories. Lamentations are an interesting case from a stylistic perspective: they used two different musical techniques, complex imitative polyphony in the Hebrew letters at the start of each verse and much simpler chordal declamation in the verses. Each office culminated with settings of the *Miserere* and the *Benedictus* in *falsobordone*, simple harmonizations in homophonic chordal style. Particularly characteristic in Rome were settings for two choirs, one of four singers and the other of five. The singers, especially the sopranos, added improvised ornaments (*abellimenti*) to their parts. The most famous example is the setting by Gregorio Allegri that was sung for centuries in the Cappella Pontificia.

The music associated with oratories has, for the most part, not survived; this can partly explain why it has largely been ignored by music historians. It was generally simple *gebrauchsmusik*, easily replaceable and not worth saving. One uniquely surviving complete set of twelve partbooks (Rome, Biblioteca Nazionale Mss. Mus. 77–88) gives an insight: packed with *falsobordone* settings of the *Miserere* and *Benedictus*; it also includes a complete set of Holy Week lamentations and responsories as well as numerous Marian antiphons and psalms, such as the penitential *De profundis* also set in *falsobordone*.[30] While this set of partbooks cannot

---

[28]   For SS. Trinità dei Pellegrini, see Noel O'Regan, *Institutional Patronage in Post-Tridentine Rome: Music at Santissima Trinità dei Pellegrini 1550–1650*, (London: Royal Musical Association, 1995). For S. Maria dell'Orazione e Morte, see A. Bevignani, *Le rappresentazione sacre per l'ottavario dei Morti in Roma* (Rome: Società Romana di Storia Patria, 1910). Details of Lenten devotions in the other confraternities will be given in my forthcoming book.

[29]   See Howard Smither, *A History of the Oratorio*, vol. 1: *The Oratorio in the Baroque Era: Italy, Vienna, Paris* (Chapel Hill, NC: University of North Carolina Press, 1977), Chapter 3.

[30]   For a full listing, see Noel O'Regan, 'Palestrina and the oratory of SS. Trinità dei Pellegrini', in *Atti del II Congresso internazionale di studi palestriniani, 1986* (Palestrina:

be associated directly with a particular Roman confraternity, its compiler, Annibale Zoilo, worked for a number of these bodies and the repertory is clearly appropriate for Lenten and Holy Week ceremonies. This circumstantial evidence is strengthened by the contents of the surviving manuscripts of the only Roman confraternity to preserve some music from the sixteenth century, that of SS. Crocifisso in S. Marcello. Because it did not own the church of S. Marcello in which it was based, it made even more use of its oratory than other confraternities and so its surviving music is most likely to have been used in that oratory. There are three motet prints by Palestrina and six incomplete sets of manuscript partbooks.[31] Between them, these contain a very similar repertory to that in the Biblioteca Nazionale partbooks: Holy Week lamentations and responsories, Holy Week motets, *Miserere* and *Benedictus* settings, Marian antiphons and psalm-motets. Two of the surviving sets originally had twelve partbooks, but only one and three, respectively, of these survive. These also contain some large-scale, more general-purpose motets for up to twelve voices that reflect the increasingly patrician nature of SS. Crocifisso's membership and its consequent need for more sophisticated music.

The resemblance between the contents of these SS. Crocifisso manuscripts and Mss. Mus. 77–88 strengthens the case for both of them as transmitting something of a Roman confraternity repertory. At the same time, this is music that has been copied and has survived and so is a repertory that its composers or the confraternity wished to retain, that is, music perceived to have some lasting value. While some settings are in simple chordal style, they represent only a fraction of the *falsobordone* improvisations that may well have been many confraternity members' main experience of music. This now-invisible repertory was heard at weekly or monthly offices and in processions, sung by singers or members with limited experience. The singing of more complex polyphony by professional singers was exceptional, confined to one or two patronal feasts and to Lent and Holy Week.

Rome's devotional confraternities were given a huge boost by the arrival in the late 1530s of two of the century's major figures for religious reform: Ignatius Loyola and Philip Neri. Loyola's influence was felt through his and his followers' support for confraternities working with reformed prostitutes, catechumens, orphans, the mentally deranged and prisoners.[32] The Jesuits were particularly supportive of the Arciconfraternita della

Fondazione G. Pierluigi da Palestrina, 1991), pp. 95–121 and O'Regan, *Institutional Patronage in Post-Tridentine Rome*, pp. 68–70

[31]   ASV, Fondo SS. Crocifisso, Q XX 3.

[32]   Lance Lazar, 'The first Jesuit confraternity and marginalized groups in sixteenth-century Rome', in Nicholas Terpstra (ed.), *The Politics of Ritual Kinship* (Cambridge: Cambridge University Press, 2000), pp. 132–49.

Dottrina Christiana, which organized the teaching of catechism to young boys and girls and used very simple music to help memorize prayers like the *Pater noster* and *Ave Maria*, as well as the Creed.[33] Sunday Schools were held in parish and other churches and, to give the children a break from learning the catechism, *laude spirituali* were sung.

In 1573, Jacques Ledesma, a Spanish Jesuit working in Rome, published his *Modo per insegnar la dottrina christiana* in that city, the preface of which stresses the importance placed on music at these gatherings, both to help memorize texts and to counteract the singing of songs with rude words:

> … In particular the reason for singing, especially in places where to sing like this is a novelty, is because thus the pupils learn more easily and especially those, who do not know very well how to speak or how to read, and those of uncouth mind, peasant boys and girls; since the memory is reinforced by singing [the material] and the teaching is made more sweet; also in places where rude (*brutti*) songs are commonly sung, [it is better] to sing those holy and good songs; we also have the example of the early church which sang in the morning and in the evening the praises of God. For these and other similar reasons, the church today causes sacred things to be sung.[34]

In 1576, in Milan, a small book of *Lodi e Canzoni spirituali per cantar insieme con la Dottrina Christiana* was published as a companion to the revised 1576 *Dottrina Christiana a modo di dialogo* published in the same city. It included a few very simple melodies harmonized in four parts that could be used for a number of *laude*. Formulae like this allowed children to memorize important prayers. For older confraternity members, memorizing key prayers and psalms was also crucial. Basic chants such as the *Salve Regina*, *Miserere*, *De Profundis* and the *Te Deum* were known to all confraternity members. Part of the founding mythology of the

---

[33]   Giancarlo Rostirolla, 'Laudi e canti religiosi per l'esercizio spirituale della Dottrina cristiana al tempo di Roberto Bellarmino', in Giancarlo Rostirolla, Danilo Zardin and Oscar Mischiati, *La Lauda Spirituale tra cinque e seicento. Poesie e canti devozionali nell'Italia della Controriforma. Volume offerto a Giancarlo Rostirolla nel suo sessantesimo compleanno*, ed. by Giuseppe Filippi et al. (Rome: IBIMUS, 2001, pp. 275–472.

[34]   '[E]t particolarmente le cause perché si canta; principalmente ne i luoghi, dove è cosa nuova cantare così; cioè perché i putti imparino più facilmente, et ancora quelli, che non sanno ben parlare, et quelli che non sanno leggere, et i rozi d'ingegno, rustici, et le donne; si perché si conferma la memoria co'l canto et si fa più soave l'imparare; et acciò in luogo di canzoni brutte, che si sogliono cantare, si cantino cose sante, et buone; si anco perché n'habbiamo l'essempio nella primitiva Chiesa, che cantavano hinni la mattina, et la sera in lode di Dio. Onde per queste, et altre simile cause hoggidì canta la Chiesa le cose sacre': Jacques Ledesma, *Modo per insegnar la dottrina christiana* (Rome, Antonio Blado, 1573), f. 8v (my translation).

Confraternita dell'Orazione e Morte contains two stories about the power of recitation and singing.[35] Its members undertook the task of searching in the Roman *campagna* for dead bodies and giving them a decent burial. In one story from the early years, some of the brothers became extremely hungry while collecting a body fifteen miles from the city. They tried a number of villages but could not get any food. Eventually they turned to prayer and recited a *Miserere* and *De profundis* for the souls of the dead; as soon as they finished their chanting a man appeared with seventeen loaves and some herrings. They offered to buy these but while they were counting them the man disappeared. This was reckoned a miracle with, of course, overtones of the multiplication of the loaves and fishes and its Eucharistic symbolism. On another occasion while out recovering bodies, some brothers took shelter in a cave. They heard a voice saying 'go outside, brothers', 'uscite fratelli', three times. They obeyed the voice and went outside and immediately the cave collapsed. Their response was to sing the *Te Deum* in gratitude.

Filippo Neri's Florentine upbringing under the influence of the Piagnoni, followers of the Dominican reformer, Girolamo Savonarola, saw him steeped in the *laudesi* tradition of popular singing of *laude spirituali* by guilds and confraternities.[36] His first confraternity involvement in Rome was as one of the founders of SS. Trinità dei Pellegrini, a confraternity devoted to the care of pilgrims and convalescents. After ordination, he moved in 1551 to S. Gerolamo della Carità, a confraternity founded by the future Pope Clement VII Medici in 1518 for devotional purposes and for the care of prisoners.[37] While there, he began to welcome people to his room for informal religious gatherings that quickly expanded and were eventually to be more formalized in the oratories of S. Giovanni dei Fiorentini and S. Maria in Vallicella (the Chiesa Nuova). Neri was very conscious of the power of music in attracting people to his meetings. He was fortunate to have the services of a fellow Florentine, Giovanni Animuccia, an extremely accomplished musician who attached himself early on to Neri.[38] Animuccia was appointed *maestro di cappella* at St Peter's in 1555 and remained there until his death in 1571. He was a regular attendee at Neri's gatherings, both outdoor and indoor, organizing

---

[35] *Statuti dell'Arciconfraternita della Morte et Oratione* (Rome: Paolo Blado, 1590), Chapter 1.

[36] Iain Fenlon, 'Music and reform: the Savonarolan legacy'. See also the same author's contribution to this volume.

[37] Lumbroso and Martini, *Le Confraternite romane nelle loro chiese*, pp. 149–54.

[38] Lewis Lockwood and Noel O'Regan, 'Animuccia', in Stanley Sadie and John Tyrell (eds), *The New Grove Dictionary of Music and Musicians* (London: Grove Publications, 2001), Vol. 1, pp. 686–8.

singers and composing music. The indoor gatherings, also known as the *Oratorio Vespertina*, became more formal as time went on, taking on many of the characteristics of the Lenten devotions in confraternity oratories. Animuccia oversaw the publication of the first Roman book of *laude spirituali*, published in 1563. This has already been given significant attention: it consisted of very simple three- and four-voiced *Laude* that responded to the need for good popular music to be interspersed between sermons and prayers.[39]

In 1565 and 1570, Animuccia published two very significant collections, both of which broke the mould in combining both sacred and secular forms, motets and madrigals or *laude*, setting both Latin and Italian texts, in the one publication. The first of these, published in Rome in 1565, was his *Il primo libro de madrigali, a tre voci … con alcuni motetti, et madrigali spirituali*; it was the first Roman publication to use the title 'madrigali spirituali'. The book was dedicated to the brothers Marco and Piero del Nero, two young men closely involved with Filippo Neri's burgeoning oratory. Its dedication is worth quoting in part, capturing as it does the ambience of Neri's own apostolate among the young:

> And if perchance, in this hot season, you find yourselves either weary from your serious studies or fatigued from strenuous exercise, or simply wishing to disport yourselves in that paradise of Arcetrum, these [pieces] will allow you some recreation which will keep my memory alive in you: this is what I would wish more than anything else and I recommend myself to the favour of you both, praying God for your happiness.[40]

The collection is evenly balanced between the secular and the spiritual, containing twelve secular madrigals, five spiritual ones and seven motets. Secular and spiritual madrigals are alike in their lightness of touch and their delight in syncopated rhythms in line with the words. Compared with Animuccia's *Il primo libro delle laude spirituali* of 1563, two years

---

[39]   Giancarlo Rostirolla, 'La musica a Roma al tempo del cardinal Baronio: L'oratorio e la produzione laudistica in ambiente romano' in Rostirolla, Zardin and Mischiati, *La Lauda Spirituale tra cinque e seicento*, pp. 1–209; Arnaldo Morelli, *Il tempio armonico: Musica nell'oratorio dei Filippini in Roma (1575–1705)*, Analecta Musicologica 27 (Rome: Laber, 1991).

[40]   'Et essi per avventura, quando voi sarete in questa calda stagione, o affaticati nelli studii più gravi, o stanchi nelli essercitii più faticosi, o veramente à disportarvi in quel paradiso d'Arcetri, vi faranno di qualche recreamento cagione; il quale terrà viva in voi la memoria di me: la qual cosa io sopra ogni altra desidero, et alla buona gratia d'ambedue mi raccomando, pregando Dio per la vostra felicità': Giovanni Animuccia, *Il primo libro de madrigali, a tre voci … con alcuni motetti, et madrigali spirituali* (Rome: Valerio Dorico, 1565), f. 2 (my translation).

previously, the music is rhythmically more complex and makes more use of imitation between the voices. The motets bring some of the lightness and freshness of the contemporary three-voice secular *canzonetta*, for instance, by pitting two high voices against a lower one. In this, they anticipate the popularity of the *canzonetta spirituale* in 1580s Rome.[41] This sort of writing can also be seen as an antecedent of the *concertato* motet for small numbers of voices which was to blossom in Rome about thirty years later: Animuccia's alto parts could easily be transposed down an octave and played on an organ, to provide a *basso continuo* to accompany the upper two voices.[42]

Animuccia's 1570 *Il secondo libro delle laudi* has justifiably received a lot of attention.[43] It was unique in *laude* collections in including settings for up to eight voices and, like the 1565 *madrigali*, it included Latin motets, many of them too for eight voices. Some of the latter are Gospel dialogues, of the type later to be much used in the oratory of SS. Crocifisso.[44] The eight-voice pieces here also represent the first embryonic attempts by a Roman composer to write music for double choir: while not consistently split into two choirs there is considerable use of antiphonal groupings, particular in the dialogue-motets. In his forward, Animuccia specifically singles out the city's patricians, 'the most important gentlemen and prelates' who, he says, are increasingly attending Neri's gatherings and for whom he thought fit to include pieces that increased the number of voices and provided greater variety. He sought to vary the texture as much as possible, and the language, while conscious of the need not to obscure the words. What he attempted was to produce a collection that, like that of 1565, combined simple popular music with more sophisticated settings. These would appeal at the same time to a more lowly and a more courtly public. He was combining the music associated with his high-ranking position as *maestro di cappella* at St Peter's with that of his more everyday outreach work for Neri's oratory. Interestingly, this approach seems not to have been particularly successful: neither publication was reprinted

---

[41]   Carlo Assenza: *La canzonetta dal 1570 al 1615* (Lucca: Libreria Musicale Italiana, 1997).

[42]   Noel O'Regan, 'Asprilio Pacelli, Ludovico da Viadana and the Origins of the Roman Concerto Ecclesiastico', *Journal of Seventeenth-Century Music*, 6 (2000) <http://www.sscm-jscm.org/jscm/v6/no1/Oregan.html> accessed 1 August 2008.

[43]   Smither, *A History of the Oratorio*, pp. 73–4; Thomas Noel O'Regan, 'Sacred Polychoral Music in Rome 1575–1621', unpublished D.Phil. dissertation, University of Oxford, 1988, pp. 145–59; Fenlon, 'Music and reform: the Savonarolan legacy'. See also the same author's contribution to this volume.

[44]   Domenico Alaleona, *Studi su la storia dell'oratorio musicale in Italia* (Turin: Fratelli Bocca, 1908; reprinted Milan: Fratelli Bocca, 1945), Chapter 11; Smither, *A History of the Oratorio*, Chapter 3.

and the idea of mixing genres and languages was not imitated by others. After Animuccia's death in 1571, the next collection of *laude spirituali* for Neri's oratory, prepared by the oratorian priest and papal castrato singer Francisco Soto de Langa in 1577, reverted to the earlier model of simplicity and small number of voices.[45] *Lauda* or spiritual madrigal and motet remained in separate compartments but the cross-fertilization was to remain important for church music.

Animuccia's two publications were important in helping to seal a paradigm shift in Roman sacred music in the 1560s. Gone was the complexity that had generally characterized Roman music of the 1550s, replaced by a directness and a consciousness of projecting the words which was to remain central to the writing of sacred music thereafter. The reformers' concerns about intelligibility coincided with a new awareness of the rhetorical powers of music, as a result of humanist interest in ancient texts.[46] This led to a more transparent musical language that was more easily placed at the service of the text; an analogous shift was taking place in secular music at the same time. Over the decades following 1563, sacred music both expanded, into settings for two and more choirs, and contracted, into solos, duets and trios with keyboard or lute accompaniment. Both trends allowed the words to be heard without sacrificing too much musical interest. At the same time, the older imitative approach (often referred to as the *stile antico* or *stile osservato*) was not abandoned entirely: it continued in use for particular parts of the liturgy such as the Ordinary of the Mass and Vespers hymns.

After his death in 1571, Animuccia was replaced as *maestro di cappella* at St Peter's basilica by Palestrina, who had given up the position to Animuccia back in 1555 when he was appointed a singer in the Cappella Pontificia. Palestrina also had the title of composer to that Cappella, granted in return for writing some music for it in the 1560s. He was now in undisputed poll position in Rome, even if his personal finances did not allow him to take full advantage by immediately pushing out a series of publications. Like virtually all musicians active in Rome, he supplemented his income by providing music for a number of confraternities on a freelance basis, using singers from the choirs of which he was *maestro di cappella*, either for patronal feast-day celebrations, or for the Corpus Christi or

[45] *Il terzo libro delle laudi spirituali stampate ad instantia delli Reverendi Padri della Congregatione dell'Oratorio* (Rome: Antonio Blado, 1577). See Rostirolla, 'La musica a Roma al tempo del cardinal Baronio', pp. 88–9.

[46] Iain Fenlon, 'Music and Society', in *idem* (ed.), *Man and Music: The Renaissance* (London: Macmillan, 1989), pp. 1–62.

MaundyThursday/Good Friday processions.[47] Among those confraternities were the Gonfalone, SS. Crocifisso, S. Giacomo degli Spagnoli and SS. Trinita dei Pellegrini. During the important decade of the 1560s, he is now known to have been involved with both S. Luca dei Pintori and S. Maria di Loreto dei Fornari, in his capacity as *maestro di cappella* of S. Maria Maggiore.[48] The sums of money involved were small: S. Luca in particular was a relatively poor confraternity. What is significant is that they provided Palestrina with an alternative source of patronage, with different requirements to the major institutions: confraternities needed music which was at once simple but bright and ear-catching, music which could impress but which also spoke immediately to its consumer-listeners.

This was also true of Palestrina's involvement with the newly established Seminario Romano to which he moved in late 1566 or 1567. Here he came into close contact with the Jesuits who were tasked with training priests in a more organized way and in a community setting; training in liturgy and in sacred music was seen as an important part of the process. Here too, the music used had to make a direct impact, different from that used in the formal atmosphere of S. Maria Maggiore or the other major basilicas. The Jesuits were at this time moving from a position of suspicion of music, caused particularly by a fear of being forced to chant the offices in choir, to a realization of its powers of attraction and use as an evangelical tool. This brought music's rhetorical powers into play, something which chimed with contemporary humanist interest in expressing the text.

These various influences can be seen to have played their part in the paradigm shift in Roman music of the late 1560s and 1570s mentioned earlier. One publication from this period which has perhaps not been given the attention it deserves is Palestrina's *Liber primus ... mottettorum, 5,6,7vv*, published in Rome by Dorico in 1569. Palestrina had previously published a conventional collection of four-voice motets in 1563. His 1569 collection is for larger forces (five to seven voices), making direct comparison difficult, since the greater number of voices naturally encouraged Palestrina to use greater contrasts in voice groupings and to experiment with texture. It is a mixed collection, bringing together pieces from the previous decade and maybe earlier. Some are retrospective in style, in the strongly imitative or canonic style of the previous generation. But many pieces in this collection show a very new concern for texture and

---

[47]   Noel O'Regan, 'Palestrina, a musician and composer in the market-place', *Early Music*, 22 (1994), 551–70.

[48]   Unpublished research by the author. Rome, Archivio dell'Accademia di S. Luca, 41 (*Libro del Camerlengo, 1548–97*), ff 67v, 69; Rome, Archivio di Stato, Fondo S. Maria di Loreto di Fornai, 20 (*Libro Entrate-Uscite del Camerlengo, 1564–76*), non-foliated.

for expressing the text through a much closer relationship between words and music.

A good example is the five-voice *Crucem sanctam subiit*, which has little conventional imitative writing. While we have no evidence for its commissioning by the confraternity of SS. Crocifisso, *Crucem sanctam* would certainly have been very appropriate for performance there: it is based on the plainsong *Magnificat* antiphon for the feast of the Invention of the Holy Cross, one of that confraternity's two patronal feasts.[49] Its block-chordal opening in breves is characteristic of a number of the 1569 pieces, particularly those beginning with vocative phrases such as *O magnum mysterium* or *Viri Galilei*. The three opening chords in *Crucem sanctam* run through a circle of fifths before breaking out into figuration that continues to be based on a chordal progression. It is a call to attention, a deliberate search for a quick reaction and brings the techniques of the *falsobordone* into more formal play. After a repeat of the opening gesture a fifth lower, the bottom four voices declaim the succeeding phrase, 'qui infernum confregit', starting in stark homophony but quickly becoming figurative under a *cantus firmus*-like line in the soprano. The next phrase, 'accinctus est potentia', introduces word-painting of the type used in the contemporary madrigal: two voices are bound together in thirds against a rhythmically contrasted third part. Then the three highest voices burst in with a high chordal 'surrexit dies tertia', in which the syncopated declamation temporarily moves from duple to triple rhythm. The three lower voices repeat the phrase antiphonally, then all five voices together sing the phrase for the third time, emphasizing 'tertia'. A short Alleluia leads to a repetition of the second half of the piece, though nothing is reiterated exactly: differences in texture and scoring ensure a subtle variety. The underlying harmony in this piece shows a new clarity arising out of the more frequent cadences that mark off the short contrasting sections, as in the Gloria and Credo of the same composer's well-known *Missa Papae Marcelli*. All is carefully calculated theatrically and the motet is an early example of a type shortly to become commonplace in Rome, by composers such as Tomás Luis de Victoria and the two sets of brothers, Felice and Giovanni Francesco Anerio, and Giovanni Maria and Giovanni Bernardino Nanino. Like them, Palestrina wrote simple *gebrauchsmusik* too, some of it published in the final volumes of the Haberl edition, for

---

49   Interestingly, the piece is included in the anthology *Responsoria, antiphonae et hymni in processionibus per annum*, published by Nicolò Mutii in Rome in 1596. This was compiled by Jean Matelart, *maestro di cappella* at the Roman basilica of S. Lorenzo in Damaso, who was very active in providing festal and processional music for confraternities. It is included in a number of pieces to be sung during the procession of the Greater Litanies on the feast of St Mark.

example.[50] The fusing of elements from courtly music with those of the popular devotional repertoire, together with approaches to the text that were honed in madrigal writing, led to a new Roman style of sacred composition in the late sixteenth century. In this process the freelance work that Palestrina and others did in the Roman confraternity marketplace played a significant part.

Musical change in sixteenth-century Rome was a gradual and organic process. There had long been a strong undercurrent of popular religion in the city that called forth its own musical response, seeking largely functional and simple music to accompany *sacre rapprasentationi*, processions and oratory devotions. In the aftermath of Trent, during the papacies of Pius V and Gregory XIII in particular, devotion became increasingly fashionable and necessary for social and religious advancement. The Holy Year of 1575, in particular, gave a strong boost to this process, with the city on show, as it were, to the thousands of visiting pilgrims. Music had long been an integral part of the urban experience, everything from the sound of bells to the chanting of friars and the playing of wind-bands and trumpeters which all accompanied ritual and devotional actions. While polyphonic Mass settings and motets may only have been heard by the few, and listened to seriously by even fewer, a much broader cross-section was likely to have heard the simpler devotional music. The fact that much of this latter music has by its nature not survived should not lead us to ignore its one-time existence. The integration of some of its strengths into art music by composers like Animuccia and Palestrina during the 1560s and later, helped lead to a renewal of sacred music in the city's major basilicas.

---

[50]   Giovanni Pierluigi da Palestrina, *Werke*, ed. by F.X. Haberl et al. (Leipzig: Breitkopf & Härtel, 1862–1907), vols 30–33.

CHAPTER 10

Liturgy as a Mode of Theological Discourse in Tasso's Late Works

Matthew Treherne

Standing between modern readers and Torquato Tasso's heavily religious work of the 1590s are a number of commonplaces and critical presuppositions. Those presuppositions might perhaps best be emblematized by Romantic images of the poet, such as Delacroix's 1839 painting of a misunderstood Tasso languishing in a cell in Sant'Anna, his writings scattered on the floor, leering faces from the ignorant world outside mocking him through the bars. This notion of Tasso's sensibility becoming increasingly restricted by his desire to be conform to the Church, at the great expense of his artistic expression, continues to echo in various ways in criticism of the poet's work – yet the assumptions underlying it are worth questioning, and in many ways hinder a full understanding of artistic and poetic expression in the wake of the Council of Trent. One such assumption is that any sign of the poet willingly conforming to the dictates of an increasingly authoritarian Church necessarily indicates a relinquishing of his authentic poetic voice, and inevitably diminishes the value and interest of his work. Perhaps because of our knowledge of Tasso's difficult personal history, and because the appeal of works such as the *Gerusalemme liberata* and *Aminta* was never matched by these later texts, modern scholars have largely neglected the possibility that the orthodoxy of the later works might represent not intellectual inhibition, but the discovery of new theological and poetic resources. Even if the poetry which emerged from that discovery failed to match the heights of the earlier works, which were so quickly established in the Western canon, it is worth taking seriously, and indeed represents a form of subtle orthodoxy which deserves attention alongside the cultural modes of resistance to the authority of the Church, which are rightly the focus of much current research on Counter-Reformation Italy.

Whatever the artistic consequences of the shift, it is undeniable that Tasso's work took a strongly religious turn in the last decade of his life. The 1590s saw the publication of his revision of the *Gerusalemme liberata*, as the *Gerusalemme conquistata* (1593), and associated writings published in defence of the new work (primarily the *Giudicio sovra la Gerusalemme riformata* (1593) and the *Discorsi del poema eroico* (1594)). This period also saw the publication of the devotional *Lagrime della beata vergine* (1593), a twenty-five stanza meditation on the Sorrows of the Virgin, and of the blank verse *Il mondo creato* (1594), a highly ambitious account of the Creation. The new religious preoccupation is demonstrated, too, by the poet's developing interest in theology, which can be traced back to his time in the hospital of Sant'Anna.[1]

Accounts of Tasso's work have tended to see his religiosity as being in tension with even his poetic endeavours dating to before that shift. Famously, the nineteenth-century critic Francesco De Sanctis was dismissive of much of the *Gerusalemme liberata*, primarily because of its religious tenor, arguing that Tasso's lavish descriptions of outward manifestations of piety revealed how superficial his religiosity was:

> What, then, is religion in the *Gerusalemme*? It is Italian-style religion: dogmatic, historical, and concerned with form. The letter is there; the spirit is not. Its Christians believe, confess, pray, go on processions; this is the surface, but what lies behind it? ... Religion is an accessory to that life; it is not its spirit.[2]

Underlying arguments such as this is a distinction between superficial form and genuine belief, the letter and spirit of religiosity (a distinction which, in the case of De Sanctis, must be seen within the framework of the critic's Hegelian scheme, according to which the Counter-Reformation imposed restrictive practices and precepts on human freedom). For similar reasons, scholarship tended to dismiss Tasso's religious feeling into the twentieth century, as shown in Eugenio Donadoni's judgement in 1928 that 'Tasso never reached a profound and living sense of religiosity.'[3] Brand, too, claims that 'one doubts the depth of his [Tasso's] religious "conversion".'[4] Recent criticism has, however, moved away from this tendency, and often acknowledges the strength and sophistication of Tasso's religiosity.[5] Some

---

[1]   Erminia Ardissino, 'Il pensiero e la cultura religiosa di Torquato Tasso', *Lettere italiane*, 56 (2003), 592–614 (p. 612).

[2]   'Che cosa è dunque la religione nella *Gerusalemme*? È una religione all'italiana, dommatica, storica, e formale: ci è la lettera, non ci è lo spirito. I suoi cristiani credono, si confessano, pregano, fanno processioni: questa è la vernice; quale è il fondo? ... La religione è l'accessorio di questa vita; non ne è lo spirito': *Storia della letteratura italiana*, ed. by Benedetto Croce, 2 vols (Florence: Sansoni, 1965), II, p. 562.

[3]   'Il Tasso non arrivò mai ad un senso profondo e vivo della religiosità': Eugenio Donadoni, *Torquato Tasso. Saggio critico* (Florence: La Nuova Italia, 1921), p. 513.

[4]   C.P. Brand, Torquato Tasso: A Study of the Poet and of his Contribution to English Literature (Cambridge: Cambridge University Press, 1965), p. 19.

[5]   Umberto Bosco set out this notion for modern scholarship, drawing sharp distinctions between the evidence of Tasso's personal correspondence, the *Rime sacre*, and *Gerusalemme liberata* ('Sulla religiosità del Tasso', *Rassegna della letteratura italiana*, 51 (1955), 1–12).

of Tasso's letters have been taken to suggest that the poet's apparent religious orthodoxy was merely a cover for his authentic, troubled inner state. Particularly suggestive in this regard has been the famous letter to Scipione Gonzaga of 15 April 1579, written in the hospital of Sant'Anna, in which Tasso admits to a profound and disturbing mix of doubt and passionate religious feeling. Such evidence suggests that his religious feeling was less simplistic than De Sanctis had argued.

Although this work has enriched our understanding of Tasso as a Christian *poet*, it has done little to alter our understanding of his Christian *poetry*. The work of Erminia Ardissino takes an important step towards putting this right.[6] Her innovation is to analyse in Tasso's poetry a category which she terms the 'sacred', a notion derived from Rudolf Otto, which she describes as:

> ... the wholly 'other', which inspires terror and attraction ... the *'mysterium tremendum et fascinans'*, which reveals itself to the religious person thanks to his propensity to perceive a more profound reality hidden behind the outward appearances of objects and events.[7]

She therefore deliberately eliminates the problems of Tasso's troubled relationship to the Church from her critical method, and opens the way towards analysing his work as a religious exploration in its own right. This approach brings significant advantages. By removing from her analysis the vexed questions raised by Tasso's life-story, Ardissino escapes the burden of scholarly obsession with Tasso's biography. She is able to integrate her analysis of the sacred into her reading of the poetry, thus producing a compelling argument that the Christianity of Tasso's work can be best discovered through the dynamics of the poetry itself.

Such a move towards a re-evaluation of Tasso's religiosity complicates any clear-cut distinctions between the doctrinal and the poetic, and troubles any value judgements that see religious expression as detrimental to Tasso's literary endeavours. Yet an emphasis on the sincerity and complexity of Tasso's religious belief, whilst welcome in its own right, in

---

Margaret W. Ferguson presents a psycho-biography of Tasso which aims to 'question the dominant critical view of Tasso as a spokesman for Counter-Reformation ideology': *Trials of Desire: Renaissance Defenses of Poetry* (New Haven, CT: Yale University Press, 1983), p. 72. See also Giuseppe Santarelli, *Studi sulle 'Rime sacre' del Tasso* (Bergamo: Centro Tassiano, 1974), pp. 11–49; L. De Vendittis, 'Ancora sul sentimento religioso in Tasso', *Giornale storico della letteratura italiana*, 145 (1988), 481–511.

[6]   'L'aspra tragedia': Poesia e sacro in Torquato Tasso (Florence: Olschki, 1996).

[7]   'Il totalmente altro che ispira terrore ed attrazione ... il "*mysterium tremendum et fascinans*" che si rivela all'uomo religioso grazie alla sua propensione a percepire una realtà più profonda nascosta dietro le apparenze di oggetti e di avvenimenti': *'L'aspra tragedia'*, p. 9.

turn brings other risks. Ardissino, for example, draws a sharp distinction between 'religione' and 'sacralità'; where the former is a system of signs which exists independently of any experience of the absolute, the latter is a pre-linguistic experience, which takes place prior to any systematization of thought or practice.[8] All organized religious practice is thus presented as less authentic than the genuine experience of the 'sacred'. But in insisting upon the importance of inner experience, on the very rich notion of the sacred, we must not dismiss too readily the fact that the Tridentine climate in which Tasso was working was heavily concerned with the ritual, formal aspects of religious practice. This was, after all, a Church which sought to codify with new clarity the liturgical forms within which worship occurred, and to underline the doctrines and principles behind the practices which represented most obviously the divisions with the Protestants: the sacraments, the use of art in churches, the place of the saints in religious life. And, for reasons which I shall outline shortly, to assume that these forms of worship should be seen as fully separate from, and in some sense inferior to, interiorized religious 'experience' is to oversimplify the possibilities both of an orthodox Tridentine spirituality, and of a poet who explicitly sets out to conform to that mode of religiosity.

Liturgy in the Late Works

Tasso's desire, in the works of the 1590s, to signal his orthodoxy is evident through the multiple allusions they contain to ritual and liturgy. *Gerusalemme conquistata*, the heavily religious rewriting of *Gerusalemme liberata*, maintains and expands the descriptions of liturgy of the earlier poem (for instance, the Mass described in *Gerusalemme liberata* XI is expanded by six stanzas, in *Conquistata* XIV). A number of new prayer-like passages appear in the text. In Canto XX, for example, Goffredo experiences a vision of the heavenly city, in which he hears the angels sing in praise of God. This is not a prayer that would have formed part of the earthly liturgy, but is rather based on the work of Pseudo-Dionysius. God is no longer presented as an actor in the plot, able to respond to prayer, but is now considered ineffable, and is evoked through a *via negativa*, the denial of the possibility of definitive statements about God. Moreover, the text is informed by an overarching allegory, which draws on an extended image

---

[8]   'Mentre per religione si intende *un sistema di credenze e di riti che si riferiscono alle cose sacre*, la coscienza del sacro precede ogni sistemazione formale ed aspetto razionale o speculativo della religione' [Whilst for religion, we understand *a system of beliefs and of rituals which refer to sacred things*, the awareness of the sacred precedes any formal systematization and rational or speculative aspect of religion]: ibid., p. 9; emphasis added.

presented by Aquinas in *De dilectione Christi et proximi*, describing five fountains.[9] Four of these represent the material elements; one represents Christ, the source of creation. In using this allegory, Tasso also makes this last fountain sacramental – in the case of the character of Clorinda, it is a figure for her baptism; for Riccardo (the *Conquistata*'s version of the *Liberata*'s Rinaldo), it represents penance.

Of Tasso's shorter religious works, the *Lagrime della beata vergine* is the most important, with seven editions appearing in its first year of publication. A twenty-five-stanza meditation on the Sorrows of the Virgin, the poem is a response to a work of art, possibly by Dürer. Its primary link with the liturgy is in its relation to the *Planctus Mariae* tradition, the most famous example being the *Stabat Mater*, which was used as a hymn by this period.[10]

My focus in this essay, however, is *Il mondo creato*. A blank-verse poem based around the Genesis account of the creation of the world, *Il mondo creato* is packed with philosophical reflection on various points of doctrine (although such reflection never deviates from Catholic orthodoxy). As well as this philosophical reflection, *Il mondo creato* has a strong liturgical feel, which derives partly from echoes of the Mass. The opening invocation of the Trinity ('Padre del cielo, e tu del Padre eterno/ eterno Figlio, e non creata prole,/de l'immutabil mente unica parte')[11] recalls the very first words of the Tridentine Mass: 'In the name of the Father, of the Son, and of the Holy Ghost',[12] as well as numerous other prayers in the liturgy.[13] Given that the invocation, like the opening of the Mass, is a call for grace, the echo is even stronger. The Creed is echoed in the description of the Trinity as 'lume pur di lume ardente'[14] (I, 5; cf.

---

[9]   In *Opuscules de Saint Thomas D'Aquin* (Paris: Vrin, 1958), pp. 462–83.

[10]   For a study of the *Lagrime* in relation to the devotional and artistic context of late Cinquecento Italy, see Matthew Treherne, 'Pictorial Space and Sacred Time: Tasso's *Le lagrime della beata vergine* and the Experience of Religious Art in the Counter-Reformation', *Italian Studies*, 26 (2007), 5–25.

[11]   'Father in heaven, and you, eternal Son/of our eternal Father, the one birth/and unmade offspring of the changeless Mind' (1–3). Citations from *Il mondo creato* are taken from *Il mondo creato*, ed. by Giorgio Petrocchi (Florence: Le Monnier, 1951); translations are by Joseph Tusiani (Torquato Tasso, *Creation of the World* (Binghamton, NY: Center for Medieval and Early Renaissance Studies, 1982).

[12]   'In nomine Patris, et Filii, et Spiritus Sancti'.

[13]   References to the Tridentine liturgy are taken from *Monumenta Liturgica Concili Tridentini*, 3 vols (Vatican City: Libreria Editrice Vaticana, 1997–99), II (1998), p. 293 (henceforth abbreviated as *Mon. Lit.*).

[14]   'Light of burning light' (I, 5).

'Only begotten son of God ... begotten not made ... light of light'[15]).
The phrase 'Signor, tu sei la mano, io son la cetra'[16] recalls the words of
the Mass, 'Upon the harp I will praise thee, O God.'[17] Throughout the
poem, comparisons are drawn between the creation of the world and the
liturgy. For instance, the creation of the oceans is compared to crowds of
the faithful coming out of Church (III, 819–26), and on several occasions,
the seven days of creation are linked with the days of the liturgical week
(for example, I, 31–33).

Liturgy as Discourse

What are we to make of such a strong liturgical flavour in these late
works? Given the assumptions underlying so much scholarly discussion
of Tasso's religious writings, it is unsurprising that these works have often
been dismissed as superficial and insincere. In the case of the most clearly
doctrinal work, *Il mondo creato*, critical reaction has been dominated
by the sense that the poem is too keen to conform obviously to doctrine
to be worth considering as poetry. For De Sanctis, the wide variety of
theological sources used in the poem indicated Tasso's lack of sincerity
and reflection: 'its philosophy is so well learned, well understood, well
laid out, set out in arguments and proper forms; but its sources and
principles are not scrutinized.'[18] Benedetto Croce, writing in the mid-
twentieth century, described the work as being 'devoid of the light of
poetry'.[19] In all of this, the strongly liturgical tenor of the poem has been
singled out as a symptom of this attachment to the superficial. Giovanni
Getto recognized the liturgical tenor of the poem, and considered this
to be a reason to dismiss it: 'a solemn liturgy seems to take shape, and
the somewhat facile tune of a choral song resounds.'[20] Joseph Tusiani
considers some of the moments in which liturgy is described to be

---

[15]   'Filium Dei unigenitum ... genitum non factum ... *lumen de lumine*': *Mon. Lit.* II,
296–7.

[16]   'Lord, you are the hand, I am the harp': I, 63.

[17]   'Confitebor tibi in cithara, Deus': *Mon. Lit.* II, 293.

[18]   'La sua filosofia è così imparata, ben capita, ben esposta, disposta in argomenti e
forme proprie, ma non è scrutinata nelle sue fonti e nelle sue basi': *Storia della letteratura
italiana*, p. 537.

[19]   '[P]rivo di luce di poesia': Benedetto Croce, *Poeti e scrittori del pieno e tardo
Rinascimento* (Bari: Laterza, 1952), p. 259.

[20]   'Sembra determinarsi una solenne liturgia, e risuonare l'aria ... *un po' facile* di un
canto corale': Giovanni Getto, *Malinconia di Torquato Tasso* (Naples: Liguori, 1979), p. 321.

'embarrassingly baroque': 'it becomes quite difficult to see where rhetoric ends and sincerity begins.'[21]

Yet there are good reasons to question the assumption that liturgy is a merely external, pietistic form of discourse. One such reason is the continued wide circulation in the Cinquecento of the extremely detailed medieval commentaries on the liturgy, which suggest ways of finding in liturgical action a broad field of meaning. In particular, the text which dominated late medieval thinking on the liturgy, the *Rationale divinorum officiorum* of William Durand (*c.*1230–96), continued to be the most widely consulted volume on the liturgy in Italy throughout the sixteenth century, and into the seventeenth.[22] (Indeed, Martin Luther attacked it as an archetypal example of contemporary Catholic thought about the liturgy.[23]) The thirteen Latin editions of the *Rationale* in the sixteenth century made it by far the most popular liturgical commentary, and speak of an enduring popularity, at least among clergy.[24] The fact that the treatise was translated into Italian in 1539 suggests that there was a move to popularize the work, and extend its reach beyond the clergy.[25] It was uniquely comprehensive: the commentary covers aspects of the liturgy, ranging from the parts of the church building, the vestments, and the liturgical calendar, to the text of the Mass itself. Crucially, not only the words of the liturgy were important: Durand breaks down the meaningful elements of the Mass into four groups: the people participating, the acts performed, the words spoken, chanted, or sung, and the objects used (*Rationale* IV, i, 13–15). Liturgy, then, was a rich field of meaning, to which both Tridentine and late medieval Catholics devoted considerable attention.

It was, moreover, a way of figuring and of representing time; and this mode of shaping temporal experience will prove central to Tasso's use of liturgical allusion in a poem such as *Il mondo creato*, for reasons that

---

[21]   'Introduction', in Torquato Tasso, *Creation of the World*, trans. by Joseph Tusiani (Binghamton, NY: Center for Medieval and Early Renaissance Studies, 1982), pp. i–xxiv (p. xiv).

[22]   *Rationale divinorum officiorum*, ed. by Anselme Davril and Timothy M. Thibodeau, 3 vols (Turnhout: Brepols, 1995).

[23]   Timothy M. Thibodeau, '*Enigmata Figurarum*: Biblical Exegesis and Liturgical Exposition in Durand's *Rationale*', *Harvard Theological Review*, 86 (1993), 65–79 (p. 67).

[24]   Roger E. Reynolds, 'Liturgy, Treatises on', in *Dictionary of the Middle Ages*, ed. by Joseph R. Stringer (New York: Charles Scribner's Sons, 1986), VII, pp. 624–33 (p. 633).

[25]   For a survey of the history of printing of the *Rationale* up to 1640, see Michel Albaric, 'Les éditions imprimées du *Rationale Divinorum Officiorum* de Guillaume Durand de Mende', in *Guillaume Durand, Évêque de Mende (v. 1230–1296): Canoniste, liturgiste et homme politique*, ed. by Pierre-Marie Gy (Paris: Éditions du Centre National de la recherche scientifique, 1992), pp. 183–200.

will be discussed. This aspect of liturgical performance was evident in a number of ways. First, in the liturgy, biblical narratives were not presented as a single sequence, but in overlapping cycles. The sequential action of biblical narratives was re-presented cyclically; within individual services, readings did not follow a single narrative, but presented alongside one another elements from different historical moments. Thus a reading from the Old Testament was given a particular place in the Lectionary, not as part of a sequential narrative, but 'predominantly for its prophetic and typological value'.[26] In applying such significance to individual moments in scriptural narrative, liturgy was consistent with other structures of Catholic religious thought. Biblical exegesis also did this, seeking for example, typological meaning in Old Testament events, or linking moments in Scripture to the life of an individual.[27] Such thinking was, one might say, embedded into the manner of liturgical performance itself.

Secondly, commentators on the liturgy made clear that the liturgical cycles themselves represented, as if in microcosm, different historical times. Each liturgical division of the day corresponded to a division of the year: so that the period from Septuagesima to Easter corresponded to night; that from Advent to Christmas corresponded to the dawn; that from the eighth week after Easter to the eighth week after Pentecost corresponded to the daytime; and that from the eighth week after Pentecost to Advent corresponded to evening (Durand, *Rationale*, III, xi). In this way, any single moment in the liturgical year was also part of the daily cycle. Liturgy did not therefore *compress* the sequential passage of time, but rather made different elements in sequential time coincide and interact.

Third, the relationship of different moments in the liturgical calendar was, in Durand's account, further overlaid by a complex set of relationships, derived from the techniques of biblical exegesis. The daily cycle represented in microcosm the fall of mankind and mankind's redemption (*Rationale*, I, x); but also figured the life of every individual, with each stage in a person's life being represented by a different liturgical service (infancy being represented by Matins, for instance; *Rationale* I, xi). Each of those moments in the cycle was related to moments in the biblical narratives. For instance, the Nocturne brought together a participation in the Passover, the birth of Christ, the arrest of Christ, the

---

[26]   Stephen J.P. van Dijk, 'The Bible in Liturgical Use', in *The Cambridge History of the Bible*, ed. by G.W.H. Lampe, vol. II, *The West from the Fathers to the Reformation* (Cambridge: Cambridge University Press, 1969), pp. 220–52 (p. 221)

[27]   The classic text on exegesis is Henri de Lubac, *Exégèse médiévale, I: Les quatre sens de l'écriture* (Paris: Editions Montaigne, 1959).

Last Judgement, and the darkness of the individual soul in sin (*Rationale*, III, i).

These features, common to both medieval and Tridentine liturgy, indeed formed a focus for controversy in the sixteenth century. The Lutheran attack on Catholic liturgy was largely aimed at Catholic notions of how biblical time could relate to liturgical time. One key aspect of this was the Eucharist, which according to Catholic theology 'made present' the crucifixion on a daily basis. The idea that the Eucharist could be a sacrifice was described by Luther as 'the supreme and most precious of the papal idolatries';[28] the liturgical rite did not participate in past events, he argued, for the salvation of humanity was achieved once and for all on the cross.[29] The Council of Trent defined the Catholic understanding of the nature of the Mass in reaction to this critique, rejecting Luther's notion decisively: 'it is the same victim, the same priest, who offered himself on the Cross and who is offering himself now through his ministers; only the manner of the offering is different.'[30]

Our awareness of the connotative, experiential and theological dimensions of liturgy has been enriched by recent work on liturgy in theological studies, which offers illuminating analysis of the liturgy as a mode of religious language, suggesting that the liturgy establishes complex relationships between the subject engaged in liturgical performance, the God to whom liturgy is offered, and the words of the liturgy itself. Such work thereby engages with liturgy as a mode of thought, rather than as a repository of received ideas. These theologians warn against any temptation to see the performance of liturgical rites as merely an articulation of set theological precepts, or a mapping-out of beliefs. They propose instead that this performance be understood as a means of situating the individual worshipper in relationship to divinity, and therefore as a theologically charged mode of discourse. Two of the most important recent books on liturgy highlight this concern. Jean-Yves Lacoste works in the philosophical tradition of phenomenology, and is concerned with the relationship between the finite experience of the individual, and the infinite truths to which the individual attempts to relate in liturgy. There can be, for Lacoste, no understanding of the

---

[28]   Cited in Francis Clark, *Eucharistic Sacrifice and the Reformation* (Westminster: Newman Press, 1960), p. 101.

[29]   Martin Luther, *Against the Heavenly Prophets*, trans. by Conrad Bergendoff (Philadelphia, PA: Fortress Press, 1958), pp. 213–14.

[30]   'Una enim eademque est hostia, idem nunc offerens sacerdotum ministerio, qui se ipsum tunc in cruce obtulit, sola offerendi ratione diversa': *Concilium Tridentinum. Diariorum, actorum, epistularum, tractatuum, nova collection*, ed. by Members of the Societas Goerresiana, 13 vols (Freiburg: Herder, 1901–80), VIII, p. 960.

'Absolute' outside this finite experience; liturgy is a means of exceeding the particular instant of liturgical performance, without leaving it. His definition of liturgy is, however, highly suggestive. Liturgy is, he argues, 'all that embodies the relationship of man to God ... Liturgy is indeed the concept which forbids us from making a ruinous dissociation of interior and exterior, of "body" and "soul".'[31] Liturgy, seen in this way, is no mere pietistic ritual, but embodies and articulates the central theological relationship between the human subject and God.

In a groundbreaking work, Catherine Pickstock presents a rich theory of the modes of thought found in the late medieval Roman Rite, and an account of how those modes of thought have been successively undermined by modern and postmodern mentalities.[32] In late medieval and Tridentine liturgy (although Pickstock focuses on the medieval context), individuals were involved in a use of language that embraced its own temporality, with various consequences. Pickstock's analysis of the Roman Rite offers several insights into the nature of liturgical language, which may enrich our understanding of liturgy. First, the liturgy establishes relationships between different types of utterance, none of which predominates. Constative, performative, doxological and self-referential utterances all interact: for instance, doxology is always tied up with a sense of the worshipping subject's limited ability to understand what she is praising. Thus the Greater Doxology ('Gloria in Excelsis Deo'), which opens with the words of the angels to the shepherds in Luke, moves into the praise of God as 'Lord God, heavenly king, God the Father almighty' ('Domine Deus, rex coelestis, Deus Pater omnipotens'), but finally to an appeal for mercy from Christ ('Jesus Christ ... have mercy on us' – 'Iesu Christe ... miserere nobis'), thereby pointing back to the sinful nature of the human speaker (p. 188). This interaction of discursive modes means that built into the liturgy is a sort of 'stammer' (p. 177). If liturgy involves the praise of God, it can only do so in the most transient of ways, constantly pointing towards the limitations of the human worshipper, emphasizing its own 'struggle to articulate itself' (p. 177).

---

[31]   'Tout ce qui incarne la relation de l'homme à Dieu ... La liturgie est en effet ce concept qui nous interdit la dissociation ruineuse de l'intérieur et de l'extérieur, du "corps" et de l'"âme"': Jean-Yves Lacoste, *Expérience et Absolu: Questions disputées sur l'humanité de l'homme* (Paris: Presses Universitaires de France, 1994), pp. 26–7.

[32]   Catherine Pickstock, *After Writing: On the Liturgical Consummation of Philosophy* (Oxford: Blackwell, 1998).

Tasso and Liturgy

There are good reasons, it is clear, to question any assumption that the liturgical feel of Tasso's late poetry is necessarily a sign of an unthinking, superficial religiosity. Accounts of liturgy, both contemporary to Tasso and more recent, suggest that liturgical performance can engage profound questions of the relation between the temporal, finite human person and an eternal God, encoding and enacting that engagement in the very manner of its performance. The relationship between the temporal subject and the eternal God is nowhere more keenly present than in Tasso's last major work, *Le sette giornate del mondo creato*. It is based on a succession of events, those of the Genesis narrative, which provides the basic action of the poem and the structural division into seven days. Yet in approaching the question of creation, it inevitably faces philosophical and theological problems of considerable sophistication: how does divine action, which must in some sense be *beyond* time, translate *into* human time? What is the relationship between the biblical representation of creation as an event in time, and theological understandings of creation as a process by which the created world is sustained in being, and indeed relies on God as the ground of its existence? These are, of course, fundamental theological problems, the very same difficulties which Augustine found in the *Confessions* of how an eternal God could be represented in the temporally finite narrative of Genesis:

> His substance is utterly unchanged in time and his will is not something separate from his substance. It follows that he does not will first one thing and then another, but that he wills all that he wills simultaneously, in one act, and eternally.[33]

The narrative of Genesis is therefore of a different order from divine action. As Augustine reports God's response to his doubts, '"what my Scripture says, I say. But the Scripture speaks in time, whereas time does not affect my Word, which stands for ever, equal with me in eternity".'[34] Human speech, and human narrative, can never match eternity: '"while you see those things in time, it is not in time that I see them. And while you

---

[33]   'Quod nequaquam eius substantia per tempora uarietur nec eius uoluntas extra eius substantiam sit? unde non eum modo uelle hoc modo uelle illud, sed semel et simul et semper uelle omnia quae uult': Augustine, *Confessionum Libri XIII*, ed. by Lucas Verhiejen (Turnhout: Brepols, 1981), XII, 15; translations from the *Confessions* are by R.S. Pine-Coffin (London: Penguin, 1961).

[34]   '"Nempe quod scriptura mea dicit, ego dico, et tamen illa temporaliter dicit, uerbo autem meo tempus non accidit, quia aequali mecum aeternitate"': XIII, 29.

speak those words in time, it is not in time that I speak them".'[35] *Il mondo creato*, too, reimagines the relationship between narrative and time. At least part of this is done through liturgy.

Nothing in the poem's reputation suggests this imaginative engagement with the question of divine action in time. The density of allusion in the text to an eclectic range of authorities has tended to give the unfair impression that the poem is a mere compilation of received ideas.[36] It is true that *Il mondo creato* is packed with philosophical reflection, and is largely concerned with providing an exposition of the way the world is. But that exposition takes place against a sustained reflection on *time*. As well as being a philosophical poem, it is also a narrative; a narrative, at that, which foregrounds problems of the relationship between time and eternity.

What precisely is the temporality represented in *Il mondo creato*? Much of the text is a narrative account of the divine action of the creation of the world. Accordingly, the account of Genesis is largely followed. Early on, Tasso asks for inspiration from God in order that he might write of 'quel primo alto lavoro'[37] carried out 'in sei giorni distinto'.[38] The division of the act of creation into six distinct days unites – as does the Genesis account – divine action and sequential time. Each day of creation contains a narrative act. For example, at the end of the action of the second day: 'Così Dio fece', the poet says, and 'e fatto insieme/fu da mattino a sera il dí secondo'.[39]

However, as Augustine's discussion of Genesis in the *Confessions* suggests, the Christian tradition complicated the notion that the creation of the world was an event confined to a particular, bounded time. Tasso's engagement with Genesis, and with the tradition of commentary on it, led him to confront the question of how time appeared in creation. Part of his response was to derive from commentaries the account of how time did

---

[35]   '"Atque ita cum uos temporaliter ea uideatis, non ego temporaliter uideo, quemadmodum, cum uos temporaliter ea dicatis, non ego temporaliter dico"': ibid.

[36]   A sense of the sheer range of sources is given by the Palatina codex, a version of the text that was annotated by Angelo Ingegneri. The annotations are transcribed in Petrocchi's edition of the text (pp. 335–8), and indicate that the primary authority was Basil the Great, in particular his *Hexameron*, as well as Denys the Areopagite, Aquinas, Origen, Augustine and Pico della Mirandola. On the influence of Boethius, see Letizia Panizza, 'Torquato Tasso's *Il mondo creato* and Boethius, a Neglected Model', *Renaissance Studies* 5 (1991), 301–14. On the possible influence of Du Bartas's *La sepmaine*, see below, and L. Erba, 'Quelques remarques à propos de *La Sepmaine* et du *Mondo Creato*', in *Du Bartas: poète encyclopédique du XVI siècle*, ed. by James Dauphiné (Lyons: La Manufacture, 1988), pp. 131–40.

[37]   'That first great deed': I, 23–4.

[38]   'In six full, separate days': I, 27.

[39]   'So acted God': 58; 'thus the second day,/from morning unto evening, was complete': 61–2.

not pre-exist the creative act, but was made with creation itself.[40] Thus the decision for the beginning of time to take place was in itself timeless: 'Già di quel ch'ab eterno in sé prescrisse/Dio, ch'è senza principio e senza fine'.[41] As Tasso puts it, in the first day, 'Era giunto il principio, e giunto il tempo/co 'l principio del tempo',[42] a formulation which attempts to create a paradoxical sense of how time emerged. Time is shown to emerge out of God's own eternity:

> Da l'eternità che 'n sé raccolta
> si gira, e di stessa è sfera e centro,
> omai prendeva il tempo il moto e 'l corso;
> quando il suo creator lo spazio al passo
> e la misura diè, lo stato eterno.[43]

Before time, then, eternity was at the same time centre and circumference of a sphere; with creation, time began to exist as movement. The creation of time was therefore the creation of space within which time could be revealed. This is perfectly conventional: the notion that time was created with creation, rather than pre-dating it, was the orthodox solution to the question posed by Augustine in the *Confessions*. But Tasso's response to the problem of the relationship between earthly time and God's eternity goes beyond that. As well as describing the narrative of creation, the poem reflects on the condition of *createdness*; and in doing so, it draws on notions of liturgical time.

The very title of the work gives some indication of the emphasis Tasso makes. Guillaume de Saluste du Bartas's poem on the creation of the world provided one possibility: *La sepmaine ou création du monde* (1587), translated into Latin as *Mundi creatio*.[44] Tasso also includes the notion of a

---

[40]   See, for example, Augustine, *De Genesi contra Manichaeos*, ed. by Dorothea Weber (Vienna: Österreichischen Akademie der Wissenschaften, 1998), p. 175.

[41]   'God, beginning with no end,/had *ab eterno* in himself decreed': I, 211–12.

[42]   'The time had come for something to begin … time was by now its own commencing life': I, 213–14.

[43]   'From eternity, rapt in itself,/both sphere and center of its own delight,/did time learn all its motion and its course/when its creator to its flux gave space,/and measure gave it never-ending state': I, 218–22.

[44]   Because there is little evidence about the circumstances and processes of the composition of *Il mondo creato*, we can only speculate over whether Tasso had actually read Du Bartas's poem. Pietro Toldi (*Due articoli letterari* (Rome: Loescher, 1894), pp. 3–51) first pointed out some similarities in wording between the poems. A translation into Italian had been completed in 1593 by Ferrante Guisoni and was published in Venice the same year. But the two poets were both working from the same source materials and so, if there are similarities between the two texts, this need not indicate that Tasso had read *La Sepmaine*.

week in his full title, but the change is crucial: *Le sette giornate del mondo creato*. The change in emphasis leads to the seven days being associated less with the act of creation, but with the very state of createdness itself. The narrated events are therefore not restricted to a clearly demarcated historical time, but rather extend into the ongoing time of the created world. This is narrative, but a narrative that locates itself in the present and future as much as in the past.

Il mondo creato's liturgical feel is evident, as mentioned earlier, in the opening lines of the text which contain, specifically, a number of echoes of the Mass – from the opening invocation of the Trinity, to allusions to the Creed, and other references. The opening of the text thus not only calls to mind the Mass; it also suggests that the narrative that is to follow should be imagined in the context of a liturgical service. As we have seen, liturgy brings events distant in time into the present, both through the Lectionary and by establishing typological relationships between the moment of liturgical action, and past and future time. By opening his description of action in a way (to cite Getto) that 'a solemn liturgy seems to take shape', Tasso is not being 'facile' (as Getto goes on to claim), but is drawing a link between the present moment of narration and the seemingly past action of creation.[45] Such a link is particularly appropriate in the case of the issue of creation. As we have seen in Augustine's reflection on the Genesis narrative, and as we shall see in what follows, it was a central part of the Christian theology on which Tasso drew that creation was *not* an event bounded in time.

Just as we have seen that medieval and Cinquecento liturgy recast and reshaped sequential time, the liturgical tenor of *Il mondo creato* draws the sequential action it describes into relationship with other times. The liturgy is frequently described as being similar to the events of creation, figuring the past event in the repeated worship of the Church:

> Ma se pur è sí bello e sí lodato
> anzi il divin cospetto il mare ondoso,
> piú bella assai festante e folta turba
> è de' fedeli suoi raccolta e mista,
> ch'anzi le porte e dentro il tempio ondeggia,
> ed offre i voti; e le preghiere al cielo
> devota sparge: onde s'ascolta un suono,
> pur come d'onda che si rompa al lito.[46]

---

45   *Malinconia di Torquato Tasso*, p. 321.

46   'Yet, if the sea seemed worthy of such praises/to God's own eye, by far more beautiful/ and festive is his faithful's gathering throng,/who now outside or in a temple's door/offer their

This relationship to earlier time is also a participation in eternity. Prayers on earth are described as a participation in prayers of the saints and angels in heaven:

> Ma come in ciel fra gli stellanti chiostri,
> in quel sacro al suo nome eterno tempio
> è chi l'adori, e con perpetuo suono
> d'alta voce immortale i lodi e canti:
> …
> così debbe qua giuso aver la terra
> adoratori, e chi in sonoro carme
> sacrificio di laude a Dio consacri.[47]

By setting up his poem in terms which recall a liturgical service, and relating the action described to the ongoing liturgy, Tasso presents the act of creation as something which reaches into the present. Indeed, he makes a link between the seven days of creation, the days of the liturgical week, and providential history. The seventh day of creation is also the day of worship in the Church (VII, 249–61). In addition, it is figured as a future event: the second coming, which will take place at the dawn of the seventh day, which will have no end:

> Piacciati ancor, che del tuo foco a l'aura
> canti il settimo dì, soave e dolce
> riposo eterno.[48]

In this, Tasso is following the analysis presented by Augustine in the *De Genesi contra Manichaeos*.[49] In addition, Tasso also introduces the notion of the eighth day – an idea he draws from Psalm VI, and Basil of Caesarea's

---

waving prayers to the sky,/and all their vows devoutly: a sweet sound/as of a breaking wave is therefore heard': III, 819–26.

[47]   'But as in heaven's ever-starry space,/high in that temple to his deathless name,/ spirits there are, who praise and worship it/with an eternal sound of happy love/ … /so must our lowly earth have worshippers/and those who make a sacrifice of praise/with their sonorous prayers to God': I, 196–9, 204–6).

[48]   'And also grant me that I sing today,/inspired by your flame, the seventh day –/the everlasting, balmy, blessèd rest': I, 31–3.

[49]   *De Genesi contra Manichaeos*, p. 195. For an account of this idea in Augustinian thought, see Julien Ries, 'La création, l'homme et l'histoire du salut', in G. Palland, G. Balido, J. Ries, A. Di Pilla and M. Marin, *'De Genesi contra Manichaeos' 'De Genesi ad litteram liber imperfectus' di Agostino d'Ippona* (Palermo: Augustinus, 1992), pp. 65–97.

Hexaemeron[50] – which is not a day at all, but a figure for eternity, lying beyond time: he describes it as the day, or even century, which becomes eternity: 'Giorno, o secolo sia, che pur s'eterni'.[51] The reflexive verb Tasso uses, 's'eterni' captures this positive view of time relating to eternity in a way that Basil's phrasing does not. Time converges into eternity. The verb recurs at the end of the Settimo Giorno: 'Abbia riposo alfin lo stanco e veglio/mondo, che pur s'attempa, e 'n te s'eterni'.[52] In *La sepmaine*, Du Bartas uses an equivalent verb: 's'éterniser'. But his use is instructively different. He uses it to describe how an artist looks over his work and finalizes it: 'the painter who, drawing a rich landscape, has put art, nature and custom into it, and has, in order to return to eternity [pour s'éterniser], added the final strokes, forgets his labours.'[53] God too is like this: 'ainsi ce grand ouvrier' 'se repose ce jour, s'admire en son ouvrage' (45, 50). In *La sepmaine*, eternity is a closure on time, whereas in Tasso's formulation, time returns to eternity.

On occasion, Tasso's invocation of God reflects this. Take this formulation, from the very opening of the poem:

> ... O tu l'insegni,
> Che 'n un sol punto chiudi i spazi e 'l corso,
> che per oblique vie sempre rotando
> con mille giri fa veloce il tempo.[54]

In this formulation, the emphasis is on the limits of earthly time and vision in relationship to God. It is close to Dante's description of God as 'the point to which all times are present' ('il punto/a cui tutti li tempi son presenti') (*Paradiso* XVII, 17–18), but God here is also a point that draws time around itself. The poet's power in relationship to God is thus utterly

---

[50] 'Scripture recognizes that day without evening, without tomorrow and without end; that which the Psalmist called the eighth day, because it is outside of time': Basil of Caesarea, *Hexamaeron*; my translation from the Italian version by Mario Naldini (Milan: Mondadori, 1990), p. 69.

[51] I, 647. Tusiani's translation ('One day? One century? Eternity!') does not convey the way in which units of time are related to, and in a sense make themselves into, eternity by the verb.

[52] 'Let this weak, aging world have peace at last,/and find its bright eternity in you': VII, 1124–5.

[53] 'Le peintre qui, tirant un divers paysage,/a mis en oeuvre l'art, la nature, et l'usage,/ et qui ... a, pour s'éterniser, donné le dernier traict,/oublie ses travaux': *La sepmaine ou création du monde*, ed. by Yvonne Bellenger, 2 vols (Paris: Nizet, 1981), VII, 1–5.

[54] ' ... Teach me all this,/O God, still holding in You [un un sol punto': in a single point]/space and wheels that, ever more rotating to and fro,/make time advance in myriads of rings': I, 27–30.

reconceived: God does not provide the impetus for sequential time as an epic actor, but time is instead represented as revolving around God, the 'punto'.

The account of the human being places time at the heart of human dignity. It is precisely because God created humans in his image that they can find within themselves rest from time:

> E se 'n terra ne l'uom quetarsi ei volle,
> fu perchè l'uomo in Dio s'acqueti al fine.
> Però quand'egli in sì mirabil tempre
> l'umanitate al suo divin congiunse,
> pose a la vita faticosa e stanca
> in se medesmo alfin dolce restauro;
> e gloria e grazia onde s'adempia e bea
> nostra natura ch'essaltar cotanto
> in lui si vide.[55]

The final temporal movement of the poem is backwards and forwards at the same time. The poem ends in prayer: an imagined prayer to God at the end of the Day of Judgement when the days of creation have come to an end. But it is also a backward-looking prayer, thinking back to the creation as a way of understanding human dependence on God. And it looks to the present, to state Tasso's sense of creation's dependency on its creator:

> O mio Signore e Padre eterno,
> che già di nulla mi creasti adorno
> mirabilmente, e mi servasti in vita
> poscia nel gran diluvio e ne gli incendi,
> io per me son caduca e grave mole,
> e ruinosa alfin, non pur tremante.
> Ma la tua destra mi sostiene e folce
> sì ch'io non caggio.[56]

This reiterates the point that Tasso does not see creation as an act in time, but as an ongoing process, in which all of the created world exists in a state

---

[55] 'He wished to rest/in mortal man so that man, too, at last,/might find his ultimate repose in God./Therefore, when He so wonderfully joined/humanity to His divinity,/He bade man's wearisome, fatiguing life/expect sweet solace in His arms alone,/with glory and with grace that would fulfil/our human nature, which He raised so high': VII, 150–58.

[56] '... "My Lord and my Eternal Father,/who from nothing gave me wondrous life,/and kept me still alive through deluges/and conflagrations; if You're not with me/I'm nothing but a grievous, trembling weight/which ultimately ruinously falls./But still your kindly hand is my support"': VII, 1086–93.

of dependency on God. You created me ('Mi creasti') (1087), the poet says; but God also *sustains* him ('la tua destra mi sostiene') and all of creation. The sustaining of creation in being by the creator is fully continuous with the *event* of creation: indeed, as Aquinas explains, drawing on a tradition of thought which had dominated Christian discussion of creation, the two are fundamentally the same act: 'The preservation of things by God is a continuation of that action whereby He gives existence, which action is without either motion or time.'[57]

Liturgical time enables Tasso to locate his poem in a relationship between historical time and eternity in such a way as to meet what might have seemed to be the irreconcilable demands of a narrative in time and the eternal divine nature. Tasso takes the notion of the seven days of creation, and without denying their status as narrative, inserts them into a liturgical structure; so that the seven days of creation become the seven days of the liturgical week, which are also figures of providential history. The entire poem is opened in terms that recall the Mass. The narrative thus speaks at the same time of the human being's boundedness in time, and of the human participation in an ongoing act of creation. It is perhaps tempting to see the prayer that Tasso presents at the end of the seventh day as a final plea of a poet who, near the end of his life, finds himself 'stanco e veglio' (1124). But that tiredness is framed within the possibilities of liturgical participation in the future. And so the very last words of the poem are an exhortation to prayer:

> Così ragiona il mondo. E sorda è l'alma
> che non ascolta i suoi rimbombi e 'l canto,
> e seco non congiunge il pianto e i prieghi.[58]

Throughout the poem, then, liturgy has been related to the condition of createdness. The days of the liturgical week have been a figure for the days of the Genesis creation narrative, making that narrative present. The poem's opening frames the narrative within phrases which make it resemble a liturgical service, once again bringing the narrative into the 'time of life' of the reader, just as the liturgy made elements of narrative present. And prayer has been described throughout as the appropriate

---

[57] 'Conservatio rerum a Deo non est per aliquam sed per continuationem actionis qua dat esse, quae quidem actio est sine motu et tempore': Thomas Aquinas, *Summa Theologiae*, Ia 104 art. 1 resp. 4; citations from the *Summa* are from the Blackfriars Edition, with Latin text and English translation. (New York: McGraw-Hill, 1964–76). On Tasso's use of Aquinas, see Basile's notes to the *Il mondo creato*, in Torquato Tasso, *Aminta. Il Re Torrismondo. Il mondo creato*, ed. by Bruno Basile (Rome: Salerno, 1999).

[58] 'Thus speaks the world. And deaf now is the soul/that does not listen to its echoing song,/and does not add its tears and all its prayers': VII, 1127–30.

response to that condition. In these ways, Tasso's use of liturgical time can be seen as part of an attempt to reconcile the Genesis presentation of creation as a succession of events, the awareness (as Augustine pointed out) that such successiveness is inappropriate for an eternal God, and the idea that God's act of creation is the ongoing sustenance of being.

Praise and Creation in *Il mondo creato*

Il mondo creato presents the act of creation, not only as the sequential narrative of Genesis, but also as an ongoing event. In so doing, it presents to the reader the world's condition of createdness, in which, as Aquinas explained, the world was maintained in its being through the very same divine act in which creation came into being. At the end of *Il mondo creato*, it is the return to the creator that brings stability; and that creator is defined as something that is self-subsistent, that does not require glory external to itself:

> … nel suo Creator pace e riposo
> han le create cose. E 'n se medesmo
> egli s'acqueta, nè d'esterna gloria,
> nè d'altro ben fuor di se stesso ha d'uopo,
> ch'è sommo bene.[59]

The response to that rediscovery of God is praise. Upon being created, the birds and animals 'facean de le sue lodi un chiaro canto';[60] the angels, too, are engaged with praise: 'Gli Angeli, dico, e le Virtù celesti/Essaltando lodar l'eterno Padre'.[61] From early on in the poem, Tasso has stated that the angels' praise should be joined by earthly praise: 'così debbe qua giuso aver la terra/adoratori, e chi in sonoro carme/sacrificio di laude a Dio consacri' (I, 204–6).

That response is ideal, rather than real, however; Tasso also describes the way in which the world struggles to find God, and thus mixes tears with praise. Faced with the work of creation, the person praises and sings ('loda e canta') (VII, 1085), but their song is marked by a sense of the person's inability to see God: 'Dove sei? Dove sei? Chi mi ti asconde?/

---

[59]   'Only in their Creator, then, can all/created things find pleasure and repose./So in Himself God rests, for He alone,/being the highest good, needs no external/glory, no other bliss outside His own': VII, 139–48.

[60]   '[B]lended their praises into one sweet hymn': VII, 1073–5.

[61]   'Angels and heavenly Virtues,/all the high Intelligences at that moment praised/the deathless Maker with exulting cries': VII, 1052–4.

Chi mi t'invola, o mio Signore e Padre?/Misero, senza Te son nulla. Ahi lasso!'.[62] Praise, therefore, is mingled with the acknowledgement of the inadequacy of the human subject; when it comes to articulating the joyful praise of creation, weeping as well as joy informs the sacrifice of praise: 'nel pianto e nel canto a te consacro/quanto leve, me stesso'.[63]

In light of this, it would seemingly be useful to alter Brand's account of *Il mondo creato*: 'the inspiration of the poem comes primarily from the material world, rather than from a desire to praise God – its subject is not the creation but the "created world".'[64] It is precisely because the poem's subject is the world, seen as created, in its very createdness, that the desire to praise God arises. This strong link between createdness and praise, though in rather different form, was frequently made in theological writing familiar to Tasso, especially that of the later Middle Ages.[65] Aquinas, in fact, had identified it as a whole strand of theological thought. In his commentary on Denys the Areopagite, he draws a distinction between two types of theology: one which aims to speak of the essence of God, and one which, reflecting on God's work in creation, arrives at truth about God through, precisely, a process of *praise*.[66]

This tradition informs texts such as St Francis's *Laudes creaturarum*, which involves a complex rhetoric of praise, expressing the desire that praise should be offered, through the natural world. It opens with a relinquishing of all praise, glory, honour and blessing to God: 'Tue so le laude, la gloria e l'honore et onne benedictione'.[67] It then goes on to work through various elements of the natural world: for example, 'laudato si', mi' Signore, per sora luna e le stelle';[68] 'laudato si', mi' Signore, per sor nostra matre terra'.[69] As my translation's recourse to multiple alternatives

---

[62]   'Where are you? Oh, where are You?/Why do You hide from me, or who or what/ takes You from me away, my Lord and Father?/Without You I am wretched, I am not': VII, 1111–13.

[63]   'Through my tears and song I give myself/to You, with all my strength to you alone': VII, 1106–7.

[64]   Brand, *Torquato Tasso*, p. 197.

[65]   On the links between praise and creation in the context of medieval Italian culture, see Matthew Treherne, 'Liturgical personhood: creation, penitence and praise in the *Commedia*', forthcoming in *Dante's 'Commedia': Theology as Poetry*, ed. by Vittorio Montemaggi and Matthew Treherne (Notre Dame, IN: University of Notre Dame Press).

[66]   Aquinas, *In librum beati Dionysii De divinis nominibus expositio*, ed. by Ceslas Pera (Turin and Rome: Marietti, 1950), p. 610.

[67]   'Yours are praise, glory, honour and all blessing' (2). Citations from Francis' *Laudes Creaturarum* are from the *Antologia della poesia italiana*, directed by Cesare Segre and Carlo Ossola, 9 vols (Turin: Einaudi, 1997–2003), I (1997): *Duecento*, pp. 22–4.

[68]   'May you be praised, my Lord, through/for/by [per] sister moon and the stars': 10.

[69]   'May you be praised, my Lord, through/for/by [per] our sister mother earth': 20.

implies, there is a fundamental ambiguity in Francis's poem, which derives from the word 'per'. Is God praised 'by' the natural world, 'on account of it', or 'by means of it'?[70] *Il mondo creato* seems to suggest a combination of all of these senses. The created world praises God; God is praised by persons because of the created world; and it is by means of reflection on the created world that Tasso exhorts his readers to praise.

Conclusion

Liturgy, then, emerges not as a turgid, pietistic ritual, but rather as a theologically charged mode of discourse, on which Tasso draws in *Il mondo creato* as part of his approach to fundamental questions about human personhood and the created world in relation to an eternal God. What this suggests is that scholarship has been too eager to dismiss the ritual elements in the text. It also suggests that in any evaluation of Tridentine spirituality, we need to be alert to the possibility that subtlety and thought might lie in the works of art, music and literature which seek to engage with the renewed emphasis on outward, codified forms of worship. After all, it is, in a sense, in liturgy that linguistic, musical and artistic forms were most carefully organized in the service of religious practice. This is not to suggest that every liturgical trope or reference in a work is a sign of a deep interest in liturgical discourse. But to assume the opposite, as has been the case in studies of Tasso, is to do the poet, and Tridentine thought and practice, a disservice. A number of the essays in this volume rightly draw attention to the multiple ways in which literary, artistic and musical culture resisted ecclesial authority in the wake of Trent. But orthodoxy, too, even in a troubled time and place, can take on forms that are subtle, rich, and worthy of attention.

---

[70]   For a summary of the issue, see Susanna Peters Coy, 'The Problem of "per" in the *Cantico di Frate Sole* of St Francis', *Modern Language Notes*, 91 (1976), 1–11.

Index

References to illustrations are given in italics.